Sport in the global society
Series Editors: J. A. Mangan and Boria Majumdar

Rugby's Great Split

D1344419

Sport in the global society

Series Editors: J. A. Mangan and Boria Majumdar

The interest in sports studies around the world is growing and will continue to do so. This unique series combines aspects of the expanding study of *sport in the global society*, providing comprehensiveness and comparison under one editorial umbrella. It is particularly timely, as studies in the multiple elements of sport proliferate in institutions of higher education.

Eric Hobsbawm once called sport one of the most significant practices of the late nineteenth century. Its significance was even more marked in the late twentieth century and will continue to grow in importance in the new millennium as the world develops into a 'global village' sharing the English language, technology and sport.

Other titles in the series

Rugby's Great Split

Since first publication, *Rugby's Great Split* has established itself as a classic in the field of sports history. Drawing on an unprecedented range of sources, the book traces the social, cultural and economic divisions that led, in 1895, to schism in the game of rugby and the creation of rugby league, the sport of England's northern working class.

Tony Collins' analysis challenges many of the conventional assumptions about this key event in rugby history – about class conflict, amateurism in sport, the North–South divide, violence on the pitch, the development of mass spectator sport and the rise of football. This new edition is expanded to cover parallel events in Australia and New Zealand, and to address the key question of rugby league's failure to establish itself in Wales.

Rugby's Great Split is a benchmark text in the history of rugby, and an absorbing case study of wider issues – issues of class, gender, regional and national identity, and the commercialisation of sport. For anyone interested in Britain's social history or in the emergence of modern sport, it is vital reading.

Tony Collins is Senior Research Fellow at the International Centre for Sports History and Culture at De Montfort University, Leicester and Editor of the journal *Sport in History*. His publications include the companion volume *Rugby League in Twentieth Century Britain*.

Rugby's Great Split

Class, culture and the origins of
rugby league football

2nd Edition

Tony Collins

 Routledge
Taylor & Francis Group

LONDON AND NEW YORK

First published 1998 by Frank Cass Publishers

This edition published 2006 by Routledge
2 Park Square, Milton Park, Abingdon, Oxon OX14 4RN

Simultaneously published in the USA and Canada
by Routledge
270 Madison Ave, New York, NY 10016

Routledge is an imprint of the Taylor & Francis Group, an informa business

© 1998, 2006 Tony Collins

Typeset in Bembo by
Keyword Group Ltd
Printed and bound in Great Britain by
TJ International, Padstow, Cornwall

British Library Cataloguing in Publication Data
A catalogue record for this book is available from the British Library

Library of Congress Cataloguing in Publication Data

Collins, Tony, 1961–
  Rugby's great split: class, culture and the origins of
Rugby League football/Tony Collins – 2nd ed.
      p. cm. – (Sport in the global society)
  Includes bibliographical references and index.
  ISBN 0-415-39616-6 (hardback) – ISBN 0-415-39617-4 (pbk.)
  1. Rugby League football–social aspects–England–History. 2. Rugby
Union football–social aspects–England–History. 3. Working class–
England–Recreation–History. I. Title. II. Series.
GV945.9.G7C65 2006
796.3330942–dc22
                                                    2006001069

ISBN10: 0-415-39616-6 (hbk)
ISBN10: 0-415-39617-4 (pbk)
ISBN10: 0-203-96997-9 (ebk)

ISBN13: 978-0-415-39616-5 (hbk)
ISBN13: 978-0-415-39617-2 (pbk)
ISBN13: 978-0-203-96997-7 (ebk)

Contents

List of figures

Series editor's foreword

For rugby union read 'tories'; for rugby league read 'whigs'; for Thomas Babington Macaulay read Tony Collins! The analogy in terms of the history of (Northern) English sport is not all that far-fetched. 'Whig history', as Hugh Trevor Roper tells us in the Introduction to his *Lord Macaulay: The History of England* in the Penguin English Library (1979), is essentially English and a historical interpretation of events imposed on the English past for reasons of legitimacy and justification. Furthermore, 'Whig history' is English insular history: *Rugby's Great Split* is an English insular historical drama.

As for Tony Collins, consciously or unconsciously, he imitates Macaulay, much in the same way, as Trevor Roper informs us, Macaulay imitated Scott in 'his use of description, of local colour or popular tradition or ephemeral literature'. It would be rather nice, of course, if Collins had Macaulay's publishing success!

One great attraction of *Rugby's Great Split*, apart from the pellucidity of the writing, is the clarity, force and persuasiveness of Collins' argument that 'Rugby itself was used to define class'. Sport not only reflects culture: it shapes it. A further attraction of the book is Collins' appreciation of the significance of ritual, symbol and myth in modern social affairs – interestingly, a point first made strongly, and subsequently widely applauded, in a recent analysis of sport in those cultural bastions of middle- and upper middle-class England – the public schools. It is good to witness ritual, symbol and myth closely examined, with equal pertinence and pertinacity, in a wider cultural setting.

Collins is to be applauded for injecting a necessary reality into the reconstruction of the history of modern soccer with his 'heretical' observation that the assumption that the folk football of pre-industrial England was the direct precursor of modern soccer, is quite simply an absurdity. It is certainly time that it was recognised that sport and the British had a rather more complicated relationship than is sometimes asserted in sports history circles, and also time that the change and continuity associated with the evolution of the great games of British society were more carefully considered.

'Whig history' does not have a lot to say directly on masculinity. It was hardly the issue it is now in past centuries, but with the canny social historian's capacity to feed the appetite of his contemporary audience, Collins makes it one of his recurring themes. And, a little to my amusement, since there is just the slightest hint of providing startling originality in his reflections on the issue, he argues that in the late nineteenth-century sport definitions of masculinity and violence were defined by class: 'Acts perceived as manly and character forming by the middle classes were interpreted differently when carried out by members of the working classes.' How true. As I remarked as long ago as 1981 in *Athleticism in the Victorian and Edwardian Public School* of the hugely popular annual Eton versus Harrow match at Lord's (no less) at the turn of the century: 'the younger supporters would clash regularly in front of the pavilion at the end of the match in a free-for-all that in a modern football ground would attract the opprobrium of a scandalised public. In those more robust times this exhibition of upper class virility was tolerated as a manly gesture of loyalty.' That muscular Corinthian tradition took a long time to die!

Rugby's Great Split is a valuable addition to the ever-increasing volume of works of quality in the history of sport. Virgil most certainly did not have Collins in mind when he penned his famous epithet: 'Lucky is he who has been able to understand the cause of things', but he might well have done.

J. A. Mangan
January, 1998

Preface to the second edition

In 1895 William Wollen exhibited 'The Roses Match', a painting based on the Yorkshire versus Lancashire rugby match played at Bradford's Park Avenue ground in 1893. Wollen was to become a renowned war artist for his work during World War One, but this painting became famous because it was believed that those players who joined the Northern Union (NU) after the 1895 rugby split had been removed from the picture. Indeed, a ghostly apparition of at least one player can be made out in the centre of the painting. During the course of the twentieth century the belief that the rebel players had been removed grew, being repeated in articles, books and even on television programmes. It was, so it seemed, the sporting equivalent of Stalin's airbrushing of Trotsky out of Soviet history.

But the story was not true. Completed shortly before the rugby split in August 1895, the painting was widely exhibited in Lancashire and Yorkshire just weeks after the split, when missing players would have been spotted immediately. More to the point, if Wollen had painted out all those players who joined the NU he would have been left with hardly any players on the field. With the exception of two Lancashire players who played for the exclusive Liverpool and Liverpool Old Boys clubs, all of the players in the 1893 match either played for clubs that were to join the NU or would switch to NU clubs. Nevertheless, the myth persists even today. For rugby union, the painting seemed to symbolise its institutional power over the league game. For league, it seemed to be yet another example of the visceral hostility it faced from the union game.

The French historian Ernest Renan's observation that 'getting its history wrong is part of being a nation' applies equally to sport: getting history wrong is an integral part of sports culture.[1] In part, it was a desire to get right the story of the split between league and union that inspired me to write *Rugby's Great Split*. Of all sports, none has a more interesting history than that of the rugby codes. The circumstances of rugby's origins and development compressed within it all the great social forces in modern society: class, nation, race and gender. In Britain and Australia, the sport became an arena for conflict between its middle-class leaders and working-class players and spectators. In Wales and New Zealand, rugby became entwined with national identity. In South Africa, rugby union became the sporting expression of apartheid. And in all countries and in both codes, it became a means for men to demonstrate their masculinity. *Rugby's Great Split* seeks to explain how these social forces acted upon rugby in Victorian and Edwardian Britain, and how they resulted in the creation of the sport of rugby league.

Yet despite a growing body of scholarly research into the history of sport, Renan's remark remains irritatingly true, and especially so of rugby union. In 2005 the newly elected president of the Rugby Football Union (RFU), LeRoy Angel, declared that 'the game has never excluded anyone from participation and it never will', blithely ignoring over a century of explicit and vigorously pursued exclusion of anyone who had participated in rugby league.[2] More insidious are the claims, repeated for example by the novelist Richard Beard in his 2004 memoir of rugby union, *Muddied Oafs*, that 'rugby league is dying'.[3] The reality is that rugby union as it existed for its first century is dead. Amateurism, which the RFU once claimed was the very reason for the sport's existence, has been abandoned, the game is now an unashamedly commercial spectacle at the mercy of television schedules, and its tactics and techniques are increasingly borrowed from rugby league. The leaders and supporters of rugby union described in these pages would not recognise today's game as theirs.

Yet, in contrast, the supporters of the NU would immediately recognise the culture of rugby league as their own, despite the tremendous changes in the playing of the game. Its working-class base of support, its distrust of the 'establishment', whether it be rugby union or the media, and its deep self-identification as a democratic sport remain as strong today as they were a hundred years ago. Likewise, those rugby league supporters who read *Rugby's Great Split* when it was first published had no difficulty in recognising events that occurred over a century ago. The book was lucky enough to receive a number of gracious reviews but perhaps the most gratifying was one that appeared in the now sadly defunct *Open Rugby* magazine, in which the reviewer commented that 'in reading the book I found an explanation for many things which I had previously felt'.[4] I hope that this new edition will further aid that understanding.

This edition carries out some essential housework to the original, such as correcting spelling and punctuation errors, but also adds new material. Chapter 6, which deals with the evolution of the Northern Union from a variant of rugby union into rugby league, has been expanded to include sections on the spread of the game to Australia and New Zealand, the failed attempt to expand the sport to South Wales, and the history of the RFU in the decade following the split. I have also added material about the levels of violence in the game in the early years of the NU. All of these topics were dealt with briefly in the original edition but the new edition presents the opportunity to explore them in greater depth. The section on the southern hemisphere enables me to incorporate groundbreaking newer work by Andrew Moore, Sean Fagan and Greg Ryan,[5] while that on Wales allows me to answer the question that is probably most often asked after 'why are there two kinds of rugby?', which is 'why did rugby league never take hold in Wales?' The section on the RFU's troubled Edwardian years squares the circle, something which space constraints precluded in the original. The history of the two games from World War One will be explored in subsequent volumes.

Although I remain indebted to those acknowledged in the first edition of the book, this new edition has benefited from discussions with my colleagues at De Montfort University's International Centre for Sports History and Culture: Neil Carter, Jeff Hill, Dick Holt, Pierre Lanfranchi, Tony Mason and Dil Porter. I owe a particular debt to Samantha Grant, my commissioning editor at Routledge, for her commitment to publishing this new edition. I also offer my thanks to many others who have helped along the way, especially Mary Bushby, Sean Fagan, Robert Gate, Tony Hughes, Chuck Korr, Greg Mallory, Kate Manson, Andrew Moore, Huw Richards, Greg Ryan, Jed Smith and Vanessa Toulmin.

Introduction

Why are there two forms of rugby? This has been asked at one time or another by anyone with even a passing interest in sport. And given the profound changes which both rugby league and rugby union are currently undergoing, the question now has an importance which transcends mere historical curiosity.

This work aims to provide the answer. It looks at the development of rugby in the social context of late Victorian and Edwardian England and tries to demonstrate how the changing nature of that society shaped the sport and led to the creation of rugby league. At its heart is an exploration of how a game that was initially exclusively restricted to public school boys was transformed into a sport that became exclusively identified with the working classes of northern England.

Although such a study is hopefully of value in itself, it also has a broader purpose. Despite the intentions or illusions of its participants, whether on or off the playing field, sporting culture reflects the society in which it is rooted and can offer us a window through which to study that society. This has been noted especially in the context of nationalism, race and gender but it is also true within the framework of class. As we shall see, rugby's growth and split brought to the fore all of these factors, but it was class that was the fulcrum around which rugby turned. This work also aims to provide insights into how attitudes towards class were expressed in ostensibly non-political, recreational situations. The fact that discourse on class took place in a sporting context meant that views were often expressed without the need for social or political diplomacy. In exploring this aspect of class, I have deliberately allowed the participants to speak for themselves. Regardless of current academic debates as to the reality of class, it is clear that the term did have meaning for those who were engaged in the debates on the future of rugby at the time.

But the debates on class that took place in rugby were not simply *about* class. Rugby itself was given broader, and widely differing, meanings by members of different classes. Rugby league and rugby union were used by their supporters to identify themselves and their class positions – and the status of others who did not share their social position. Rugby itself was used to define class. The traditional 'union = middle class/league = working class' dichotomy, which is shared even today by partisans of both sports, is not simply a creation of bar-room sociologists, but was a quite conscious social construction that has its roots in the class relations of the late Victorian and early Edwardian period. This construction was not solely the creation of one class or a section of a class but rather a product of the interplay and conflict between the classes – thus the place that rugby league occupied in working-class culture was in part defined by the attitude of the middle classes to the game. Conversely, the relationship between the middle classes and rugby union was shaped by the experience of the influx of the working classes into the sport. In other words, the culture of one class, or section of it, was not shaped by itself alone. This work is therefore an exploration of both middle-class and working-class cultures and the uses to which rugby was put by these cultures.

Much of this work builds on themes in late nineteenth century British social history that have been explored by historians such as Eric Hobsbawm, Gareth Stedman-Jones and Eileen and Stephen Yeo; in particular, the question of the development of modern working-class culture. I share Hobsbawm's view that the late-Victorian and Edwardian periods were crucial in defining working-class culture and leisure patterns, yet, as others have pointed out, there were many continuities from earlier times in this culture and many influences impacting on it from outside of the working class. Stedman-Jones has argued that working-class culture in London during this period was being depoliticised by the influence of the music hall, yet in their edited collection *Popular Culture and Class Conflict*, Eileen and Stephen Yeo have claimed that recreational activities were sites of conflict as important as those in the workplace. In the case of rugby in the north of England however, it does not seem that involvement in rugby was an inhibitor of social or political disaffection – the 1890s, the moment of rugby's greatest popularity in the north, was a period of widespread and often violent class conflict in Lancashire and Yorkshire. Conversely, there is no evidence that working-class rugby players or spectators viewed the sport itself as an arena of class struggle to rank alongside the mill or the mine – although there is evidence that middle-class rugby supporters viewed the game as a microcosm of a wider struggle.

The 'turn to language' in investigations of class and class consciousness during the 1870–1914 period has shifted the focus away from structural analysis of class to one in which words and symbols and their uses are central to understanding the process of the creation of class identity. While this may open the door in an idealist way to discursive analysis isolated from material conditions, it can also open up new possibilities for social and cultural historians. Patrick Joyce's work on northern factory culture and the importance of language in the study of working-class culture is crucial to understanding the various components of working-class culture and their interaction on each other. For a social historian of sport, an area of culture that is communicated and preserved largely through oral tradition, folk memory and ephemeral press reports, Joyce's work provides a tool that can take our understanding of sport beyond mere recounting of data and towards an understanding of the role of sport in the creation of class culture and, at a deeper level, why it was important to those who participated on the field or on the terraces.

The best work on the social history of sport has drawn on these themes. Tony Mason's work on soccer and Wray Vamplew's analysis of the development of professional sport have established the social history of sport as a legitimate area of study. Gareth Williams has illuminated the links between rugby union and the growth of Welsh national consciousness. Richard Holt's work has followed more directly the work of historians such as Joyce and his *Sport and the British*[1] is perhaps the only major work so far to attempt to situate the history of British sport in the broader context of the development of society. Nevertheless, there is much work still to be done in the field of sports history, especially if the discipline is to break free of the celebratory/statistical strands of work that have dominated 'amateur' sports history and are still occasionally to be found in works claiming academic credibility.

As will be seen, this book is written largely in a narrative, rather than thematic, format, unlike similar work on other sports of this period – for example Tony Mason's *Association Football and English Society 1863–1915* and Keith Sandiford's *Cricket and the Victorians*.[2] There are a number of reasons for this, the most obvious being that the chronology of rugby's rapid development leading to the 1895 split and subsequent evolution into two distinct sports lends itself perfectly to the narrative format. Without wishing to exaggerate, there is drama in the story. However, there are also methodological reasons for this approach. History is created by men and women pursuing their perceived interests in circumstances that are beyond their choosing. The danger of working in a thematic framework is that change, discontinuity and individual actions are ignored or underplayed in an attempt to uncover 'long waves' of historical development or to elaborate theoretical constructs. Periods separated by relatively short spans of time can be profoundly different, especially as perceived by the participants – a fact that is especially true of late Victorian sport. Rugby league in particular has a history that is defined by sharp twists and turns of fortune fashioned by the changing times in which it found itself.[3]

This should not be interpreted as a rallying cry for the primacy of empiricism over theoretical investigation, nor for history as a discipline over that of sociology. Rather it is an acknowledgement that without a firm grounding in the detail of historical events, any attempt at theoretical elaboration must remain at the level of speculation. Indeed, the weight of empirical data presents, in my view, compelling evidence for the primacy of the driving force of class relationships in the development of modern, mass spectator sports and for the crucial importance of the uses made of sport, both formally and informally, by wider social forces.

One example of the tendency to subsume the conflicts, contingencies and disjunctures that mark the social development of sport is the way in which most historians of the various codes of football have telescoped the current balance of power between the rival footballs back into the past. The most absurd example of this is the widely held assumption that the folk football of pre-industrial society was the direct precursor of modern soccer. On a less egregious level, Tony Mason's outstanding history of soccer in its formative period gives little indication that, as we shall see, the north of England was dominated by rugby until the mid-1880s or that soccer's prominence was only established after a struggle for supremacy with rugby. Although not wishing to engage in speculation of the 'what if' variety, I do hope to demonstrate that the relative weights of the football codes were not inevitable but were contingent on both objective and subjective factors.

In passing, it should be noted that this emphasis on change and continuity has an impact on language. I have used the word 'football' in the sense it was used at the time; both as a generic term for all forms of football – folk, association, rugby union and Northern Union – and as signifying the dominant code in rugby-playing areas. Football as a nationally used synonym for association football appears to have been a post-World War One phenomenon. As a child, I found it mystifying to hear my grandfather refer to rugby league as 'football': now I know why he did so. No doubt to the chagrin of devotees of the round ball code, I refer to association football as soccer, which is not an American term as many claim but the word commonly used for the sport in rugby areas during this time, although I have shied away from its alternative spelling of 'socker'.

The narrative structure is therefore based largely on chronological order. Chapter 1 begins with the folk antecedents of modern football and seeks to demonstrate the deep roots of these early forms of football. In a sense, this is a pre-emptive strike against the belief that rugby football was the exclusive property of the public school-educated middle classes, a view which is examined in the latter part of the chapter, which looks at the uses to which football was put by the public schools. The chapter moves on to discuss the spread of rugby from the public schools to the north of England and links the rapid growth of the sport to the sense of civic pride that prevailed among the industrial towns of the North and Midlands. Finally, the chapter ends at the moment at which rugby began to gain a following among the working classes in the late 1870s.

This new-found popularity, and the disquiet it provoked among rugby's leaders north and south, is the theme of Chapter 2. It analyses the means by which working-class men and women became involved in the sport and looks at the nature and activities of the rugby crowds of the period. Its key focus is on the ways in which working-class cultural practices became part of the fabric of the sport and the counter-development of the ideology of amateurism as a method of suppressing this, culminating in the Rugby Football Union's introduction of its first set of regulations intended to stamp out incipient professionalism.

Chapter 3 examines the 'golden age' of northern rugby union in the late 1880s and early 1890s. By now the game in Yorkshire and in many areas of Lancashire was supported by all classes but with the working-classes making up the majority of players and spectators. The chapter highlights how the demands of working-class players and the growing commercialism of the sport in the north undermined amateurism and made its implementation, despite the vigorous efforts of its partisans, impossible.

The breakdown in the consensus among rugby's leaders about how to deal with mass working-class participation and the events leading to the 1895 split are the focus of Chapter 4. This looks at the debates that took place about the role of working-class players, about amateurism and professionalism and also about broken-time payments and unfettered professionalism. Much of the latter half of this chapter is taken up with tracking the events and political manoeuvring that took place in the two years following the RFU's 1893 Annual General Meeting, as it became clear that there was no longer room for compromise between the supporters of pristine amateurism and those of broken-time.

The aftermath of the split is dealt with in Chapter 5. As well as looking at the initial successes of the Northern Union and the devastation of northern rugby union, it attempts to explore the reasons for the marginalisation of the NU, placing it in the context of a multiplicity of national and class-based forces. After examining the role of players in the game and the NU's reluctant steps to open professionalism, the chapter details the helplessness of the sport in the face of the tidal wave of soccer in the early 1900s.

The final chapter looks at the development of the NU as a separate sport, as it moved away from being merely a professional version of rugby union. It details the rule changes that created a new sport, its expansion to other countries and the growth of the game's distinct ideology. It examines the class composition of the sport's leadership and looks at the way in which it became identified almost exclusively with the working classes and how working-class cultural norms came to predominate, both on the field and in the crowds that watched the game.

Within this structure, certain themes are explored on a recurring basis. The organisation of the material in this way helps in understanding the changing nature of rugby and the society that shaped it. For example, at various points the relationship between rugby and masculinity is looked at in the context of public school rugby, under rugby union rules and Northern Union rules. I will argue that, first and foremost, definitions of masculinity and violence were defined by class. Acts perceived as manly and character-forming by the middle classes were interpreted differently when carried out by members of the working classes: thus hacking was viewed as courageous between former public school boys, yet outrageous when perpetrated by miners. Conversely, the predominantly working-class supporters of the NU found tripping and kicking unacceptable. The growth of imperial nationalism towards the end of the nineteenth century had a crucial impact on notions of masculinity: not only did it tie rugby closer to the felt need to prepare for war, but it also had the effect of both excluding NU rugby from the pantheon of acceptable manly pursuits and of halting the significant support for the game given by women in the 1880s.

Similarly, the North/South divide is examined throughout the work. Again flowing from an understanding of the primacy of class relations to the development of the game, I will suggest that the importance of regionalism to rugby's 1895 split has been exaggerated – although the post-1895 period is a different matter. Certainly up to the late 1880s there was almost total unanimity between

North and South on the need to oppose professionalism and, indeed, for many the proposal to introduce broken-time payments was an attempt to safeguard this unity. It was only in the early years of the twentieth century, as the Northern Union began to develop its own ideology, that 'Northernness' became an important factor in northern rugby.

Although class is viewed as the dynamo that ultimately drove rugby to schism, the role of civic pride, of both the working and middle classes, and of commercialism is also examined in the changing contexts of the period. It was the growth of clubs seeking to represent their towns that opened the door for working-class involvement in rugby and it was the twin engines of civic glory and mass working-class involvement that provided the basis for the rapid growth of commercialism in rugby in Lancashire and Yorkshire in the 1880s. The clash between commercialism and amateurism is central to the first half of the book, as the exigencies of commercialism and the civic pride that it could bring became the wedge that split the RFU leadership's previous consensus over how to deal with the working-class influx.

The activities and motivations of players and crowds under the RFU and NU regimes are also highlighted separately throughout the work. The practices and cultural norms that working-class players and spectators brought to the game were crucial in undermining both middle-class control of rugby and the belief of some middle-class rugby administrators that the classes could be accommodated on the rugby field. But such practices were not fixed and the development of the NU was accompanied by subtle changes in the behaviour of players and spectators, especially in the way the game was played and in the behaviour of spectators to rival supporters.

The sources for this work came primarily from newspapers of the time, in particular *Athletic News* and the *Yorkshire Post*. This reliance on newspapers has its weaknesses; even in the late nineteenth century the sporting press had its own agendas and reporting was probably as selective and superficial as it is today. Any historian must be highly suspicious of such material. Nevertheless, both of these newspapers had a reputation for accuracy and from 1877 the *Yorkshire Post* carried detailed reports, and sometimes verbatim minutes, of the leading bodies of not only Yorkshire rugby union, but also of the Lancashire, Welsh and English rugby unions, as well as the Football Association and Football League. In this, it was far more comprehensive than *Athletic News*, which was less inclined to involve itself in the politics of rugby or soccer. I have also made extensive use of the literary weeklies that flourished in Yorkshire in the 1880s and 1890s, which as well as often producing dialect material, carried detailed reports of football and its culture. Curiously, the equivalent Lancashire journals of the time carried little football coverage, possibly reflecting the fact that rugby never occupied as central a place in the culture of the county as it did in Yorkshire. This lack of minutiae about the day-to-day activities of Lancashire clubs in the 1880s has forced me at times to place an unintentional focus on Yorkshire clubs during this early period.

By and large, I have deliberately avoided using such works as club histories. While there are honourable exceptions, a number of which are listed in the bibliography, it seems to me that many of these works are poorly researched and, especially when written about rugby union clubs, serve little purpose other than to assure supporters that their club can claim some form of dubious apostolic succession from the mists of time. In contrast, and no less flawed, most rugby league club histories assume a big bang theory, whereby the pre-split period was an unknowable primordial soup out of which clubs sprang fully formed in August 1895.

Sadly for the historian, and posterity, very few club records from the period have survived. The few that have are generally to be found in local libraries and archives. As many have pointed out in relation to other sports, the administrators of clubs and sporting bodies unfortunately seem to have little sense of the importance of preserving their history. I have made use of the minute books of leading committees at the headquarters of the Rugby Football League and the Rugby Football Union; while useful, these are usually little more than a written record of decisions made. The usefulness of the Rugby League's records is also undermined by the fact that they hold no minutes of the first four years of its existence − a crucial period in its development. Thus the reliance on newspapers was consequently both enforced and by choice.

Finally, I have avoided direct polemic with other authors unless absolutely necessary, although I have referenced their works where appropriate. This is for two reasons: first, there is an urgent need to establish the historical record. Too much work on sport has been produced that relies on secondary sources and half-digested myth. In the case of rugby, Frank Marshall's admirable but flawed *Football − the Rugby Union Game*, first published in 1892, has too often been used uncritically.[4] Where prominent works are factually incorrect, I have pointed this out in footnotes. Secondly, I hope that where its analysis and conclusions differ from others, this work speaks for itself. Certainly, the rise of professionalism, the reasons for the 1895 split and the class composition of the Northern Union are viewed from a different perspective from previous researchers.[5] Nevertheless, there is a sense in which I am indebted to all previous scholars and researchers of the social history of sport. Without their example, the task of exploring how and why men and women found twenty-six players in pursuit of an oval ball so fascinating would have been so much more difficult.

Although the writing of this work has been a singular exercise, it would not have been possible without the help of many people. I would particularly like to thank John Baxendale, Cathy France, Robert Gate, Trevor Delaney, John Jenkins and Piers Morgan for their support above and beyond the call of duty. For help, assistance and suggestions, my thanks also go to Tim Auty, Terry Bambrook, Bernard Booth, Walter Chamberlain and Heather Menzie, J. G. Davies of Leeds Grammar School, John Drake, Dave Fox, Mike and Lesley Gardner, Trevor Gibbons, Elaine Hall, Chris Harte, Richard Holt, Rex King at the Rugby Football Union, Michael Latham, Tony Lewis, Tony Mangan, Tom Mather,

John Mitchell of St Peter's School in York, Colin Price and team at Leeds Local History Library, Alex Service, Karl Spracklen and the Rugby Football League's Neil Tunnicliffe, not forgetting the staffs of Barrow, Batley, Bolton, Bradford, Brighouse, Burnley, Castleford, Dewsbury, Huddersfield, Hull, Keighley, Manchester, Oldham, Preston, Rochdale, Salford, Wakefield, Warrington, Widnes and Wigan libraries, the British Library in London and Wetherby, Colindale Newspaper Library, the Public Record Office at Kew, and the city archives at Hull, Leeds, Wakefield and York.

Chapter I

From folk football to civic pride: Origins to 1879

Rugby league football, like all modern forms of football, has its roots in the folk football of pre-industrial society. Many of the areas that became strongholds of the game had long histories of folk football going back far into the past. Hull, Huddersfield, Manchester, Rochdale, Whitehaven, Workington, York and many other towns in Lancashire, Yorkshire and the North West can all record football games from at least the seventeenth century.[1]

These early forms of football were intimately connected with the fairs, festivals and holidays of a predominantly rural nation. Shrove Tuesday, in particular, was the favoured day for many football matches across Britain. Christmas Day, New Year's Day and the Easter holidays too were popular dates for football. Other than two sides and the propulsion of a ball to a goal, the playing rules of the game could differ enormously from area to area. In some regions, the ball was driven primarily by foot. In others, the ball was carried or thrown. Quite often a mixture of the two was allowed. But against those who would imagine folk football was a direct precursor to soccer, Montague Shearman's *Athletics and Football*, published in 1887, noted that 'there is no trace in the original form of [football] to suggest that nothing but kicking is allowed'.[2]

Folk football was primarily a game for large numbers played over wide distances, often involving the majority of the male population. In Derby, the game often involved around a thousand men, while the Sedgefield game involved 400 men per side. The goals were three miles apart for the Ashbourne game, while Whitehaven's goals were set at the docks and a wall outside of the town. These organised games were also generally occasions for social mixing between the classes. The level of organisation required in many matches was considerable, often involving the closing of roads, prizes, arrangement of fields, suspension of regular business and newspaper advertisements, necessitating the patronage of local squires or landowners. But whatever its rules or wherever it was played, that folk football was extremely violent and disorderly, even in its most organised form, there can be no doubt. Fighting, bloodshed and broken bones are words rarely absent from reports of football matches, and death was not an uncommon occurrence. It is fair to say that Joseph Lawson's description of the Pudsey street game of the 1820s and 1830s could apply to almost any area in which the game was played:

> Down-towners playing up-towners; in wet weather, bad roads and played through the village; breaking windows, striking bystanders, the ball driven into houses; and such 'shinning', as they called kicking each other's legs. It was quite common to see these up and down towners kicking each other's shins when the ball was a hundred yards away. Of course, many received serious injuries.[3]

By the early 1800s, the growth of industrial capitalism had begun to undermine the traditional social basis for folk football. The anti-Sabbatarian Horatio Smith, writing in 1831, described the way in which the urbanisation of London had driven out the possibilities for popular recreation:

> Every vacant and green spot has been converted into a street; field after field has been absorbed by the builder; all scenes of popular resort have been smothered with piles of brick; football and cricket grounds, bowling greens, and the enclosures or open places set apart for archery and other pastimes have been successfully parcelled out in squares, lanes or alleys.[4]

But it was not simply lack of green spaces that removed opportunities to play. Football had developed in a rural, feudalistic setting. The way in which it was played – the involvement of large numbers of people playing and watching, taking place over large areas and for long hours – ran counter to the discipline, order and organisation necessary for urban capitalism. As a critic of the Derby football game complained in 1832, 'it is not a trifling consideration that a suspension of business for nearly two days should be created to the inhabitants for the mere gratification of a sport at once so useless and barbarous'.[5] In 1835 the Highways Act banned the playing of football on public highways, imposing a maximum penalty of forty shillings. Religious objections to the playing of the game grew too, especially from nonconformist denominations who saw in football only licentiousness, debauchery and violence. Just as importantly, the old relationships between the classes no longer existed. The 1830s and 1840s saw the rise of the Chartists, attempts at armed insurrection in England and Wales and widespread fear of revolution crossing the channel, reducing to a negligible level the opportunities for social mixing across class lines. The gathering of large numbers of working-class people, for whatever purpose, was viewed with some suspicion by the authorities. Threats to public order were often cited as the reasons for the banning of football, as, gradually, most of the remaining outposts of the traditional game succumbed to the exigencies of capitalism.[6]

Despite the vast differences in modes of play and methods of organisation between pre-industrial football and its late-Victorian forms, it is important to stress that many continuities and survivals from these earlier times became bound up in the culture of modern football. For example, there is little doubt that it was associated in the public mind with the common people. In 1720, *Stow's Survey* spoke of football as something with which 'the lower classes divert themselves', along with 'throwing at cocks and lying at alehouses', amongst others.[7] Joseph Strutt's 1801 survey of British sports describes football as 'formerly much in vogue among the common people of England'.[8] Occasionally football was used as a pretext for the gathering of large crowds to protest against a variety of injustices. A protest against enclosure at White Roding, Essex, in 1724 was initiated under the guise of a football match, while at Kettering in 1740 a match was organised as a pretext for the attempted pulling down of a local mill.[9] The importance of the game to some sections of the nascent working class can be seen in an 1845 comment of a working man in Derby responding to attempts to ban the annual game: 'It is all disappointment, no sports and no football. This is the way they always treat poor folks.'[10]

The decline and suppression of folk football was not without opposition nor was it totally successful. In Derby, for example, a protracted struggle took place in the 1840s against the local authority's outlawing of the Shrove Tuesday game, including the reading of the Riot Act and the calling out of troops in 1846.[11] Indeed, despite Strutt's belief in 1801 that 'of late years [football] seems to have fallen into disrepute, and is but little practised', a number of games survived until well into the mid-nineteenth century.[12] These survivals continued primarily in villages and rural communities where the straightjacket of inflexible working hours was not so tight. This was especially true in areas where pre-industrial forms of capitalism such as outworking predominated, and where, more often than not, the patronage of a local landowner could be relied upon to provide the authority to ensure folk football's continuation; for example, the Duke of Northumberland rescued the Shrove Tuesday game at Alnwick in Northumberland in 1827 by providing a field for the game to be played upon and presenting the ball before the match.[13]

It is also clear that survivals of unorganised football, in the form of kickabouts in the streets or fields, continued to be played throughout the period of folk football's decline. Certainly, football was still played in the 1840s in villages near Huddersfield and Leeds.[14] In 1842 the Royal Commission on Children in Mines and Manufactories found that football was played widely, but informally, in the West Riding coal fields. It is also clear that in the mid-nineteenth century knowledge of football survived among the working classes in parallel with the development and growing influence of public school-derived football. For example, in Sutton, a village just to the east of Hull, a form of folk football was played up until at least 1871, and was the introduction to the game for at least one Hull FC player of the 1880s. Such evidence highlights the degree to which continuities and survivals of pre-industrial practices coexisted alongside urban, industrial culture. It may well be that this residual consciousness of older forms of football was one of the reasons for the alacrity with which organised rugby and association football were taken up by the working classes in the latter part of the century.[15]

But as organised football faded almost to insignificance in urban society, it was beginning to acquire the utmost significance in the life of British public schools. By the time the Royal Commission on Public Schools had published its report in 1864, muscular Christianity's cult of games in the public schools had reached full maturity – and football occupied a central position in its pantheon of character-building sports. Nowhere was this more true than at Rugby school. Football had begun to be played by the boys of the school around 1800 and it is probable, although no definite proof exists, that the game they played was inspired by the annual New Year's Eve game played by the people of the town of Rugby in the 1700s.[16] Initially, the boys played the game with little or no interest from the school authorities but headmaster Thomas Arnold's reshaping of the school ethos in the 1830s led his successors to ascribe to football a central position in the school curriculum. Organised by the praeposters, the school's senior boys, football gradually came to occupy a key position not just as a winter recreation but also in the boys' hierarchical 'fagging' system.[17] While its origins at the school may be unclear, there is little doubt as to a key reason for football's popularity among the boys who played it or the partisans of muscular Christianity who championed it – its violent appeal to masculinity.

As Philip Mason has noted:

> the [public school] process aimed above all at *hardening*. The public schools were meant to produce a ruling class, and there was a wide-spread view that great empires of the past had fallen because the ruling classes had grown luxurious and effeminate.[emphasis in original][18]

As if in practical demonstration of this, the Rugby school game was marked by an almost obsessional belief in players 'hacking' at each other's shins. Known as 'shinning' in the more plebeian forms of folk football from which the practice was taken, hacking became one of the issues that divided the rugby-playing schools from the devotees of 'dribbling' forms of football, such as Eton or Harrow, at the founding of the Football Association in 1863. The importance of hacking to the Rugby game cannot be underestimated: reminiscing about his school days in the 1860s at rugby-playing Blackheath Proprietary School, Rugby Football Union (RFU) president Harry Garnett recalled how boys practised hacking in their dorms at night. 'Boots were made specially with an extra sole piece at the toe, pointed like a ship's ram, and hardened against the bars of the fire, or with a hot poker,' and opponents were hacked 'with the utmost violence'. Throughout his playing career, Garnett played in bare legs, deliberately disdaining protection. Once when playing for Otley, Garnett told a team mate who was wearing a shinguard 'If you don't take that off, I will see if I cannot hack it off,' adding that his colleague 'deemed it prudent to take the shin guard off at once'.[19] The Reverend E. H. Dykes, an archetypal footballing muscular Christian, went to Durham School during the same period, where:

> hacking and tripping were allowed to any extent. 'Hack him over' was the cry when anyone was running with the ball, and it was the commonest thing to see fellows hacked off their feet. A scrummage was mainly an opportunity for hard hacking.

He claimed that the hardest hack he ever took was from a future Bishop of Calcutta, although he took the precaution of preparing for school games by 'solemnly hammering my shins with a poker to make them hard'.[20]

As these examples from Blackheath and Durham demonstrate, by the 1850s the Rugby school game had quickly acquired adherents in other schools. Spurred by the popularity of Arnold's teachings (despite the fact that he personally showed no interest in football) and the proselytising zeal of old Rugbeians who became teachers, public schools across the country, especially the newer schools such as Clifton, Haileybury, Wellington, Marlborough and Cheltenham, took up the game. Public consciousness of the Rugby game was raised significantly in 1857 with the publication of old boy Thomas Hughes' *Tom Brown's Schooldays*, which sold 11,000 copies in its first year. While the game's initial popularity may have in part been due to its association with Arnold's reputation and Hughes' book, it was the distinctiveness of its rules which cemented its popularity among its players.

In 1845, a levee, or general meeting, of the sixth form published the rules to Rugby school football, highlighting the essential difference between their game and those of the other leading public schools: running with the ball. Whilst other schools did not totally forbid handling the ball, only Rugby allowed a player to catch the ball and run with it. How this point of difference arose has become possibly the most famous example of myth-making in British sport. Ostensibly, as recorded in a plaque at Rugby school erected in 1900, one William Webb Ellis 'with a fine disregard for the rules of football as played in his time, first took the ball in his arms and ran with it, thus originating the distinctive feature of the Rugby game' sometime in late 1823. Unfortunately, no facts can be adduced to support this proclamation. The Rugby game had originally not allowed carrying the ball but by the early 1830s it had become an accepted feature of the game. There is no way of knowing who first ran with the ball at Rugby, but whoever did the deed was only continuing the age-old traditions of folk football. If anyone could claim the mantle of originator of the carrying game at the school, it would be Jem Mackie, a pupil who became well known for his exploits as a ball-carrier in the late 1830s. Soon after, in 1842, carrying was formally legalised by a levee.

Ellis's name was first advanced in 1877, and again in 1880, by Matthew Bloxam, an old boy keen to prove that the Rugby game was unique to itself and was not a variant of older folk football. Other than in Bloxam's writings, Ellis's name is not mentioned in connection with the Rugby game in any work on the subject published before 1895. Even the 1895 inquiry of the Old Rugbeian Society into the origins of the game, which endorsed Bloxam's theory and led to the erection of the commemorative plaque, could not find a single witness who either saw Ellis's act or could provide even hearsay evidence of it. Although it has been suggested that the Rugbeians had a need for a heroic, Carlylean figure with whom to credit the origins of the game, the acceptance of Bloxam's myth and the invention of the Webb Ellis tradition served a broader function for both the school and the Rugby Union authorities at that time.[21] The school itself had ceased to play other schools at the game in 1876 after a series of losses, claiming that their opponents were playing non-school boys, only reviving inter-school games two decades later. The Webb Ellis myth allowed the school to do something it had been unable to do on the playing field: reassert its leading position in public school football over its more successful imitators. More importantly for the broader perception of the sport, the myth served to anchor the Rugby game as separate from the older traditions of plebeian folk football, creating a distinct middle-class lineage for the sport at a time when the middle classes in general were seeking to create exclusive recreational havens for themselves outside of the prevailing mass sporting culture.[22] This explains why the myth was taken up with such alacrity and why previous claims to historical lineage were so quickly dropped – such as the Reverend Frank Marshall's in his 1892 history, *Football – the Rugby Union Game*, that rugby was:

> the most ancient of British sports ... the legitimate refinement of the rough and crude games which in their main features are undoubtedly the source from which the Rugby game and the Rugby game alone are the true issue.[23]

The legend also helped to de-legitimise the 1895 split of the Northern Union by seemingly proving that rugby football was indeed the property of the middle classes. And by implying that Ellis was playing a form of soccer when he picked up the ball, it unwittingly lent support to the claims of association football that it was the continuator of the folk football of the masses.

But these developments lay in the future. As pupils and masters left Rugby and the schools that had adopted the Arnoldian spirit, many took with them a continuing enthusiasm for the philosophy of 'Mens sana in corpore sano'[24] and the game they had learnt as boys. The sport had become, as one old Rugbeian put it in 1863, 'an enthralling, engrossing passion that seems to madden all who come beneath its influence as the Thrysi of Bacchus frenzied the Maendes of old'.[25] It was this enthusiasm that was to lay the basis for the formation of the football clubs which were to bloom in the 1860s and 1870s.

A game for gentlemen throughout the land

It therefore did not take long for the spread of Rugby School football to reach Yorkshire and Lancashire. But this did not happen in a vacuum. The expansion of the middle classes in the mid-nineteenth century and the subsequent development of leisure time led to a corresponding demand for recreational activities from those engaged in white collar work. In this 'new leisure world',[26] there was a growing interest in physical activity, especially from former public school boys upon whom the importance of healthy minds and healthy bodies had been impressed from an early age. Physical recreation was, wrote a correspondent to the *Leeds Mercury* in early 1864:

> a subject which is becoming more and more recognised as one of the greatest importance to one class in particular ... viz., the young men who are all day engaged in the dispiriting and enervating employment of the shop, the office, and the warehouse, in our busy manufacturing and commercial towns.[27]

The formation of the Rifle Volunteer movement in 1859 as a precautionary measure against the threat of a French invasion played an important role in both meeting and extending this demand. After the initial fear of invasion had passed, the Volunteers quickly enlarged their scope of activities to take in athletics, gymnastics and other sports. Their training grounds and fields were to provide the first playing pitches for Hull, Huddersfield and many other football clubs of the period.[28] Across England, organised athletic clubs were being founded, the formation of the Amateur Athletic Club in 1866 marking the start of attempts to regulate the sport.[29] Gymnasia had also been introduced into a number of northern towns by this time, such as one opened in Huddersfield in 1850. The success of these ventures – Huddersfield Athletic Club recruited over 150 members within a month of its foundation in 1864 and Leeds Football Club attracted over 100 in six weeks in the same year – was proof of the fertile ground into which the seeds of football were being planted.[30]

The first recorded non-school football match under Rugby School rules in the region took place in December 1857 at Edge Hill cricket ground in Liverpool, when old Rugbeian F. A. Mather and Richard Sykes, the current football captain of Rugby School, organised a 'Rugby versus the World' game. Around fifty players took part, most being Rugbeians, many being sons of Liverpool's merchant class and all being drawn from the upper echelons of society. This so encouraged Mather and his fellow-participants that it appears a Liverpool football club was formed some time after the match.[31] Sykes, who was actually a native of Manchester, was also one of the central movers in the foundation of Manchester FC in 1860, being its first captain. Like the key figures in the Liverpool club, Manchester's founders had learnt the game at public school, particularly at Rugby itself and at rugby football-playing

Cheltenham College.[32] Hull Football Club was founded in a similar fashion in 1865 when a group of Rugby School boys returning home for holidays, led by the scion of one of Hull's leading ship-owning families, W. H. H. Hutchinson, decided to form a football club.[33]

The widespread diffusion of Arnold's supposed ideals amongst public schools also meant that by the 1860s Rugby School was not the only school playing its version of football. Leeds Grammar School had formed a football club to play the game as early as 1851 and St Peter's School in York had published its football rules, modelled on Rugby rules, in 1856.[34] Pupils and former pupils of these schools were instrumental in founding the original Leeds club in 1864, the York club in 1868 and Leeds St John's in 1870, which was to become the Leeds club in 1890. Hull's founders also included pupils of St Peter's and Cheltenham College. The first Broughton football club in Manchester was founded as a team of Broughton College school boys in 1869 and, a year later, boys from Victoria Park and Chorlton High schools began the Manchester Free Wanderers club.[35] And, as with the old Rugbeians, boys sent away to rugby-playing schools returned to the region with a desire to start their own clubs: Harry Garnett, the unreconstructed enthusiast of hacking, was educated at Blackheath Proprietary School in London (his younger brothers all went to Rugby) and brought back to Yorkshire an enthusiasm for the game he had played at school, as did former pupils of Mill Hill School and Finchley Christ College in London and Durham School.[36]

As can be seen from this roll-call of public school alumni, the social character of these early clubs was uniformly middle class, albeit encompassing a wide spectrum of occupations and professions. Liverpool's leading lights were cotton merchants and articled clerks and Manchester's founders came from similar backgrounds. Robert Christison, the instigator of the York club, was a solicitor, while Huddersfield's Harry Beardsell was a wool merchant. In comparison to the sons of shipping magnates and clergymen who led Hull FC or the heirs to textile manufacturers who formed the Bradford club, the Leeds club was founded by members of the less exalted sections of this class. Henry Jenkinson, who placed the advertisement in the *Leeds Mercury* calling for the formation of a football club, was a clerk with the North East Railway company, although he later became a moderately successful author of walking guides, and of those who responded to his advertisement, one was a partner in a cap manufacturers, one a carting agent and another a bank employee. Barrow FC's team for their first match in December 1875 included seven old boys from Lancaster Grammar School, a solicitor, a clergyman, an accountant, a customs officer and a future Justice of the Peace.[37]

The narrowness of the social strata upon which these clubs were based can also be seen from the family relationships of many of the clubs' players and officials (although at this time they were usually one and the same). Christison was one of three brothers who founded York FC. At Hull three separate sets of brothers played for the club, three members of the Huth family played for

Huddersfield, three Cariss brothers graduated from Leeds Grammar School to the Leeds club and four sets of brothers were involved in the founding of the Harrogate club.[38] And where the ties of family or school were lacking, the social connections of business could substitute. On being questioned as to the respectability of his fledging Bradford club, textile dye works heir Oates Ingham replied, 'Well, you know me, and do business with my firm.'[39] More practically, the subscription money to join one of these football clubs was usually sufficient to restrict membership to the middle classes – Manchester charged ten shillings and sixpence, Rochdale ten shillings and Liverpool five shillings, rising to ten in 1875. Even the two shillings and sixpence charged by Bradford, Huddersfield and Hull would probably have been beyond the reach of the wider population.[40] Rational recreation, the attempt by sections of the middle classes to take their idea of culture and recreation to the working classes, was most definitely not part of the ethos of any of these early clubs.

Indeed, the clubs formed in the 1850s and 1860s existed solely for the enjoyment of their members alone. Few, if any, spectators watched them play and the clubs paid little attention to those that did – not one of the twenty-one provincial football clubs is listed as charging an admission fee to their ground in the *Football Annual* of 1868. Play was organised according to the needs of members; the Leeds club practised every morning at 6.30am and in the evening at 7.30pm, attracting up to 60 players for the early session and 150 at night, with a fine of 6d for latecomers being 'strictly enforced for a time'.[41] Up to the mid-1870s, players would usually play the game in their ordinary clothes; Leeds's J. G. Hudson even played his entire career wearing spectacles, breaking them only once. It was only around 1870 that some clubs began to insist on players wearing a uniform, Hull's 1870 rule book specifying 'a striped scarlet and white jersey, a scarlet and white cap (if any), with white flannels'.[42] Even as late as 1874 Halifax played their first ever game, at Leeds Athletic, in everyday clothes.[43] Because inter-club games were initially infrequent, although less so between school teams, clubs were more likely to play games between different categories of members. Liverpool played Rugby and Cheltenham versus the Rest, Bradford played Captain's side versus Secretary's side, the Leeds club in 1870 held a match between Dixon's Blues and Turner's Reds, and many clubs played A–M versus N–Z or some other alphabetical combination. St Helens in the early 1870s even played Fair versus Dark.

This preponderance of footballers playing Rugby School rules in the major cities of Lancashire and Yorkshire effectively meant that anyone wishing to play football in the region usually had to choose rugby – thus confining soccer, up to the 1880s at least, to pockets in eastern Lancashire and around Sheffield in south Yorkshire. The high social status of clubs led by old Rugbeians also meant that significant social cachet was beginning to become attached to the playing of the game, giving newcomers to club football another incentive to play under Rugby rules. The dominance of the rugby code can be seen in the subsequent sporting activities of old boys of Bramham College near Leeds.

Founded by the Liberal, non-conformist Dr Haigh in 1843 and based on a firm belief in muscular Christianity, it played a version of association rules and, indeed, became one of the first teams in Yorkshire to join the Football Association.[44] However, its old boys earned a place in the football history of the area for being the founders of rugby football clubs: Oates Ingham and Alfred Firth founding the Bradford club in 1863, R. J. Wade being instrumental in Hull FC and Harry Beardsell being a key mover in Huddersfield Athletic Club's formation of a football section.

Despite a common enthusiasm for the Rugby version of football, there existed wide variations in the rules, clubs each having their own greater or lesser peculiarities. This was not confined to the Northern clubs; there were similarly wide variations in the rules of the London-based clubs.[45] For example, there was little agreement on the number of players per side. At the extreme end of the spectrum were Leeds, who according to one of their founders 'did not trouble too much about [rules]' despite writing to Rugby School's head-master, Dr Temple, seeking a game with the school.[46] More particularly, hacking, despite its popularity amongst some footballers, was frowned upon by many. Rochdale, Sale FC and Preston Grasshoppers were by no means unusual in playing non-hacking Rugby rules; even Hull, founded by Rugbeians, allowed tripping but not hacking. In contrast, York maintained the zeal for hacking, on one occasion playing the shinguard-wearing York Training College and, upon failing to convince them to discard their protection, proceeded 'to make them look a good deal worse for wear' by the time they removed the shinguards after the game.[47] Despite being founded by non-hacking association-playing Bramham old boys, Bradford also played full Rugby rules, including hacking. The original rules of St Peter's School in York allowed hacking too, although this was outlawed in 1873. The St Peter's rule book was also the source for one of the more bizarre statutes to appear in a club rule book – Hull FC's rule 20, stating that 'no player may stand on the goal bar to prevent [the ball] going over'.[48]

But as the number of clubs and players grew, so too did the desire to play new opponents. This necessarily led to compromises in rules and even the playing of other football codes: 'we played any mortal code possible with other clubs away from home so long as we could get a game of some sort,' remarked Hull's William Hutchinson.[49] As late as 1873 Bradford still set aside two Saturdays a season on their fixture list for 'association practice'.[50] The most common arrangement in such situations was that which pertained amongst the public schools of the area, whereby the rules of the home club would be played. This presented little problem for games between clubs such as Leeds and Manchester, who first played each other in 1865, where there was common agreement as to the form of the game if not the precise rules. However, greater difficulties were experienced by clubs when they sought to organise matches with sides outside of the rugby-playing areas.

The most popular source of non-rugby opponents was Sheffield, a stronghold of football but of the dribbling variety, as defined by the rules of the Sheffield

Association, which had been formed in 1857, six years before the Football Association.[51] The FA itself had initially investigated the possibility of forging a unified football code but this had been scuppered by supporters of dribbling rules, who pushed through the adoption of the 1863 Cambridge University rule book; motions to adopt running with the ball and hacking by supporters of Rugby rules were decisively voted down by members of the FA. Nevertheless, the difference between rugby and the dribbling forms of football did not appear to be so wide as to make rapprochement impossible. Neither the Cambridge rules nor the FA rules forbade touching the ball with the hands, only running with it. The Sheffield code also allowed for use of the hand to hit or push the ball. And both the FA and the Sheffield rules even allowed players to make a 'fair catch' of the ball in general play, entitling him to have a free kick unchallenged by members of the opposing side. However, hacking, holding, pushing and tripping were explicitly forbidden by both sets of rules.[52]

In reality however, the disparity between the two forms of football and players' familiarity with their own code meant that the usual result was a victory for whichever side was playing at home under their own rules, giving an unwelcome predictability to such matches. In 1864 Leeds played Sheffield, winning at home and losing at Sheffield. Four years later Manchester easily defeated Sheffield by a goal and eight touchdowns to nil on home territory but lost two goals to nil in south Yorkshire. Similar difficulties afflicted Hull FC, whose football hinterland extended south of the Humber into association-playing Lincolnshire. Their first away game took place under association rules at Lincoln in 1866. Hull White Star, the club with which Hull FC would eventually merge, suffered in the same way, playing rugby rules at home, association when playing at Brigg and Market Rasen and, more acceptably, a twelve-a-side variation of rugby at Gainsborough.[53] Gradually however, as the rules of the two games became more codified and as the players acquired skills developed specifically for their form of football, the desire and occasion for such hybrid matches declined.

By 1870, public interest in football was beginning to develop beyond the narrow circle of those who had played the game at school. Press reports of matches began to appear in local newspapers and, in particular, major matches, such as those between clubs representing towns, began to attract significant numbers of spectators. Like the players, the spectators at this time came almost exclusively from the middle classes. A match between Liberals and Conservatives organised by the Huddersfield club in 1869, with the teams being chosen by prominent local Liberal Edward Brooke and Tory C. E. Freeman was 'attended by nearly all the well-known ladies and gentlemen of the town, while the residents generally evinced an extraordinary enthusiasm for the encounter'.[54] That same year, 3,500 people had attended a match between Huddersfield and Leeds Grammar School. Given such numbers, it is probably safe to assume that some of these spectators came from the working classes, yet such interest was still very limited – and in some areas the working classes showed no interest at all in organised football. Jack Shaw, an early member of the York club, described how at the start of the 1870s:

all the sport in which the working men of York seemed interested was rabbit coursing. Hundreds of them used to assemble on the Knavesmire on a Saturday afternoon to indulge in this so-called sport and when they saw the football players they made jeering references to the 'silly fools who kicked the ball about in the wet'.[55]

This sentiment probably extended beyond York, because rabbit coursing, pigeon shooting, foot racing and 'knur and spel', a game in which a long-handled club was used to hit a wooden ball as far as possible, all commanded a great deal of support and involvement from the working classes at this time.

Testimony to the popularity and growth of football amongst the middle classes was provided by the playing of the first Yorkshire versus Lancashire match in March 1870. The success of the annual games between Leeds and Manchester, including an exhibition match staged at Huddersfield in 1867, and the rise in the number of clubs on both sides of the county border, led to the suggestion that a county match be arranged. Responsibility for organising the game fell to J. G. Hudson, one of the founders of the Leeds club, who, along with Yorkshire captain Howard Wright, attempted to make the Yorkshire side as representative as possible of the county's footballing prowess by inviting players not only from the senior Yorkshire rugby clubs, Bradford, Huddersfield, Hull and Leeds, but also from the dribblers of the Sheffield club, about whom Hudson was later to remark, 'played as if they had never seen a rugby ball'.[56] In all probability, it was the Sheffield players' ineptitude in this match which signalled the end of any serious attempts at collaboration between the rugby and dribbling codes in Yorkshire.

Played on the ground of the Leeds club, the social tenor of the occasion can be gauged from the handbill produced to advertise the game: 'Lancashire will be represented by Gentlemen from Manchester, Rochdale, Preston, Burnley and other towns. Yorkshire by Gentlemen from Bradford, Huddersfield, Hull, Sheffield and Leeds.' To add to the prestige of the event, the match was played 'under the distinguished patronage of Sir A. Fairburn, Lieutenant Colonel Swinfen and the officers of the 5th Dragoon Guards'. The admission price of sixpence was not so low as to encourage the merely curious, yet the game attracted 'a good attendance of admirers ... there also being a large number of the fair sex who graced the ground with their presence'. Played with twenty men on each side, the game itself was conducted with characteristically cavalier attention to the rules – the first half lasted forty-five minutes and the second was played for an hour. The admissibility of hacking also came under question. The Lancashire captain, William MacLaren, Manchester merchant and uncle of Lancashire and England batsman Archie MacLaren, approached Howard Wright and explained that 'many of his men were in situations and it would be a serious matter for them if they were laid up through hacking, so it was mutually agreed that hacking should be tabooed'. Wright agreed, only to find that the Lancastrians began hacking as soon as the ball was kicked off.

In modern terms, the match was hardly a spectacle. At this time, rugby was played with each side fielding sixteen forwards and four backs, who rarely handled the ball because of the continuous scrummaging by the forwards, the aim being to push the opposing forwards as far back as possible. Heeling the ball out of the scrummage was virtually unheard of. Even at this early stage in rugby's development, it was recognised that the 'dreariness of heavy brigade scrummaging' was hardly an attractive feature of the game. Notoriety surrounded the 1871 Roses game at Huddersfield at which 'the spectators had to be content to hear the shouts and desperate grunts of the huge pack of humanity that struggled for possession of the ball most of the afternoon'.[57] In such circumstances, there were plenty of opportunities for indulging in the less savoury aspects of the game, as Richard Sykes later remembered: 'Anyone who played in the match at Queens Park [in Liverpool] in or about 1865 would remember it as we were overmatched and roughly handled. Some of us had to be helped out of the railway carriage on arrival at Victoria Station.'[58] Passing the ball by hand between players was also extremely rare, the role of the backs at this time being largely confined to punting the ball into the opposition's half to set up another scrummage or, when within range, to attempt to score a goal by drop-kicking the ball. Matches were decided solely on goals scored, which often led to a team that had conceded numerous tries winning a game by kicking a lucky goal. Even then, this anomaly was recognised by the fact that most newspaper reports recorded goals, tries and touchdowns – the latter being number of times a team was forced to touch the ball down behind its own goal line – in order to give a more accurate assessment of matches.

Unsurprisingly, disputes over scoring or illegal play often arose and, because the rules made no provision for referees, were decided by discussion between the two captains. This apparently gentlemanly method of settling disputes in fact simply gave the upper hand to the more loquacious of the two disputants, as a participant described in the 1890s: 'some captains would jaw away until they gained their point by sheer blarney, the opposing side giving in merely to get some more play.'[59] As Robert Christison admitted, this necessarily meant that 'the more plausible and argumentative a player was, the more likely he was to be considered as a captain'.[60] Arguments between captains over disputed points had become so common by 1870 that it was accepted practice to add time on to the length of a match to cover the time lost for play.[61] In such an atmosphere gamesmanship, or the art of gaining maximum advantage from the letter of the law, flourished. No greater an exponent existed than Blackburn cotton magnate A. N. 'Monkey' Hornby, captain of England at both cricket and rugby, who became notorious for his behaviour at the 1878 Roses match when, with Lancashire defending a slim lead, he continually kicked the ball into touch. 'Damn it Hornby,' protested Yorkshire's Harry Garnett, 'we've come here to play football, not to watch you punt the ball into the next parish,' to which Hornby replied, 'You go to the devil Garnett. We've won this match and we are going to stick to it.' Indeed, the violence and gamesmanship of middle-class football of this period must cast doubt on the reality of the so-called gentleman's code of playing the game purely for the

Figure 1 Football, of whatever code, and violence were inseparable in the public mind from the 1860s onwards, as depicted here in *The Yorkshireman* in 1883.

game: the self-image of the middle-class sportsman, who, in Richard Holt's words 'saw himself as someone who could hold his passions in check and for whom the enjoyment of the game was more important than the result,' bore little relationship to the hacking, argumentative and rule-bending ex-public school boys who populated the football fields of the 1860s and 1870s.[62] As we shall discover later, they may have articulated these ideals when telling *others* how to play football, but for themselves winning was the supreme goal.

Civic pride and football's 'gigantic strides'

The first Roses match was won by Lancashire by the margin of a goal, two tries and a touchdown to nil, but the game's true significance lay not in the result but in the fact that it established football as a respectable recreation in the two counties. The football rivalry between towns and counties mirrored precisely the great growth in civic and commercial rivalry in the decades immediately following 1850.

Writing in 1896, Talbot Baines, grandson of the Liberal founder of the *Leeds Mercury*, commented on:

> the existence in Northern parts to a degree elsewhere unknown, of the 'element of local corporate unity'. In its most pronounced form it is found in some great towns in Yorkshire, Lancashire, and the neighbouring counties; and its presence begets a public spirit fruitful in all manner of good civic deeds, a wholesome rivalry between communities and a healthy local pride.[63]

The quest for civic pride, embodied in the erection of town halls and other municipal buildings, reached its zenith during this period: Leeds opened its town hall in 1858, Bradford in 1873, Huddersfield in 1879, Wakefield in 1880. Manchester had been accorded the status of a city in 1853, followed by Liverpool in 1880.[64] Nor was this a process confined to the large metropolitan areas: stung by the incorporation of Dewsbury in 1862, the adjoining town of Batley campaigned for incorporation, succeeding six years later and thereafter basked in superiority over its neighbours because it could boast its own town hall. Much of this rivalry was based on trade. With the partial exception of Hull at the eastern extremity, textiles were the backbone of the regional economy. Although areas tended to have their own speciality, the greatest example being the cotton/woollen cloth division between Lancashire and Yorkshire, growing overseas competition from 1870 increased the spirit of rivalry. For example, despite specialising in different markets, Bradford's manufacturers took the opportunity of a strike by Huddersfield operatives in 1883 to capture a portion of the men's worsted cloth market. And in the smaller towns between Leeds and Huddersfield, based primarily on the production of 'shoddy' low-quality textiles, competition was intense. As we have seen, the vast majority of the principals of the first football clubs in the region were intimately connected with the textiles trade. Bradford, Huddersfield, Leeds, Liverpool and Manchester were all founded in part or in whole by the sons of textiles manufacturers or merchants and thus, in a limited sense, football rapidly became the recreational medium for municipal and trade rivalry.[65]

The sport's growth in popularity and its identification with inter-town rivalry meant that clubs were, on the whole, no longer formed to be private recreational associations for young gentlemen but were created to represent towns or districts. 'We saw reports in the papers of football matches being played at Leeds, Bradford and elsewhere, and we thought that Halifax ought to have a club also,' was how the founder of the Halifax club, Sam Duckitt, described his motivation for forming the club in 1873.[66] The previous year Wigan FC had been formed, under the patronage of the mayor, explicitly to play matches against other towns. After six weeks' practice, they took to the field against Warrington.[67] Four years later Oldham FC was founded in similar circumstances, the chief constable and a local peer being present at the founding meeting.[68] In contrast to later years, this rivalry between towns was highly localised and focused on neighbours or near-neighbouring towns – at this time there was no suggestion that football could be a conduit to national prominence, even for the larger towns and cities such as Manchester or Leeds. The 1870s saw a whole swathe of clubs formed to represent their towns and led by the sons of textiles manufacturers: Brighouse, Dewsbury, Halifax, Rochdale, Swinton and Skipton being just a fraction of those clubs founded in this way. Although working-class participants were as yet few and far between, all of these clubs exhibited a high level of unity among the upper and middle classes that provided their backbone: Tories and Liberals, merchants and manufacturers were to be found gathered together in virtually all of them. The strength of local pride and desire for corporate unity can also be gauged by the contrasting fortune of Cavendish FC, who moved from Moss Side to Salford in 1879. They 'wrote to the local gentry for their patronage and support, [but] received the reply that they did not know any of the members of the club or recognise the club as a Salford club'.[69] By 1875, at least thirty-two towns and cities in Lancashire and Yorkshire had a rugby-playing football club claiming the town's name, not to mention those representing junior teams, local districts, Rifle Volunteer regiments or church organisations.[70]

If the rise in the number of football clubs was spurred by feelings of civic pride, it was facilitated by the works of the municipal age. In particular, the creation of public parks extended the scope for both playing and watching football. Most of the early clubs had relied on either local landowners or the grounds of the local Rifle Volunteers for playing surfaces. One exception to this was the Leeds club, which had played near the centre of Leeds on Woodhouse Moor public park, known as 'the lungs of Leeds'. This had been opened in 1857, followed rapidly by Bradford's Peel Park six years later, Huddersfield's Beaumont Park in 1866 and the more famous Roundhay and Lister parks of Leeds and Bradford in 1872 and 1873 respectively. In Manchester, the first public parks had been opened in 1846. The provision of transport, especially the railways, expanded dramatically during this period, increasing the ability of teams, and spectators, to travel between towns and so enhancing the nature of local rivalry. On a smaller scale, the widespread introduction by many towns of public transport such as horse trams in the 1870s meant that rivalry between different districts of towns could be indulged with the maximum of ease.

These manifestations of civic pride were joined in their facilitation of football by that other great passion of the nineteenth-century middle classes: cricket.[71] Initially this took the form of out-of-season cricket pitches being used by football clubs – as in the case of Liverpool FC who played on Edge Hill cricket ground until 1879, or York who used the Yorkshire Gentleman's Cricket Ground in the 1880s – but as the popularity of the winter game grew, cricket clubs themselves began to look at it as a complementary form of recreation and formed football sections of their own. Swinton and Widnes were two of the better known clubs formed in this fashion. In 1876 Halifax, who had originally loaned Ovenden cricket ground for matches, joined forces with the local Trinity Cricket Club to form Halifax Cricket and Football Club. Although not all Cricket Clubs welcomed these developments – the chairman of Oldham's

Figure 2 Civic pride in football boots: a caricaturist's impression of the 1884 Bradford versus Manchester game, from *Toby, the Yorkshire Tyke*.

powerful Werneth Cricket Club warning, a few months after the formation of Oldham FC, that football 'was calculated to irritate the players and when their feelings got wound up it no doubt led to angry displays' – this symbiotic relationship between cricket and football clubs was to continue with increased strength throughout the 1880s.[72]

Cricket, of course, was seen by the Victorians as the highest state that muscular Christianity had yet attained. Many of the public school boys who did not follow their classmates into business had gone into the church and taken an enthusiasm for rugby football into their work. The Church of England's attempts to reach out to the working classes in the 1850s and 1860s through 'rational recreation' had continued through the provision of Sunday schools, Bible classes and Young Men's Societies, from which the principles of muscular Christianity were propagated.[73] It appears that two types of clubs were formed by church bodies. The first were those founded by middle-class Sunday-school members themselves, such as that started in 1870 at St John the Evangelist church in Leeds by members of the church cricket team seeking something to do in winter. Its founders were all pupils at Leeds Grammar School, two of them becoming headmasters of public schools, one a partner in a printers and another a prominent local Conservative politician. In effect, it functioned in the same way as other teams founded by public school boys. Its 1874 report contained a catechism of the public school ethic that exhorted members to: 'let no voice be heard in matches except that of the captain' and 'however much provoked, never to lose temper, but to remember that, as St John's FC they have a character to maintain as well as for good conduct as for good play.'[74]

On the other hand, there were also clubs started by the clergy to encourage the working classes to participate in church activities. For example, Wakefield's Holy Trinity church provided a wide range of self-improving classes, including bookkeeping, shorthand, languages and 'electricity', as well as running a cricket team. At its annual prize-giving ceremony in November 1872, the Reverend William Madden announced that the Society was to form a football club, after which his colleague Dr Browne spoke of the need to 'preserve to the working class those sturdy thews and sinews which their ancestors possessed and which were supposed to make one Englishman equal to five Frenchmen,' adding that 'science, literature and art would be of comparatively little avail without muscular exercise'. Within the month the new team played its first game against Leeds Grammar School, although the fact that the Trinity side could only muster twelve players to the school's fifteen suggests that, initially at least, not all parishioners shared Dr Browne's enthusiasm for thews and sinews.[75] Founded on similar principles was the Leeds Parish Church club, where the football team was formed directly out of a recreation club attached to the church's 'A' Division Bible Class in 1874. Led by E. H. Dykes, the former Durham School hacker, the club was held to be 'the embodiment of that sane doctrine of Muscular Christianity'. The forerunners of the Salford, Runcorn, Radcliffe and Sowerby Bridge Northern Union clubs also had similar origins.[76]

How successful these exercises were in imparting Christian values to the working class will be seen later, but a foretaste of the problems to come were experienced by Heckmondwike FC. Formed by the vicar of Heckmondwike as part of the church's athletic club, the team became notorious by the late 1870s for the rough play of its team and the violent behaviour of its spectators. In 1876

Halifax walked off the pitch in the midst of a game at Heckmondwike 'owing to the rough and ungentlemanly play' of their opponents.[77] The following year Leeds St John's followed suit only to find themselves come under a hail of stones and clods of earth from the disgruntled crowd.[78] Although at this stage of the sport's development, such behaviour was rare, the church-based sides quickly found themselves having to compromise on the question of club membership. Almost all of them had originally allowed only members of their congregations to play but within a few years, as Dykes was later to ruefully point out, 'force of circumstances led to the introduction of outsiders'.[79]

These circumstances were the massive increase in the popularity of rugby. Just three years after its formation, a note in Wakefield Trinity's cash book commented that 'the interest taken in the club by the public of Wakefield is something extraordinary' and recorded a profit on the season of thirty-one shillings, despite the fact that the club made no charge for admission to games. Such success was now common to many clubs.[80] For major games involving the better known clubs, crowds could rise to upwards of two thousand people. This growth of interest was given a fillip in 1875 when the RFU decided to reduce the size of teams from twenty to fifteen per side. Other than in county games, fifteen-a-side had been the most common line-up for matches played in the region, but the official sanction to the change gave clubs added incentive to move away from the traditional heavy scrummaging game, making the game a more palatable spectacle for the onlooker. In the 1877 *Football Annual*, it was noted that:

> Football in the North of England ... has made great strides during the past season, and in addition to Manchester, Liverpool, Preston, Huddersfield, Leeds, etc, etc, there are many clubs less widely known in Yorkshire and Lancashire which can turn out a fifteen both strong in play and possessing a good knowledge of the science of the game.[81]

In Yorkshire, the game was also helped by the creation of the Yorkshire County Football Club (YCFC) in 1874, which gave the sport both a structure and a higher profile. Formed at the instigation of Bradford's Harry Garnett, the newly appointed county captain, the YCFC initially set out to ensure the efficient organisation of county games and the selection of the county side. Unlike Lancashire, where the organisation of county matters was firmly in the hands of the Manchester and Liverpool clubs, the YCFC consisted of representatives of the Bradford, Huddersfield, Hull, Leeds and York clubs.[82] Although appointed by no-one other than themselves, as the oldest clubs in the area they possessed sufficient authority to give the burgeoning game a direction it had hitherto lacked. The YCFC's first major action was to organise a trial match for places in the county team in 1875 but it was an idea of Arthur Hudson, the son of a Leeds woollen manufacturer, who had joined the committee a year or so after its formation, that was to change the face of football in the county. Neither original nor revolutionary, it was a proposal to start a knock-out cup competition for the leading teams in Yorkshire. The association code's FA Cup had begun in 1871 and three years later in London rugby-playing medical students had begun competing for the Hospitals' Cup. Both had succeeded in bringing their sports to wider audiences and, according to Harry Garnett twenty-five years later, Hudson had convinced the YCFC of the idea by explaining that 'we will make football the game for every boy in Yorkshire and Yorkshire shall be able to play the rest of England and beat it'.[83] Hurriedly organised for December 1877, sixteen teams were invited to compete for the Yorkshire Challenge Cup, although no medals were to be presented to players because it was felt that this smacked too much of professionalism.

In the first round, an unprecedented 8,000 people packed into Halifax's Hanson Lane ground to see the defeat of Wakefield. A week later, five hundred Halifax supporters went by special train to Wakefield to watch their team overcome Trinity. Such scenes were repeated across the county. Of their second round tie at Heckmondwike, Hull's William Hutchinson recounted:

> There was so much excitement over the match among the local public that we really were fortunate in getting away from the ground without having to fight our way out ... the spectators swarmed all about the field and there was a scene that up to that time we had not been accustomed to.[84]

Three thousand people paid to see the semi-final between Bradford and Halifax, but:

> the arrangements for taking the gate money were very inadequate, the result being that a number of those travelling with the Halifax team, rather than bear the infliction of waiting until it came to their turn to pay, leaped over the walls of the field and thus obtained access free of charge.[85]

Unfortunately, due to snow, the final between Halifax and York had to be switched at the last minute from Huddersfield to Holbeck in Leeds, attracting a disappointing crowd of 3,000 to watch Halifax, a club not represented on the YCFC committee, carry off the trophy. Nevertheless, no-one could argue with the verdict of the *Yorkshire Post* that 'the object the Yorkshire football committee had in view when they offered this cup – viz. the further development of football in the county – has been fully realised'.[86]

The following season's competition was even more successful. Twenty sides entered and the semi-final – only one was played because Kirkstall were given a bye into the final – attracted 10,000 to Wakefield Trinity's ground to see them overturn their previous season's defeat by Halifax, with special trains bringing spectators from Halifax, Leeds, Bradford, Dewsbury and Huddersfield. Despite expecting a one-sided game, 12,000 turned up for the final at the Halifax ground to see Trinity victorious. Thousands travelled on trains from Wakefield and Leeds, paying sixpence or a shilling to see the match. As soon as the news of Trinity's victory was received in their home town;

> the Parish Church bells began to ring in honour of the event. On the arrival at Wakefield of the special train, the victors were met by the Parish Church Association band and an immense concourse of people, and marched from the station to the Woolpacks Inn, the cheering in the streets being again and again renewed.[87]

This explosion in popularity brought with it a set of entirely unexpected pressures. The first and most obvious was the growth in spectators. As the 1877 Bradford semi-final demonstrated, few clubs could cope organisationally with large crowds. The days when, as in Halifax, crowds could be controlled 'by a few friends parading on horseback', were now gone.[88] The partisanship engendered by the cup competition led to disorderly and rowdy crowd behaviour. As a referee, Harry Garnett had to be escorted from grounds by the police following Yorkshire Cup ties after supporters had sought to dispute some of his decisions with him personally. Most notoriously, the Wakefield Trinity team had been attacked by Halifax supporters after their 1879 final victory in revenge for Trinity's semi-final defeat of Halifax, breaking a window and almost overturning their carriage.[89] The determination of spectators to see their side win was also shared by many of the competing teams. From the beginning of the competition, the YCFC had warned clubs against importing players specifically to play in cup ties but controversy surrounded the transfer of star half-back Rufus Ward from Wakefield Trinity to Halifax in the winter of 1877. His move was variously explained by his falling out with the Trinity committee over an athletics meeting or by the fact that his girlfriend lived in Halifax, but others suspected that he had been offered an inducement to switch clubs, a practice known as 'kidnapping':

> Well Rufus hed nobbut nicely gotten browt aht afoor he fell aht wi' some o' t'Trinity chaps an' fell in wi' Halifax. Nah doan't be sa sharp. Ah didn't say 'at t'Cup started t'kidnapping bizness. Only this is t'fust case 'at I knaw, an' it wor just ta help Halifax ta win t'Cup t'fust time, like. Two an' two, ye knaw – fower.[90]

Whatever the truth of these accusations, it was clear that some clubs were adopting new methods of improving their chances of cup success. Halifax held a special training session the night before the 1877 Cup Final and Wakefield Trinity began to meet before matches to decide on tactics. Such methods did not find favour with those players who still viewed the game purely as a recreation – in contrast to the Halifax team, York captain Robert Christison spent the night before the 1877 final at a dance in Harrogate.

The Yorkshire Cup had brought with it an influx of new players, new spectators and new playing methods. The success of Halifax in the inaugural final had been followed by:

> clubs springing up like mushrooms on every side. People saw that the 'blue and whites', after a paltry connection with the sport of three years standing, had earned so much distinction, and why shouldn't they succeed in the same manner?[91]

The quest for civic pre-eminence embodied in football clubs and the new competition was also beginning to be embraced by those social strata normally excluded from its pursuit. Although expressed in a different manner and often undertaken by different means, the search for civic glory was enthusiastically taken up by the working classes – indeed, in many ways, attendance at their town club's football matches was one of the few practical methods they had of expressing local pride. The Yorkshire Cup now meant that football and civic honour were now tightly bound together: 'I copt t'fooitball fever at t'same time as monny a hundred moor did – when t'Yorkshire Cup wor first laiked for thirteen year sin, and what's moor – or less, if owt – I've hed it ivver sin,' was how one rugby fan summed up the impact of the cup.[92] But the people who now began to pour into the game, both as players and spectators, were of a distinctively different class to the former public school boys who had hitherto thought of the game as their own. Rugby was now poised to re-occupy the position of mass popularity that had been held in pre-industrial times by folk football. Slowly but surely, a perceptible threat to the middle-class exclusivity of the game was beginning to be felt. How they were to deal with these newcomers was an issue that was to occupy the leaders of rugby for the next two decades.

Chapter 2

The coming of the working classes: 1879–1886

Beginning with the Ten Hours Act in 1847, the working class had slowly clawed out periods of free time from their employers. Although in many areas 'Saint Monday', whereby workers would simply not go into work or not work at full capacity on Mondays, was an informal method of reducing the heavy burden of long hours of factory work on working people, the needs of disciplined, ordered production meant that such informal practices were gradually suppressed and, in effect, replaced by the Saturday half-holiday. In 1850 textile workers were granted a two o'clock end to work on Saturdays, which was further reduced to one o'clock in 1874. A year later the August Bank Holiday was institutionalised by an act of parliament. The Saturday half-day holiday became the norm for most, but not all, trades during the economic boom of the early 1870s.[1] This upturn in economic fortunes also saw working-class standards of living begin to rise, providing working-class people with not only the time but also the means to enjoy it, effectively laying the basis for the growth of most modern forms of working-class leisure over the following years.[2] Along with the music hall and seaside trips, football of both varieties became a focus of interest for those with new time to spend, as Moses Heap, a Lancashire cotton spinner, wrote:

> For a while we did not know how to pass our time away. Before it had been all bed and work; now in place of seventy hours a week we had fifty-five and a half. It became a practice, mostly on Saturdays, to play football and cricket, which had never been done before.[3]

As we saw in the previous chapter, working-class players had begun to enter the rugby game in the late 1870s, at roughly the same time as the beginning of the Yorkshire Cup. It appears that the first player without a public school background to be selected for the Yorkshire county side was Wakefield Trinity three-quarter Harry Hayley, who made his representative debut against Middlesex in 1878 while still a pupil teacher at a local Wesleyan school.[4] The rapid advancement of working-class players in the game was acknowledged in 1880 by RFU secretary Arthur Guillemard, who somewhat haughtily pointed out that:

> the recent foundation of a large number of clubs in the North has resulted in the drafting into club fifteens a large proportion of tyros, who may know how to drop and place kick, but are unlearned in the various points of the game.[5]

This 'diffusion'[6] of the game down from the middle classes was made possible not only by the increase in working-class leisure time but also by the relative reduction in class conflict, which had prevailed in England since the defeat of the Chartists following 1848. It was a period of 'forty years of slumber' for the English working-class, to quote Engels, who described the suppression of previous antipathies in the decades up to the 1880s:

> a gradual change came over the relations between both classes. The Factory Acts, once the bugbear of all manufacturers, were not only willingly submitted to, but their expansion into acts regulating almost all trades, was tolerated. Trades Unions, lately considered inventions of the devil himself, were now petted and patronised as perfectly legitimate institutions and as useful means of spreading sound economical doctrines amongst the workers. Even strikes, than which nothing had been more nefarious up to 1848, were now gradually found out to be occasionally very useful, especially when provoked by the masters themselves, at their own time.[7]

This did not mean that class conflict had been abolished or that the leisure pursuits of the classes were interchangeable Nor did it mean that harmonious relations between the classes were the norm. Practically, it meant that the reduction in social tensions created a greater possibility of members of different classes playing sports together, certainly when compared to the pre- and post-1848 periods. In rugby, this process manifested itself in factory owners and factory workers playing the same game and occasionally in the same teams. The Tyldesley side that won the West Lancashire Cup in 1888 included eight colliery workers and two sons of colliery owners.[8] A flavour of this unusual social mix was captured by Richard Davies, one of the founders of Dalton FC, near Barrow in Furness: 'The occupations [of the players in the 1880s] were varied in the extreme – professional men, mechanics, miners, carpenters, town clerks, butchers, masons, clerks, labourers, landlords, chemists and schoolmasters.'[9] This lowering of barriers between the classes was highly transient and, in the eyes of rugby's middle-class leadership, dependent on the new working-class participants accepting their leadership and set of values. So while the massive upsurge in rugby's popularity among the working classes of Lancashire and Yorkshire was initially welcomed by the game's rulers, it was also accompanied by tensions and conflicts over the direction the game was taking.

If the growth in leisure time and a reduction of class tensions were the culture medium in which the downwards diffusion of rugby took place, what were the agencies which facilitated this change? The Yorkshire Cup undoubtedly inspired the formation of countless new clubs; at the beginning of the 1882–83 season the *Yorkshire Post* reported that it had received 120 fixture cards from teams in the region.[10] There were doubtless many others who lacked the means or the ambition to print such cards. By 1886 most large urban regions in West and East Yorkshire also had their own local cup competitions with which to fan the flames of football fever, as did the West Lancashire area, against the wishes of the Lancashire rugby union authorities. Yet it appears that few clubs were formed spontaneously by working-class people – rather, they generally made use of existing clubs or existing recreational channels, such as the church, the workplace or the pub. Many teams were also formed on the basis of local streets and districts, although a district name often concealed a link with a pub or church. Stuart Barlow had identified over seventy such teams in the Rochdale area in the 1880s.[11] Typical of this type of side was Hull Southcoates, formed by a local shopkeeper, publican and board school teacher, and based on the Courteney Street area of east Hull. They survived for a decade competing against other local Hull sides and were 'invariably composed of horny-handed sons of toil'. Looking back at their history, an old player proudly remarked that the side had fulfilled at least one useful function, 'and that was in training the manual labourer and in educating his mate to take an interest in the game'.[12]

The spread of church clubs based on muscular Christian principles accelerated in the 1880s, as the clergy sought to capitalise on the football boom and set up their own teams. This growth was not limited to Anglicans; Roman Catholic churches also began teams, such as Wakefield St Austin's, which was set up as an alternative to Wakefield Trinity. The names of junior clubs such as Dewsbury Shamrocks and Leeds Catholic Institute also demonstrate the non-sectarian nature of football's popularity. It is also evident that many of these clubs quickly slipped their bonds with the sponsoring church. When the Yorkshire Church Temperance Challenge Shield was started in 1887, one of its rules was that players must be bona fide members of a church, church school or Anglican temperance society, no doubt in order to ensure that the participants' enthusiasm for football was matched by their devotion to the scriptures.[13] Indeed, it was not unusual for churchmen, after having formed a football club, to lose their enthusiasm for the game when faced with the less than Corinthian zealotry of their new recruits, as a Bradford curate discovered after forming a youth side and suffering:

> complaints and reproaches from the mothers of his protégés about black eyes, sore bones and all the other luxuries accompanying the game. He was so intimidated that he now wants to back out, but these exuberant youths, having tasted the sweets of victory, insist on going on.[14]

As working-class influence grew, it seems that many ostensibly church clubs were operating under little more than a flag of convenience, with only minimal involvement from the clergy. This certainly became the case with the Leeds Parish Church club and it was also true at a lower level, as the superintendents of Nether Green Sunday School in Leeds admitted after an inquiry into the violent on-field activities of their football club:

> we have not kept a sufficiently close connection with and oversight of the football club which uses the name of the school. Matters have been left too much to the management of the players themselves, with the result that, contrary to the original intention of the officers of the school, the team is largely composed of those who have no connection with it. We feel that it would be incumbent on us to re-organise the club and bring it under more immediate control.[15]

Similar problems affected sides formed by companies for their employees. The most famous works club was probably St Helens Recreation, formed as the football section of Pilkington Brothers glassworks recreation club. For a subscription of one penny a week, the recreation club provided football, cricket, bowls and library facilities, but that provision was tightly controlled by the company, who, for example, refused to allow the side to participate in the West Lancashire and Border Towns Cup, despite the desire of their players to do so. As captain Monsey Parr explained, Pilkingtons' management 'said we'd better give up cup ties and such things; and you must do as your masters want or else shut up shop . . . Th' masters don't like us drinkin' and they won't allow committee meetings to be held in public houses.' Indeed, the side was viewed as the personal property of the Pilkington family, with established members of the side sometimes having to step down when a Pilkington son decided he fancied a game.[16] More fundamental problems faced the men of Wakefield Glassworks, who, after having made an impressive start to their inaugural season, were forced to disband after their employers decided that they could no longer afford to allow men to take time off work to play.[17] In Huddersfield, a number of employers ran their own clubs, such as Charles Brooke's Meltham Mills team, or actively helped to subsidise the local junior sides.[18] Other clubs soon broke the link with their benefactors. For example, the apprentice boiler-makers who formed Kingston Amateurs in the west of Hull in 1882, quickly left the control of their employers to eventually become Hull Kingston Rovers, the city's second senior side. Even more successful was the club formed in 1878 for employees of Barkers' Mill, one of only two factories in the village of Thornes, just outside Wakefield. Although the company donated a field in which to play, those employees wishing to make use of it had to subscribe tuppence in order for the club to buy a ball. Nevertheless, the team advanced so quickly, thanks in large part to the tactical genius of warehouseman and three-quarter Harry Wigglesworth, that in 1882 they produced possibly the greatest upset ever in

English rugby by defeating five-to-one on favourites Wakefield Trinity in the final of the Yorkshire Cup.[19]

Other than the church and the factory, the pub was the most important medium for the entry of working-class players into rugby. Of the forty-five clubs listed in the 1881–82 *Yorkshire Football Handbook*, only five did not have their club headquarters in a pub. By 1885–86 the number of clubs listed had risen to eighty but those without a pub as their headquarters remained at five.[20] While some of these clubs may have chosen pubs for their convenience, the growing importance of the pub in promoting football can be gauged from the fact that four of the twenty club secretaries of this period that I have been able to trace were publicans or beer retailers, as detailed in Table A.1 of the Appendix.

The pub had long been the focus for recreational activities in working-class areas and, in particular, the pub landlord often played the role of the recreational entrepreneur, organising sports and sponsoring contests. Unsurprisingly, therefore, pub landlords were not slow to capitalise on the football boom, especially those in possession of land adjoining their pub. Typical, if somewhat hopeful, was a Mr Boniface, a licensee at Woodchurch near Dewsbury, who fenced off a football ground behind his pub and 'is now anxiously waiting for the thousands to flock to this place whenever he turned his showy colours on to the field'.[21] History does not record whether, like Shoeless Joe Jackson in *Field of Dreams*, players, or indeed spectators, came to the field. Initially more successful was the landlord of the Cemetery Tavern in Hunslet, Mr Cusworth, who in 1883 offered the cricket field behind his pub as a winter pitch for rugby after an unsuccessful foray into soccer. Two local sides Excelsior and Albion merged under the auspices of Woodhouse Hill Cricket Club to play on the pitch as Hunslet FC. Support for the team grew so quickly that two years after their formation they took over £100 in gate money at a Yorkshire Cup tie in which they defeated Leeds St John's – and Cusworth promptly raised the rent to an unheard of £365 per year. Although he later relented and asked for only £200, the Hunslet committee decided that if they were going to pay such an astronomical sum, they might as well move and find a ground of their own.[22] A similar falling-out occurred between Woodhouse FC in Leeds and the landlord of their local pub, The Swan with Two Necks, who sued them for non-payment of £39 for beer and cigars he supplied, contrary to RFU regulations, to the players after matches.[23]

Unlike the church and works teams, where football was largely seen as an adjunct to moral or business imperatives, it was in the environment of the pub that working-class cultural practices came to the fore. In particular, sport for money – and for food prizes such as geese and legs of mutton – was an integral part of working-class cultural life across the North of England. Shooting competitions were especially popular. The Crown Hotel in Dewsbury offered '£10 to be shot for at four birds each' in December 1879, one of fourteen pubs offering cash prizes for shooting rabbits, sparrows or pigeons on one weekend. Prize money of £20 was on offer to the winner of a contest between H. Moorhouse and

J. Woodhouse to shoot twenty-one sparrows.[24] Open foot-racing contests were common; a typical example being at the British Oak Inn at Chickenley Heath near Dewsbury, which offered £7 and 10 shillings to the winner of a 137 yards race, competitors paying a one shilling entrance fee.[25] Dog racing for money was also highly popular, as was cock fighting; a challenge match between cocks from Chester and Ulverston being fought for £50 a battle.[26] On a larger scale, 1,200 people gathered in 1879 at the Black Horse Hotel at Tyldesley, near Manchester, to watch a wrestling match that was being contested for £25.[27] One of the leading sports in working-class communities at this time was knur and spel, sometimes known as Northern Spel. A long-handled club, similar to those used in golf, was used to knock a wooden ball into the air and, in an almost simultaneous movement, hit it as far into the distance as possible. The best players were able to fire the knur, as the ball was known, between 250 and 300 yards. The sport attracted large crowds and substantial cash prizes were offered to winners of competitions. For example, on one unexceptional weekend in February 1880, J. Wade beat M. Smith at Halifax to win £40, whilst H. Wainwright and R. Beresford battled it out at Barnsley for £50.[28] Needless to say, gambling was an attendant part of all these pastimes.

Consequently, as working-class men took up the rugby game, they brought with them a range of cultural practices that were based on the necessity of selling their labour power in whichever way was the most lucrative, including the utilisation of sporting prowess. 'Spoort's gooid lads, but brass is better,' was how a dialect story of the time summed up this attitude.[29] A greater clash with the ideals of public school sport could not be imagined, especially for those who sought to utilise football as a medium for moral improvement. The centrality of the cash nexus in working-class sport also gave rise to the apparently paradoxical situation of working-class players supporting the operation of market forces in rugby and capitalist mill owners opposing them. In the main, the middle-class leaders of the game saw the working-class professional sportsman as a form of prostitute: 'We shall always view with the gravest apprehensions the intro-duction of the *paid* element into a game which up to the present time has been played for sport – or rather for the love of sport – alone' warned the *Yorkshire Post*.[30] The popularity of the game, and especially the Yorkshire Cup, was therefore viewed with a degree of ambiguity by its leaders. This was both because the sport that they had learnt 'with their Latin grammar' at school was no longer exclusively theirs, but also because increasing working-class involve-ment was changing the nature of the game itself – as was acknowledged by the secretary of Goole FC in 1882, who wrote to arrange a fixture with York and reassuringly pointed out that 'as our club is pretty nearly free from the working-class element, you have nothing to fear about a rough or noisy game'.[31] The national leadership of the Rugby Union itself had long expressed doubts about the popularity of cup competitions, turning down an offer from the Royal Military Academy to supply a trophy for a national cup competition in 1875. Rowland Hill, the secretary of the RFU, believed that cup ties caused 'an evil spirit

A NEW PLAYER.

LITTLE AITCHLESS, *a Bradford limb of the law, goes to the Bradford v. Oxford University Football Match, and, hearing all the partisans of the University shouting "'Varsity, 'Varsity," asks another limb of the law :* "I say, old fellow, which of the players is the fellow called ''Varsity'?' Seems to be a big favourite anyhow."

Figure 3 Across the social divide I: the cross-class appeal of rugby and its subsequent confusions are captured by the cartoon from *Toby, the Yorkshire Tyke.*

to arise, and that sometimes men are influenced more by the desire to win rather than to play the game in the true spirit'.[32] Arthur Guillemard echoed these sentiments in 1880, pointing out that:

> the fact that by far the greatest number of disputes occur in the northern counties shows that by the minor clubs the game is far from being properly understood. There is also a great deal of partisanship afloat, and the umpires have by no means a pleasant time of it on occasions.[33]

The threat that cup competitions represented to the exclusivity of the game was widely understood. Participation in a knock-out cup meant that a club could no longer choose its opponents and the prospect of defeat by ostensibly lesser teams helped to animate the socially exclusive clubs' opposition to cup ties. In Yorkshire, the core of the original Leeds club, now known as Leeds Athletic, transformed themselves into the Yorkshire Wanderers in 1881, refused to play in cup competitions and generally restricted their fixtures to exclusive middle-class clubs. A series of heavy defeats led to them disbanding in 1883. The Rugbeian leaders of Hull FC also gave up the game in 1881 after a string of crushing losses to the socially open Hull White Star, against whom they had declined to play for some seasons previously.[34] The ex-public school leaders of York FC underwent a similar loss of faith in their club, merging in 1882 with their conquerors, York Melbourne, a side 'composed of strong burly workmen, who gradually but surely made a better name for good exciting matches than the old York club'.[35] The YCFC committee even discussed abandoning the Yorkshire Cup in 1880, when Arthur Hudson, spoke in favour of its suspension.[36] Although it was decided to continue, doubts remained. In 1882 Dewsbury, Halifax and Huddersfield declined to enter that year's competition. Huddersfield also boycotted the following season's competition and Bradford's annual meetings perennially discussed withdrawing, but the cup exerted such a powerful draw for both players and spectators it was difficult for a club not to compete and retain credibility.[37]

In Lancashire, despite several attempts by clubs to force the county leadership to emulate Yorkshire, the controlling Manchester and Liverpool clubs steadfastly opposed cup football and became notorious for refusing fixtures with clubs they felt to be socially inferior; in Manchester's case this was especially directed against local rivals Salford and Swinton. After years of attempting to arrange a match with their illustrious neighbours, Swinton were finally granted the honour in 1878. In a match that was as significant for Manchester rugby as Blackburn Olympic's 1883 FA Cup final defeat of Old Etonians was for soccer, Swinton, nicknamed the Colliers, won by a try to nil. The disquiet about the stranglehold of Lancashire county rugby by the Liverpool/Manchester duopoly came to a head in March 1881 when Broughton's William Bell called for other clubs to be involved in selecting the county side. Manchester refused the request point-blank and declined to meet with their critics. In May, twelve clubs therefore formed a Lancashire Football Union and arranged representative matches with Lanarkshire and Midland Counties. Sensing that their control of the game could slip away, Manchester eventually reached an arrangement with the rebels in December and the Lancashire County Football Club was formed. Given the nature of the agreement it could hardly be called a compromise: for two years, Manchester were automatically entitled to the positions of president, vice-president, secretary and treasurer, and Liverpool were guaranteed two committee seats. To cap it off, all home county fixtures were to be played at Manchester's Whalley Range ground.[38]

At the time, this refusal to countenance cup competitions and broaden the leadership of Lancashire rugby seemed to have little consequence. Rugby's popularity towered over soccer in the North. For example, in the first week in

November 1876 the *Athletic News* published the results of fifty rugby matches and just two association games that had taken place the previous weekend in Lancashire and Yorkshire. At the beginning of the 1877–78 season its directory of football club secretaries listed 141 rugby clubs in Cheshire, Lancashire, Yorkshire, the North East and the North West, six association clubs, one club playing both codes and thirty-nine playing Sheffield Association rules. While this was clearly an underestimation of the number of active soccer clubs in the region – it named just two clubs in Lancashire – it underlined the lead that rugby had established. Even as late as 1882, the upcoming fixtures for the weekend of 11 February listed 133 rugby and 39 soccer matches in the two Pennine counties.[39] Indicatively, when the *Manchester Guardian* discussed the growth of the two football codes in the same year, it felt compelled to describe the association game, but not the more familiar rugby, for its readers: 'in East Lancashire the dribbling game (kicking the ball along the ground when running) only is cared for.'[40]

Such dominance was not to last. Although at its formation in 1878 the Lancashire FA had just twenty-eight clubs, the overwhelming majority coming from the three towns of Blackburn, Bolton and Darwen, it grew rapidly because of the appeal of the Lancashire FA Cup competition, begun in 1879, and its plethora of local competitions. More importantly, the success of Blackburn's Olympic and Rovers in the FA Cup had demonstrated the nationwide interest it was possible to create through success in a national cup competition and, given the lack of any countervailing attractions in the rugby game, the impact of Blackburn's success on its neighbouring towns was too great to withstand. Preston had been a rugby town at the beginning of the decade but, following the example of Preston North End's conversion in 1881, virtually all its football clubs had switched to the dribbling code by the end of the 1881–82 season. Burnley FC too had begun as a rugby club before changing codes in 1882 and Chorley FC made the same switch in 1883.[41] In fact, many of the key personalities in Lancashire soccer had begun their sporting careers as rugby players, including Scotsman Fergus Suter, possibly one of the first two soccer players to be paid for playing. Other prominent ex-rugbyites included Preston's William Sudell, a key mover in bringing professionalism to soccer, T. Y. Ritson, the founder of Bolton and District FA, and future Football League presidents Charles Sutcliffe and John McKenna and secretary Tom Charnley.[42] Whilst many of them will have swapped their allegiances because of the association game's greater simplicity and openness of play, the stranglehold of the patrician Liverpool and Manchester clubs over rugby in the region may well have proved a disincentive to the entrepreneurial spirit of men like Sudell and McKenna, who, unlike the leadership of Lancashire rugby, were from the less socially exalted echelons of the middle classes and were envious of the prestige that cup competitions and imported players had brought to the Blackburn area. The success of Lancashire clubs in the FA Cup and the civic recognition it brought to towns was the springboard from which soccer became able to overtake and eventually dwarf rugby, as 'The Free Critic' wrote in 1893:

> Up to 1877 there was not a large amount of interest taken in [association] football so far as the North was concerned, and it was not until Darwen made their journey to play the Old Etonians in the English cup ties that we in Lancashire commenced to think of popularising the game.[43]

By the mid-1880s the growth of soccer in Lancashire had become a cause for concern and at the 1886 LCFC Annual General Meeting, a number of speakers expressed alarm at its progress. Werneth FC, based near Oldham, had proposed without success that a Lancashire Cup be instituted, modelled on the Yorkshire Cup, in order to rekindle interest in the game.[44] In Liverpool an association cup competition had attracted twenty teams in its inaugural season in 1886 and had shaken the popularity of rugby in one of its bastions. The fear was that Liverpool might go the same way as Preston. Werneth reiterated their call for a cup competition the following spring, their delegate to the LCFC meeting stating that 'the association game was progressing rapidly and [that] the only way to help the Rugby game in Lancashire was by a cup competition'.[45] Yet again, the county authorities turned their faces against this move to popularise the sport. But behind this apparent stubbornness lay the hope that soccer's advances could help reassert the social exclusivity of rugby:

> in some districts ... the Rugby game is losing ground among the working class and Association spreading in its place, owing to the pecuniary advantages to be reaped from the latter game. The loss of followers to the grand old game is regrettable, yet looking at the present state of all professional sports, we cannot but think that this possible loss is far preferable to legalising professionalism.[46]

Monster crowds and howling mobs

As working-class players came into the game, so too did working-class spectators. We have already seen the first five-figure crowds for football matches in Yorkshire in the late 1870s and this growth in crowd sizes continued unabated in the 1880s. It was estimated that in excess of 50,000 people saw the sixteen first round Yorkshire Cup games in the 1882–83 season, with five-figure gates being recorded for the later rounds at Dewsbury and Halifax. The following season, estimates suggested that over 100,000 had seen the first round matches, with the Dewsbury versus Wakefield Trinity tie attracting more than 15,000 spectators paying nearly £354 to get into the ground. This was, proudly boasted the *Dewsbury Reporter*, 'a larger attendance than has ever before been present at a match in Yorkshire'.[47] A few weeks later, the same paper drew attention to the fact that the Blackburn Rovers versus Queen's Park 1884 Cup Final drew only 10,000, while 15,000 had gathered at Halifax to see Bradford's semi-final defeat of Batley: 'it will be noticed that the Yorkshire monster attendances are far in excess of those of the metropolis with its millions of inhabitants.'[48] The crowds continued to grow in subsequent years, 20,000 jamming into Bradford's Park Avenue ground to watch the 1885 cup tie against Hull and 14,000 (with 3,000 locked out) packing Cardigan Fields at Leeds to see the 1886 final between Halifax and Bradford. On a smaller, albeit equally noteworthy, scale were the 5,000 spectators at Thornes, near Wakefield, who watched the local side play Dewsbury in 1883 – despite the fact that, according to the 1881 census, the population of Thornes was less than 3,500! The growth of the game in West Yorkshire was such that the *Football Annual* for 1881 devoted a special chapter to the game in Yorkshire, in which it claimed that 'Yorkshire can boast of being "second to none" in its support of the popular winter pastime'.[49] By 1887 the *Yorkshire Post* could speak confidently of 'the million who follow the game in these parts' and Arthur Hudson calculated that a total of 350,000 people had attended the sixty-three ties in that year's Yorkshire Cup competition.[50] Lacking the focus of a county cup competition, attendances in Lancashire were slower to take off but their rapid growth can be seen in the rise in gate money takings of Salford and Warrington during the early to mid-1880s. In 1883 Salford took £160 in gate receipts, rising to £570 four years later, an increase of over 256 per cent. Warrington's growth was even more remarkable, rising from just £34 to slightly more than £1,234 in the same period, due in no small part to the introduction of the West Lancashire and Border Towns cup competition in 1886.[51]

This rise in attendances reflected rugby football's increasing popularity among all sections of society, not just among the working class. Football, particularly during cup competitions, had become a focus for outpourings of civic pride and inter-town rivalry that transcended class and political divisions. Describing Warrington's triumphant return from Liverpool with the West Lancashire Cup, the local newspaper stated that 'We have witnessed many processions and receptions in Warrington, but with respect to excitement, enthusiasm and numbers, all have been eclipsed by the monstre[sic] which took place on Saturday evening.'[52] There are no data available for us to determine the exact social composition of the rugby crowd but descriptions of crowds at this time all note the wide social spectrum of spectators at matches.[53] Reporting on the 1884 Bradford versus Manningham derby game, an observer noted that amongst the crowd were 'clergy and ministers, pastors and deacons, very good people and some that were only so-so; lawyers, doctors, magistrates, tinkers and tailors, soldiers and sailors, tag, rag and bobtail'.[54] Further evidence of the cross-class appeal of football can be seen in the behaviour and organisation of the crowds, as this 1881 report of a football crowd in Bradford describes:

> On the road near, an endless stream of people goes flowing on. There are enthusiasts munching the last mouthfuls of their dinners and speeding to be

in time for the 'kick off'. From all quarters and directions do they come. Old men and maidens, matrons and children, and young men of every degree. Already the lower walls of the field are surmounted by an unbroken line of spectators, who form a sort of human railing, and, regardless of the drizzle and biting wind, and the somewhat uncertain character of their seats, amuse themselves with pipes, occasional bottles, and the interchange of not too delicate pleasantries with passers-by, while the belligerents in the grandstand strip for the fray.[55]

One piece of evidence that does help us gain an insight into the backgrounds of *supporters* – rather than *spectators* – of the game is an 1887 list of subscribers to a fund to commemorate Wakefield Trinity's fourth triumph in the Yorkshire Cup. Supporters of the club were asked to donate upwards of a shilling and the proceeds were used to buy momentoes which were presented to members of the team.[56] The picture that emerges from Table A.2 of the Appendix is ample testimony to the broad support of rugby.

Almost a third of those contributing came from the gentry and professional classes, while 43 per cent came from the lower section of the lower middle classes, particularly the pub- and shop-owning sections. Given the identification, even by 1887, of the game with manual workers, it may seem surprising that only 16 per cent of identifiable subscribers fall into that category but by asking for money over and above admission charges, the fund would automatically exclude members of the poorer sections of the working classes who attended games.

That many spectators were cautious about paying money to clubs can be seen by the common last-minute rushes to get into grounds. Particularly when visiting teams were travelling some distance, the vagaries of the transport system and the unwillingness of some players to make long journeys meant that crowds often waited for confirmation of the opposing team's arrival before parting with their admission money. Financial disaster seemed to be looming at the opening of Wigan's new ground in 1886 when few people had paid admission before kick off time, but as the *Wigan Observer* pointed out:

> it is quite evident that Wigan people are wise in their time and like to see a team turn up before going on the ground, consequently when the [Wakefield] Trinity players arrived in the town there was a great rush to the field.[57]

At most grounds, the cost of attendance for first class games was usually 6d, with boys being admitted for 3d and women free. Admittance to enclosures or grandstands, which were being erected with increasing frequency at this time, more often than not cost one shilling, the price differential helping to both regulate demand and preserve social distinctions amongst the crowd. For lower ranking games prices were cheaper: the two junior sides sharing Manningham's Valley Parade ground charged just 3d and 2d to get in. The price of admission was often a controversial topic, and as early as 1880 there were complaints that an admission charge of one shilling for the North versus South match at Halifax 'does not give the working class a chance of patronising the match'.[58] Dewsbury opportunistically doubled their prices for the visit of Bradford in 1886 and suffered a disappointingly low turnout. They did not repeat the price rise. Nevertheless, enterprising supporters were always keen to cut the cost of attendance. Fake Bradford season tickets were discovered in 1886 and many club members indulged in the practice of dropping their season tickets over the perimeter walls of a ground to friends outside, who could then enter for free. Led by Leeds Parish Church, clubs eventually got wise to such activities and introduced a match voucher system for season ticket holders.[59]

For many spectators, the cost of going to a match included travel to a game. From the earliest days of the Yorkshire Cup, when Halifax supporters made the journey to Bradford by train, spectators travelling between towns to support their sides had become commonplace. By 1880 this was such a regular occurrence that a minor controversy broke out when Great Western Railways refused to run special trains from towns in Lancashire and Yorkshire for the Roses game at Huddersfield. The ensuing letters of complaint to local newspapers caused them to reconsider their stance and trains were laid on for the North versus South match at Halifax later that season.[60] Bradford in particular were quick to spot the commercial opportunity provided by supporters keen to travel: their regular excursions to clubs in Manchester cost two shillings and threepence for return rail journeys. For one shilling, enthusiastic Huddersfield supporters could, in 1886, travel by train to Leeds to see their side take on Leeds St John's.[61] For those with the time and money to follow their side further afield, Bradford's 1884 journey to Cambridge University was charged at nineteen shillings and elevenpence, while their 1886 tour to London and the Oxbridge Universities cost twenty-five shillings and ninepence.[62] Although it is impossible to estimate the numbers going to away games regularly, it is clear that for important cup matches, travelling supporters could be numbered in four figures: 'thousands' of Hull supporters were said to have journeyed to Bradford for the 1885 Yorkshire Cup first round tie, while Halifax laid on six railway coaches for their match at Park Avenue the following year. At the beginning of 1886 it was noted that many West Riding pubs had formed savings clubs to enable patrons to pay for their trip to the forthcoming Yorkshire Cup final. Even an end of season friendly saw St Helens Recreation take two train loads of supporters to Warrington.[63] The scale of regular travelling support can also be judged by the disappointment felt by the local press that only a hundred Dewsbury supporters went with their side to a key game at Halifax.[64] For those who could not afford to travel with their sides, town-centre shops and pubs would post regular telegrams reporting the play and results, often as regularly as every ten minutes. Sometimes the crowds awaiting the telegrams approached that at the matches, most notably on the day of finals. Waiting for telegrams to be posted during the Manningham versus Batley Yorkshire Cup final in 1884 in the centre of Bradford, the assembled crowd found themselves harangued by the Salvation Army as it tried to march through the town. The outcome was inevitable: 'Natural result – a collision in which the Army suffered a reverse with the loss of their flag, which was torn up. A football crowd is not to be trifled with.'[65]

It is important to note that football spectating was not an exclusively male activity; women were an integral part of the football crowds of this period. As far back as the first Yorkshire versus Lancashire game in 1870, the presence of female spectators was deemed noteworthy by the press and this continued throughout the 1880s. In 1884 *The Yorkshireman* suggested that one-quarter of a 5,000 crowd at the Manningham versus Hull game were women. The numbers of women attending games may be gauged by the decision of the Bradford committee to start charging women for admission to the grandstand, unless accompanied by a club member, suggesting that some women attended matches without male company.[66] While women's attendance at matches may have been encouraged by the fact that most grounds allowed women into matches free, it is clear that many women were active spectators and keen supporters of their chosen teams. This was pointed out by a journalist at the 1883 game between Yorkshire and Cheshire:

> Don't imagine that all the spectators were men, for they were not. Indeed, the female element was very largely represented and the comments from this portion of the gathering were as numerous and as critical as those of their brothers, husbands and fathers.[67]

In 1885 it was reported that the Bradford captain, Fred Bonsor, had received a letter from 'young ladies' in Wakefield accusing his side of cowardice for their refusal to play Trinity that season.[68] Football clearly appealed not only to young women either: 'it is somewhat surprising that so many mature matrons patronise the sport, and what is even more surprising is the extent of their knowledge of the game and the pitch of enthusiasm to which they work themselves up.'[69] When Pontefract returned home after winning the Yorkshire Cup in 1891, one correspondent noted that the crowd contained a 'great number of the fair sex. Old girls and new, young and pretty, old and, er, well, er, respected.'[70] Although there was a chauvinist attitude to the reporting of women's involvement as football spectators, often implying that it was somehow unfeminine, that same year the football columnist of *The Yorkshireman* was moved to protest about a 'men only' meeting for Keighley FC 'comrades': 'What about the ladies who patronise the Highfield Lane enclosure? . . . are they not comrades as well?'[71] Women's behaviour at matches often did not meet Victorian ideals of womanhood, the chairman of Swinton criticising female supporters for their 'bad manners and rowdiness' in 1888. Nor were women adverse to participating in hooliganism – after winning a cup tie at Horbury in 1884, the Batley team found themselves being pelted with red-hot coals by a woman as they left the ground.[72] But despite an obvious high level of interest, there is no record of women actually playing the game at this time.

Figure 4 In the 1880s, women were prominent in northern rugby crowds and were often more than willing to make their presence felt (from *The Yorkshireman*).

It is also clear that previously exclusive clubs, such as Bradford and Huddersfield, began to open the doors of membership wider. This was spurred on by the growing importance of clubs in a town's civic life and their desire to expand their influence, not to mention the financial benefits that subscription monies brought clubs: thus many made considerable efforts to recruit new members. Bradford doubled their membership from 1,271 to 2,500 in the three years to 1888, despite the fact that membership cost ten shillings.[73] In preparation for the opening of their new Valley Parade ground, Manningham offered the prize of free membership for seven years for the recruitment of the most members, which was won by a Mr Jackson who recruited ninety-four new adherents, the next best being thirty-five. This turned out to be a highly successful promotion as it doubled the club's membership to over 1,200. The benefits of membership were usually free entrance to all home club matches and a vote at general meetings, although it seems the former was the motivation to join for most people – for example, less than half of Bradford's membership bothered to attend their 1888 special meeting called to discuss the vital issue of whether to withdraw from the following year's Yorkshire Cup.[74] This indifference to administrative workings was acknowledged by a number of clubs, who, in order to attract more working-class members yet maintain social differentials, introduced tiers of membership. Salford, whose membership grew from just over a hundred in 1883 to over 2,100 in 1890, had four levels of membership: voting honorary members, voting playing members, non-voting season ticket holders and non-voting youths, paying six shillings, four shillings, five shillings, and two shillings and sixpence respectively.[75] Such distinctions often led to resentment, as Halifax discovered when they distinguished between subscribers, who paid £1 per season, and members, who paid half that. This came to a head at their 1887 annual meeting when the chief topic of debate was 'whether the "top nobs" are to be allowed the exclusive use of the large and handsome pavilion' on the ground.[76] This influx of lower-class members into clubs had the overall effect of diluting the control of the game by the upper middle classes.

The behaviour of football crowds in the North became an increasing cause for concern for rugby's leadership throughout the early 1880s. The prevalence of betting at grounds was a particular source of great disquiet among those who led the game. As early as 1883 it was noted that at the Dewsbury versus Halifax Yorkshire Cup tie 'the amount of betting was enormous' with hundreds of pounds changing hands, and many contemporary reports point to the presence of bookmakers at most senior grounds.[77] When Halifax pulled out of the 1882 Yorkshire Cup competition, they cited as a reason 'betting men' who had wanted to see their players lamed, and both Wakefield Trinity and Batley complained that bookmakers had tried to influence their players, although no proof was ever produced in any of these cases.[78] At the end of the decade the Yorkshire committee threatened to take legal action against any bookmaker found plying their trade at matches. But, while betting was undoubtedly a common feature at matches, the paucity of the evidence produced by its opponents would seem to indicate that their concern had something of the character of an ongoing moral panic. Writing in the *Clarion*, former Salford and Swinton player A. A. Sutherland pointed to his journeys throughout the football grounds of the North and argued that:

> Of course there are times when a fair amount of money may change hands, but that it would be worth the while of any bookmaker to 'square' the players, I am inclined to doubt. The matter is hardly to be taken into serious consideration when discussing the dangers to the game.[79]

As the partisanship of crowds and the importance of games increased, referees became a regular target for disgruntled crowds and 'sodding', throwing clods of earth at them, became a popular post-game pastime for some supporters. Holbeck, a Leeds team, were barred from the 1885 Yorkshire Cup because of their supporters' anti-referee activities, while Dewsbury almost lost their right to stage a county game at their Crown Flatt ground after a serious outbreak of mud and stone throwing following a match.[80] Unsurprisingly, many referees made sure that adequate recompense was received, some charging between ten shillings and

Figure 5 Even in 1885 the referee's lot was not a happy one (from *Toby, the Yorkshire Tyke*).

one guinea to take control of a game, as one club secretary discovered at the conclusion of a match: 'How much are we indebted to you?' Referee: '15/-please.' Secretary: 'Rather high isn't it?' Referee: 'Do you suppose I referee for my health?'[81] As Table A.3 of the Appendix shows, theirs was not a negligible risk.

Of the twenty-four incidents reported to the Yorkshire Rugby Union between 1887 and 1895, seventeen involved attacks on referees. Of the remaining, five involved fights between spectators and players, a phenomenon particularly common among smaller clubs, where spectators were often separated from the action only by a rope. Up until 1885, lesser matches were sometimes played without referees, giving rise to similar risks, as Bradford's second team discovered in 1882 when, during an on-field dispute between the two opposing captains, 'spectators crowded on to the ground, hustled the players and the umpires and converted the game into a 'fratching'[fighting] match'.[82]

Certainly, in the early 1880s visiting sides and their supporters, especially those who proved to be victorious, could find themselves attacked by crowds. In 1881 the rivalry between Batley and Dewsbury spilt over into fighting after the two teams had disputed the final of a nine-a-side competition in Batley. Similarly, violent rivalry led to the 1884 Swinton versus Salford derby match being abandoned. Visiting Hunslet supporters invaded the pitch and attacked Liversedge players and supporters near the end of their 'friendly' game.[83] Pudsey supporters lay in wait for Ossett players and supporters as they made their way back to the railway station after their 1884 Yorkshire Cup match. Batley's retreat from Horbury, a village outside Wakefield, in the same year gives a flavour of the fury generated by supporters of a defeated team:

> the occupants of waggonettes, as well as foot passengers, were assailed by a number of cowardly ruffians who hid themselves behind walls and other barricades, from whence they threw large pieces of dross and other missiles. Even the tradesmen could not refrain from venting their spite in a similar manner, a member of that usually respectable body actually coming to the door of his premises in order to fling something at the Batley players as they drove past on their way home.[84]

However, such events may have assumed an importance in the minds of contemporary commentators, which their frequency, or lack of it, did not deserve. Indeed, the local constabulary sent only one policeman to the Wakefield Trinity versus Bradford game in January 1884, a match that attracted a crowd in excess of 10,000, suggesting that the threat of violence was not seen as serious by the police.[85] Although, as Robert Storch has pointed out, the role of the police during this time was to act as a 'domestic missionary' in attempting to control and curb working-class leisure activities, they seem to have played little role in regulating the behaviour of the football crowd. Other than escorting harassed referees or teams from the pitch, there is little to suggest that the police sought to impose middle-class values on crowds by, for example, curbing gambling or bad language inside football grounds. Indeed, the presence of significant numbers of middle-class spectators may have meant that the police did not view football crowds as threats to public order.[86] Without exception, judgements about the behaviour of crowds, or more particularly the working-class sections of crowds, were made by middle-class commentators and it is noticeable that, certainly during the period leading up to 1886, the vast majority of the criticisms of crowd behaviour are not about violence but about the language and enthusiasm of working-class spectators. 'When I say that the home spectators were simply a howling, surging, abusive mob, I don't exaggerate one whit,' wrote a reporter sent to cover a Castleford versus Bradford match, although he was unable to report any violence before, during or after the match.[87] As one might expect, the imagery of the 'mob' loomed large for those unused to, or afraid of, working-class people gathering in their thousands. Although there was neither suspicion of nor actual reason to assume that there was any subversive intent behind such gatherings, the sharp contrast in the behaviour of the classes was seen as a disincentive to middle-class players and spectators: 'If "mob law" is permitted to run riot on the football field, however great the provocation, the pastime will become no game for gentlemen', wrote the *Yorkshire Post* sternly in 1886.[88]

The first laws against professionalism

The disquiet about the changing nature of rugby was first expressed publicly in November 1879, when it was somewhat breathlessly reported that:

> a certain well-known Yorkshire club has in its ranks a *paid* man. Such a startling statement as this we can hardly give credence to, since it is so entirely opposed to the hitherto recognised notions of what has hitherto always been considered a purely amateur pastime.[89]

The name of the player in question was not reported, nor was any overt sanction taken against him. The dreaded paid man was in fact Wakefield Trinity's C. E. 'Teddy' Bartram, a cricket professional who had initially played for Harrogate's football team. His prowess with a rugby ball, both drop-kicking and running with it, soon came to the attention of other clubs and he played for York in the 1877–78 season. His experience of the amateur ideal was grounded in the harsh working life of a professional in cricket, and he stopped playing for York when they could not pay for his railway ticket from Harrogate. He resumed playing for Harrogate and, after an outstanding display for the club at Wakefield early in the 1878–79 season, the Trinity committee persuaded him to switch clubs by agreeing to pay his rail fare if he joined them. Although not officially recorded, they also lent him money. Trinity had recently merged with the formerly socially exclusive Wakefield club and were anxious to make their mark among Yorkshire's leading sides. Teddy was such a key player in helping the club to consecutive Yorkshire Cup victories in 1879 and 1880 that by the end of the following season they invented the position of assistant secretary for him, paying an annual stipend of £52. This remuneration was something of an open secret in Yorkshire rugby circles and there is no doubt that he was deliberately left out of the Yorkshire side in the 1879–80 season because of his status. Despite his outstanding reputation as the best three-quarter in the North – he was probably the most gifted three-quarter to play the game in the region until the career of Dicky Lockwood – he was never selected for England, because, as was noted in 1882, 'there is too much of the professional about him for their [southern selectors'] genteel ideas, football being solely intended, according to their notions, for public school or university players'. He was eventually banned *sine die* from the game in 1889 for professionalism after being found guilty of receiving loans from the club.[90]

Anxious to maintain the sport's reputation, the YCFC immediately introduced the first rules anywhere in the rugby game – or indeed in any code of football – to outlaw professionalism. Because the RFU had no rules on professionalism at this time, they turned to cricket's governing body, the MCC. On 22 November 1879 the YCFC committee passed a motion stating that:

> no player who is not strictly an amateur shall be allowed to play in the Challenge Cup ties, or in any match under the direct control of the County

Figure 6 Wakefield Trinity's C. E. 'Teddy' Bartram, probably the first rugby player to be paid to play (from *Toby, the Yorkshire Tyke*).

Football Committee; the definition of the term 'amateur' shall be the same as that adopted by the MCC.[91]

The committee quoted the MCC's definition of an amateur:

That no gentleman ought to make a profit by his services in the cricket field, and that for the future, no cricketer who takes more than his expenses in any match shall be qualified to play for the Gentlemen versus Players at Lords; but that if any gentlemen feel difficulty in joining in the match without pecuniary assistance he shall not be barred from playing as a gentleman by having his actual expenses defrayed.[92]

As the YCFC committee was to discover later, such a definition was so broad as to allow virtually any payment as long as it was related to 'expenses defrayed'. Indeed, almost the same form of words was used a decade later by the supporters of 'broken-time' payments. But the real difficulty with the MCC rule was that it served only to define categories of gentlemen and said nothing about working-class players who were not full-time professionals. The structure and deep roots of cricket in English society meant that its distinctions between gentlemen and players could be rigidly maintained, but the rapid development of rugby made similar controls impossible. The main discussions about working-class participation in middle-class sports in the 1860s and 1870s took place in athletics and rowing, where the debate was overtly about whether to exclude the working classes from participation. The 1861 *Rowing Almanack* defined an amateur by listing the educational establishments and institutions to which they belonged and excluded absolutely 'tradesmen, labourers, artisans or working mechanics'.[93] The Amateur Athletic Club, the forerunner of the Amateur Athletic Association (AAA), also explicitly excluded anyone who was 'a mechanic, artisan or labourer' from its definition of amateurism.[94] In 1883 the AAA even barred professional cricketers from its events. On the whole, the tenor of middle-class opinion was opposed to working-class participation on an equal footing in those sports thought of as their own. But in rugby, burgeoning mass working-class interest meant exclusion was out of the question. Instead, the leaders of the sport decided that involvement in the game had to be on their terms:

the [mechanic, artisan and labourer] must not forget that the rules now governing the game have attained a definite form ... The chief object – we might say the only object – for which the game is fostered by those who, combining ability with responsibility, control its destinies, is a recreation – a pleasure, in fact – that shall produce, in a most acceptable form, relaxation for both mind and body.[95]

Invariably, the word 'professional' was used as a synonym for working class in both cricket and rugby. The MCC definition of amateurism implied that a middle-class professional was almost a contradiction in terms: as the *Bradford Observer* pointed out, 'the player who has had a [public] school training ... is not likely to develop into the exponent who intends to make a living out of the game'.[96] Of course, many of the leading amateurs of the time found sport a lucrative pastime thanks to expenses payments. In later years W. G. Grace and the high levels of expenses which he commanded became a favourite target of the advocates of broken time payments to rugby players, as did the Surrey and England cricketer W. W. Read, who on the 1887–88 tour of Australia received £1,137 in expenses payments.[97] On a less lucrative scale, middle-class athletes often competed amongst themselves for cash stakes. For example, in the 1860s members of the Stock Exchange, civil servants, army officers, solicitors and other professionals competed for money at Brompton, Hackney Wick and Bow.[98] For the middle-class defender of the amateur ethos, therefore, the question of receiving payment for play was secondary to that of the social class of the player who received the money.

The ramifications of the new regulations were not immediately understood and did not stop payments being made to players. In March 1880 Arthur Hudson, secretary of the YCFC, wrote to the *Yorkshire Post* to publicly condemn Heckmondwike FC for offering cash prizes of £5 for a six-a-side rugby competition to be held over Easter. Threatening to ban them from the forthcoming Yorkshire Cup competition, he claimed that the club's offer of money for a game of football was:

> the first that has ever been made, and I do not think that even any respectable athletic club has gone so far as to openly offer money prizes at its annual meeting ... my personal vote would most certainly be given against any club whose proceedings thus (in my opinion) tended, not to the advancement but rather the prostitution of a game which has happily been played for sport alone.[99]

Heckmondwike quickly apologised and substituted the cash for gold medals, but their original offer of cash prizes for a sporting contest was nothing more than standard practice in working-class communities – indeed, less than three months earlier the same club had advertised for participants to run in a foot race for a prize of £10.[100] Hudson's claim that football had always been amateur was one that was to be taken up regularly over the next decade. Backing the YCFC's stand, the *Yorkshire Post* claimed that since 1300, football 'has stood out in bold relief among the many manly games indulged in by the British youth as being the only example where the competitors engaged are solely and exclusively amateurs'.[101] This was simply not true: in folk football monetary reward was common. In 1773, a 'grand foot-ball match' was played at Walton, near Wetherby, in Yorkshire for the not inconsiderable sum of twenty guineas.[102] After the completion of the Workington Shrove Tuesday game, 'the successful party [was] treated with a sum of money'.[103] In 1765, contestants in West Haddon played for 'a Prize of considerable value and another good prize'.[104] At Alnwick, the best players on each side were rewarded with individual prizes. And as late as 1848, a game was played at Holmfirth, near Huddersfield, for a stake of £5.[105] As they searched for reasons to control the influx of working-class players and attitudes into the game, Hudson and his supporters had engaged in what Hobsbawm and others have identified as 'the invention of tradition' in order to legitimise their authority and instil 'value systems and conventions of behaviour' into rugby.[106] It was this response to working-class involvement in the sport that signalled the start of the development of rugby union's amateur ideology.

But the road to amateur purity was a rocky one. The civic importance now ascribed to football, especially in connection with cup competitions, had increased the pressure on clubs to find the best players and adopt playing methods that enhanced their prospects as a successful team. So although the leading clubs continued to be controlled by the middle classes that had established them, they found themselves having to adopt many of the norms of working-class sport, albeit surreptitiously, in order to attract and retain the best players. By the early 1880s, payments for time lost from work due to playing and training – what became famous in the 1890s as broken-time payments – were regularly made and regarded in some quarters as legitimate expenses: the *Leeds Mercury* even included such payments as acceptable 'ordinary expenses' in a discussion of the FA's legalising of professionalism.[107] During the time spent training for cup matches or on tours to play teams outside of the Yorkshire or Lancashire area, players were often paid expenses for time lost at work.[108] In November 1881, the Wakefield Trinity committee, possibly aware of the attention that was being paid to their activities in the light of the Teddy Bartram affair, passed a resolution stating that 'for the remainder of the football season, no money to be paid out of the funds of the club to any member on account of "broken time" and that a notice be posted in the rooms to this effect'.[109] Hull FC's 1883–84 *Report and Accounts* actually listed as expenditure £18 spent on 'players' loss of time, through accident and attendance at matches' and the committee minutes for that season, in which they reached the Yorkshire Cup final, show that broken-time payments were paid on at least three occasions during their cup run, including for the final itself when all players were asked not to work on the morning of the game.[110] In December 1885, the York committee decided, after hearing an appeal from a player who had travelled up to Middlesborough for a match, that 'a day's wage be allowed him in consequence of having to get a man to do his work'.[111]

The YCFC felt sufficiently worried by this situation to further amend the bye-laws of the Yorkshire Cup for the 1884–85 season, tightening the definition of expenses by forbidding players from 'receiving any money over and above expenses actually out of pocket'.[112] But in January 1885, *The Yorkshireman*'s rugby correspondent was stating confidently that 'I could mention some dozen players who (if report is to be believed) all receive money over and above their actual expenses'.[113] The Manningham team was so widely believed to be in receipt of cash during its 1886 Yorkshire Cup run that Arthur Hudson felt compelled to publicly denounce the rumour mongers.[114] In the same season it was also reported that there was 'a grave rumour afloat' that Batley had given half the gate money of the match against Barrow to the players to share amongst themselves.[115] Unofficial rugby competitions for money, like the one organised by Heckmondwike in 1880, also began to be played again – one of the more notable being a full fifteen-a-side contest in Leeds on Whitsuntide Monday in 1883 that offered a first prize of £15 to the winning team with 15 shillings to each player and £1 each to every team winning its first round match.[116] Even those competitions that provided winners with medals or other non-monetary prizes, for example clocks or suits, were careful to advertise the precise monetary value of such items.

Cash payments, however, were not the most common form of remuneration for players. They smacked too much of 'hard' professionalism for many clubs and, more to the point, were a drain on club finances. Much more popular were payments in kind. In 1881 Dewsbury began the practice of rewarding players with a leg of mutton for each game won in the cup.[117] This quickly became standard practice, and better performances merited even greater rewards. A two-try performance by a Batley player in 1885 earned him 'one leg of mutton, two bottles of port and two shillingworth of eggs'.[118] Mutton was seen as a vital aid to training for the cup too. A Leeds team was reported to have begun regular training for cup matches and given each of their players a leg of mutton every week.[119] Unfortunately, lamented *Toby the Yorkshire Tyke* in March 1884, 'neither mutton nor Blackpool were any use' to Manningham in their Yorkshire Cup loss to Bradford that year.[120] As *Toby* implied, the more ambitious clubs were also taking their players to the seaside for a week to prepare for important cup clashes. But mutton, port and seaside trips were not the only rewards available. 'There is the providing of a man's outfit and a plan which seems to have been adopted of paying for teas for some poorer members of the team after "at home" matches' reported the *Leeds Mercury* disapprovingly.[121] Such was the importance attached to such payments that if a team performed badly, doubt was raised as to whether their players were receiving their weekly reward. 'They nobbud want a leg of mutton and two bottles of wine apiece, an' then they'll laik,' allegedly complained one Dewsbury supporter after a poor performance from his side. 'Aye, an' if I had t'brass they sud hev it an' all,' replied his companion.[122]

Inducements to players to leave one club and join another also became a central feature of the sport. In September 1882 *The Yorkshireman* published a rumour that Bradford, one of the game's most patrician clubs, had offered a player 'a free ticket, a new rig out and a place in the County [team],' if he signed for them.[123] Although the magazine was forced to withdraw the allegation in its next issue, the fact that it could confidently be stated that even Bradford were indulging in such practices illustrates the extent to which the rules were being ignored. During the 1884 close season it was reported that a Leeds club had 'sent out invitations to join its ranks to a number of players, offering them a solid inducement, euphemistically termed "expenses"'.[124] The following season saw 'kidnapping' become rife. Rumours spread about inducements being offered to players by Wakefield Trinity,

Manningham and Bradford. Both the Mirfield and Thornes clubs publicly complained about 'large baits' being offered to tempt players away.[125] In Lancashire,
Wigan became notorious for their 'kidnapping' of players from Aspull, causing the
local paper to comment sarcastically that 'the most cordial relationships at present
exist between Wigan and Aspull ... so much so that the latter have lent the other
team one of their very best men for the rest of the season'.[126] The *Leeds Mercury*
highlighted the underlying reasons for the growth of inducements, pointing
out that:

> there may appear no reason whatever why [a player] should suddenly join
> another organisation. But he is a poor man, and the club which he has joined
> has found him work in their town at increased wages on condition that he
> plays for them.[127]

Nowhere was this more true than in the importation of players from South
Wales. Unlike the predominantly middle-class southern English and Scottish clubs,
South Wales shared a similar social basis for the game with Lancashire and
Yorkshire, and links between the two regions had been forged in the early 1880s
when the leading Yorkshire teams arranged small tours to play clubs in the
Principality. Again, evidence is sketchy but the first reported Welsh import
appears to have been the international full-back D. H. 'Harry' Bowen of Llanelli,
who signed for Dewsbury in February 1884. Despite being highly regarded,
he played only a handful of games for the club before returning to Wales.[128]
At the beginning of the 1884–85 season Dewsbury announced that they had
signed another Welsh international full-back, Alfred Cattell, but he does not
appear to have played any games for the club.[129] The following year the Wales and
Newport back James Bridie signed for Manningham, after he had independently
found work in Bradford. He played one game for Manningham and then turned
out for their local rivals, Bradford. Presumably mindful of his original obligations,
he then went back to play for Manningham! Bradford's poaching caused so much
animosity between the two clubs that it inspired Manningham supporters to
compose a song:

> Bridie was a Welshman,
> Bradford was a thief.
> Bradford came to our house,
> And now we are in grief.[130]

Perhaps the most sensational signing was that of Wales and Cardiff half-back
William 'Buller' Stadden, along with his team mate Angus Stuart, by Dewsbury
in September 1886. Their stated reasons for signing seemed unremarkable. They
were 'out of employment, and having made a few friends during Dewsbury's tour
of the Principality, they naturally steered for Yorkshire and got employment and
a place in the Dewsbury team'.[131] The amount of lucky coincidence involved

in this chain of events was not surprisingly called into question. When it was discovered that Stadden's and Stuart's employer was none other than Newsome, Sons & Spedding (Blanket Manufacturers and Woollen Spinners) of Dewsbury, many smelled a rat – Mark Newsome, one of the sons in the company title, was also president and former captain of Dewsbury FC. Despite widespread condemnation of the club, the Yorkshire committee found itself powerless to act because there was no evidence of money having changed hands and, as Newsome knew, there was, as yet, no rule that forbade players working for members of a club committee.[132]

The October 1886 General Meeting of the RFU

By 1886 the tattered nature of the amateur flag and the increasing influence of working-class players and spectators on the game in the North, especially in Yorkshire, had become a cause for much concern in the leadership of both the RFU and the county rugby unions. In January, press reports spoke of 'the appearance on the scene of the much dreaded and detested professional footballer – the man who plays not for love and honour but for gain' and disclosed that it had 'an array of convincing evidence' of at least two examples of such players.[133] Sure enough, in what appears to have been a pre-planned action, Pudsey appealed against their defeat by Manningham in the first round of the Yorkshire Cup on the grounds that their opponents had fielded J. Birmingham and W. Pulleyn, two players who, Pudsey claimed, 'were being paid over and above expenses actually out of pocket'. Both had originally played for Selby, some thirty miles from Bradford, and, as one witness testified, had 'received broken-time payments, rail-fare and a sovereign' to play for Manningham. Pulleyn had even been heard to state publicly that he 'would play for the club that paid him best' and that 'football paid better than working'.[134] Interestingly, both Pulleyn and Manningham's captain admitted that the club had promised to find him a job, something that was illegal by the end of the year but over which the committee took no action. Manningham reacted by presenting six sworn statements that the two had not been paid and the YCFC committee, unable to find a smoking gun, found the case not proven but thanked Pudsey for bringing the matter before them.

As the 1886–87 season began, the *Yorkshire Post* summed up the mood:

> the professional question last year was assumed to have reached very grave dimensions. It is scarcely possible for matters to continue in the present unsatisfactory condition.... The RFU is determined to purify the game in these parts by the combined legislative action of its members after careful consideration.[135]

The *Bradford Observer* wondered if the game had become 'over-popular' and *The Year's Sport* annual called on the RFU to 'exclude the professional football player from their ranks'.[136] Arthur Budd, a member of the RFU committee, took up the argument in that year's *Football Annual*:

> Only six months after the legitimisation of the bastard [of professionalism] we see two professional teams left to fight out the final [FA] cup tie. To what does this all end? Why this – gentlemen who play football once a week as a pastime will find themselves no match for men who give up their whole time and abilities to it. How should they? One by one, as they find themselves outclassed, they will desert the game and leave the field to professionals. . . .
>
> The Rugby Union committee finding themselves face to face with the hydra have determined to throttle it before he is big enough to throttle them. . . . No mercy but iron rigour will be dealt out.[137]

Budd was not merely speaking for himself. He was a member of a sub-committee that the RFU had set up to draft new laws to illegalise all forms of payment for the October 1886 General Meeting. Along with Budd, the committee consisted of Frederick Currey, the RFU president, James MacLaren of Manchester, William Cail of Northumberland, Rowland Hill of London, Arthur Hudson, the Yorkshire secretary, H. W. T. Garnett of Bradford and George Thomson of Halifax. The presence of three of Yorkshire's leading administrators on the sub-committee – in fact, only Budd, Currey and Hill came from the south of England – underlined the fact that a primary aim of its work was 'to meet the evils existing in Yorkshire'.[138]

As Budd's article implied and the debate before the October meeting made clear, the fact that some players received money for playing the game was not necessarily the major issue. The RFU had sanctioned the payment of second class rail fares for players travelling to matches as legitimate expenses in 1880.[139] But the amount of expenses payments received by southern teams travelling north for matches had subsequently become a source of great controversy. Rowland Hill had congratulated the Yorkshire clubs in 1885 for 'doing good work to the cause of football by spending some [of their money] in the necessary expenses of those bodies who have great difficulty in finding money', yet the double standard involved was not lost on other commentators.[140] 'People are now asking how it is that over £100 was spent in this way for a team composed of amateurs', wrote the northern rugby correspondent of *Pastime* about payment received by the Middlesex team before their game against Yorkshire at Dewsbury in 1885:

> Yet, forsooth, Mr Rowland Hill says the Yorkshire Executive is doing good work in this matter, and in the same breath is indignant because several members of a cup team received last season a small recompense for incidental expenses received while in training![141]

What animated Budd and the RFU was the fear that the influx of working-class players would mean that gentlemen would no longer be able to dominate the game as they had done in the past. The eclipse of the public school-based association football clubs was seen as a dreadful warning of the shape of things to come.[142] Professionalism and payment for play would allow the working classes to dominate rugby in the same way. The *Yorkshire Post* rugby correspondent, who generally reflected the views of the YCFC, continued Budd's arguments:

> rough and unfair play, a disregard to the rules, and abuse of the umpires and referees, can all be traced directly and indirectly to the presence of the paid professional, to whom a love of the game and fair play are of very small importance as compared to the necessity of winning a match.[143]

Working class players and spectators should know their place:

> Why are so few public school men and clergymen found in our leading fifteens? It is because the associations of the game are now becoming thoroughly distasteful to any gentleman of sportsmanlike feeling. They do not care to be hooted and yelled at as part and parcel of a sixpenny show or to meet and associate with men who care nothing for the game other than as a means to an end. We have nothing to say against the mechanic, the artisan or the labourer, who as long as they indulge in the game for sport and not for profit, are an ornament to the game.[144]

The proposed rule changes declared illegal any payment, either in cash or in kind, to players for playing or training. The new regulations also forbade the employment of a player in any capacity by his club or by any member of the club. Unsurprisingly, they met with little resistance at the October general meeting. Arthur Hudson led the discussion, euphemistically referring to 'a small cloud which has appeared on the horizon'. Rowland Hill claimed that 'even in the poorest communities' players opposed professionalism and Budd, in character-istically pointed fashion, prophesied that if they compromised with professionalism, 'the game would eventually resolve itself into a distinct game for both professionals and amateurs, as the latter would be in time completely outclassed'. To a Yorkshire delegate who argued that 'the very existence of his club, composed almost entirely of working men, would be threatened if they were held to the letter of the new laws,' Bradford's Harry Garnett bluntly replied: 'If working men desired to play football, they should pay for it themselves, as they would have to do with any other pastime.'[145]

Horace Lyne of Welsh club Newport, supported by Dewsbury, opposed the new regulations because of the impact they would have on the working-class player. He 'thought the rules too stringent, especially with regard to the payment of expenses. A large number of Welsh clubs were composed of working men and they could not afford to lose time when engaged away from home,' and he went on to 'urge payment for lost time'.[146] An amendment from the Lancashire county club, originating from Oldham, that 'a player receiving compensation for injuries sustained while playing for his club should be excepted from suspension' was accepted, but only four clubs voted against the new amateur regulations.[147]

Thus was laid the foundation stone of the RFU for the next 109 years. In direct response to a flood of working-class participation, the leaders of the RFU had drawn a line beyond which they were not prepared to compromise. Although rugby's leaders were perfectly prepared to allow working-class people to participate in the sport, and many, especially those with a church background, sought to encourage it, such involvement was to take place solely on their terms – hence the codification of amateurism. As Garnett's speech implied, compromise with working-class cultural practices was not part of the RFU's agenda: if the working classes did not like it, they could leave it. This intransigence reflected the fact that the rational recreation shoe was on the other foot; instead of middle-class reformers attempting to change working-class leisure, the impact of the working class on a formerly exclusive middle-class leisure pursuit was changing rugby. Far from middle-class values being imparted to its new participants, working-class values and traditions threatened to overwhelm the sport, especially given the importance of proletarian players and spectators to clubs that now carried the weight of civic pride and expectation with them.

As the RFU leadership realised in its own fashion, working-class people brought to the sport different ways of participating in football, whether it was on the terraces or on the pitch. While violence, dissent and competitiveness were also integral to middle-class ways of playing rugby, for the working class to engage in such practices – with no little success, it should be added – was to undermine the accepted sporting order. More particularly, working-class expectations of monetary or material reward for their on-field endeavours was directly counterposed to the Arnoldian spirit that underpinned much of rugby's appeal to the middle classes. Thus the reaction of working-class players to the new regulations was summed up by a Batley player who declined to discuss the terms of an offer to switch clubs until he had heard the outcome of the RFU conference: 'Who's bahn to provide t'mutton; becos noa mutton, noa laaking, not me.'[148]

Off the field, working-class spectators also attached alternative meanings to watching the sport. Although they shared with the middle classes the sense of civic pride in their football club, their behaviour at matches – the barracking of the referee, the booing of the visiting side, the resorting to low-level violence when things did not go their way – all suggest that they saw themselves as *participants* in the match ritual, rather than mere observers. And, just as working-class players sought monetary value for their efforts, working-class spectators saw the match as a spectacle and demanded value for their monetary outlay. Although not articulated as such, rugby football had become a site of conflict between the expression of working-class cultural practices and the dominant cultural codes of the public-school ethos.

Chapter 3

'King Football': 1886–1893[1]

In the autumn of 1896, Talbot Baines, grandson of the Liberal, non-conformist founder of the *Leeds Mercury* Edward Baines, published a series of articles in *The Times* on the North of England. In its introduction to the first article, the newspaper summed up popular thought on the matter by stating that 'North of the Trent, it is often suggested are found most of the backbone and manly virtues of the country: south of that line exists what amount of good is consistent with somewhat invertebrate moral strictures'.[2] These mutually interdependent images of the North and South of England had a long history predating the industrial revolution – some have even claimed to have found early manifestations of North/ South rivalry in the eighth-century writings of the Venerable Bede – but they had been rekindled and given renewed impetus by the coming of the factory age.[3] The dominant image of the North of England in the nineteenth century had been expressed in literature ranging from Blake's dark satanic mills to Dickens' Coketown and Gaskell's Darkshire – most notably by the words of the latter's John Thornton in *North and South*:

> We are Teutonic up here in Darkshire in another way. We hate to have laws made for us at a distance. We wish people would allow us to right ourselves, instead of continually meddling, with their imperfect legislation. We stand up for self-government, and oppose centralisation.[4]

For those living in the South of England, Baines argued that 'many of them still feel that, collectively, the points of contrast to be met with in the North of England produce an atmosphere as really, if not as profoundly, distinct from that of their own native districts as is the atmosphere of one of the continental nations'.[5] These supposed differences in attitudes and perspectives of the geographical halves of England have been summed up by Donald Horne in terms of metaphors:

> In the Northern Metaphor Britain is pragmatic, empirical, calculating, Puritan, bourgeois, enterprising, adventurous, scientific, serious, and believes in struggle.
>
> . . .

In the Southern Metaphor Britain is a romantic, illogical, muddled, divinely lucky, Anglican, aristocratic, traditional, frivolous, and believes in order and tradition.[6]

But this was at worst caricature and at best based on attitudes that had more credence in the early to middle part of the century. Certainly the idea that northern industrialists were merely pounds, shillings and pence pragmatists with few interests beyond the factory gate is mistaken, as a glimpse of mid-Victorian architecture and artistic patronage of urban centres of Lancashire and West Yorkshire will testify. And, as Patrick Joyce has demonstrated, the culture of the northern factory itself included a variety of social and recreational activities provided by employers.[7] In fact, by the mid-1890s, northern industrialists of the type described by Dickens and Gaskell were few and far between, if they had ever existed at all, and Baines thought it wise to point out that regional differences:

> apply primarily and exclusively to the middle and working classes. Such differences in type as may have existed between the upper ranks of society in North and South have not survived in any appreciable form the fusing of public school and university education.[8]

Certainly in rugby up to the late 1880s, there was no 'North/South divide' among the RFU leadership, as the framing of the 1886 anti-professional rules had demonstrated. In Lancashire the Liverpool/Manchester axis was firmly based on former pupils of Rugby and Cheltenham, and to a lesser extent Eton and Harrow. The founders of Yorkshire rugby were largely educated at southern public schools. Those who had attended private schools in the north, such as Leeds Grammar School, Manchester Grammar School, St Peter's in York or Bramham College, had been educated firmly in the tenets of the Arnoldian tradition, and many of them, such as Lancashire's J. H. Payne or Yorkshire's W. E. Bromet, had also completed their education at Oxbridge. Nor was opposition to professionalism based on antipathy to an urban, industrial culture. Most of these men represented the northern bourgeoisie par excellence, coming from families that had made their money from industry, particularly textiles, or as merchants. The backgrounds of three of the North's presidents of the RFU, and most determined fighters against professionalism, were impeccably industrial: Harry Garnett of Yorkshire was a paper manufacturer, William Cail of Northumberland was manager of a chemical works and J. W. H. Thorp of Cheshire was a textile manufacturer. But while they may have been proud of their northern roots, they shared with their colleagues living in the south a generalised disquiet about the growth of working-class self-confidence, demonstrated by a rising tide of industrial militancy and political organisation, and the impact of the working class on their leisure pursuits.

The North/South divide is therefore a seductive yet unhelpful metaphor in understanding the development of rugby. Although there were local and regional rivalries, the erosion of rugby's national consensus was, as we shall see in this chapter, caused primarily by the growth of differing attitudes towards working-class participation. Given that the vast majority of working-class rugby players were based in Yorkshire and Lancashire, it was inevitable that its geographic focus would be on the northern counties. Similar tensions existed everywhere that rugby had a significant working-class following. In the southwest of England, Gloucester and clubs in Torquay were investigated in the 1890s and found guilty of violations of the amateur regulations. In the Midlands, there were investigations into payments for play throughout the 1900s involving the Leicester and Coventry clubs, one of which resulted in the resignation of RFU president Charles Crane in 1908 after he called for expulsion of the miscreants. Clubs in the Scottish border towns were suspected but never convicted of being more than generous with expenses payments to players. And of course, Welsh rugby union was plagued with accusations of professionalism for almost as long as Lancashire and Yorkshire, eventually managing to partially suppress the contradiction by covertly legitimising informal payments to players. But the situation in the North of England differed because the sheer scale of working-class involvement and the impossibility of controlling payments for play were increasingly perceived by the RFU leadership as a direct threat to their control of the game.

This is not to deny that there were rivalries and jealousies between different regions. However, in the main, these tended to involve Yorkshire and the county's perceived slights by either the metropolitan rulers of the sport or their fellow-northerners across the Pennines. Both Lancashire and Yorkshire had grievances against the southern-based RFU leadership: southern county sides often turned up in the North with sides weakened owing to players withdrawing because of the long journeys involved and accusations of southern bias in the selection of the England team were commonplace, even after the RFU had introduced the North versus South game in 1874 as a trial match to make selection fairer.[9] There were also disputes over the rules, Yorkshire seeking stricter off-side and penalty laws. But the major source of friction in the 1880s was due to the massive growth of the game in Yorkshire and the county committee's consequent belief that they were entitled to a major place in the national leadership of the sport. This was primarily expressed through the call to hold the Union's general meeting alternately in the North and South. As early as 1881 the YCFC had circularised it member clubs asking them to meet before that October's RFU general meeting, emphasising 'the importance of Yorkshire clubs acting in unison' and the calls for general meetings to be held in the North continued throughout the 1880s. Relations between the Yorkshiremen and the RFU hit a low point in 1887 when the RFU refused to accept Mark Newsome as a member of its executive and the Yorkshire Rugby Union (YRU), to which the YCFC had changed its name in 1888, almost gave its support to Scotland in its dispute with the RFU the following year.[10] Despite this, there was never any suggestion that the leadership was anything less than unswerving in its commitment to the RFU's philosophy, if not its personnel. We have already seen that it was Yorkshire representatives who played a central role in drawing up the 1886 amateur regulations. As this chapter will demonstrate,

Yorkshire's pursuit of the 'veiled professionals' among its players was second to none and earned it the respect of the RFU leadership. If anything, the fact of being the nation's leading rugby county meant that Yorkshire leaders felt they had a duty to be 'more royalist than the king'.

The rivalry with Lancashire was not simply due to traditional enmities but was also a result of the county Palatine's greater influence on the game's ruling bodies; throughout the 1870s and most of the 1880s Lancashire were allocated more seats on the RFU executive than the white rose county. The Lancastrians were also felt to be too strong in their support of the RFU – the Lancashire union repeatedly voted against Yorkshire's proposals for alternate annual meetings to be held in the North, most notably in 1891 when a Yorkshire motion for alternate meetings was passed by 143–106 but did not carry because it failed to get the necessary two-thirds majority. Lancashire clubs were conspicuous in voting against the motion, including representatives of future Northern Union clubs Broughton Rangers, Oldham, Runcorn, Salford, Swinton and Wigan.[11] For their part, those to the west of the Pennines felt that Yorkshire rugby was intent on self-aggrandisement and the domination of rugby for its own ends: 'they were trying to make the Union an accessory of Yorkshire' protested a delegate to the 1891 Lancashire AGM.[12] To Yorkshire rugby enthusiasts, it was not a question of North versus South but of Yorkshire versus the Rest. This was the case for Yorkshire regionalism in general during the late nineteenth century, as expressed in the plethora of weekly and monthly magazines with the word 'Yorkshire' in their title during this period: *The Yorkshireman*; *Toby, the Yorkshire Tyke*; *Yorkshire Owl*; *Yorkshire Chat*; and *Yorkshire Busy Bee* to name only those that had significant coverage of football. These magazines were concerned to demonstrate the virtues of the Yorkshire character – *The Yorkshireman* even carried a column entitled 'What Yorkshiremen are inventing' at one point – rather than sing the praises of an abstract North, although this did not stop them denouncing the perfidy of an equally abstract South.[13] A similar point can be made about regionalist feeling west of the Pennines – one can find little trace of northern corporate feeling in Lancashire's journals and newspapers of the time. Unsurprisingly, the Lancastrian partisans felt that they too were a unique entity, with possibly more cause than the latter day Yorkists, as a recent historian of the North has pointed out: 'Always an isolated and insular county, Lancashire never quite got into step with the rest of the North. It moved towards alignment belatedly, as so often in the past; and still never quite got into place in the end.'[14]

But despite the misgivings of its leadership, the growth of the sport in Lancashire and especially Yorkshire in the 1880s was nothing short of phenomenal. At the start of the 1885–86 season a Yorkshire journalist remarked that:

> Goal posts and mill chimneys seem in some quarters to vie with each other in profusion. A friend of mine residing in the Girlington district [southwest of Leeds] tells me he can count the goal posts of twenty football clubs within a radius of 500 yards.

Between 1887 and 1890 the number of teams entering the Yorkshire Cup doubled, from 64 to 129, and the number of local and junior cup competitions experienced a similar growth – the turn of the decade saw almost every sizeable town or district in Yorkshire (except Sheffield and Middlesborough) able to boast its own cup, including Barnsley, Bradford, Castleford, Dewsbury and the heavy woollen district, Halifax, Huddersfield, Hull, Keighley, Leeds with three, Wakefield, Wharfedale and York. The popularity of these competitions with spectators can be gauged by the fact that the Bradford Charity Cup was able to hand over a clear profit of £700 to local hospitals in 1887.[15] That same year, the Yorkshire Church Temperance Shield competition began with thirty-two of the county's church-based teams and in 1888 the West Riding Public Schools Challenge Cup was inaugurated, private schools thus emulating the initiative of their board-school cousins in Bradford, who had begun their own competition in 1886. A cup for board schools in Leeds began in 1891, organised by the local branch of the National Union of Teachers. There were also competitions for members of those trades that still had half-day holidays during the week: ties in the Yorkshire Tradesmen's Cup were played on a Tuesday afternoon, while other half-holiday clubs played on a Wednesday afternoon. As a visitor to the county suggested in 1893, rugby had become the 'national game' of Yorkshire:

> I found the entire population of the place arguing madly about place kicks, dropped goals, referees, off-side play, tackling, punting, dead balls, and I know not what else. . . . I have travelled through this great county and from end to end thereof [and] have heard no scrap of rational converse. Nothing, absolutely nothing, but strange weird gibberish until my reason tottered on its throne.[16]

In Lancashire, because of the encroachment of soccer and the complete opposition of the county authorities to cup football, the rate of expansion did not match that of Yorkshire – in 1890 the YRU had 198 affiliated clubs whereas the Lancashire union never had more than fifty.[17] But despite the lack of a county-wide cup competition to focus popular appeal, at a local level cup competitions flourished. The nearest equivalent to the Yorkshire Cup in Lancashire was the West Lancashire and Border Towns Cup, which became the focal point of the season for clubs in its region. Begun in 1886 by the semi-autonomous West Lancashire and Border Towns Rugby Union its later rounds consistently attracted five-figure crowds.[18] The core teams of the competition – Wigan were the most northerly side with the remaining eleven teams drawn from the Merseyside area, including St Helens, Warrington and Widnes – had been stung into action by the growth of soccer and the cup was a deliberate attempt to maintain rugby as the dominant football code by increasing local interest. Such was the enthusiasm aroused that in 1889 a league competition was begun and a knock-out cup for junior sides started, the first year's entrants totalling forty. The South East Lancashire Union, formed in 1884 with members coming from the Manchester district, quickly followed its westerly neighbours. Catering for junior sides in the area, its cup was withdrawn by its sponsors, the *Athletic Journal*, in 1889 after a dispute over the allocation of competition profits and an investigation by the Lancashire Rugby Union into allegations of professionalism against the Union's officials.[19] The trophy reappeared later in the year as the Manchester and District Charity Cup. Although not as widespread as in Yorkshire, town-based competitions also sprang up in Lancashire. Eighteen thousand people watched the final of the Wigan Challenge Cup in 1886. Sixteen sides contested the first Rochdale Charity Cup in 1887 and thirteen sides contested the Warrington junior cup competition in 1888, by which time it was estimated that 10,000 people watched that year's final of the Rochdale Cup.[20] These competitions assumed a double importance for the game, by countering the appeal of soccer's plethora of cup competitions and also by granting a degree of autonomy from the constraints of the Lancashire Rugby Union. Provided their paths did not cross too often, the leaders of the Manchester and Liverpool clubs showed little interest in the activities of these local competitions, allowing the more dynamic and entrepreneurial clubs to explore ways of promoting the sport which were forbidden at county level. Nevertheless, as the captain of Warrington argued after they had won the West Lancashire Cup in 1886, what was needed for rugby as a whole in Lancashire was a competition that emulated the Yorkshire Cup.[21]

Professionalism on trial in Yorkshire . . .

The impact of the 1886 amateur regulations took time to filter through to Lancashire and Yorkshire – indeed, in Lancashire it was to be another four years before any formal action was taken by the authorities. When the anticipated storm eventually broke in Yorkshire in March 1888, it concerned a factory worker, Jack Clowes of Halifax.[22] Along with fourteen other northern players (and six southern-based players), Clowes had been approached by the England cricket professionals Alfred Shaw and Arthur Shrewsbury to take part in a football tour of Australia and New Zealand, to play both Rugby and Victorian (Australian) rules. Unapproved yet unforbidden by the RFU, the tour was an unambiguously commercial venture from the start, as Shaw conceded openly: 'We arranged the trip in the hope of making money.'[23] Unfortunately for Clowes, Dewsbury's president, Mark Newsome, was determined to feed fat the grudge he had borne against Halifax since 1883.[24] Newsome withdrew Dewsbury's tourists Stuart and Stadden from his side to play Halifax in the second round of the Yorkshire Cup, which Dewsbury lost, and then appealed against the result on the grounds that Halifax had fielded a professional: Clowes![25]

When called before the Yorkshire committee, Clowes openly admitted everything and even offered to pay back his £15.[26] The RFU declared him a professional, but he had already set sail with the touring party, placing him in the unfortunate position of being a tourist yet unable to play in any games. But it was an open secret that Clowes was not the only member of the touring party to receive money. Its most famous player, England rugby and cricket captain Andrew Stoddart, who took over the tour captaincy after the original captain, Broughton Rangers' Bob Seddon, was drowned, had been 'bound' to the tour by a down payment of £50, with more to follow.[27] How much Stoddart eventually received is unclear but can be gauged by the fact that two lesser-known amateurs had been offered £200 in expenses to make the trip.[28] Of those who did go, W. H. Thomas of Cambridge University and Wales was paid £90 for the thirty-week tour and tried to negotiate a further £3 per week when the tour was unexpectedly lengthened.[29] There were other advantages to being a gentleman amateur on tour, as can be seen from Shrewsbury's request to Shaw, who had recruited the players, to identify which 'amateurs you have promised to pay their wine and refreshment account at dinners'. Unfortunately for Shrewsbury, Shaw had failed to organise such social distinctions adequately en route, resulting in an on-board drinks bill of £68.[30] But as soon as they arrived down under, Shrewsbury imposed a hierarchy of players – at one point even threatening to stop sending the wages of Rochdale's Johnny Nolan home to his family unless he 'behaved himself', despite the fact he was the tourists' leading try scorer – with the unfortunate Clowes at the bottom of the pile: 'he won't be able to play in a single match and we shall have all his expenses to pay.... He is a dead head, and of no use to us at all.'[31] For sharp entrepreneurs such as Shaw and Shrewsbury, the RFU's amateur regulations suited their purposes perfectly, as Shrewsbury admitted before the tour began, 'if the rugby union can get players to come out without paying them anything, all the better for us'.[32]

On their return in November 1888, having won twenty-seven of their thirty-five rugby matches and nine of the nineteen Victorian rules games, confusion surrounded the tourists' status. The YRU, fully expecting the RFU to take disciplinary action, advised clubs not to play such players until the situation had been clarified. Salford telegrammed Rowland Hill to ask if their four tourists would be allowed to play. To everyone's surprise, the RFU lifted the ban on Clowes and merely called on the other tourists to sign declarations that they had received no money other than expenses while on tour. Needless to say, all of them swore that they had not received a penny and the matter was dropped.

The reason for the RFU's reluctance to act was simple: any investigation into the financial arrangements of the tourists would have implicated Stoddart and the other amateurs on tour. If the charges of professionalism had been pursued, the RFU would have had to ban one of England's leading sportsmen and declare illegal the generous advantages of the gentleman amateur's expenses. And to have maintained the ban on Clowes but taken no action against Stoddart would have been to admit openly that different, unwritten, rules applied to different classes of players. Nevertheless, by ignoring both their own regulations and the over-whelming evidence of payments, the RFU had laid bare the underlying class bias of the amateur ethos – a middle-class gentleman was by definition an amateur, whether he was paid or not, and was not to be judged by the standards of other, working-class, men.

Figure 7 The Reverend Frank Marshall is caricatured trying to turn back the tide of professionalism (from *The Yorkshireman*).

This failure to act against 'one of their own' was met with anger by the supporters of amateurism in Yorkshire and seized upon as the opportunity to promote the county as the most determined and consistent proponent of amateurism.[33] The YRU had been under considerable pressure for some time to clean out its Augean stables and since the unexpected death of Arthur Hudson in January 1888 had been dominated by its newly appointed treasurer, the Reverend Frank Marshall, the headmaster of Almondbury School near Huddersfield, apostle of muscular Christianity and scourge of the 'veiled professional'. In October 1888, the committee laid charges of professionalism against Leeds St John's, alleging that it had induced F. L. North to transfer from Kirkstall through the promise of a job. This time the case was watertight. St John's secretary George Smith had been foolish enough to send North a letter offering him a job, which the player gave to the Kirkstall secretary. Caught in the act, St John's were suspended for six weeks.

This was a tug at a loose thread that began to unravel the rugby tapestry. Instead of accepting their punishment, Leeds St John's claimed they had been scapegoated and accused the YRU committee, and especially its president Mark Newsome, of hypocrisy. Other clubs claimed that the suspension was too harsh because it deprived them of lucrative games against St John's.[34] Undeterred, the YRU then suspended Brighouse Rangers for professionalism after they had induced Herbert Hartley, a miner, to join them from Liversedge in exchange for a job in which he would 'learn a trade'.[35] A few weeks later, Cleckheaton also found themselves suspended. Their crime was to have encouraged players to attend training sessions during the summer by offering them cloth with which to make up suits. '*No professionalism* is still the cry of the hour – town, village and country being consumed with a zeal for football purity', proclaimed the *Yorkshire Post* with its usual zealotry.

Purifying or not, it was obvious to all that the suspensions were playing havoc with the season and that serious financial losses would be faced both by suspended clubs and their opponents. And, given the widespread nature of the offences for which the three clubs had been suspended, the direct threat of suspension now hung over the head of virtually every club in the county. Faced with the bitter fruits of the amateur regulations, a number of Yorkshire's leading clubs began to campaign for reform. Led by Captain Bell, vice-president of the Halifax club who had led the defence of Jack Clowes, the dissidents forced a special general meeting of the YRU in February 1889 to discuss the suspensions. Bell called for clubs found guilty of professionalism to be punished by the forfeiting of home games only, thus avoiding the loss of fixtures by their opponents. However, he went on to propose a general solution:

> He yielded to no man in his opposition to professionalism and he thought if clubs established some common ground of action they might do something to prevent it. One of the ways to prevent it in its gross form was to give compensation for loss of time. The idea was contrary to the present law but he thought it was worthy of consideration. He put it to them whether it would not be better to give compensation for loss of time to the working man, who enjoyed his football in the same way as the rich man.[36]

The genie was out of the bottle. Although Bell commanded support from much of the meeting, no vote was taken because the YRU committee came up with a compromise scheme. The meeting also heard suggestions that county games should be held on weekdays, to avoid players missing Saturday club matches, and that clubs hosting county fixtures should be entitled to a larger share of the gate money. For the first time, a section of the senior clubs had openly called for change on the basis of commercial, club-centred, interests, denying the primacy of county games and amateurism, the twin pillars of Yorkshire rugby tradition.

Despite the qualms of these leading clubs, the YRU continued to hunt down violators of the amateur code, enthusiastically backed by the RFU. Speaking after refereeing the 1889 Roses match, Rowland Hill declared that it was his aim 'to drive a nail into [professionalism]'[37]. Perhaps not surprisingly, the next two clubs to be suspended, Wakefield Trinity and Heckmondwike, were among those most involved in the campaign for the February special meeting. Trinity had also been at the forefront of moves to start a Yorkshire league. Their offence was to offer Teddy Bartram a testimonial, now an offence under the RFU rules. They were suspended for six weeks. Bartram, about whom it was common knowledge that he had been paid by the club for ten years, was barred from playing *sine die*.[38] Heckmondwike were charged with directly paying players, and, although not publicly admitted at the time, one player in particular: Dicky Lockwood.[39] The YRU had overwhelming circumstantial evidence against the club. Their accounts showed that gate money from the grandstand always came to an even amount and that, despite having a successful side with three England internationals in it, in only two games during the previous season did they appear to take more than £20 at the gate. Not only did they not have a bank account but the treasurer confessed that he never counted the gate money. Further questions were also raised as to how three players who had transferred to Heckmondwike all worked at the same dyeing factory in the town. Eventually the club and its players were suspended for three months.

The bloodletting went on. Over the next four years, the YRU held over twenty trials for offences against the amateur regulations. Only twelve of these hearings returned guilty verdicts. Bizarrely, the enthusiasm of the committee to track down miscreants led them to investigate wedding presents given to J. W. Moore of Leeds St John's and George Broadbent of Holbeck. Most disappointingly for advocates of rugby's moral role, the Leeds Parish Church club was suspended in January 1890 for sinning against the commandments of amateurism. Their secretary denied paying the players but, as *The Yorkshireman* revealed, the truth was somewhat more ornate:

> The items for cigars, champagne, oyster suppers, drinks, etc., and the comfortable fashion in which they encouraged their players by giving them contracts, shows that the church militant is by no means given to mortification of the flesh, nor meant to allow its players to be left out in the cold when a nice little job was knocking about.[40]

As the YRU's pursuit of the professional spectre gathered pace, the situation grew more complex as calls for league competitions began to be heard from senior clubs. In May 1889 Wakefield Trinity called a meeting of eleven of the county's senior sides to discuss the formation of a Yorkshire Football League. Although it did not win a great deal of support, it highlighted the growing realisation that soccer was not going to collapse after legalising professionalism and that the formation of the Football League in 1888 had been highly successful. The growth of local cricket leagues in the North also served to underline the benefits to be gained from formal organisation of the season's competition.[41] By 1892 the pressure to form a Yorkshire league had become irresistible, both because of envy of the burgeoning crowds attracted by the Football League but also because of the Yorkshire Cup triumphs of the relatively junior Otley and Pontefract clubs, in 1889 and 1891, were seen as diminishing the cup's credibility as the true championship of Yorkshire.[42] In May of that year ten of Yorkshire's leading clubs – Batley, Bradford, Brighouse Rangers, Dewsbury, Halifax, Huddersfield, Hunslet, Leeds, Liversedge and Wakefield Trinity – met to form the Yorkshire Football Alliance. Based explicitly on the organisation of the Football League and with a paid secretary to ensure efficient proceedings, its declared aim was to create 'a real fight for the Yorkshire championship'.[43] Despite intense opposition from both the YRU and RFU nine of the clubs stood firm for the new venture. The one exception was Leeds, of whom YRU secretary James Miller was a leading committee member and whose commercial commitments to the Headingley grounds made them chary of opposing the rugby authorities. Faced with clubs determined to form a league, the YRU backed down and agreed to the formation of a Yorkshire Senior Competition (YSC) – the word 'league' being avoided because it was felt to carry too strong an implication of professionalism – on condition that the YRU had ultimate control over its activities. There was then a rush to form lower divisions by the not-so-senior clubs. In a few weeks, the unpretentiously titled Number Two Competition had been formed and by September 1893 almost the whole of Yorkshire rugby was organised on a league basis, with sixty teams participating in county-wide leagues.

As expected, the YSC proved to be an outstanding success. In its first month Bradford, Halifax and Hunslet all attracted five-figure crowds. In fact, just about the only loser in the whole affair was the Leeds club, whose abandonment of the Yorkshire Football Alliance was rewarded by their erstwhile allies with exclusion from the first season of YSC. Naively, they assumed that they would be able to counter this reversal of fortune by arranging fixtures with the leading London sides, who showed no interest at all, so Leeds were reduced to playing friendly fixtures with some of the North's more junior sides. Needless to say, the season proved to be a financial disaster with losses of more than £800 leaving the club determined never to be placed in a such a risky position again, a desire that was to shape the history of the club for the following two decades. But for the other senior clubs, there were no such problems: gates, revenue and public interest grew. At the end of the first season of the league system A. W. Pullin addressed the question of whether competition football had proved a success and answered 'with a monosyllabic "Yes"'.[44]

... and in Lancashire

In Lancashire, the campaign against professionalism was slower to develop, partly because the sport had effectively been 'socially zoned' for many years: day-to-day contacts between the public school-based clubs and those that relied on working-class players and support were few and far between, especially given the absence of a county cup competition.[45] The situation in Lancashire also differed from Yorkshire in that the growth of soccer offered an alternative to those seeking rewards for their sporting prowess. As a letter to the *Oldham Evening Chronicle* put it: 'the association game is slowly but surely taking our best men, as it is only likely that they will play where they can be paid.'[46] Nevertheless, by 1890 rumours of payment for play had become so widespread that the Lancashire committee, also under pressure to emulate the zeal of the YRU, was forced to act. Acting in concert with the LCFC, Mossley FC charged Werneth with inducing their star player, Abe Ashworth, to join them in exchange for a job. Conducting the case on Mossley's behalf, LCFC secretary J. H. Payne, a Cambridge-educated Manchester solicitor, described how Ashworth, a weft carrier in Mossley earning £1 a week, had obtained a job as an iron dresser at Werneth's Hartford iron works for twenty-seven shillings per week. Determined to make an example of their first successful prosecution, the LCFC banned the unfortunate Ashworth *sine die* and suspended Werneth for sixteen weeks. The severity of the sentence, which in the case of the club was greater than anything handed down by the Yorkshire committee, shocked observers and caused outrage in Werneth, where 3,000 people signed a petition calling for the sentence to be lifted.[47]

Invigorated by their success, Payne and the LCFC committee planned a series of investigations into professionalism.[48] However, in October they found their hand forced by the Reverend Frank Marshall, who publicly demanded that accusations of professionalism against Oldham be investigated by the Lancashire authorities. Oldham had long had the finger of suspicion pointed at them, especially given their success in recruiting players from Wales – the first being international three-quarter Bill McCutcheon who signed in 1888, swiftly followed by fellow international Dai Gwyn at the end of the next season.[49] Marshall, keen to build on his reputation as 'the man with bell, book and candle [facing] the evil spirit of professionalism', seems to have believed that the club would make an easy target.[50] However, it soon transpired that Marshall had absolutely no evidence for his, albeit probably correct, accusations and, in a move widely regarded as cowardice in Lancashire, refused to make public his evidence, saying that he would call witnesses to back up his accusations only when the LCFC committee pressed formal charges. After interviewing the club's three Welsh imports, who of course denied any hint of payment, the LCFC committee decided to take no further action.[51]

Marshall's ham-fisted attempt to extend the YRU's war on professionalism effectively halted the LCFC in its tracks. Such was the outrage of the Lancashire clubs that any attempt to pursue further investigations would have been treated with scorn, particularly because the accusers would have been seen as a tool of the Yorkshire rugby authorities. Even the *Manchester Guardian*, a determined opponent of any concession to professionalism, felt it necessary to oppose Marshall's attack on Oldham.[52] Antipathy towards Yorkshire had become intense, and not simply because of the two counties' traditional sporting rivalry. The strength of the white rose county had come to dominate northern rugby, toppling Lancashire's former leadership, with the YRU now commanding more seats on the RFU committee.[53] By causing the fight against professionalism to be identified as a Yorkshire issue, Marshall had so seriously weakened the LCFC's case that it was to be another four years before they felt strong enough to pursue the matter again, although when the battle was finally rejoined in 1894 its purpose was to hasten a split in the union.

Nevertheless, rumours of professionalism in Lancashire continued unabated. The most famous rumours centred on the mercurial brothers David and Evan James and their attempts to transfer from Swansea to Manchester's Broughton Rangers in 1892 for a reputed, and astronomical, signing-on fee of £250. As with many Welsh players, the avowed reason for moving north was work, as Broughton's secretary explained:

> They left Swansea in search of work. One of them had been out of employment for some time. The other was in work but you know how things are in Swansea. Trade is bad and the wages the one in work got were not of the highest. So they came to Manchester in search of employment. Is there anything extraordinary in that?

However, a well-placed source in Swansea informed the *Clarion* that 'the talk of them leaving Swansea in search of work is moonshine. They were idolised in Swansea but their demands were too exorbitant.'[54] The LCFC blocked their move after Swansea claimed that the brothers had indeed demanded money from the club. It was also rumoured that Huddersfield, after having had their offer turned down by the brothers, had tipped the wink to the RFU.[55] Six weeks later the RFU overturned the decision and gave them permission to turn out for Rangers. But following pressure from the Welsh Rugby Union to make an example of the brothers, the RFU changed their minds in January 1893 and decided that, even if no money was received, the act of asking for payment was an act of professionalism and promptly banned the brothers as professionals.[56]

As in Yorkshire, the campaign against professionalism was complicated by calls for league competitions – but in Lancashire, the clamour for league competition was even more heartfelt. Here, the astonishing growth in support for soccer caused not only envy among rugby clubs but also fear. Rugby, which in 1880 had dominated the county (with the exception of Blackburn and its hinterland), was by 1892 in danger of being overwhelmed by the popularity of the round ball game. The failure of the county authorities to promote the game was causing it to wither on the vine, as A. A. Sutherland lamented at the end of the 1891–92 season:

> Less than ten years ago not a single association club could be found either in Manchester or district. Now both Newton Heath and Ardwick are high up and making big names for themselves at the dribbling code, and have innumerable imitators in their districts. To go further afield, Preston, Southport, Bolton, Bury, Chorley, Little Lever, Bootle, Walton and other clubs which stood high up in Rugby circles have all been absorbed by the associationists. ... The conservatism evinced by rugby footballers in the Palatine is astounding and those who profess to look after the best interests of the game are content to sit still whilst the tide of association football makes great inroads into the stronghold of the rugby game.[57]

Sutherland himself called for a sixteen team league to be formed of the best clubs in Cheshire, Lancashire and Yorkshire and in 1891 began to compile his own merit table, 'Muff's Rugby League' in the *Clarion*. Nor was he alone in calling for radical change; the *Salford Reporter* noted that soccer's 'introduction of leagues, alliances and the English association cup, not forgetting the recognised professional, [has meant] that the rugby game has soon received the go by in public favour, especially in the county Palatine'.[58] Some rugby areas had taken matters into their own hands and set up their own district or regional leagues: the Manchester and District, North West, South East Lancashire and West Lancashire leagues all being in existence by 1892. But district leagues alone could not stem the tide of soccer into rugby areas. What was necessary, so the senior clubs thought, was an elite league based on the principles of the Football League. In June 1892 Swinton called a meeting in Manchester to discuss the formation of such a competition. The nine clubs which attended not only included the most senior commercially minded clubs – Swinton, Salford, Broughton Rangers, Oldham, Warrington and Wigan – but also three of the exclusive, public school-based clubs, Liverpool, Liverpool Old Boys and Broughton, which had led Lancashire rugby since its inception. Faced with almost unanimous support for the introduction of leagues, and with Liverpool and Manchester conscious of the fact that if they tried to oppose them they would simply be pushed aside, in September the Lancashire Rugby Union voted to sanction a league system.[59] Thirty-five of the county union's thirty-eight affiliated teams applied to join the three division championship, the only exceptions being, unsurprisingly, Liverpool, Liverpool Old Boys and Manchester, although Broughton also withdrew a couple of seasons later because, in the words of its committee's statement of resignation, it was 'trying to raise the social tone of the club.[60]

Masters, servants and players

With the mass popularity of rugby also came popularity of the players. Like so many other developments in northern football, players had become famous names at the time of the introduction of the Yorkshire Cup. Upon securing the services of Rufus Ward from Wakefield Trinity in 1877, Halifax had put up posters around the town bearing the legend: 'Ward, the great Yorkshire half back, will appear at Hanson Lane today'.[61] As the fame of footballers grew so did their rewards. Until banned by the RFU, testimonials for players regularly raised upwards of £100. Weddings of players, in particular, were an occasion for much celebration by their supporters – hundreds of Bramley supporters followed local hero Harry Bradshaw to church for his wedding in 1894, blocking roads and turning the event into a minor civic celebration.[62] By 1889, Bradford's Joe Hawcridge was appearing in advertisements in the local press 'recommending' Goldsborough's herbalist embrocation.[63] The late 1880s also saw the introduction of football cards showing pictures of famous players and the crests of notable clubs, the most well known being those produced by J. Baines and Co. in Bradford, and these quickly became immensely popular. Few players could match the claim of Huddersfield's Jack Dyson who, after scoring the winning try in a Yorkshire Cup quarter-final, discovered that a local shop had made a model of him out of butter![64] Although public fame for sportsmen was not a new phenomenon, the new found fame of rugby footballers differed somewhat from the adulation of, for example, W. G. Grace, in that it was predominantly focused on working-class players. While the cult of Grace was seen as a national asset, the cult of the footballer was different: 'Nowadays people make too much of football players,' argued the *Hull and East Riding Athlete* in 1890:

> There is too much 'hero worship' knocking about. A crack footballer is looked upon as a little god – his name is never mentioned without admiration, and he cannot take the air in the street without being as much stared at as a model in Madame Tussauds.[65]

No player was as famous in northern rugby football nor so symbolised the rise of the working-class player in the game as Richard Evison 'Dicky' Lockwood. Born to a labouring family in Crigglestone, near Wakefield, he made his debut as a right wing three-quarter for Dewsbury at the age of sixteen in 1884 and rapidly established himself as a sporting phenomenon. Known as 'the Little Tyke' and 'Little Dick, the World's Wonder', partly because of his age and also because of his diminutive stature – he was only five feet, four inches tall – Dicky played for Yorkshire, the North and England at the age of nineteen. Fleet of foot and deadly in the tackle, observers praised his knack of being in the right place at the right time. Playing for a losing Heckmondwike side in a Yorkshire Cup tie against Batley, he turned in a performance of such virtuosity that he left the field to the applause of both the winning and losing sides. An astute tactician, he was responsible for introducing the Welsh-originated four three-quarter system into the Yorkshire county team and for popularising the tactic of running after the ball after he had punted it in order to put his forwards on side.

Unlike his nearest equivalent of the time as a regional sporting hero, Welsh rugby union captain Arthur Gould, Dicky was unambiguously proletarian, a serious handicap to gaining the respect of those who ran the game: 'Dicky doesn't sport sufficient collar and cuff for the somewhat fastidious members of the committee,' it was reported in 1891.[66] In 1889 he shocked his supporters by moving to Heckmondwike who, thanks to an aggressive policy of attracting players through match payments and jobs boasted one of the best teams in the county. Despite the club being suspended for professionalism, Dicky survived two trials for the same charge, and the feelings of his supporters could be gauged by the fact that 'hundreds of people collected in Heckmondwike market place and its approaches, and the news of his acquittal was received with an outburst of cheering, the gathering in all respects resembling those witnessed at an exciting political election'.[67] Despite captaining England earlier in the season, he was barred by the RFU from playing in a club match in 1894. He had been forced to withdraw from the England side to face Scotland because he could not take time off work to travel north but wanted to play for Heckmondwike on the Saturday of the international. This caused a considerable furore in Yorkshire, especially given the fact that Eton housemaster Cyril Wells had been allowed in similar circumstances to play for Harlequins after pulling out of the Rest of England team beaten by Yorkshire the previous season.[68] Dicky, a man who knew his own worth, had little time for the RFU, commenting in the twilight of his career that 'there was always a strong feeling against us', yet his talent was sufficiently prodigious to almost outweigh blind prejudice and between 1887 and 1894 he was an automatic choice for the England selectors. But the tension between Dicky and the game's authorities epitomised the relationship between the supporters of amateurism who ran the game and working-class players who had come to dominate its playing.

That working-class players made up the majority of Lancashire and Yorkshire rugby players by the mid-1880s is attested to by all contemporary commentators, included those who welcomed and those who opposed this development. But, unfortunately, we have no way of empirically testing this fact. Few players of the time can be traced by address and those club records that are available do not hold details of players' occupations or addresses. The best we can hope to do is to use the scanty evidence available to discover what sections of the working class these players came from. This existing evidence tends to suggest that there was no particular occupational strata from which they were drawn. Tony Mason[69] has speculated that professional association footballers were drawn mainly from the ranks of the skilled working classes, yet the evidence for rugby players is not so strong, as Table A.4 of the Appendix suggests.

As can be seen from this small sample, there is no great distinction between the number of players working in jobs classed as skilled, semi-skilled or unskilled.

Nor is there any marked difference between players in Lancashire and players in Yorkshire. As could be expected from the geography of the game, miners and millworkers make up a significant proportion of the occupations identified but no clear pattern emerges. It would appear to be the case that players came from all sections of the industrial working classes in Lancashire and Yorkshire. Why the occupational structure of players in the two football codes should differ is not clear, particularly as the two sports drew their players and support from the same communities. Much of the evidence in Table A.4 is drawn from transcripts of hearings into charges of professionalism against players where great attention was paid to the precise occupation of players. In the hearings they would not be allowed to gild the lily by claiming to be skilled tradesmen as would be possible in press interviews. Mason himself notes that none of the soccer players in his samples described themselves as labourers or unemployed, whereas seven players, or almost 15 per cent, are categorised as such in this sample. The reason for these differences may well be found in association footballers' seeking to appear respectable when faced by the press, something that their rugby cousins could not do when faced by a rugby union kangaroo court.[70]

Slightly broader conclusions can be drawn from an admittedly much smaller sample of Welsh players who 'went North' to play for clubs in Lancashire and Yorkshire prior to the split. Of the thirteen whose occupations can be traced (of which seven were internationals) four were factory workers, three miners, three clerks and the others a boilermaker, a storeman and a teacher. The teacher and two of the clerks came North in the 1880s, which would give a more proletarian hue to those following in the 1890s, as the showdown over professionalism grew near and an air of unrespectability attached itself to playing in the north. It may also be the case that the economic difficulties of the 1890s hit South Wales harder than the North of England, forcing players who worked with their hands to look further afield for economic security.

This influx of working-class players seemed to many middle-class rugby followers to put the future of the game in doubt unless a firm hand was exercised, especially when dealing with players who appeared to want to profit from the game. Commercial realities, public-school morality and class prejudices combined in the attitudes shown to players by officials. The great Yorkshire three-quarter Teddy Bartram's suspension from the game in 1889 had been precipitated by his impending testimonial at Wakefield. The club president, and leading YRU executive member, Barron Kilner had approached him and said 'Now Bartram, it's come to this: will you allow our club to head your testimonial with £50 and retire, or will you go on playing as an amateur and have nothing?' Unsurprisingly, Bartram, now in his thirties, opted for the money and a ban.[71] More egregiously, in 1892 Tadcaster, captained by Yorkshire captain, Oxford blue and England international William Bromet, suspended one of their own players, who was unemployed, for professionalism. He had sung in the club bar after a match, passed the hat round for a collection and received twelve shillings. The club insisted that he pay it back before he could play again.[72]

These attitudes were thrown into especially sharp relief when players were called to answer disciplinary charges before the YRU committee. The committee was both judge and jury, adopting a high moral stance towards those brought before it. For example, swearing and bad language were considered to be especially serious offences, whether directed at the referee or not. Thus the entire Skipton club was banned from playing for three weeks in 1892 after being found guilty of using bad language ... in their own dressing room, half an hour after their match had ended![73] When a player called Leech was brought before the committee in October 1890 for playing whilst suspended, he was asked two questions: 'Are you Leech?' and 'Did you play in this match?', and upon answering in the affirmative was told that he was suspended for the rest of the year. When he protested that he had not had a chance to defend himself, the committee increased his suspension to the end of the season for 'impertinence'.[74] Beechcliffe, the club he had played for, was not even a member of the YRU. The fact that almost all of the players brought before the committee were working class and that the core of the executive consisted of two public school masters, James Miller and the Reverend Frank Marshall, and three local industrialists, Mark Newsome of Dewsbury, Barron Kilner of Wakefield and Harry Garnett of Bradford, carried distasteful connotations for many. Ted Southall, summoned before it to answer somewhat convoluted charges of professionalism (he was the paid secretary of Leeds Cricket Club and also played for their football section), refused point-blank, saying that 'I prefer to sacrifice football altogether rather than submit to the indignity of appearing before the county committee.'[75]

The hearings into allegations of professionalism give us an especially rich insight into the relationship between players and officials. Disheartened by the difficulty of turning up hard evidence of payments to players in the cases immediately following the 1886 anti-professionalism rules, Marshall proposed in January 1888 that the burden of proof of innocence should rest with the player.[76] At the start of the 1889–90 season the YRU announced that, if asked, players would henceforth have to show cause for their move to another club, even if no charges were pressed.[77] In effect, players were considered guilty unless they could prove otherwise – because, as the *Yorkshire Post* explained:

> the character of the players themselves has to a very great extent changed, and changed, we are sorry to say, for the worst. A great many players who pass as amateurs are not only professionals, in truth of fact, who make money out of the sport, but, what is more, they are making a living out of it by dishonest means.[78]

The attitude of the players towards these hearings was shaped by the treatment handed out to Jack Clowes, who, as we saw earlier, had innocently answered his cross-examiners truthfully. Subsequent defendants took this lesson to heart and the practice of stonewalling the inquisitors rapidly developed into an art form. No-one was more successful in this than Dicky Lockwood, who managed to survive two inquiries and the suspension of his club and still emerge with his reputation intact. His second trial lasted for three days and the 'prosecution' case was conducted by the Reverend Frank Marshall:

Marshall: What year were you asked to go to Morley?
Lockwood: 1886 about.
Marshall: What was the inducement?
Lockwood: Nothing.
Marshall: Do you know Mr Crabtree of Morley?
Lockwood: Yes.
Marshall: What did he offer you?
Lockwood: He did not offer to apprentice me to him. I was not paid anything. If anyone stated I was paid it would be wrong.
Marshall: A gentleman has stated that you were paid 10s a week.
Lockwood: Well, that gentleman is wrong. . . .
Marshall: I want you to be very particular about this. I have positive information that you were paid after refusing to go to Morley.
Lockwood: I was not, sir.
Marshall: I understand you were paid £1 for exhibition matches.
Lockwood: That is wrong.
Marshall: Were you in a position to go to these matches and lose your wages?
Lockwood: Then I was, sir. . . .
Marshall: I want to be explicit on this point, as to the meaning of 'dinners'. Have you ever been told that, seeing that you were not so well off, you could have 'dinners' if you went to play with any club?
Lockwood: No, never.[79]

In general, those who followed Lockwood's example usually avoided sanction, while those who engaged in detailed explanations were less successful. A former Doncaster player called Foster who had moved to Bradford and sought permission to play for Manningham found himself discussing how his prospects as a painter would be improved by his move and had his request turned down.[80] Teddy Bartram exasperatedly confessed during cross-examination that if he had known that IOUs he gave to the club for a £32 'loan' had to be repaid he would not have borrowed the money in the first place.[81]

Players were also at risk from unscrupulous clubs who could utilise the ambiguities of amateurism to blackmail them. Kirkstall's F. L. North, uncertain of how to react to Leeds St John's written promise of a job if he played for them, gave the letter to the Kirkstall secretary, who told him, 'as long as you remain true to us, no-one shall see this letter'. Needless to say, a few weeks later the player changed his mind and the letter was used against him.[82] Richard Earnshaw, a half-back with Shepley, was told that if he left the club his employer would sack him. Eventually he signed for Huddersfield and, as threatened, was sacked. Any doubts as to the cause of his sacking were dispelled when his job was given to Harry Hill, a former

Huddersfield player who had moved to Shepley.[83] Few players would have disagreed with one commentator's 1890 observation that 'the amateurs playing under the Yorkshire Rugby Union laws really have less liberty than the professionals in Association, and a comparison of the rules and bye-laws of each will prove this up to the hilt'.[84]

There was some resistance by players to such treatment, although the amateur status of the players meant that there were never any moves towards the formation of a players' trade union. We have already seen how Ted Southall refused to appear before a YRU investigation into professionalism. His example was followed by Salford captain Frank Miles in 1894 who, accused of being offered thirty shillings a week to play for Wigan, told the Lancashire committee that: 'I do not intend to give any evidence at all in any shape or form. I do not care if I get suspended or not. I am not going to turn Queen's evidence against anybody.' He was immediately banned from the game for professionalism.[85] In 1890 a number of players in the Hull team threatened to go on strike over the levels of expenses payments for a game at West Hartlepool, but were eventually persuaded to play – although it is not recorded if they won an increase in payments.[86] Wakefield Trinity, Harrogate and Armley experienced players' strikes over team selection policies. None was successful and the Trinity strike resulted in six players being expelled from the club the following week.[87] In 1891, a pseudonymous letter writer protested against the YRU executive's decision to stop a player's transfer, despite their admitting that there was no evidence of any inducement, by calling on players and club members to 'declare open war and defy the county committee'.[88] Such activities were rare exceptions however, discontent being more likely to be expressed by individual, albeit illegal, bargaining for better terms or by changing clubs – such as the player who told the YRU executive that he wanted a transfer because he did not like being forced to wear a collar and tie at his current club and that 'If I'm noan good enew to laake fooitball wi'em baht collar and 'dickey', I'm noan bahn to laake at all.'[89] John Sutcliffe, Heckmondwike's international three-quarter, gave up rugby altogether after the YRU suspended the club for professionalism. He immediately switched to soccer, signing for Bolton Wanderers and eventually became one of only three men to be capped for England at both rugby and soccer.[90] The capacity for collective action was also seriously undermined by the secrecy involved in remunerating players and the divisions that created amongst them. As a Northern Union commentator looking back at the days before the split pointed out:

> a player who had it in his power to make things awkward for his club received the lion's share indeed; whereas each member of the rank and file had usually to be content with a half a crown which someone, quite accidentally, let fall into his boot or pocket.[91]

The one aspect of the relationship between players and clubs where players did make their presence felt was in the pressure towards payment for play. There is little doubt that the vast majority of working-class rugby players favoured some form of professionalism: there was a 'burning anxiety amongst them for compensation and for even more than that, for professionalism outright' and it was confidently stated that 'ninety-nine out of a hundred players in Yorkshire' favoured a system of payments. In Lancashire, Swinton captain and England international Jim Valentine spoke for many players when he said, 'a working man cannot be expected to give his working time for nothing and nobody should ask him to do it'.[92] As the practice of payment in cash or in kind spread, so too did the bargaining power of the players – and, as we saw earlier, with it came a distrust of the motives of those players. There was no doubt that the threat of professionalism came first and foremost from working-class players: 'To men of small means, the question no doubt suggests itself whether football cannot in some way or another be made to pay.'[93]

The 'question' indeed suggested itself most strongly when players changed clubs. Dicky Lockwood was reputed to have said that 'he had got all he could out of Dewsbury and that he was going to Heckmondwike to see what he could get there'.[94] J. H. Gordon of Pocklington baldly told the YRU executive that he would play for the club that found him the best job because every man should do the best he could for himself.[95] In 1885 W. Pulleyn was overheard telling friends in a local pub in Selby that 'he would play for the club that paid him best' before he transferred his services to Manningham.[96] F. L. North allegedly arranged his move across Leeds from Horsforth to Wortley because he believed that the latter were the best club in the city 'for tipping'.[97] The provision of a job on condition a player turned out for a particular club was especially common. The depression of the early 1890s in the textile trades meant that for many players their best chance of finding work was by trading their footballing skills. In Lancashire, Radcliffe were able to attract players because their president, J. C. Hamer, owned a cotton factory employing over 700 people and would give jobs to players through a subcontractor.[98] Three of the Heckmond-wike team suspended for professionalism in 1889 worked at the same textile mill in the town but, apart from their football ability, they were little different from 200 other textile workers who had moved there over the past three years to find work.[99]

Much the same applied to the influx of Welsh players into the game from the late 1880s. Bill Keepings came all the way from Cardiff to Halifax to take up a position as a boiler-maker and three Welshmen moved to Leeds to play football for Leeds Parish Church and to work at the nearby Waterloo Colliery in 1893.[100] The appeal of Oldham to Welsh players could be found in the continued success of 'Spindledom'.[101] One enterprising Welsh player even advertised his services in the classified pages of the *Yorkshire Post*:

> General Clerk requires a situation, knowledge of French; highest refer-
> ences; wing-three-quarter Welsh team. Address P28, The Yorkshire Post,
> Leeds.[102]

While advertising publicly was unusual, letters to clubs from players seeking jobs were not. W. Thorne, a Dewsbury player hailing from Cardiff, sent a circular around local clubs asking them to:

> kindly inform me if you are in a want of a wing three-quarter back. I am from Cardiff, and have been playing with the Dewsbury club, whose officials do not seem to be in a hurry to find me a situation. I can kick with either foot, and am a sound tackler, and have a good turn of speed. I have been accustomed to office work. An early reply will oblige.[103]

In Cumberland, the transfer of J. Alderson from Whitehaven to Westoe in County Durham was vetoed by the county committee when it was informed of a letter Alderson had written to the South Shields club offering his services if they could find him a job or a pub.[104] To the supporters of amateurism, using football talent in this way was anathema:

> these alien recruits, who are said in one or two instances to be pit men, are striking a hard blow at the pastime. In one way or another, it is made profitable for them to go outside their districts, there receiving a good round sum under the elastic term of expenses.[105]

In the 1890s, as the game's influence increased, it became a commonplace for players transferring their services to another club to mysteriously become pub landlords, where their fame could be sure to attract customers keen to bask in the reflected glory of their heroes. In 1893 Harry Varley, a miner in Liversedge, moved to Oldham and took over a pub, as did Edmund Buckley of Halifax on his transfer to Rochdale. Halifax and Bramley became especially famous for the number of publicans playing for them.[106] Nor was the practice confined to clubs in Yorkshire and Lancashire. In August 1893 the Manningham forward Edward Redman moved to the Leicester club to take up a pub in the city.[107] Out of thirty-five players who appeared for Yorkshire in the 1892–93 season, ten were publicans.[108] Frank Marshall claimed that Bradford's 1893 Yorkshire Senior Competition winning side contained eleven publicans, and in January 1895 the *Yorkshire Owl* facetiously titled an article 'How to spend a football evening', listing eleven pubs in the centre of Bradford that were run by or connected with players from the city's two senior clubs.[109]

How much players were paid by clubs is difficult to ascertain given the secrecy under which payments were made. In the early part of the 1880s payment in kind, through the ubiquitous legs of mutton, bottles of port and other items of food and drink generally out of the everyday reach of most of the players, colloquially known as 'presents', became the norm. This tradition continued and, as RFU rules on payments tightened, the methods used to recompense players became more inventive. As can be seen in the case of Dicky Lockwood, even the provision of dinners for players came under the scrutiny of the YRU. More imaginatively,

Elland ran a prize draw in which each player miraculously won a prize every week and Harrogate players received their Christmas 'presents' from the club via the apparent generosity of a certain Mrs Marsden.[110] For winning the Yorkshire Cup in 1888, Halifax presented their players with gold medals, marble clocks and gold watches worth 100 guineas.[111] And, as the Teddy Bartram case demonstrated, clubs were not above 'loaning' money to players who had little intention, or means, of paying it back. Sometimes items noted in the account books of clubs stretched credibility to breaking point. Heckmondwike's accounts showed 4d per player being allowed as refreshments for players' meetings – unfortunately for the club, the Reverend Frank Marshall pointed out at a YRU hearing that a rough calculation would show that the club must have held sixty players' meetings in December 1888 alone![112]

Although vigorously denied by all, a scale of cash payments prevailed amongst wide sections of the sport by the late 1880s, as a study of the YRU's hearings of alleged cases of professionalism shows. A Manningham player called Birmingham claimed to be paid twenty-eight shillings a week in 1885, but this would seem to be an exaggeration on his part.[113] However, Wortley, a junior club in Leeds, allegedly offered F. L. North five shillings a week to play for them in 1889.[114] The aforementioned England international John Sutcliffe reputedly received ten shillings a match from Heckmondwike, whilst household-name Dicky Lockwood could command £1 a match from the same club.[115] These rates compared favourably with those paid by the openly professional association football clubs, and in some cases were even better. Stoke City paid their players two shillings and sixpence a week in the 1885–86 season and when Sheffield Wednesday turned professional in 1887 they paid nine shillings for home games and eleven shillings for away.[116] By the 1890s the going rate for good players had increased, as was illustrated by the trials that engulfed Lancashire rugby in the autumn of 1894. Salford's Frank Miles, an outstanding but uncapped player of the period, was offered thirty shillings a week in the off-season by Wigan. Leigh paid international forward Tom Coop £1 a game, another player seventeen shillings, their two Welsh imports twelve shillings and sixpence, and seven shillings and sixpence respectively and the rest of the team between five shillings and two shillings and sixpence.[117] As these figures demonstrate, rugby had developed a sophisticated, albeit informal, market place in which players, usually acting according to Brecht's axiom that 'time is short and so is money' sought to maximise their earnings potential before the inevitable onset of old age, injury or loss of form.

'Science' on the football field

The profound social changes that had taken place in the world of rugby football could not but be reflected in the way the game was played on the field. We have seen in previous chapters how the game up to the late 1870s had been dominated by scrummaging. Yet by 1887 the passing game was so prevalent in the North that the *Scottish Athletic Journal* could remark that the touring Batley side 'throw the ball boldly, and with as much calculated judgement as a first-class cricketer could throw a cricket ball'.[118] Historically, the credit for developing the passing game and placing the game on a 'scientific' basis has gone to Henry Vassall of Oxford University and England, who introduced passing among the team and dribbling by the forwards to the Oxford University side of the early 1880s. Developing this theme, most histories of rugby state that the first pass from a half-back to a three-quarter was made by Lancashire's J. H. Payne to Teddy Bartram during the 1881 North versus South game, and that it was not until 1886 that Bradford centre three-quarter Rawson Robertshaw initiated the practice of centres passing the ball to wingers.[119] It is clear that tactical innovation and experimentation became widespread in the mid- to late-1880s, moving the game away from constant scrummaging and kicking towards a 'scientific' playing style, defined by the predominance of passing and running with the ball in order to score tries.

Perhaps most daring of the early innovative teams was the Thornes side of 1882, which overcame the much-fancied Wakefield Trinity in that year's Yorkshire Cup final. Marshalled by warehouseman and three-quarter Harry Wigglesworth, Thornes planned their games in a way previously unheard of. Eschewing the traditional practice of forwards taking whichever position was available when they arrived at the line-out or scrum, known as 'first man up gets his head down', the Thornes forwards were assigned positions that they varied according to where on the pitch play was taking place and what the score was at that particular time. Anticipating the 1905 New Zealand rugby union tourists, Thornes used a form of 'wing forward' play whereby the wing forwards would not pack down in the scrum but waited at the side of the scrum in order to tackle the opposing scrum-half or to shield their own. Unusually for the time, they also scrummaged with just three players in the front row of the scrum, enabling them to gain more momentum for pushing. The side also used previously arranged code words and signals to indicate a change of tactics, such as the direction of a kick or a direct heel out of the scrum. Nor were they unaware of the importance of psychological factors, so effectively riling the notoriously short-tempered Trinity captain Barron Kilner, who before the final had facetiously asked 'Who, where, what and which is Thornes?', that his performance was severely under par.[120] But despite the success of Thornes, which was ultimately short-lived because of the ease with which richer clubs plundered their players, wing-forward play was widely disliked, one critic calling it 'reprehensible', because it was seen as a spoiling tactic that prevented the ball moving away from scrum. Nevertheless, it had a long history in Yorkshire, Brighouse Rangers using two wing-forwards in conjunction with four three-quarters to defeat Halifax as late as the 1893–94 season.[121]

The rise of the Thornes team highlighted the advantages to be gained from having a well-prepared, organised side. By the mid-1880s clubs had started to develop training techniques to enhance their players' abilities, especially for the Yorkshire Cup competition. By 1885 specialist trainers were employed to improve players' fitness. In 1886 Dewsbury appointed Tommy Conlon, a former professional runner, to train the team, a method emulated by Bowling Old Lane when they took on the famous professional sprinter Harry Richardson a few years later.[122] The following year Batley, one of the first teams to appoint a 'medicine man' to attend to the team, announced that they would be training at night under electric torches.[123] St Helens Recreation trained every Tuesday and Thursday in the late 1880s, combining both dumb-bell exercises and boxing. Summer training was popular too, although the providing of incentives to players to attend such sessions was to see Cleckheaton suspended for professionalism. 'Most football teams have a property manager, a trainer and a medicine man' reported *The Yorkshireman* in 1892, which later the same month revealed that Hunslet were using the revolutionary method of a blackboard and chalk for pre-match tactical discussions.[124] Nor was diet neglected. The Batley team raised eyebrows at a celebratory dinner when they refused the pudding because it contained brandy and the club president, himself a medical man, insisted that 'physical training required abstention from excess both in food and drink, and if this was not carried out, there was no chance of going on to victory'.[125]

In contrast, such training was felt to be unnecessary by the middle-class amateurs who led the game. 'The Rugby Union officials, apart from other considerations, have a strong objection to training for football, contending that if a player abstains from foolish excess and takes moderate exercise, he will always be in condition,' it was stated in 1886. But the rise of the working-class player demonstrated that, to remain competitive at least, this was simply no longer the case. How much working in a physically demanding job helped when it came to playing rugby is unclear, but certainly many of the players felt it to be an advantage. St Helens Recreation captain Monsey Parr observed in 1889 that 'only those as are used to working hard can tackle it' and pointed to the decline of middle-class players in the game as evidence.[126] As much was admitted in 1892 by 'A Londoner' when he examined the reasons for the North's playing superiority: 'How is it done? Why, by converting the indigenous talent into an enthusiastic machine and by insisting on the fact that that machine is always in working order.'[127]

But fitness and organisation did not necessarily make for an exciting, open game. Rugby still maintained a large measure of dourness carried over from its early days of mass scrummaging. Under pressure from Yorkshire delegates, the March 1882 general meeting of the RFU ruled that players not in the scrum had to retire five yards behind it in an attempt to open up the game, but the lack of neutral referees (which were not made compulsory until 1885) made this rule something of a dead letter. Another suggestion at this time to make the game more open, touted in both north and south, was to play the game with a round ball to allow forwards more opportunity to dribble the ball as in soccer, although this was never taken up.[128] But as the game became more competitive, the need to develop new tactics and styles of play took precedence and the advantages of the passing game quickly became apparent. By the mid-1880s the growing dominance of passing movement and team play was leading some to question the importance attached to the goal in the winning of games. Before the 1886–87 season, the only way a game could be won was by one side scoring more goals than its opponent, regardless of the number of tries scored by either side. Hence it was not unknown for a team to dominate a game, scoring several tries but no goals, yet lose a game to an inferior team because the latter had scored a lucky goal. In the Yorkshire Cup, 'minors', or touchdowns by a defending side behind its own try line, were used to decide drawn matches but the South East Lancashire Cup took the logic to its fullest extent and introduced a points system that awarded four points for a try, eight for a goal, six from a drop-goal and one for a minor, the winner being the side that scored the most points rather than the most goals.[129] In October 1886 the RFU decreed that three tries would equal a goal, which still meant that four tries had to be scored to defeat a goal (although in September 1891 this was changed to make three tries superior to a goal). That this marked the beginning of an important change to the traditional nature of the game was noted in 1888:

> The acme of good play is when a skilful three-quarter or half back finishes up a skilful or dashing run by dodging a full back and planting the ball over the line. In the North, no other part of the game is more applauded than this, and anything in the rules tending to lessen the kudos of the same cannot but injure the style of play and make the game less scientific and more of a blind dropping into touch exhibition.[130]

This is not to say that forward play did not change. Northern forwards, especially those from Yorkshire, become noted for their size, mobility, dribbling ability and skills in wheeling the scrum to enable a quick heel out to allow the scrum-half to set up an attack. Internationals Harry Bradshaw and Donald Jowett, nicknamed 'the baby elephant', both weighed over nineteen stones yet were famed for their ability to move quickly around the field. Indeed, of forty-four players from Lancashire and Yorkshire who were selected for England between 1886 and 1895, twenty-three were forwards. Against Scotland in 1892, the pack consisted of seven forwards from the two counties, as well as four backs from Yorkshire. Yet despite the considerable success of what was known as the 'fast forward' game, it increasingly came to be felt in the north that too many matches were dominated by forward play, especially cup ties when the necessity to win meant that sides kept the ball tight in scrummages to lessen the risk of their opponents gaining possession. The 1891 Yorkshire Cup competition became notorious for this type of play: in the Batley versus Dewsbury local derby neither half-back made a single pass to his backs, and Wakefield Trinity and Ovenden managed seventy-nine scrums and fifty-four line-outs in their allotted eighty minutes.[131]

Clubs had been aware of this problem from the mid-1880s and various attempts had been made to overcome it. In 1889 Halifax had experimented with three half-backs and just eight forwards, using it to good effect to defeat the 1888 touring New Zealand side. However, when faced with the speedier, more skilful forwards of the senior Yorkshire sides, they found their less numerous pack overwhelmed and abandoned the idea, although others continued their experiment up to 1895.[132] Two full-backs was offered as an alternative but never gathered much support. The dominating influence of northern forwards also meant that clubs were reluctant to move to the four three-quarter system pioneered in Wales and first used by the Welsh national side in 1886.[133] 'Buller' Stadden had unsuccessfully introduced the system to Dewsbury when he moved there in 1886, but Oldham were the first northern side to use it regularly when Bill McCutcheon joined them in 1888 from Swansea.[134] Even then, there was still widespread doubt in Lancashire and Yorkshire as to its efficacy – despite northern admiration for the back play of clubs like Newport, it was believed that its success in Wales was due to the poorer quality of Welsh forward play, especially in comparison to club football in the north of England. When it came to be widely, although not universally, accepted in the early 1890s, it was partly due to Dicky Lockwood who introduced the system to the Yorkshire county side and captained the 1894 England side against Wales that used four three-quarters to beat the Welsh 'at their own game'. It was also part of a broader move to make the sport more attractive to spectators and counter the increasing threat of soccer. The need for change was well spelt out by a former player in 1891:

> The public . . . don't want to witness only scrimmages nowadays but fast, open play, and nothing will tend to bring about this more than playing four three-quarters. . . . The association game is no doubt in a healthy state and in places has sounded the death knell to Rugby football. Why is this? Simply because the public want a game where they can see plenty of the ball. If four three-quarters is not generally adopted, then I contend that the number of players should be less.[135]

A few months later, addressing a conference of Yorkshire referees, YRU secretary James Miller called for a reduction in the number of players in a team to thirteen. Recalling the improvement to the game that the reduction from twenty-a-side to fifteen-a-side in 1875 had made, Miller argued that the 'pushing age' of dominant forwards had come to an end and that 'instead of admiring the physique and pushing power of those giants which took part in the game in the early stages . . . in the future they would be able to admire the skilful and scientific play of the game'. He returned to the theme in 1894 when speaking at a dinner in honour of Manningham, that year's Yorkshire champions: 'Let [the game] be of an open, skilful and scientific character and not the slow monotonous game which people would not go and watch,' and reiterated the need to reduce the number of forwards in the game, 'where most of the illegalities and transgressions occur'.[136] In addition to his native county, where his successor as secretary, William Hirst, had spoken forcibly in favour of thirteen-a-side at Huddersfield's AGM that year, he found much support for his ideas in Lancashire, ranging from staunch defenders of the amateur ethos such as the *Manchester Guardian* to outright advocates of open professionalism like the *Clarion*.[137] More so than Miller, who had just seen soccer establish its first beachheads in Yorkshire, Lancashire clubs were acutely aware of the need to make the game more attractive in order to hold back the tidal wave of soccer now sweeping through their region.

But although the RFU was prepared to travel a little down the road of reform – the deciding of games by points scored instead of solely by goals had been introduced for the 1889–90 season, a goal being counted as three points and a try as one, although this was raised to two in 1891 – radical moves such as those proposed by Miller and his supporters in the north were beyond the pale. There were even those, such as Loretto headmaster H. H. Almond, who advocated a return to the days of twenty-a-side, fearing that rugby had become nothing but spectacle and was in danger of losing its purpose as a means of keeping fit for boys and young men.[138] Although those engaged in the debate had no way of knowing it, it was to be the Northern Union, freed from the constraints imposed by the RFU, that would continue and put into practice the discussion about reform of the game and its playing.

The business of rugby

The sheer weight of interest generated by the game led inevitably to very rapid commercialisation. 'Who would have been believed ten years ago if he had prognisticated that £260 and £270 would be received as "gate money" at Saturday afternoon football matches?' remarked one observer in 1884.[139] Nowhere was this more true than in Bradford. By 1885 Bradford FC were forced to appoint a second paid part-time secretary due to the administrative burden now placed on the club by its success. In 1887 the club took £2,049 in gate money but was also estimated to have lost another £1,000 due to matches cancelled because of widespread snow that winter. The following season they took £2,500 and their gate money income never dropped below £2,000 until 1892. Although it was undeniable, but not publicly stated, that some of this income found its way to the players, it was of such little importance that for nine years, until 1892, annual profits never fell under £1,000 and actually topped £2,000 in 1886. In 1887 the club announced it had paid off a capital debt of £8,000 that had been used to develop the Park Avenue ground and a year later the accounts showed that a cash balance of £4,331 was available at the bank. In 1890 that figure had risen to £7,000. They were, it was claimed with little fear of contradiction in 1887, financially the strongest football club of any code in England, a fact acknowledged in a roundabout way by the Inland Revenue in 1893 when they chose to investigate Bradford and Aston Villa for non-payment of taxes.[140] Other clubs also found themselves in a world of riches that would have been unimaginable in 1880. Manningham's income topped £1,500 in 1888 and continued to rise. In the same season Hull FC took over £1,900 through their gates. Halifax's gate money rose to over £2,000 during the 1888–89 season and the new Headingley-based Leeds club took over £2,200 in gate money in the 1891–92 season. Although such amounts were not generally equalled in Lancashire, at least by rugby-playing football clubs, the growth in gate money receipts was still startling. Salford, despite playing in close proximity to both Swinton and Broughton Rangers, saw their income from gates almost double to over £1,000 in the five years to 1891. Warrington's gate money after 1887 stayed constantly around the £800 mark, with St Helens averaging around £600.

Where did this money go? Some went in one form or another to the players, although such money was not always included in recorded receipts – as the *Bradford Observer* confided, 'the trick [of paying players] can be done by manipulating the gate money before it becomes a cash book item'.[141] However, as many clubs discovered later in the Northern Union, there was a great deal of difference between an informal agreement to pay cash in hand, or in kind, and legal contracts obliging clubs to pay a weekly wage bill. Aside from any ethical attachment to amateurism, most clubs opposed professionalism because of its sheer cost – one look at the wage bills of the professional soccer clubs was enough to persuade any rugby club official of the dangers of 'open' professionalism. Being under no obligation to pay players regularly meant that, at least up until the late 1880s, labour costs were a minor drain on resources. In fact, the greatest source of expenditure was the purchase, improvement and maintenance of grounds. Fuelled by the massive inflow of capital to the game and necessitated by the ever-increasing numbers watching the sport, rugby clubs initiated a ground development boom from the mid-1880s. Halifax, Manningham, St Helens, Leeds St John's, York, Warrington, Swinton, Wigan, Rochdale Hornets, Leigh, Keighley, Hunslet and the two Hull sides were merely the most prominent clubs of the time to have moved grounds in the decade before the 1895 split. Halifax spent nearly £5,000 buying their Thrum Hall site and erecting a pavilion. Hull eventually paid £6,500 to acquire the Hull Athletic Grounds, renaming it the Boulevard.[142] Manningham spent £1,400 to make their Valley Parade ground playable before a ball was passed. Huddersfield spent over £8,500 improving their Fartown complex. By 1896 Oldham had spent almost £3,500 building a pavilion, stand and terraces at their Watersheddings ground. Bowling Old Lane, a successful Bradford junior side, were faced with a bill for £1,000 to develop a new ground before local volunteers and supporters pitched in to help reduce the cost to £300. And, although not directly funded by the Leeds St John's club, their new home at Headingley cost £25,000 to build and develop.[143]

Once installed at an appropriate ground, clubs also faced high levels of expenditure for its upkeep. Bradford and Leeds regularly spent between £100 and £200 per season on straw to protect their pitches from the unwelcome visitations of the northern weather. Advertising costs were also a significant outlay: for example, Salford never spent less than £100 on advertising after 1887 and in 1888 Hull spent over £300 on this item. Turnstiles were probably first used by Hull and Wakefield Trinity in 1883 and by 1890 most senior clubs had installed them, often creating the need to pay gatemen or 'money takers' as they were known; although an unusual example because of the size of the ground, Leeds paid out £61 in gatemen's wages in 1892. Nevertheless, claims that crowds were under-reported remained constant and the 1892 Widnes AGM saw vociferous appeals for more 'checkers' to be appointed.[144] Those clubs not sufficiently endowed to commission their own purpose-built grandstands would buy them, usually from agricultural shows. Dewsbury bought their original stand from the York Show in 1883 before replacing it with the memorably titled, 130-yards-long, 'Noah's Ark', which they bought from Preston for £170 in 1885, and Castleford purchased their two stands from the nearby Pontefract Show.[145]

In fact, commercial reality dictated that once a club had decided to become part of the football world and compete in cup competitions, develop a successful side and attract public support, it found itself caught in a spiral of increased crowds and rising expense in order to be able to cope with the growing number of spectators. And from a civic point of view, success was not merely attained through the winning of matches, it also required a ground of which its locality could be proud. Hence the constant rivalry between Bradford, Huddersfield and Leeds for the title of the north's leading rugby arena, and the large amounts poured into the construction of pavilions, access to which was invariably restricted to the more socially exalted supporters of the club. But the exigencies of football economics also meant that this drive for bigger gates and better facilities undermined many of the social exclusivities of the game. Although gate money meant that clubs were no longer dependent on members for the whole of their income, members' subscriptions still played an important part in club finances. As commercial realities began to dominate clubs' thinking, the need to increase membership brought in larger numbers of working-class and lower-middle-class members, diluting the social cachet of club membership and further weakening the control of those who had founded the clubs.

Other than gate receipts and membership subscriptions, the most usual ways of attempting to raise additional income were summer sports days and annual balls. Sports days, usually held around Whitsuntide and the August bank holiday, focused on athletic events, not least because the playing of football in the summer months was barred by the RFU regulations (in fact the YRU suspended eight teams for this very offence in 1890), and more often than not offered cash prizes.[146] Even a relatively minor side like Pudsey could offer £40 in prize money for their annual athletics meeting in 1889.[147] How successful these ventures were in raising cash is unclear, Warrington only once making more than £27 from their August Monday sports day in the years up to 1895.[148] Likewise for the annual balls that many clubs organised, which seem to have been at best public-relations exercises and at worst excuses to spend club money on the more senior members. In 1887 Huddersfield's annual ball attracted 550 'of the elite of Huddersfield' including such civic worthies as H. F. Beaumont MP, the Lord Mayor, the Town Clerk of Leeds and various titled members of the local community. It is not recorded how much money, if any, was raised for the club. The club also organised a series of smoking concerts for members, which included piano and banjo recitals, but which were abandoned after losses were experienced.[149] After two loss-making balls, Warrington dropped them completely in 1890.[150]

Figure 8 Even in the mid-1880s, matches at Bradford's Park Avenue ground were still viewed as social occasions for the local middle classes (from *The Yorkshireman*).

Other sources of income available to clubs were, by and large, highly marginal. The sale of franchises to sell refreshments inside grounds was common. Halifax raised £80 this way in the 1887–88 season but this appears to have been an unusually high figure; when Dewsbury tried to sell their franchise in 1885 for the previous season's price of £40 they found no takers and were forced to settle for £25.[151] Other clubs no doubt used the rights to sell refreshments as a form of payment in kind to players. Jim Slevin, Wigan captain in the mid-1880s and mine host at the Bull's Head, was also the sole agent for the sale of refreshments inside the Wigan ground.[152] Some money could also be made during the summer close season. Hull's ground was used as grazing land for sheep and, at one point, Batley allowed a local farmer to keep poultry under the stand but balked at a request to allow pigs to use the pitch. But again, the amounts that could be made through such enterprise were strictly limited, Hull receiving just £11 for grazing rights.[153]

Despite this high, if not always fruitful, level of commercial activity, there is little indication that any rugby club in the north saw itself, or indeed acted, as a profit-maximising institution. Most clubs, and especially the most senior ones, saw themselves as akin to a civic institution, bringing honour to their town and providing a focal point for local sporting endeavour – yet another manifestation of the sense of civic pride that had spurred the formation of clubs. Hence the number of clubs that combined football with cricket and/or athletics, very often with the football section subsidising the less well patronised cricket sections. As *Athletics News* commented in 1887, 'in ninety-nine cases out of a hundred . . . football helps cricket over the stile of financial embarrassment'.[154] Halifax in particular spent considerable sums subsidising their cricket section, which, it was widely admitted, would have gone bankrupt if not for football's helping hand. This sense of a broader civic importance was also manifested in the close relationship between many clubs and local charities. In 1890 Huddersfield donated £2,000 from its profits to local charities, topping its previous best donation by £800. Bradford made similar donations over the years and at one point in the mid-1880s the Bradford committee discussed whether the club should become a charitable institution run solely for the benefit of local good causes.[155] The Yorkshire Rugby Union itself was the epitome of this charitable instinct, devoting on average almost 90 per cent of its profits from county games and the cup final and semi-finals to charities across the county.[156] Salford manifested another aspect of this sense of civic duty when in 1891 it decided to purchase £300 of local corporation stock despite sustaining a loss on the season of nearly £30.[157]

However, the necessity and expense of developing and improving grounds increasingly eroded many of the financial commitments that clubs had made to charitable and civic purposes. By the early 1890s, 'business-like' was becoming a vogue phrase among rugby's administrators, and one of the constant criticisms from the northern clubs of the RFU was that it was 'unbusinesslike' in its dealings.[158] In 1891 Wakefield Trinity discussed merging with Wakefield Cricket Club partially because their combined resources 'would secure better management' for the club.[159] The year after Huddersfield had made the £2,000 donation to charity, the exigencies of extending its Fartown ground led the club to reduce this amount to just £184. Park Avenue had cost Bradford so much to acquire, a phenomenal £13,000, that its donations to charity slowed to a trickle. The demands of capital investment for ground improvements meant that senior clubs had little choice but to become incorporated and convert themselves into limited liability companies so as to minimise risk and make the raising of loans easier. Huddersfield had become an incorporated body as early as 1879, but this was not connected with the raising of capital. In practical terms, Manningham led the way in 1886 when, as part of their move to their new Valley Parade ground, they were granted a Board of Trade licence of incorporation. The cost of leasing the ground from the Midland Railway Company and its development into a football stadium cost the club almost £2,000, £1,350 of which was paid off by 1888, thanks to the success and popularity of the club, despite their sharing the city with Bradford, the game's biggest crowd pullers.[160] But even this incorporated status did not lead to a drive for profit accumulation or individual speculation, as Bradford's *Weekly Telegraph* somewhat gushingly explained:

> The club is now, therefore, a corporate body, with a common seal and permanent succession, the funds are protected against misuse, and the profits of the club cannot be divided either amongst the committee or the members, but on the winding up of the club the funds must be divided up amongst the charitable institutions of the town. It will be seen, therefore, that the work of the committee is pure love, and they cannot receive anything for their services.[161]

In fact, the only direct financial benefit gained by the individuals of the committee due to incorporation of the club was the limiting of individual liability to twenty shillings per member. Again, it can be seen that even in this move to greater commercial awareness and organisation, the articles of association specified that local charities would be the beneficiaries in the unlikely event of the club failing and having assets to distribute.

The success of Manningham's experiment with limited liability and the incessant financial toll of providing facilities for the tens of thousands watching football led others to follow their lead. In 1891 Huddersfield put their company status to work in order to raise capital for ground expansion plans by issuing 5,000 £1 shares bearing 5 per cent interest per annum. Unsurprisingly, considering the size of the football bubble at the time, the issue was massively oversubscribed.[162] Three months later Bradford announced their intention to incorporate in order to raise money to complete the purchase of Park Avenue. Most notable, however, both for its long-term impact on the history of football and cricket and its demonstration of the tension between commercial realities and the sense of civic duty pervading rugby, was the foundation in 1890 of the Leeds Cricket, Football and Athletic Company Limited, the first rugby football club to be formed as a limited liability company.

Despite being the centre of rugby football in the north of England – for example, on one weekend in 1891 eighty-nine teams from the immediate Leeds area had their match results recorded in the *Yorkshire Post* – uniquely, Leeds did not have a team that was representative of the whole of the town.[163] Clearly, given the importance football now occupied in the cultural life of Yorkshire, the lack of a team that could carry the honour of the town was sorely felt, not just by football enthusiasts but also by those civic dignitaries eager to promote the virtues of the municipality. For it was not just in football where Leeds found itself lacking. In cricket too, the town had no ground to match Sheffield's Bramall Lane, or Bradford's Park Avenue, and was felt to have conceded by default to Sheffield the title of 'the home of Yorkshire cricket'. And on a broader scale, its status as a town, rather than a city, was believed to be injurious to its standing as a commercial centre, especially given the rise to prominence of Birmingham, granted cityhood in 1889, and to a lesser, but probably more keenly felt, extent Sheffield. The Conservative MP W. L. Jackson, who was also a founding member of the Leeds club's board of directors, led the town's first attempt to upgrade its status in 1890, but it was to be another three years before Leeds acquired the title of city.[164]

At the beginning of the 1886–87 season, members of Leeds St John's, which had now established itself as the town's leading club through a combination of playing success and social status, being led primarily by ex-Leeds Grammar School boys, voted in principle for the formation of a Leeds football, cricket and athletics club. In 1887, following the defeat of St John's by Wakefield Trinity in the Yorkshire Cup final, the clamour rose for something to be done about getting 'a club of first-rate standing' in the town.[165] In November of that year, the formation of the Leeds Cricket, Football and Athletic Sports Company Limited was announced, with the intention of raising £25,000 for the purchase of Lot 17a from Cardigan Estates, comprising twenty-two acres of land in the Headingley area. By January 1889 sufficient funds had been raised and the sale was complete – although the issue of 25,000 £1 shares was never fully taken up and the outstanding £8,000 was loaned by a local businessman. A month later 400 members packed into an extraordinary meeting of the St John's club and voted to join the new club as its football section. On 20 September, the new Leeds side played its first game at the Headingley ground, which, with a capacity of 30,000 offered 'unrivalled accommodation to all classes of spectators' according to the club's first annual report, and in June 1891 the Yorkshire county cricket side made its debut on the new ground. Facilities were quickly expanded to include athletics, bowling, tennis and cycling (and also, a little later, soccer) as the club sought to provide a complete range of sporting activities and attractions for the town.[166]

The board of directors of the club was composed of prominent local businessmen, most of whom also played some form of role in the civic life of the town. The chairman was Lord Hawke, the patrician ruler of Yorkshire county cricket for forty years. His vice-chairman was Charles Tetley of the brewing family, and other members included the aforementioned MP, W. L. Jackson, John Gordon, former president of the St John's club and a local Tory councillor, two solicitors, a merchant and the owners of textiles, gas burner and engineering factories. Despite Leeds being a stronghold of the Liberal Party, of the three members whose political affiliations can be traced, all were Conservatives.[167] Two of the directors had a direct commercial interest in the ground: J. Tweedale's architects firm designed the main stand and George Bray designed the popular south stand. Although it was the most commercially minded of all rugby organisations, even the Leeds club did not have profit maximisation as its raison d'etre. It never issued a dividend to its shareholders until 1927 and, perhaps inevitably, its football section generally subsidised its other sections, including cricket on occasions, most of which were designed to provide a service to members rather than attract spectators. The size of the debt incurred in the buying and development of Headingley did however put the club under serious financial pressure and there was a constant drive to cut expenditure, the biggest component of which was usually termed 'players' expenses'. In theory this covered travel, medical and outfitting costs but it was of course widely assumed to include payments for play. Indeed, it was only after the formation of the Northern Union that players' expenses showed a significant decrease![168]

As the Leeds example makes clear, although rugby clubs were not run as profit-maximising organisations, and were viewed more as civic institutions, the exigencies of running a successful football side meant that the rigours of the market place came to bear more and more on clubs. So while it would be untrue to describe even the most cost-conscious club as a classical capitalist enterprise – not least because no director or administrator ever got rich running a club, although some did get poorer – the need to raise funds, to control expenses and to attract new custom were just as great as for any other form of company. As the chairman of Warrington pointed out at his club's annual general meeting in 1887, 'as in cricket and all other exercises, so it was in football, success in the balance sheet meant success in the game'.[169] It was the clash between this commercial reality and the practical implications of the sport's ostensibly amateur ethos that began the unravelling of the ties that bound together the RFU and most of its northern clubs.

Chapter 4

Schism: 1893–1895

By 1893 Britain was a very different society from that which it had been in 1886. Relationships between the classes had changed profoundly. The relative harmony that had characterised British society in the decades following the early 1850s had given way to a social climate in which industrial conflict and class antagonism were to the fore. Beginning with the Trafalgar Square riots of 1886 and followed by the matchgirls, dockers and gas workers' strikes of the late 1880s, a new tide of class conflict spread rapidly across the country, spearheaded by the 'new union' movement. In 1890 cavalry attacked a demonstration supporting striking Leeds gas workers. Later that year a protracted strike took place at Manningham Mills in Bradford, when over 5,000 men and women struck for almost five months in protest against pay cuts.[1] In 1892 cotton manufacturers in Lancashire locked out their workers. The following year in Hull, striking dockers were confronted by naval gunboats in the Humber. Rugby's heartland of Cheshire, Lancashire and Yorkshire experienced the UK's highest incidence of strike activity in 1892 and 1893, culminating in the 1893 miners' strike, during which troops shot dead two and wounded sixteen more at Featherstone, near Wakefield.[2] On a political level, indications of working-class self-confidence were seen in the growth of the Social Democratic Federation in Lancashire and the formation in Bradford of the Independent Labour Party in 1893. For the upper and middle classes, their old certainties were disappearing and the fear of the mob was rising. It seemed that Matthew Arnold's semi-ironical warning of 1869 was about to bear fruit:

> The working class which, raw and half-developed, has long lain half-hidden amidst its poverty and squalor, and is now issuing from its hiding place to assert an Englishman's heaven-born privilege of doing as he likes, and is beginning to perplex us by marching where it likes, meeting where it likes, bawling what it likes, breaking what it likes.[3]

Rugby found itself a direct participant in the events that symbolised the changing times. Matches were played to raise funds for the Manningham Mills strike in 1891 and three of Bradford's international players were special constables

Figure 9 The Yorkshireman depicts the new 1893 rugby season starting amidst growing social unrest.

who, along with the Durham Light Infantry, helped to break up demonstrations supporting the strikers.[4] Later that year, striking miners set fire to the glassworks belonging to Pilkington Brothers in St Helens, patrons of the St Helens Recreation football club. Hunslet captain Albert Goldthorpe and Castleford captain Harry Speed, later to become a Liberal councillor, organised a benefit match in Leeds for locked-out Castleford glassworkers in 1893.[5] The Yorkshire Rugby Union (YRU) committee itself was divided over an appeal for aid by striking West Yorkshire miners when Castleford Liberal councillor Arthur Hartley, later to become president of the RFU, called on the YRU to make a donation to the miners' relief committee. In a debate that continued over two days, Hartley was backed by the delegates from Hunslet and Bradford but opposed by Dewsbury's Mark Newsome and the YRU secretary James Miller, whose uncompromising declaration that: 'the time had now come when the responsibility for the distress must go back to those who caused it, and ought to be laid at the door of the men themselves,' gathered sufficient support to ensure that the miners' supporters were defeated.[6]

These heightened class tensions were manifested throughout the game. As working-class players and spectators continued to flock into the game, the involvement of former public school boys continued to decline. By 1892 even Bradford, a club long regarded as having the most socially exalted players in Yorkshire, had a team that with a couple of exceptions was entirely composed of working men.[7] As one commentator declared regretfully in 1889:

> This Rugby football movement, which commenced in Yorkshire with the 'classes' and first drew its strength from the public schools and the middle classes, has finally, like other movements and fashions, good or bad, spread downwards to the 'masses'. It is this which has led to the corruption of the sport, which has in some districts tended to drive gentlemen out of the field.[8]

Not surprisingly, given such attitudes, friction between the classes flared up in various ways. As early as 1886, Bradford's AGM heard complaints that working-class players did not get a fair chance."Talent must prevail" is their motto on what is known as the "collar and cuff question" said *The Yorkshireman*.[9] At Halifax the following year, working-class members of the club complained that they had been barred from the club pavilion, while at Manningham the same year a section of the membership ran a 'working man's candidate'. The following year they called for votes to committeemen who would 'put their hands dahn for t'players'.[10] On a more basic level, class antagonism could also act as a catalyst for violence on the field, as the Otley Clarence team claimed after being accused of 'foul and low' behaviour by the Leeds Good Shepherd team. Clarence blamed 'one of the [Good Shepherd] players, who considering himself a cut above the others, had to be accommodated in a special dressing room' as the cause of the trouble.[11]

Irritation was also regularly expressed that middle-class players allowed their outside interests to interfere with match preparations, the most famous example being Bradford captain and half-back Fred Bonsor's late arrival at the 1885

Yorkshire Cup semi-final, and by the late 1880s the demands of regular training led to a steady stream of middle-class players giving up the game because of business pressures. Throughout the 1880s most of the captains of the leading clubs were ex-public school boys, in much the same way as captains of county cricket sides were always amateurs, but even this tradition was now challenged. Much outrage was expressed in 1891 when Dicky Lockwood, the most famous rugby player in Yorkshire, was passed over for the county captaincy in favour of Oxford-educated William Bromet. One correspondent complained:

> It is simply a case of pandering to social position, nothing more nor less. We thought we were "all fellows at football"; yet an alleged democratic Yorkshire committee can still show a sneaking fondness for persons who are – we had almost said in a better social position than ourselves.[12]

Eventually talent did prevail and Lockwood went on to captain both Yorkshire and England.

Although sometimes trivial, all of these examples highlighted growing working-class self-confidence in the sport and the gradual development among working-class participants of a consciousness that they had contributed as much to the game, if not more, than the middle classes that had hitherto dominated it. The middle classes found their authority challenged on the playing fields and, to a certain extent, in the committee rooms. It was undeniable that it was working-class players that had made the sport so popular in the north, as Robert Blatchford's *Clarion*, founded in 1892, pointed out:

> the prosperity and popularity of the game dates from the time the working man commenced to interest himself in it, both physically and mentally. His success at the game may not be quite suitable to the tastes of the Corinthian, but it is nevertheless a fact that since he poked his nose into the recreation football has come on in leaps and bounds.[13]

The middle class, the working class and the amateur ethos

Once again, therefore, the debate on the future of rugby in the 1890s centred on the role of the working man within the game. Characteristically, it was Arthur Budd who put his finger on the central point of the debate. 'Since the working man has become so prominent an element in our game, there are many who advocate the introduction of professionalism in toto, and others, the moderate party, who are in favour of compensation for loss of time.' He was not sympathetic however:

> The answer, then, to those who urge that the working man ought to be compensated for 'loss of time' incurred by his recreation is that, if he cannot

afford the leisure to play a game, he must do without it. ... 'What would happen if stockbrokers wanted compensation for loss of time? Compensation commensurate with earnings would create a scandal. AB, the stockbroker, has therefore to stop at home at his desk because he cannot afford to play, but CD, the working man, is allowed his outing and compensation for leaving work.[14]

Given the level of expenses demanded by middle-class London clubs for matches against northern clubs, this latter point was somewhat disingenuous. Budd re-emphasised his 1886 arguments that professionalism would mean the middle-class player being unable to compete with working-class players, arguing that 'while you allow a man to play for money, you prevent another playing for love of the game without emolument'. It was not hard to see why Budd felt that middle-class players were in danger of being driven from the game. Top-class rugby in England was becoming dominated by the working-class player. The over-whelmingly working-class Yorkshire side's stranglehold on the county champion-ship from 1889, relieved only in 1891 by the equally proletarian Lancashire team, and the growing importance of working-men players to the England team – eleven of the fifteen members of the English side that defeated Scotland in 1892 were from Lancashire and Yorkshire and ten of those were manual workers – only served to confirm his fears. But, as A. A. Sutherland waspishly pointed out in reply to Budd, if playing the game for enjoyment, rather than victory, was the thing, why was the gentleman player so worried about failing to triumph over working-class professionals? 'It might reasonably be said, by the same line of argument, that amateurs who cannot afford the leisure to practise to keep up to the standard of professional play, must do without the game,' he suggested archly.[15] However, the crux of Budd's argument was not, in truth, about payments but about control of the game: 'no professional sport under its own government, and independently of amateur supervision, has ever yet permanently prospered in this country.'[16] In his eyes, sport had to be administered by the middle classes. Professionalism would undermine their control by making them inferior to the working classes on the field of play and thus destroy the credibility of their governance.

Nowhere was this clearer than in his reply to those, like Amateur Athletics Association founder Montague Shearman and, by implication, FA and Surrey County Cricket Club secretary C.W. Alcock, who pointed to cricket as a sport that had accepted professionalism and not sunk into moral turpitude.[17] 'Our best amateur cricketers devote quite as much time to [playing] as the professionals. As a consequence, while they are able to maintain an equality of play, they are at the same time able to retain a monopoly of government,' he claimed. This, of course, was true, but only because, as many of the supporters of broken-time pointed out, W. G. Grace, Andrew Stoddart and many other of cricket's leading gentlemen amateurs made much more money from sport than any professional cricketer or association footballer. In essence, Budd's position meant excluding working-class players from the higher echelons of the game. Without financial assistance, argued the supporters of payments for play, working-class players could not play at the sport's most competitive levels. England international forward Donald Jowett was one of the better examples of such circumstances. He was forced to step down from representative matches because:

> to keep some of these engagements he had to break two or three days' work. His employers took no deep interest in football, and regularly stopped his wages for the time broken. He could not afford to lose this money and hence his request to the authorities not to select him.[18]

Rowland Hill supported Budd in denying that useful parallels could be drawn between cricket and rugby. Whereas cricket could be played for many years with jobs as coaches, groundsmen or umpires available upon retirement, rugby, he claimed, did not have the same long-term prospects. A professional rugby player would find for a time: 'that it is more remunerative to play football than to follow his regular occupation,' but when he retired from the game:

> he then realises that football has unfitted him for other work, and finds it very difficult to get any employment; and if he is able to get work it will probably be at a much smaller rate of pay than he would have received if he had from the first stuck steadily to work.[19]

He offered no evidence for this view – indeed, given the boom in rugby and association it was quite probable that the expanding infrastructure of football would provide opportunities similar to those for former cricket players. And, as we have seen in the previous chapter, many rugby players in Lancashire and Yorkshire had in fact discovered that their prominence as footballers had enabled them to acquire employment opportunities previously unavailable.

However weak his argument, Hill's concern for the future prospects of players was not simply cynical. Like the Reverend Frank Marshall and many other supporters of amateurism Hill believed that the middle classes had a debt of responsibility to those below them. It was his duty to protect the lower orders both from themselves and those who would needlessly exploit them. He summed up this belief a few weeks after the Northern Union split in 1895:

> I saw gradually coming up a new class – the working class – taking a deep and great interest in our game. As one who has always held some good old-fashioned Tory notions [in fact he was a Conservative councillor in London for many years], in good friendship to the working classes, I looked with passionate delight upon this development. But unfortunately dangers have come. Those who ought to have led the working men properly have, I deeply regret to say, led them astray. It is for that class that I feel so keenly sorry today – these men who but for a few years will not be able to take payment for broken-time or for anything else.[20]

Hill's view of his relationship to the working classes was exactly that which John Stuart Mill had described thirty years earlier as being a typically English one of 'dependence and protection':

> The relation between rich and poor, according to this theory..., should be only partly authoritative: it should be amiable, moral and sentimental: affectionate tutelage on the one side, respectful and grateful deference on the other. The rich should be *in loco parentis* to the poor, guiding and restraining them like children.[21]

This feeling that the lower orders were child-like was very common amongst the supporters of amateurism, Frank Marshall being the most explicit: 'I look upon [Rugby] for the working man much as I regard the same game for my boys at school.'[22] At the 1893 AGM discussion on broken-time, Lancashire's Roger Walker, a future RFU president, and Mr Hobson from the Midland Counties RFU spoke with gushing condescension of working-class players viewing the game as a 'little holiday' and not desiring payment. The *Rugby Union Football Handbook* for the 1894–95 season spoke in similarly patronising terms, declaring that:

> there is no keener sportsman than the bona-fide working class amateur; he is ready to give time (which is money to him) in pursuit of his amusement, as far as he can, and is the last person to ask for exceptional privileges.[23]

Much of the philosophy behind this type of relationship between the classes came, of course, from the Church of England, of which Hill was a 'devoted adherent'.[24] But by 1893 much of the enthusiasm previously shown by its clergy for northern rugby was beginning to wear thin. The Yorkshire Church Temperance Challenge Shield, begun in 1887 to 'promote an interest in football among the younger churchmen of Yorkshire and, secondly, to keep them out of the public houses' and open only to teams affiliated to Anglican churches, church schools and temperance societies, had rapidly become notorious for its entrants' cavalier attitudes to its rules. In 1888 it was forced to revise its rules to bar clubs that had pubs as team headquarters, but even this did not stop Hull Britannia from proudly displaying the trophy in a Hull pub.[25] By 1892 it had given up the ghost and abandoned the competition. Leeds Parish Church, arguably muscular Christianity's flagship in the North, were suspended for professionalism in 1890 and later that year had their ground closed for a month after an angry crowd had attacked a referee. The following season Cosmo Lang, the future Archbishop of Canterbury then working as a curate at the church, was forced to appear before the YRU to answer charges of violent play by the team on a tour of Ireland after their hosts had threatened to bring criminal charges.[26] There was little surprise therefore when the Bishop of Chester, on a pastoral visit to Leeds in 1890, chose to use the pulpit to denounce professionalism in football 'even at the risk of giving offence to

A GOOD LIVING IN THE CHURCH.

Figure 10 Muscular Christianity meets its match: *The Yorkshireman* highlights the failure of the Leeds Parish Church side to meet its Corinthian ideals.

every working man in England'. Nor was he alone, as a disillusioned muscular Christian, writing under the pseudonym of Orestes, made clear:

> In the brave days of old, in the public games of the Spartans and the Athenians, the victor was crowned with a wreath – not of gold – but of the leaves of the wild olive. But in these degenerate days, after 1800 years of the high moral teaching and influence of Christianity, our young city athletes

are to be bribed to victory by the secret application of 'palm oil' and to have their morals corrupted and their minds debased.[27]

Continuing the theme, the vicar of Farsley, near Leeds, denounced football in 1893 as 'a fascination of the devil and the twin sister of the drink system'.[28] Some of this hostility was due to a residual suspicion of sports among the more puritan-minded clergy that dated back to the first half of the century, but it was undeniable that by the mid-1890s muscular Christians had begun to doubt rugby's usefulness as an agent of evangelism among the urban working classes. Although not all clergymen were opposed to the course the sport was taking, Bradford committee member Reverend J. E. Leighton being a notable exception, the exodus of men of the cloth from involvement in the game was such that, speaking at a Church Congress in Exeter in 1894, Rowland Hill called on clergy to stop criticising from the sidelines and 'make their influence felt' by playing a role in the sport once more.[29]

In fact, the RFU was experiencing the same phenomenon that afflicted the Church of England in its dealings with the urban working class and that had frustrated the efforts of the purveyors of 'rational recreation' in their attempt to bring middle-class culture to the masses a generation earlier. As we saw in the previous chapter, dutifully supplicant members of the working class were difficult to find and the feelings of those who thought themselves to be *in loco parentis* were not always reciprocated by their ostensible charges. Marshall himself faced deep hostility from almost all sections of the game, being heckled by players at after-match dinners, confronted at railway stations and regularly stoned by youths on his way to and from Almondbury School.[30] Despite the best efforts of the muscular Christians, working-class culture remained firmly rooted in the pub and the local community. And when the working-class player failed to match up to the idealised vision of him held by those controlling the game, the friendly patronage soon turned to something more vicious. No longer was the rhetoric of the 'honest working man' employed by the purveyors of the amateur ideal. 'Hordes', 'herds', 'howling mobs' and 'seething masses' were commonplace terms used to describe working-class players and spectators who did not fulfil their appointed role. Indeed, such people were viewed in the same light as those subject to British imperial rule overseas: 'I could not expect worse from the heathens of darkest Africa,' claimed J. H. Jones after his refereeing had been hooted and catcalled during a match at Hull.[31] Oft expressed anxieties about large crowds at matches in Lancashire and Yorkshire – although such concerns were rarely voiced about international matches or major games held in the South, where spectators tended to be middle class – were also to a large extent based on a deep distrust of working-class participation. The legalisation of broken-time payments would, as B. F. Robinson put it, force players to 'pander to the howling mobs that crowd the circular stands of some Yorkshire coliseum'.[32] Behind such language lay a fear that had been so alarmingly described by Mark Rutherford in 1885: 'Our civilisation is nothing but a thin film or crust lying over a volcanic pit. . . [it is to be wondered] whether some day the pit would not break up through it and destroy us all.'[33]

When it came down to it, a working class that did not accept its place in the social order of the sport was not welcomed at all. The dual cricket and rugby international, and Yorkshireman, Frank Mitchell asked:

> The Rugby game, as its name implies, sprang from our public schools. It has been developed by our leading London clubs and universities; and why should we hand it over without a struggle to the hordes of working men players who would quickly engulf all others?[34]

'Creston' poured scorn on:

> those pampered members of society, the British lower classes, who can apparently only regard any form of sport as it assists them to make money. It was an ill day for the game when the northern labourer diverted his attention from quoits and rabbit coursing and pigeon flying and turned it to football.

He went on to claim that 'the lower class player is the greatest adept at breaking laws when the referee is not looking'.[35] Nor were such sentiments confined to those residing in southern England: writing in the *Yorkshire Evening Post*, an opponent of broken-time payments was moved to write that:

> the seething mass of humanity, monopolising the streets, obstructing traffic, shouting and yelling the coarsest language, and behaving like the herds usually associated with prize fights are not necessary for the success of southern football . . . If Yorkshiremen cannot afford to play the game they boast so much about, pay them for their services but let them . . . start a union of their own, where they can quarrel amongst themselves, find employment for the many out of work, and indulge in strikes, trades unions, and a general disinclination for honest work so dear to the average north country working man.[36]

Similar attitudes could also be found across the Pennines. A correspondent in the *Salford Reporter* argued:

> if the working man cannot afford to play, he must do as other people have to do who want things they cannot afford – do without. Football is a luxury, not a necessity . . . the said working man, by the way, being too often a man whom a thoughtless crowd has spoiled for the dry drudgery of everyday life.

Even the ostensibly socialist readership of Blatchford's *Clarion* was not immune from such prejudice: 'The individuals who would benefit under professionalism and payment for broken-time would still be the working man who does not work, the cadgers, drawers of ale, ostlers, billiard markers, and that species', wrote one reader in 1893.[37] As usual, it was Budd who cut to the essence of the argument of the supporters of amateurism when he warned that:

> [if] blind enthusiasts of working men's clubs insist on introducing professionalism, there can be but one result – disunion. . . . And if this black day comes, which I hope it never will, it will be the duty of the Rugby Union to see that the division of classes dates from the dawn of professionalism.[38]

Rough play, chivalry and manhood

One of the central issues in this debate was the assertion, made by Rowland Hill and many others, that professionalism would lead to unacceptable levels of rough play, an argument which had also been used against cup competitions. 'The necessity to win will be felt more by the paid player than by the amateur, the necessity to win will create a determination to win at all hazards; this will inevitably result in rough play,' argued the RFU secretary. In the *Fortnightly Review* 'Creston' advanced the same argument, albeit somewhat more colourfully: 'The Rugby Union professional would be the most appalling character seen in England since the Mohocks. A man who collared us for his daily bread would be perfectly unbearable.'[39] The *Manchester Guardian* blamed the allegedly growing roughness of the game for the decline of middle-class players in the North: 'it is undoubtedly a fact that after leaving college many of our finest players have given up the game simply on the ground of the roughness which has been imported into it.'[40] The RFU were acutely sensitive to accusations of roughness and to the emotive power of such accusations on the wider public. In its early years, the game had been haunted by perennial accusations of violent play; indeed, one of the catalysts for the formation of the RFU had been calls in *The Times* for the game to be banned because of its ferocity. Gradually however, as an anonymous contributor to the *Football Annual* of 1881 pointed out, 'as the game began to be better understood, and played with greater perfection, those prejudices were removed'.[41]

But as working-class players began to flood into the game in the early 1880s, the old accusations began to be voiced again. In 1883 Rowland Hill criticised the cup competitions for encouraging rough play and the Reverend E. H. Dykes, captain and founder of the Leeds Parish Church team, had protested about the dangerous use of spiked boots, despite being an enthusiast of schoolboy hacking.[42] Rough play came to be explicitly associated with those clubs seen as working class. Thornes became known as 'the doctors' friends' for their allegedly over-vigorous play, Manningham going so far as to cancel their fixture with them in 1884. Horbury, a mining village team from near Wakefield, gained a similar reputation.[43] But despite such claims, violent play was not the sole preserve of working-class players, nor an outgrowth of recent trends towards professionalism. Indeed, many felt that professionalism would reduce the incidence of rough play: 'with the same stringent regulations in force as at present there would be a minimum of rough play, for the simple reason that the suspension of the professional would mean a matter of life and death,' wrote 'Nomad'.[44] A. W. Pullin also pointed out that the first season of the new Yorkshire Senior Competition league, held by the RFU to be the next worst thing to professionalism, had seen only two or three players reported for foul play.[45]

In fact, many of those former public school boys who now complained at the roughness of their working-class opponents prided themselves on their ability to give and take hacking. As A. A. Sutherland pointed out:

> the football of our school days was a very crude and cruel thing and would not be tolerated for one moment. Time was when it was perfectly legitimate to single out an opponent and hack him over in a style that would have done credit to the 'purring' propensities of the corner cads of Liverpool.[46]

And even during this period, violent play was not the preserve of the lower orders. Remembering an 1881 game for Blackheath against a northern club, C. B. Grundy recalled that:

> Their idea evidently was, 'There's a team of southern amateurs, let's frighten them by playing rough'. And they did play rough! But they never made a greater mistake in their lives. At half-time Blackheath had thirteen men left and the others eleven. The rest had been take in cabs to the nearest hospital.[47]

Similarly, on their 1885 tour of Scotland Bradford encountered 'some of the foulest play ever perpetrated' in 'a display of coarse play far from creditable to the followers of the Rugby code' from the resolutely middle-class Edinburgh Academicals.[48] Testimony to the fact that rough play was not unique to the 1880s was also provided by a veteran of rugby's early days:

> 'Chivalry', they call it! Well I can see no harm in giving pretty names to uncouth subjects; but it seems to me that if the bare-faced (and bare-shinned) hacking prevailed now to the same extent as in the halcyon days that I am speaking of, that little Rule 47 [penalising foul play] in the new rule book would have to be slightly enlarged. At this very moment I possess one of these 'chivalrous' tokens, below the knee, as a memento of a game which took place upwards of fifteen years ago.[49]

The charge that rough play was the fault of the working classes was difficult to sustain not only because it was empirically untrue, but also because violence was an integral part of the 'manly' philosophy of the middle-class administrators of the sport. 'Rough' sports were seen as healthy and character-building – after all, it was only in 1871 that hacking, seen by its proponents as the true mark of the manly game, was made illegal. As early as 1876, following calls to ban the sport after two deaths during matches, *Athletic News* had responded by stating that football could never be outlawed 'as long as English youths inherit the traditional pluck and energy of their race'.[50] The uneasy tension between class and the aggressive demonstration of masculinity was no better expressed than by the rugby correspondent of the *Yorkshire Post* who, two months after blaming the veiled professional for rough play, denounced those who wished to see 'chances of accident' taken out of the sport and warned that:

> our athletic youth and manhood will have to subside into dominoes, bezique, croquet or other gentle crafts and our playing fields will no longer serve to educate in those important elements which have done so much to make the Anglo-Saxon race the best soldiers, sailors and colonists in the world.[51]

As with payments for play, approval of masculine aggression was dependent on who was doing what to whom. Physical toughness was widely admired among the middle classes. The reputation of J. G. Ashburner, a leading Barrow player of the 1880s and a scion of one of the town's leading shipbuilding families, was based largely on his brute strength and aggression:

> He was set on by a bullock in a loose box, and ... lifted it bodily and downed it. On one memorable occasion, when Barrow were playing Bradford, Fred Bonsor, the international half back, tried to tackle him. Out came that powerful arm, down went Bonsor, minus a few teeth.[52]

Halifax's three-quarter Doctor Robertson was praised for 'an exhibition of true British courage' by the *Athletic News* for playing throughout a game in which he had sustained three broken ribs.[53] For a team of miners from Horbury or textile workers from Thornes to subject a team of former public school boys to a rough game was to upset the natural order of class relationships. But for teams of ex-Rugby and Cheltenham boys to hack at each others legs until the blood ran, as Manchester FC did until the late 1870s, was to stiffen the sinews of the imperial character. This contradiction was unwittingly, but neatly, encapsulated by a former public school pupil in 1886:

> a great many of the Horbury team were artisans and colliers. Now, I don't object to any working man – collier or whatever he may be – as long as he understands the game he is playing, but when in ignorance he puts on his working boots, which, combined with betting on the event [and] brute force ignorance of the game of Rugby Union ... I am not surprised at smashed legs ... it is a disgrace to the prestige of 'Dear Old England' for time-honoured fair play.[54]

Working-class aggression was seen as legitimate only when it occurred within a framework of national, racial and imperial identity as defined by the middle-class leaders of rugby. 'I believe that football is a thing which will encourage men to be brave *in whatever position of life they are placed* [my emphasis],' stated the Warrington president after his team's cup victory in 1886, as if to emphasise to his predominantly working-class players that their superiority on the football field extended no further than the touch line.

This ambiguity towards rough play in the game can be seen in the statistics for players' offences reported by referees to the Yorkshire Rugby Union (YRU) executive in the 1890–91 season. On average, players were suspended for shorter periods for reported acts of rough play than for acts of open violence or dissenting from referees' decisions. Of the 198 teams in membership of the YRU before the start of the season, forty-six had players appear before the disciplinary committee. Of seventy-six offences reported, rough play accounted for twenty-four, yet the average period of suspension handed out by the committee was a mere two-thirds of a week. Fighting, kicking and striking an opponent – violent offences differentiated from rough play in that they were clearly outside the rules of the sport – made up twenty-six of the offences and, excluding one life ban, carried an average suspension of two weeks. Most surprisingly from a modern perspective, twenty-four players, almost a third of the total, were reported for dissent. This may suggest that referees were seeking to impose standards of behaviour on players that they were reluctant to accept. The average suspension for such offences was a week and two-thirds, but there were also two season-long bans and one life ban for this offence. In fact, the three lengthiest bans were for dissent and only two other players received bans of more than five weeks, for kicking and rough play respectively.[55]

Similar ambiguities towards working-class physicality could be seen in the attitude of the rugby authorities towards insurance schemes set up for injured players. While there were suspicions that such schemes were used as a means of covertly paying players, in many cases justifiably so, there was also a feeling that it was somehow unmanly to receive money for injuries sustained on the football field. The image of the work-shy labourer also figured strongly in this worldview, as expressed by YRU president and leading glass manufacturer Barron Kilner when cross-examining an official of the Leeds district rugby union about their insurance scheme in 1890: 'Did it not strike you that such payments [of £1 a week to injured players unable to work] might lead to "shamming" for a week or two?' In the early 1880s a number of clubs had taken out insurance policies for their players, to some extent spurred on by the enterprising Employer's Liability Assurance Corporation, which in 1882 offered insurance policies at annual premiums of ten and five shillings each. The following year Manningham took out ten shilling policies for their first team, three-quarters of the premium being paid by the club and the rest by the players. For that, an injured player would receive fifteen shillings a week for total disablement or seven shillings and sixpence for 'partial' disablement. This was certainly not an amount which could support an injured player for any length of time and, perhaps mindful of such problems, in 1883 Salford set up their own insurance scheme for players, contributing 15 per cent of the gate takings from each home match to the insurance fund. In 1886 York voted to pay injured players ten shillings a day insurance money and Warrington took out insurance policies for both its first and reserve teams, the benefits being thirty shillings a week plus the payment of all doctor's fees for injured players.[56] After some debate as to whether receiving an insurance payment was itself an act of professionalism, insurance payments of no more than ten shillings a day were legally sanctioned at the RFU's 1886 Annual General Meeting. But in order to avoid clubs setting up their own schemes as a means to pay players covertly, it was ordered that only schemes run by bona fide insurance companies would be recognised. Despite these restrictions, suspicions about players 'undeservingly' receiving insurance pay-outs continued, fuelled by the commonly held belief among the leaders of the Rugby Union that players who could not afford to play, and consequently run the risk of injury, should not play. [57]

But as fears of war came to the fore in the 1890s, the controlled aggression of rugby was widely seen to have a military purpose, both for the middle classes and working classes. In 1894 the St Helens team were told by their local MP that:

> the Duke of Wellington once said that the battle of Waterloo was won on the playing fields of Eton. That was, of course, when football was largely confined to the public schools. If the Duke had been here today, he would have said that any future battles of Waterloo would be won on the playing fields of St Helens.[58]

B. F. Robinson even praised the sport as an alternative to conscription for the working classes:

> Perhaps the best feature of this enthusiasm for Rugby football which has grown up among working men is the delight in hard exercise and the consequent self-denial that it has taught him. A man cannot spend his nights and his wages in the public house if twice a week he has to face a hard struggle of forty minutes 'each way'. Many foreigners, amongst whom the German emperor stands conspicuous, have recognised the advantages of artisan athletics. But it must be remembered that they have an excellent substitute in their military system. . . . It seems probable that without such games as football we should gradually sink from our present *premiere* position in masculinity among the European nations.[59]

The practical outcome of this line of thought was to be seen a couple of decades later in a letter from Colonel Davidson of the 1/10th Liverpool Scottish regiment to the sisters of a young lance-corporal, Jack King, who had been killed in action in France in 1916:

> It was a sad day for football. We can ill spare men like these, but if another game of football is never played in Britain, the game has done well, for after

two years' command in the field, I am convinced that the Rugby footballer makes the finest soldier in the world.[60]

The attempts to direct working-class physicality as expressed on the football field towards public school-defined 'manliness' and nationalistic and military ends also meant seeking to marginalise the importance of women to the game. As we saw in the previous chapter, women made up a significant proportion of rugby crowds in the 1880s and 1890s, yet they played no role whatsoever in the structures of the sport. Given the sheer weight of the double social oppression facing working-class women during this time, it is unlikely that there would have been large numbers of women seeking to be involved in the sport, even if they had been encouraged to do so, but, nevertheless, fear of feminine influence ran deep in the minds of rugby's rulers. Even in pursuit of his bête noire, the veiled professional, Frank Marshall refused to countenance taking evidence from a woman during an investigation in 1889: 'We have no dealings with women here', he reportedly told a woman who was prepared to offer evidence of players receiving cash from the Wortley club in Leeds. Marshall himself was described by a former pupil as 'a thoroughly manly man, and one whose manliness appealed to his boys'.[61] In general, there was widespread mockery of women's interest in football, and this increased in the mid-1890s as women's participation in sports began to grow. The perceived difficulty of women participating in such a 'manly' sport, in contrast to cricket for example, was seen as one of rugby's strengths, as the president of Salford explained in 1891: 'It was perhaps the only game that was absolutely masculine in the country. Women took part in cricket and other pastimes but he had never yet heard of them playing football.'[62] The necessity of sexual segregation in rugby in order to develop truly masculine men – and, in a common piece of circular logic, of the necessity of truly masculine men to maintain rugby's manliness – was most perfectly expressed by H. H. Almond who saw rugby as a means to develop 'robust men' with 'manly sympathies', pronouncing in 1892 that 'I have never yet known a genuine Rugby forward who was not distinctively *a man*'. Whether he regarded backs as 'unmanly' is not recorded.[63]

How violent was rugby in reality? To some extent such judgments are subjective, especially given the absence of documentary evidence about the extent of player injuries. However, in *Barbarians, Gentlemen and Players*, Eric Dunning and Kenneth Sheard quote a set of figures that appear to suggest an horrific rate of 71 deaths and 366 broken limbs among Yorkshire rugby players between 1890 and 1893.[64] To be blunt, these figures are wrong. They were taken from two paragraphs that appeared in the 'Football Notes' column of the *Wakefield Express* of 8 April 1893. The column does *not* state that the deaths occurred solely in Yorkshire or while playing the rugby code of football. Indeed, the columnist saw fit to reproduce the figures without comment. In fact, although the *Express* did not mention it, the figures were taken directly from a series of articles that had appeared in the *Pall Mall Gazette* over the preceding three years entitled 'The Butcher's Bill'. These articles were part of a campaign to prove the dangers of football and were widely commented on at the time as being unreliable, not least by the editor of the *Gazette* itself who felt compelled to add a disclaimer to the 1892 article stating that 'neither we nor the author can vouch personally for the accuracy of the following statements'.[65] The articles, which consisted of lists of accidents, covered the whole of the British Isles, and even some football incidents in Australia in 1892, included both association and rugby, and encompassed everything from school games to international matches. Entry to the lists was indiscriminate and arbitrary – one related baldly that an unnamed Blackburn Rovers player 'was hurt' in a November 1891 match while another claimed a death due to peritonitis was 'caused probably by a kick on the football field'. The rigour that was applied to the compilation of these articles can be gauged by the inclusion of an accident of a match at Warriston 'the nature of which was not stated'.[66]

If these figures for Yorkshire are wrong, what is the true figure? Between 1890 and 1893, a total of seven fatalities occurred in Yorkshire rugby, one tenth of the figure quoted by Dunning and Sheard, out of a total of thirteen deaths directly linked to playing the game between 1886 and 1895. Table A.5 of the Appendix sets out the details – unfortunately, information about serious injuries, such as broken limbs or internal injuries, are not recorded on any systematic basis and levels of insurance payments, because of their use as a way of paying players, are unreliable. All of these fatalities were attributed to accidents rather than deliberate foul play and all but one occurred in games involving junior clubs, suggesting that at the higher echelons, with better standards of refereeing and well-disciplined, organised teams, the game was neither more nor less dangerous than before or after this period. Two of the deaths, Dougherty and Scoley, appear to have occurred as a result of complications setting in after injuries. No deaths occurred in matches in Yorkshire Cup or Yorkshire Senior Competition matches, supposedly catalysts for rough play because of the high degrees of competitiveness that they engendered. Interestingly enough, in none of the cases of rough play investigated in the 1890–91 season was a serious injury recorded as having occurred to the 'innocent' party.

Nevertheless, even an average of one and a half deaths per season is shocking, yet players and officials tended to be scornful about accusations of roughness, other than when making specific accusations against individual clubs. Possibly with one eye on the class bias underlying many such accusations, the rugby correspondent of the *Wigan Observer* quoted figures showing that ten deaths had occurred during the previous two hunting seasons: 'From a statisticians point of view, it is by a heavy percentage safer to play at football than to ride after hounds or shoot the beasts of the field or the birds of the air.'[67] Lees Knowles, president of Salford, used a similar argument five years later, pointing to figures that suggested that there were more serious accidents in riding, cricket and cycling than in football.[68] John Gordon, a former Leeds St John's player and the first president of the city-wide Leeds club formed in 1890, seems to have summed up the attitude of most players when he claimed that the critics of rough play 'really do not know anything about football'.[69]

Broken-time or open professionalism?

For the majority of those who controlled rugby in its northern strongholds, the issue of amateurism was not as simple as the leaders of the RFU believed. As we have seen, the attempts by the YRU to purge itself of all traces of professionalism in the late 1880s had created an atmosphere of paranoia in the sport. Team selections were subject to the arbitrary banning of players and, even worse from the point of view of the club administrators, fixture lists could be decimated by the suspensions of opponents or of the club itself. While the ideal of amateurism was viewed as a noble aim, it was widely realised that the practicalities of implementing it could only result in working-class players being driven out of the game. To embark on such a course was unthinkable, for it would decimate rugby's popularity in Lancashire and Yorkshire, as an anonymous player pointed out in 1891:

> In the North the game is essentially dependent upon working men, both for its exposition and its support. It is a game by the masses for the masses. It is a cosmopolitan institution, in which all have an equal interest. . . . To carry out such an abstract idea [amateurism] to its logical conclusion would be to depopularise the game and make it the selfish possession of the silver-spooned classes. Moreover, it would deprive the pastime of its ablest and most numerous exponents, who are essentially the working men of the North, and of its most enthusiastic supporters, who are undoubtedly the wage-earning classes.[70]

Since the early 1880s the fabric of rugby in the North had been woven from the cloth of working-class participation and the day-to-day reality of rugby was rapidly eroding support for the philosophy of amateurism. The mass popularity of the sport meant that the game had become a spectacle, much to the chagrin of amateurists. 'There was too much consideration for the spectators and too little for the players,' argued Scotland's captain after the 1893 Anglo-Scottish match at Headingley.[71] But in the North of England, large crowds and rugby were synonymous. What was good for one was necessarily good for the other and the spectacular nature of the game was freely acknowledged. 'Football now ranks as a popular entertainment, and spectators consequently have the right to get the best article they can for their money. That can only be provided by professionals. No one goes (often) to the theatre to see amateur actors,' stated a supporter of open professionalism, using a line of argument pursued by 'Nomad' of the *Bradford Telegraph*:

> if these [players] are not fit subjects for remuneration, then all I can say is this, viz: that the thousands who flock to witness their performance ought not to be charged any admission fee . . . those who provide the play ought, if they require it and by every human law (except those framed by the

Rugby Union), to receive a share of the spectators' contributions. If it were so the players would naturally return the compliment by giving as good a display as possible.[72]

By the spring of 1891, the discontent over the broken-time issue, combined with the pressure for the formation of league competitions in Lancashire and Yorkshire, had begun to coalesce into a campaign. 'Something *must* be done in the direction of compensating men for the loss of working time,' pleaded *The Yorkshireman*.[73] 'A Professional in Mufti' issued a call to arms in March of that year: 'I say, therefore, to the clubs of the Yorkshire Union, and to footballists generally, let payment for loss of time be your battle-cry and watchword. And what Yorkshire says today, England will accept tomorrow.'[74]

The demand for payment for loss of time, or broken-time, was explicitly *not* a call for open professionalism on the model adopted by the Football Association. The formula sought a return to the pre-1886 days when payment for time off work for training was more or less an accepted part of the game. Its advocates stopped short of proposing out-and-out professionalism because it was felt in northern rugby circles that soccer-style professionalism would lead inevitably to spiralling costs, wage inflation and regular bankruptcies. It was hoped that broken-time payments could be a middle road between Spartan amateurism and the jungle law of open professionalism. Politically too, it was felt that there would be more chance of broken-time being adopted by the RFU because it was merely a way of reimbursing the expenses of playing the sport yet would not allow a player to earn his living or make a profit from the game. Support for the idea was quickly forthcoming. 'That this meeting is in favour of the payment of football players for broken time' was carried at Batley's AGM in May 1891. Applause greeted Wakefield Trinity president Barron Kilner's speech in favour at his club's AGM. It was even suggested that the Reverend Frank Marshall might support broken-time payments as a way of preserving the amateur ideal.[75] YRU secretary James Miller made a rousing speech in favour of the proposal at a meeting of Yorkshire club secretaries that same April:

> Football is no longer the pastime of the public schools and the leisured classes alone; it has become the sport of the masses – of the wage-earning classes in our great manufacturing centres. That being so, football legislation ought not to be for the 'silver spoon' fraternity but for working men and the Union clearly cannot legislate on the same lines for the latter as they could for the former classes. It is unreasonable to expect the same 'amateurism' from the wage-earning classes as from public school men. It is unfair to expect working men to break time to play football without their being remunerated.

But despite the rhetoric about the rights of the working-class player, the broken-time principal was conceived as one that if implemented would *reduce* the influence of the players in the game, as Miller made clear. He felt that it was pressure from the players that was leading rugby towards professionalism and therefore proposed three methods to combat the threat. First:

> [to] limit the migration of players or transfer of services; secondly to grant reasonable concessions by allowing men to be paid for the loss of wages by breaking time, and lastly to increase rather than diminish the penalties imposed for professionalism. If these three remedies were applied the ground would be cut from under the feet of such players who not only advocated professionalism but were working to bring it about.[76]

That the broken-time proposal was seen as a means for tightening control over players was emphasised in November of that year when the *Yorkshire Post*, whose representative had been made a non-voting member of the YRU committee the previous month, commented on a speech by Miller on broken-time by stating: 'whether the game flourishes on a deceptive basis or not – and how tired we are of hearing the term veiled professionalism – the time has arrived when players are to be put in their places and kept there.'[77] Indeed, the whole thrust of the arguments of the advocates of broken-time was that its introduction would be a better safeguard against the spread of professionalism than the pristine amateurism of the RFU. Miller and the leadership of the YRU shared the RFU's concern about the growing influence of the working class on the game – the differences were over how to deal with it.

This need to exert greater control over players was also bound up with the developing business exigencies of running a major rugby club. As the clubs became bigger enterprises and sought to secure their long-term futures through the purchase of grounds and through incorporation, so too did they desire to put their relationship with the players on a more business-like footing. The broken-time scheme would allow clubs to better plan their financial futures by putting the payment of wages on a fixed and orderly basis while avoiding the perils of professionalism. Despite the popularity of the game, financial losses were a common occurrence, especially for those clubs outside of the Lancashire and Yorkshire elite crowd-pullers. For example, Batley's profit of £227 in 1887 was entirely due to a bumper attendance at their Yorkshire Cup tie with Wakefield Trinity that brought in over £300. The club only made a profit once more before joining the Northern Union in 1895, when they were forced to hold a bazaar to raise funds to clear off an accumulated debt of more than £600. Throughout the 1890s much concern had been expressed about the ability of players to extract payments from clubs but clubs could not exert financial discipline over players without breaking the RFU's amateur regulations. As the *Bradford Observer* argued in 1893:

> Professionalism is worked on recognised lines. Amateurism simply pretends to be and what the difference amounts to in money today no man can tell.

Unless a decided check is put upon the lavish expenditure of clubs a general state of bankruptcy must ensue before long. There will at least be a fixed scale of payment limiting the liability, whereas some of today's amateurs appear to involve their clubs in costs which can never be properly estimated beforehand.[78]

In short, broken-time would help to put the running of clubs on a firm capitalist footing.

This was the key to the apparently contradictory spectacle of middle-class businessmen and professionals making stirring speeches in defence of the rights of the working man. For clubs to become successful and stable businesses the rules of the RFU had to be modified. The sanctions against infringements of the amateur code put clubs' futures at the mercy of the zealots of amateurism. The need for secrecy and behind-the-scenes dealings with players meant that financial planning and wage control were almost impossible. Strictures against cup and league competitions, especially in Lancashire and at a national level, resulted in valuable opportunities for revenue and expansion of the sport's influence being lost. Pure amateurism meant that clubs were not in control of their own destinies. And, because the RFU's decision-making annual general meetings were always held in London, it was felt that patronage and social connection played too strong a role in determining the development of the sport. The northern clubs' call for equality for the working man was part of a general desire to see market forces – the equality of the cash nexus or 'bourgeois equality' – play a greater role in the overall administration of the game. Hence the call for broken-time was based both on a desire to tightly control wages and to compromise with an RFU that had declared many times before that it would not relinquish its principles.

Unlike the support for amateurism, the movement for broken-time had no clear ideological basis. Its ranks included those who believed that broken-time would defend amateurism; those who wished to return to pre-1886 practices; those who felt that broken-time was a viable option in itself; and those who felt that broken-time would give the game some breathing space to prepare for the inevitable arrival of open professionalism. For this latter group the discussion was about expediency and economics. 'Professionalism will come, must come; and when it does arrive Rugby clubs will benefit by the mistakes and the experience of the Association forerunners,' wrote A. W. Pullin in March 1893. 'But the time has not come yet, and a means to postpone it – not to obviate it, for that is impossible – is to grant payment for bona-fide broken time.'[79] Much of this debate was informed by Charles Edwardes' widely noted 1892 article 'The New Football Mania', which pointed out that even the most successful soccer clubs were unlikely to make money and that the cost of paying players had proved crippling to many.[80] The following year, The Times had also highlighted the detrimental financial effects that professionalism had brought to soccer.[81] Those in favour of broken-time payments argued that their scheme would meet the demands of the players whilst avoiding soccer-style bankruptcies caused by clubs having to pay wages. The *Yorkshireman* argued:

> Yorkshire football supporters ... have no desire to see Yorkshire Rugby football sink to the commercial level of the Association game, to see clubs lose their local connection by the wholesale importation of either Scotch, Welsh or even Irishmen. What they do desire, however, and what they will eventually insist on, is that a working man player shall not be placed under restrictions which make it impossible for him, in many instances, to assist either his country, county or club.[82]

The possible economic impact was explored in detail in an article published just two weeks before the 1893 RFU AGM at which the motion to legalise broken-time payments was to be discussed. 'OPQ' warned that 'professionalism has proved ruinous to Association clubs' and that rugby clubs could not afford to pay the huge wage bills professionalism would bring.

> Even Bradford could not afford to pay their men, and that club is the most successful financially in connection with the Rugby game. At the end of last season they had a balance to the good of about £1164; but supposing they had to pay their men how far would that go? As I have already pointed out, Everton pay £3529 in wages, Blackburn Rovers £2156 and so on. It is plain to be seen, therefore, that once professionalism were adopted the balance of even the Bradford club would be so much on the wrong side as it is on the good.

He concluded by saying that:

> some reform is necessary, I admit, but the experience of Association clubs warns us from the payment of players as professionals unless we are anxious to rush headlong into bankruptcy. The solution of the difficulty is to be found in the payment for broken time, and a maximum rate per day should be fixed for that.[83]

But, according to the advocates of open professionalism, the figures quoted by 'OPQ', like many of the assumptions of the broken-timers, did not tell the whole story. 'He quotes figures from the balance sheets of Rugby Union clubs' argued a knowing critic, 'but does he imagine that these balance sheets faithfully show every penny received? They are cooked, and what is shown is only the balance of what is left after deductions have been made for payments already made.' 'Where do the funds come from for the many presents given to play?' he asked. 'From the club receipts of course, and there is no difficulty in so arranging matters that there shall not be the slightest trace of them in the books.'[84] Moreover, to the supporters of professional rugby, the experience of soccer was something to be admired.

'Nomad' pointed to the strides forward taken by association since the introduction of professionalism:

> I noticed the other day that 25,000 spectators assembled at Sheffield to see a cup-tie between Sunderland and Aston Villa – two out-and-out professional teams. What a reflection on the alleged 'waning interest' and 'hopeless state of affairs' which the dribbling game is said to have developed.[85]

To 'Nomad' and his co-thinkers, professionalism had raised the playing standards of soccer and the same would occur in rugby, with the increased wage bills being paid for by larger gates brought about by improved spectacle on the field.

It was also argued that broken-time payments would not substantially benefit the working-class player. If it was paid just for playing in matches, it would hardly be noticed as most matches were played on Saturday afternoons when no one was at work anyway. Nor would three or four hours' payment at his normal wage rate compensate him for losing the quite valuable food, drink, clothes, etc., that players often received. And mere compensatory payments would not put him on an equal par with the middle-class amateur:

> The pure amateur should accept only his railway fare and the price of his bed, if that. But your 'amateur' as a rule takes far more than the working man player does in 'expenses'. Would the 'broken-time' compensation bring the working man player up to a level with the amateur? Not at all. But under professionalism, legalised and properly regulated, the player would have at least a fair and fixed remuneration.[86]

Others felt that the broken-time proposal was simply a manoeuvre by clubs wishing to postpone the fateful day: 'If we are to have professionalism let us have it and be honest about it. But don't let us go for miserable bastard subterfuges and legalise professional practices in an amateur game up a back street.'[87] A. A. Sutherland, with a clarity shared only by Arthur Budd, his polar opposite in the debate, spoke up for the players:

> We've heard too much rubbish about the working man and his loss of wages, and to talk about the injustice done to him is so much rot. The top and bottom of it is, the working man does not care a rap for the payment for broken-time dodge … what the working man requires is hard cash for services rendered, and in view of the money the clubs make, his demand is fair and legitimate.[88]

From their own vantage point, the leadership of the RFU understood these arguments well and, despite protestations that it would safeguard amateurism, the broken-time proposal was totally unacceptable to them. Far from being a supporter, as had been hoped, the Reverend Marshall continued to press the

YRU to seek out violators of the amateur ethic and at the 1891 RFU general meeting had proposed draconian rules to outlaw inducements to players to change clubs. These laid down that a player suspected of merely discussing such inducements had to prove his innocence of the charge before his county committee. The new regulations 'would not restrict the liberty of the undoubted amateur' argued Marshall, but 'men under a suspicion of professionalism would not be able to migrate unless they were prepared to give a satisfactory account of themselves'.[89] Three months later the RFU declared its intention to look into the status of insurance payments to injured players, with a view to determining if they allowed players to profit from their injuries. The leadership of the RFU were determined to turn back the tide. Marshall, writing in the 1892 *Athletic News Annual* declared that: 'it is far preferable to have two bodies, one amateur and the other professional, than to have the methods of the Association imitated by the Rugby Union.' When the YRU voted overwhelmingly in the summer of 1893 to put the broken-time issue to that September's RFU annual general meeting it was clear that he and his co-thinkers were not prepared to compromise, and Arthur Budd's 1886 call to arms – 'no mercy but iron rigour' – became their watchword.

The 1893 Annual General Meeting of the RFU

Nevertheless, the supporters of broken-time payments still felt that they could win over a majority of the Rugby Union. Arithmetically, the clubs in the north were felt to outnumber those in the south, and as the RFU AGM approached, an unprecedentedly high level of unity had been forged in northern rugby around the theme of equality of treatment for the working class player. Rumours even circulated that Northumberland's William Cail, the RFU president, backed the proposal.[90] The Lancashire AGM voted to support broken-time because 'the game is both supported and played extensively by the working classes, and their players feel as keenly as ours the pinch of the shoe in the loss of broken time,' with the delegates from Rochdale Hornets, Swinton, Warrington and Wigan going so far as to speak in favour of open professionalism.[91] The issue was summed up in microcosm at a meeting of the Huddersfield District Union five days before the AGM, when a supporter of the Reverend Marshall, speaking as a representative of the Old Almondburians club, spoke against broken-time payments. Responding, 'Mr Crosland [of the Paddock club in Huddersfield] pointed out that the Old Almondburians were in no need of compensation for broken time, as they were not working men.'[92]

To ensure the biggest possible turnout, the YRU chartered a special excursion train to take the delegates from Yorkshire to the AGM, to be held as usual at the Westminster Palace Hotel in London. Costing delegates ten shillings for the day or fifteen shillings for a four-day ticket, the train consisted of twelve coaches and stopped at eleven of the major towns in West Yorkshire. Disappointingly for the YRU, although 'every compartment was well-filled', it was not sold out and some of the tickets were sold off the day before the meeting at five shillings each.[93]

The *Evening Post* special correspondent accompanying the delegates on the train reported 'a look of determination about every man which told of his zeal in the cause of broken time', cataloguing their origins in mock-Carlylean tones: 'From the distant parts of Hull and Goole came the wise men of the East, from the fastnesses of Brighouse, or the lesser-known regions of the Calder Valley, on they came.'[94]

At the meeting James Miller moved the motion, 'That players be allowed compensation for bona-fide loss of time'.[95] He argued that the changed conditions that the RFU now faced were due to the success of the leaders of the game in fostering and popularising it. The sport was no longer confined to the public schools and universities but had been taken up by working men. But:

> having introduced the new type of player, the RFU at once did him an injustice. These men were constantly called upon to lose their wages in order to play for their county or their club and at the same time they were debarred from recompense for the loss of time involved. Why should not the working man be able to play the game on level terms with the gentleman?[96]

He cited the case, although he did not name him directly, of Harry Bradshaw, a forward from Bramley and a worker at Newlay Dyeworks in Leeds, who had played for England against Ireland in Dublin the previous season. Although his travel and accommodation had been paid for, he still lost three working days' pay journeying to and from the match. In contrast, the gentlemen who played in the team with him lost nothing. This could not, Miller claimed, be called playing on level terms:

> the game should be played as a sport and not as a source of income but it did not mean that these players should play it at a loss. If it was legitimate to refund expenses, why not refund wages lost?[97]

He concluded by asking delegates not to pooh-pooh the idea because it came from Yorkshire and vote for a 'simple act of justice' that would both satisfy the working man and raise the strongest banner against professionalism yet devised.

William Cail of the Northumberland RFU moved the amendment to Miller's motion, 'That this meeting, believing that the above principle is contrary to the true interest of the game and its spirit, declines to sanction the same.' He claimed that only one of the northern counties fully supported the motion and that Miller's citing of Harry Bradshaw was 'entirely fallacious' because he too had been at the same match and had succeeded in getting back to work on Monday morning. He concluded by asking any of the players present if they would like to become professionals to be bought and sold. Mark Newsome of Dewsbury seconded Miller, 'At present the working man was the only man who suffered anything by playing football. He did not play on a level with the other class of players.' The motion 'would put them on an equal footing.'[98] Indeed, the whole discussion

FOOTBALL   FREAKS.

No. I.—THE STRICT GRAMMARIAN.

Scene :—*Blackheath, last Saturday. The Bradford v. Marlborough Nomads Match.*
Real unadulterated Bradfordian (to very gentlemanly South Country " Nomad") : " Nah then, what's ta jarrin' at ?
Fotch t' umpire ; *he'll* sooin sattle all this here threeapin' an' fendin' and provin' ! " (*Utter consternation of
South Country Nomad.*)

Figure II Across the social divide 2: social mixing on the field of play did little to break down
the mutual incomprehension of southern-based middle-class players and the predominantly northern working-class players (from *Toby, the Yorkshire Tyke*).

revolved around the position of the working-class footballer. Mr Hobson of
Midland Counties RFU said that his teams were almost entirely composed of
working men who did not desire payment, former RFU president Roger Walker
of Lancashire doubted that 'honest working men' wanted any alteration to the
rules and from Devon the Reverend Warner opined that the amateur gentleman
often lost more playing football than the working man. J. W. H. Thorp, president
of Cheshire RFU, declared that:

> the pseudo-working man and the bastard amateur do not represent the
> working man of this country. The latter, and I don't mean the working man
> who gets a transfer from one club to another which places him in a public
> house, do not want this miserable subterfuge of broken-time payment.

The Reverend Frank Marshall, who was so roundly heckled by the Yorkshire
delegates that the chairman had to tell Wakefield Trinity secretary J. H. Fallas

to sit down, told the meeting that the aim of the motion was to allow Yorkshire clubs to continue to break the amateur rules with impunity. Like Walker, he called on those who wanted professionalism to form their own union.[99] Almost unnoticed, Mr Northin of the Bowling Old Lane club in Bradford spoke against the Yorkshire proposal on the grounds that his club could not afford to pay players and that payments would force many small clubs out of existence.[100]

In defence of broken-time payments James Gledstone of Otley appealed to the RFU 'as English sportsmen [to] recognise that it was their duty to place the working man on the same level with the other classes,' and Joe Mills of Swinton explained that 'the working man, who chiefly composed the teams in Lancashire and Yorkshire, felt that they had a grievance' and that the motion would put matters right.[101] Following the Swinton delegate's claim that broken-time payments would help to avert full professionalism, Harry Garnett of Bradford, who at the 1886 RFU AGM had suggested that if working men could not afford to play the game they should not play at all, rose to reluctantly support the motion as a way of delaying the inevitability of professionalism for at least a few years. Ominously, virtually all the speakers against the motion, including Rowland Hill, Walker and Marshall, warned that the Union would split if agitation for broken-time or professionalism continued. However, the debate had no material bearing on the outcome of the vote, which went against broken-time payments by 282 to 136. Immediately after the AGM the leadership of the RFU convened a special meeting to amend the constitution, so that henceforth the first bye-law of the Union allowed membership only to those clubs 'entirely composed of amateurs'.

Doubtless intense lobbying and vote procurement played a major role in this result, but is it the case that H. E. Steed of Lennox FC was charged by the RFU with collecting proxy votes from clubs opposed to the motion and raised a total of 120, as claimed by former RFU executive member George Berney in 1925 and by subsequent historians?[102] There is no contemporary evidence for Berney's claim. *Pastime*, the shrillest of all supporters of amateurism, did not mention any arrangements despite an editorial entitled 'All Hands!' which darkly warned that 'the club which does not send a delegate . . . may incur a heavy responsibility'.[103] In fact, most commentators of the time blamed the defeat on the softness of the Yorkshire voting bloc rather than the machinations of the RFU. The *Leeds Daily News* claimed that some Yorkshire delegates had been so disgusted with the insults from their opponents that they had walked out prior to the vote and later pointed to the bad organisation of the vote by the YRU, which had seen some of the region's delegates vote against their own motion.[104] The *Leeds Mercury* reported a widely believed rumour that a number of delegates 'took advantage of the cheap excursion to London to enjoy themselves and never went to the meeting'.[105] As to whether a number of Yorkshire delegates lost their way en route to the meeting, as is claimed in Titley and McWhirter's history of the RFU, there is no contemporary confirmation. The ease of the RFU's victory was also assisted by a lack of Yorkshire-style zeal for the motion on the part of the Lancashire clubs – although a number of them voted for broken-time there was no attempt to mobilise support, possibly because the matter was so identified as a Yorkshire issue.[106] The evidence would suggest that Berney's memory was mistaken and that he was actually referring to the following year's special general meeting. In December 1894 Steed organised a circular signed by eleven supporters of amateurism – including former Yorkshire captain W. E. Bromet and Barbarians founder W. P. Carpmael – which asked those clubs opposed to broken-time but unable to attend the meeting to send their proxies to Steed. The reaction in Yorkshire to this circular was outrage but, significantly, no one in either camp spoke about voting arrangements at the 1893 meeting, implying that such overt electoral planning was a new feature of rugby's civil war.[107]

The reaction of the supporters of broken-time to this defeat was controlled anger. *Clarion* remarked that the arguments of the anti-broken-time speakers were nothing more than 'a re-assertion of the typical British snob's comfortable belief that The Business Of The Working Man Is To Work; Providence made him a purpose; play was intended only for Us – Us Gentlemen'.[108] There was no doubt amongst the advocates of broken-time that the reasons for their defeat revolved around the question of class. The AGM, wrote OPQ in *The Yorkshireman*,

> has cleared the ground of many side issues and laid bare the position assumed by those who oppose the payment of out-of-pocket expenses to the working men. We have at last been boldly told the truth . . . if a man cannot afford to play he has no right to; that Rugby football is a game for the classes and, in effect, that the masses are neither more nor less than intruders.[109]

Whilst expressing their outrage at the stunning blow they had received, most northern commentators cautioned against splitting from the RFU. 'Fortunately,' said the *Yorkshire Evening Post*, 'Yorkshiremen and Lancastrians, having been beaten at the vote, can take their defeat philosophically.'[110] A. W. Pullin hoped for a 'practical compromise' and OPQ told the Yorkshire clubs that it was their 'duty to manfully stand by the cause they have espoused'.[111]

But the door to internal reform was now locked. Having won the decisive battle, the victors were in no mood to be magnanimous. The *Manchester Guardian's* comment on the AGM was that 'jerrymandering is not palatable in politics or football, but it is sometimes excusable, and this was a case in point'. *Pastime* gloated that 'it remains to remove suspected clubs, at the discretion of the committee, from membership, to expel all those which avowedly sympathise with professionalism or refuse their heartiest co-operation for its detection and suppression'. 'Creston' waxed lyrical:

> The victorious citadel of amateurism requires to be vigorously defended, and the North and South should combine to hold it, vigorously expelling any club from the Union that directly or indirectly or indirectly favours money-making at the game. The legislation of Messrs Budd, MacLaren and Rowland Hill . . . was at the critical moment admirably strong.

From Scotland, the president of the Scottish Union 'expressed a hope that the watchword with regard to professionalism would be *no surrender*'.[112] There was to be no repeat of the post-1886 failure to rid the game of the professional threat, as the *Yorkshire Owl* warned darkly:

> The English Rugby Union, as such, comprising the universities, the schools and the many clubs formed afterwards by the old school brigade, will never stand professionalism in the game, whatever name it is cloaked under. ... It would have to sacrifice many fine exponents of the game doubtless, but it would not hesitate. It would lose a good many international games, but it would still not hesitate.[113]

The road to 1895

Less than two months after the AGM the RFU charged Huddersfield, one of the most senior and widely respected clubs in the North, with professionalism for allegedly offering John Forsyth and George Boak, two players from Cummerdale Hornets in Cumberland, thirty and twenty-five shillings per week respectively to play for them, plus jobs at the Reed, Holliday chemical works. After an acrimonious hearing lasting five and a half hours, the club was banned from playing until the end of 1893. Only the votes of the Yorkshire representatives on the RFU prevented its immediate expulsion.[114] An uneasy truce prevailed for the following twelve months, as attention in Yorkshire shifted to the matter of automatic promotion and relegation in the Yorkshire Senior Competition. But it was in Lancashire where the first moves took place of the endgame that was ultimately to resolve the conflict in the Union. The social gulf that divided the leadership of the LRU from the majority of its member clubs and the aborting of the 1890 investigations into professionalism had resulted in the build-up of great stores of combustible material on both sides. Amateur zealotry, as personified in the election of Manchester's Roger Walker as RFU president in September 1894, and a well-entrenched system of covert payments, not to mention the successful example of local professional soccer, were the tinder to which the spark of political necessity was added in August 1894.

The week before Walker's election, the Lancashire committee charged Leigh with making illegal payments to players, ranging from £1 to two shillings and sixpence, and paying the board and lodgings of their two Welsh players, Dai Fitzgerald and Charlie Wilding. Although the club was suspended for ten weeks, the committee also ruled that they would automatically be placed at the bottom of the first division of the Lancashire Club Championship and barred from charging admission to any games rearranged because of the ban.[115] Three weeks after the Leigh ban, Salford were also charged with professionalism for offering Joe Smith, a Radcliffe player, twenty-five shillings a week to switch clubs. They too were found guilty and received the same punishment as Leigh. James Higson, the Salford chairman, felt that his club was being scapegoated and promptly escalated the dispute by counter-charging Radcliffe and accusing Wigan, Swinton, Tyldesley, Broughton Rangers and Rochdale Hornets of the same offence.[116] On 13 November Wigan suffered the same fate as Leigh and Salford when they too were found guilty of professionalism for offering the latter's Frank Miles thirty shillings a week to play for them.[117] There were now only three Lancashire first division clubs not involved in the dispute: and the contradiction between the RFU's amateur regulations and the day-to-day commercial interests of the Lancashire clubs was at breaking point. A split appeared to be imminent; the *Wigan Observer* predicted schism in the Union 'within ten weeks'. These explosive events had not gone unnoticed across the Pennines. Rumours of a professional league being formed in Lancashire by the end of November were given credence when reports surfaced of Leigh officials visiting prominent Yorkshire players. Leeds even held a special general meeting to discuss the new situation. Clearly, if Lancashire went professional, Yorkshire would be forced to follow suit to prevent the loss of their best players.

Into this conflagration the RFU threw a six-point 'manifesto' on amateurism, which announced that henceforth clubs or players charged with professionalism would be treated as guilty unless they could prove their innocence. Guilty clubs would be expelled from the Union. The key clauses read:

> 2. That offences committed by clubs after the issue of this circular, whether through themselves, their agents, officials, members or ticket-holders, shall be punished by the expulsion of such clubs and the permanent suspension of all their members and officials.
>
> . . .
>
> 4. That having regard to the notorious methods of concealment hitherto adopted by offending clubs, this committee will, in dealing with future cases, consider that the burden of proof of innocence lies on the club or person charged.

It was, commented the *Yorkshire Post*, 'draconian and unbending in [its] severity'.[118] The manifesto was sent to all member clubs, with the request that they sign a declaration announcing their support for the measures. Only the Yorkshire representatives on the RFU executive voted against the manifesto but it was greeted with opposition not only in Yorkshire and Lancashire but also in Durham, Gloucestershire and the Midlands, all of whom voted it down. On 21 November, the leading twenty-one clubs in Lancashire and Yorkshire met to organise opposition to the manifesto and called for a special general meeting of the RFU at the end of December to vote on the document. Despite H. E. Steed's attempts to organise pro-manifesto proxies, the outcry against the 'un-English' clauses transferring the burden of proof proved to be so strong that the RFU dropped the contentious fourth clause two weeks before the special general meeting. But at the meeting, held on 28 December 1894, it was made clear by the RFU that this was merely a tactical retreat. Rowland Hill explained that they had backed down because:

> they did not want to have a split with those they believed to be favourable to the cause of amateur football and that if they could bring such clubs into line with them by the sacrifice of some points not of a fundamental character, the cause they had in view would be aided.

Former RFU president William Cail advised:

> Keep your nerves strung up, as although it is only a sparring match tonight, it may be that when we next meet the gloves will be thrown aside and we shall be called upon to hit out as hard from the shoulder as we can.[119]

He announced that a sub-committee was to be formed to redraft the anti-professional laws, on the lines of the original manifesto, for introduction in September 1895. The tenor of the meeting can be gauged from the fact that an unsuccessful motion to offer £20 to anyone providing information about alleged acts of professionalism, proposed by Philip Maud and W. P. Carpmael of the Barbarians, gained 163 votes. Whether those receiving money for informing would thereby professionalise themselves was not stated.

For the supporters of payment for play, in any form, there were now only two options: succumb or secede. This future was clear to all, as was pointed out by the *Yorkshire Post*, 'if the obnoxious "class" feeling introduced at last Friday's meeting by men who should know better is allowed to have its full sway, the inevitable result is a split in the Union'.[120] For some, such as A. A. Sutherland of the *Clarion*, it was time for the northern clubs finally to grasp the nettle:

> There's either a lamentable want of brains or honesty – perhaps a want of both – in all [the Lancashire and Yorkshire clubs'] movements and people are getting heartily sick and tired of the whole thing. There are two courses open for the clubs to take – either amateurism or professionalism ... what we do want and pine for is the honest official bold enough to give prominence to the wishes of the majority of the working men players, and strike out for professionalism.[121]

Throughout January meetings of the leading northern clubs took place to decide on the next steps to take. Various schemes to form a northern rugby league were suggested and on 30 January the George Hotel at Huddersfield hosted a meeting of representatives of Brighouse Rangers, Batley, Dewsbury, Huddersfield, Hull, Leeds, Liversedge, Manningham, Wakefield Trinity, Broughton Rangers, Leigh, Oldham, Rochdale Hornets, Salford, Swinton, Tyldesley, Warrington and Wigan. Bradford, Halifax, Hunslet and St Helens sent their support to the gathering, which voted to form a 'Northern Union', a 'sort of mutual protection society', to organise the playing of an annual challenge match between the Lancashire and Yorkshire club champions and regulate transfers between member clubs.[122] No one was fooled by these apparently innocent intentions and it was no surprise when details leaked out of the meeting's secret resolution:

> In the event of any club in this Union being expelled, or in any way punished by the English Rugby Union or the respective county Unions, such club shall have the right to appeal to this committee, who shall investigate the matter, and if it be decided that they have been unfairly dealt with, this Union will support the club so treated.[123]

Seeking to follow the letter of the RFU's constitutional law, if not its spirit, the new body, which had officially titled itself the Lancashire and Yorkshire Rugby Football Union of Senior Clubs, submitted its rules, minus the secret caveat, to the RFU for its approval. In doing this, some clubs hoped the RFU would accept them in the same way that the Football Association had accepted the Football League. The outcome, however, was inevitable, as had been predicted by an increasingly hysterical *Pastime*, which opined that the clubs must 'forever renounce that particular form of professionalism to which they once pledged themselves – broken-time. They must profess their obedience to the county unions. ... On the whole, it seems to be a beautiful case for the Everlasting No!'[124]

As the hostility towards the new organisation grew, so did the doubts of some of its participants. Bradford, Huddersfield and Leeds – the three most wealthy clubs in Yorkshire – distanced themselves from the project by the device of signing the new union's agreement but not affixing their company seals, thereby rendering their agreement not legally binding. Salford and Swinton also withdrew their support.[125] The murky waters of the battle were further muddied by the coming to a head of the disputes over automatic promotion and relegation that had been brewing in the Yorkshire Senior Competition and the Lancashire Club Championship.

From its formation in 1892 the YSC had been a self-elected body, entry to which could only be granted by a vote by its clubs. The subsequent creation of the second, third and other junior Yorkshire leagues had put pressure on it to allow automatic promotion for the winners of the Second Competition – and consequently relegation of the bottom side. While accepting the principle in theory, the YSC had voted against any changes at the end of its first season in 1893. Unsurprisingly, this did not go down well with either the Second Competition clubs or the YRU, which had taken up the cudgels for the smaller clubs in order to reassert its own power. When the same thing happened at the end of the 1893–94 season the YRU pressurised the YSC to accept the playing of a test match between the bottom YSC club and the top Second Competition club to decide the issue. However, when the YSC came to incorporate this change into its own rules, a rider was added stating that a club finishing at the foot of the table because of 'unforeseen circumstances' may be excused the necessity of playing in the test match. In truth, this clause was added to guard against a club finishing at the bottom of the table owing to its suspension for professionalism, as had almost happened to Huddersfield and which was to happen to three Lancashire clubs the following season. This dispute allowed the defenders of amateurism to pose as the protectors of the little clubs – speaking at a Liberal rally during the 1895 general election, Castleford's Arthur Hartley, a future president of the RFU, railed against the 'unelected House of Lords which the YSC has become' and denounced its refusal to accept the YRU's call for 'equal rights for all'.[126]

Although this issue became a bitter struggle, which some have claimed was the real reason for the 1895 split, and directly resulted in the YSC clubs resigning en bloc from the YRU in July 1895, it was in fact a battle for position before the inevitable showdown over payment for play.[127] This was demonstrated by the moves in Lancashire by the attempts of the First-Class Competition clubs to assert control over promotion and relegation to their ranks following the suspensions of Leigh, Salford and Wigan in 1894. Although automatic promotion and relegation had been accepted from the start of the Lancashire league system in 1892, the suspensions and the placing of the miscreant clubs at the bottom of the First-Class league meant that clubs found guilty of professionalism found themselves facing economic ruin through relegation and the resulting loss of attractive fixtures. Perhaps not as prescient as their Yorkshire counterparts, the First-Class clubs now fought a rearguard action to avoid being picked off one by one by the Lancashire authorities. Eventually, in July 1895, the First-Class clubs, with the exception of Salford and Swinton but with the addition of Widnes, resigned from the competition.

These resignations effectively cleared the way for the formation of a rival rugby union, the necessity for which was underlined on August 12 when the RFU published a draft of the new rules on professionalism that it was to present for ratification to that September's annual general meeting. They were simply a more thorough rendering of the previous year's manifesto and, despite hopes by some in the YRU that some arrangement could be reached, represented the RFU's final nail in the coffin of compromise. Nevertheless, the waverers in Bradford, Leeds and Huddersfield still remained to be convinced. Bradford's hand was forced by their players threatening to strike if the club did not support the new union and by petitions, many of them prominently displayed in the pubs of Bradford players, raised by supporters calling on the committee to back the split.[128] At Leeds a special general meeting was held, which voted decisively to support the splitters, resulting in the resignations from the club of W. A. Brown and James Miller, current and former secretaries of the club respectively, the latter having made a passionate but forlorn appeal to the club's players. A disgruntled Leeds shareholder captured something of the class dimension of the decision when he complained that:

> it is questionable if any of the football committee are shareholders of the club and, at any rate, it may be safely assumed that they do not hold £50 of shares

among them; yet they by their conduct may, and are, jeopardising £30,000.[129]

Any hopes the vacillators may have had of a sympathetic hearing from the Rugby Union were dashed by a letter from the RFU secretary, Rowland Hill, which told them that even if they remained loyal they could not expect any fixtures with the leading southern clubs.[130] Faced with their two allies joining the rebels and, like them, fearful of being unable to generate sufficient revenue to protect the large investments made in their ground, Huddersfield issued a statement announcing their decision to join the new union, blaming it on the RFU's new laws against professionalism, which they characterised as 'too drastic in nature, and make an apparently small offence magnified into one of the gravest kind'.[131]

At 6.30 pm on Thursday, 29 August 1895 at the George Hotel in the centre of Huddersfield, representatives of Batley, Bradford, Brighouse Rangers, Broughton Rangers, Dewsbury, Halifax, Huddersfield, Hull, Hunslet, Leeds, Leigh, Liversedge, Manningham, Oldham, Rochdale Hornets, St Helens, Tyldesley, Wakefield Trinity, Warrington, Widnes and Wigan met and unanimously adopted the resolution 'That the clubs here represented decide to form a Northern Rugby Football Union, and pledge themselves to push forward, without delay, its establishment on the principle of payment for *bona-fide* broken-time only.' Although not at the meeting, Stockport were asked to join and immediately dispatched a representative to take part in the gathering. All the clubs present, except Dewsbury whose committee had not had time to discuss the matter, handed their letters of resignation from the RFU to Oldham's Joe Platt, who had been elected acting secretary, for him to forward to Rowland Hill. There was now no going back – the game of rugby was utterly and irrevocably split.

Chapter 5

The rise and decline of the Northern Union: 1895–1905

The Northern Union was born into a world in which the pace of change was becoming increasingly rapid. English society was becoming much more centralised and culture, of whichever class, increasingly became nationally based. New levels of economic integration and the growth of the role of the state undermined regionalism and activities of a purely local character. Industrial conflict in the 1890s, for example the 1893 miners' strike, quickly took on a national dimension, a development that was highlighted by the growth of national trade unions and employers' federations, and also by the keenness of the state to intervene in disputes. This keenness was not only due to national considerations but also to international ones; the decline of Britain's trade position relative to its major competitors meant that serious industrial troubles at home could affect its economic position abroad. And, of course, the increasing weight of London in national affairs was a reflection of its position as the centre of a global, and still expanding, empire.

This centralisation of British life was demonstrated in myriad ways. The rise in working-class living standards during this period had created a market that saw the growth of national retail chains, such as the Co-op stores, Boot's the Chemists and Lipton's grocery stores. The advertising and branding of goods became nationally based, so that many items available in shops in Manchester, especially newly mass-produced clothing, footwear and food, were also likely to be available in shops in London. Partly owing to the growth of literacy after the 1870 Education Act, weekly magazines, such as *Tit-bits*, *Answers* and *Pearson's Weekly* began to sell in hundreds of thousands across the country. More importantly, the launch of the *Daily Mail* in 1896 signalled the beginnings of the national newspaper, and the concomitant decline of the previously popular regional and dialect press.[1] Made possible by the development of rotary presses and mechanical typesetting, the *Mail* symbolised the creation of a national, albeit London-led, medium and, as if to underline this, was by 1900 being printed simultaneously in the capital and in Manchester. Nowhere was this growth of a nationwide culture more apparent than in the unprecedented rise of soccer, spurred by its national FA Cup and Football League competitions, and in the ubiquitous influence of the music hall, possibly best highlighted by the popularity of the song 'Ta-ra-ra-boom-de-ay', which, as an Edwardian commentator wrote: 'lit at the red skirts of Lottie Collins, spread like a dancing flame through the land, obsessing the minds of young and old, gay and sedate, until it became a veritable song-pest.'[2]

But this was not simply a structural change. As institutions and activities took on a national dimension, so too did many become suffused with a nationalist fervour. From the late 1880s there had been a growth of militaristic patriotism throughout society, based on the growth of empire and an awareness that Britain's hegemonic world position was in decline. 'Nowadays, nothing goes down better than a good patriotic song', said music hall star Vesta Tilley in 1888 and, at the other end of the scale, J. A. Mangan has identified a shift by the mid-1880s towards the glorification of the 'warrior-patriot' in public-school magazines.[3] By the close of the century and the outbreak of the Boer War, nationalistic jingoism was at its height: songs, novels, boys' stories, poetry and the national press, in particular the *Daily Mail*, were sodden with the shrill and baying glorification of war and empire. Sport was central to this ethos. Sir Henry Newbolt's *Vitaï Lampada*, with its injunction to 'Play up! play up! and play the game' on both the cricket field and the battle field, was only the most famous of works drawing the explicit links between sport and its use as a form of military training. While the focus of exhortations such as Newbolt's was towards the public schools and the next generation of the officer class, the importance of rugby to military preparedness among the working classes, as we saw in the previous chapter, was not forgotten. It was, explained a letter to *The Times*, 'the game of all games that calls for all the qualities that go to make a true Briton' and 'the best trial of the relative vigour and virility of any two or more opposing countries'. The fact that Cecil Rhodes himself had underwritten the expenses of the 1891 tour of South Africa was ample testimony of the importance of rugby to the imperial mission.[4]

It was therefore unsurprising that the formation of the Northern Union met with accusations that its actions were at best damaging to the national interest and at worst downright unpatriotic. According to Arthur Budd, the NU was embarking 'on a policy of revolution' that 'depreciated the value of the game as a means of muscular culture'.[5] A. W. Pullin asked 'are all the Yorkshiremen of the future, therefore, to sacrifice their birthright − the right to their national affairs and the national honours − for a mess of six bob pottage?'[6] Even those who did not invoke patriotism against the NU deemed it guilty of practices that marked it out as 'un-English'. In the North, so described Ernest Ensor:

> a system began of petty treachery, mean cheating and espionage, which almost passes belief. ... The miserable game was played until convictions became too numerous. The defected ones met together ... [and] ... left the old school, and started one in which bribery might be not only unpunished, but compulsory.[7]

The use of such language became the dominant form of discourse when the NU was discussed by its opponents. 'Purity' and 'cleanliness' were popular ways of describing the RFU and its policies, whilst 'evil' and 'mercenary' sufficed for the professionalism of the NU and its players. Faced with growing numbers of local players opting to join NU clubs, the Cumberland Rugby Union president, Roger Westray, declared that 'such men might be an advantage to the Northern Union but they were a disgrace to their own county' as his union sought to 'scrape its keel of mercenary barnacles'.[8] Tom Broadley, England international and Yorkshire rugby union captain, crossed over to Bradford NU club in late 1896 and was consequently described by James Miller as being 'wanting in the chief characteristics of a man and a sportsman'.[9] By such denigration, its critics sought to prove that the NU's actions, indeed its whole existence, were inimical to traditional English values as expressed through the ethos of public-school games. This was not based solely on class prejudice towards the NU's overwhelmingly working-class players and spectators, but also on a belief that the new union undermined the importance of the role that rugby played in British national life. In the eyes of its critics, the Northern Union no longer played the game for the physical training and moral development but for pounds, shillings and pence.

Of course, the Northern Unionists were no less patriotic than Arthur Budd and his co-thinkers, but the effect of such rhetoric in a period in which the framework for much of modern British national identity was being established, coupled with the new organisation's lack of links with the public schools and other national institutions, was to lock it out of the mainstream of British sport. The Amateur Athletics Association barred NU players from competing at its meetings, despite the fact that its rules outlawing the receipt of any expenses whatsoever also technically excluded rugby union athletes.[10] In 1898 policemen were forbidden to play NU football by order of the Conservative Home Secretary Sir Matthew White Ridley, because, as the Chief Constable of Halifax pointed out on his behalf, 'it would be highly derogatory to the best interests of the service for police officers to be allowed to play as professionals in football matches, considering the rowdyism and betting that are carried on in connection with football matches'.[11] The RFU even held talks with the Football Association to discuss the possibility of banning NU players from playing soccer.[12] The importance of national interest and identity to rugby union's attempts to undermine the NU game can also be seen in the later 1900s when the new game was spreading to Wales and New Zealand. The New Zealand Agent-General C. Wray Palliser even went so far as to deny that NU football could represent the nation when he denounced the impending 1907 tour of the UK by New Zealand NU 'Professional All Blacks': 'it will in not the slightest degree represent either the rugby union football of New Zealand or the sporting community of the colony . . . it comes with no sort of credit from the colony of New Zealand.'[13] Although such attempts at exclusion were to play a central role in the formation of a distinct Northern Union ideology, they more importantly succeeded in questioning the legitimacy of the sport and pushing it into a position where it could be portrayed as an aberrant strand of national sporting culture.

From split to domination

The leaders and supporters of the NU were well aware of the approbation that the split would bring, if not its long-term effects. Their response was to argue that they were the ones who had washed their hands of subterfuge and hypocrisy. At last, their dealings were honest and above board. 'The clubs who have struck a blow for freedom are to be commended for throwing off the cloak of hypocrisy, conceit and subterfuge, and standing out for those essentially English characteristics – honesty and straight forwardness,'[14] said a correspondent to the *Hull Daily Mail*. 'Freedom from the thraldom of the Southern gentry was the best thing that could happen,' was the *Wigan Observer*'s comment, while an unnamed Northern Union supporter wrote to the *Yorkshire Post* to proclaim:

> I say with Mark Twain's bold, bad boy, that we glory in the sentence of outlawry pronounced on us, as freeing us from the tyrannical bondage of the English union, and we breath pure air in being freed from the stifling atmosphere of deceit in which we previously existed.[15]

George Harrop, a referee who volunteered to officiate at one of the first Northern Union matches, 'expressed his delight that he would thus be the first member of the Huddersfield club to fall under the ban of the English Rugby Union'.[16] Brighouse's Harry Waller, the textiles manufacturer who had been elected the NU's first president, spelt out the necessity for the split later that season: 'Rugby football in the North – for every part of the Kingdom in fact where there was a preponderance of working class players – could not be honestly carried out under the existing by-laws of the English Union.'[17]

The formation of the NU was undoubtedly popular with players. As we have seen, Bradford were effectively forced into joining by the actions of their players. At Broughton Rangers, the motion to join the NU was moved by the club captain and seconded by another senior player. Harry Barker, captain of Liversedge, said, 'I think the Northern Union is a champion move and I think the committee should have been justified in making the move a year ago.' Echoing the call for honesty, Bradford's international three-quarter Tommy Dobson stated, 'All Yorkshire owes a debt of gratitude to the seniors [i.e., the senior clubs] for speaking out so plainly in favour of what should be the leading element in sport – truth.' Dewsbury's decision not to join the NU was met by one of their players with the question, 'What wages are yer paying up here?', and upon receiving the reply 'None', he responded 'It's no use me stopping here then'. In Huddersfield, it was reported that 'the players naturally champion the [Northern] Union and a very large section of spectators of matches take the same side'.[18] This was also reflected among members and supporters of clubs throughout the new organisation. Hunslet, St Helens, Manningham, Hull, Leigh and Broughton Rangers all recorded unanimity at general meetings called to vote on joining the NU, while most of the other member clubs tallied only a handful of votes against. In Dewsbury, despite the club committee's reversal, a local journalist reported that, 'there wasn't a single supporter who wouldn't say "Let us have the Northern Union and the sooner the better" '.[19] The clamour for the NU was demonstrated at a special meeting of the Hull and District RFU in September, which voted 33–24 to resign from the RFU in support of the NU, even though the NU had as yet no means by which district bodies or junior clubs could affiliate.[20] The only club at which significant opposition was encountered was Bradford, which still clung to remnants of its patrician past, where three committee members and four senior players, one of whom, Edgar Dewhurst, was also a committee member, resigned in protest.[21]

Despite this acclamation by players and spectators, the new body firmly denied that it was about to introduce professionalism to rugby. Indeed, the six shillings broken-time payment had been fixed to equal the maximum daily insurance payment currently allowed by the RFU's professionalism rules. Ernest Gresty, Broughton Rangers secretary and member of the NU Emergency Committee, asked, 'How can it be professionalism? The man that receives bare recompense for the loss of his wages makes no money by so doing. It is no more than saving him from losing anything.' William Hirst, secretary of Huddersfield, stated that he was 'as strongly opposed as ever to professionalism' but 'held that payment of working men players for loss of wages through playing in a match was not professionalism'.[22] In September, to demonstrate its fealty to the amateur ideal, the NU turned down applications to play from Sam Hall of Swinton and J. Smith of Radcliffe, both of whom had been banned as professionals the previous season by the Lancashire Rugby Union. Indeed, it is apparent that at least some sections of the NU hoped that an accommodation could still be reached with the RFU on the lines of the FA's relationship with the Football League; Tony Fattorini, Manningham's representative on the NU committee, told a meeting of his club that:

> if the new union were properly conducted, the Rugby Union would have to recognise professionalism in some form or another in the future or they would find ere long the only support they received would be from the universities and the public schools.[23]

Given the attitudes of the RFU this hope was forlorn in the extreme, yet it was to be a recurring theme over the next decade.

Despite the hostility of the rugby union authorities and its desire not to appear too radical, the NU's first season was highly successful. Although Joe Platt's claim that twenty of the twenty-two NU clubs made a profit in the first season seems to be an exaggeration, there can be no doubt that most of the rebel clubs experienced higher crowds and increased profits. Platt's own club

Oldham was the most successful, returning a record £1,148 profit. Hull also made their highest ever profit, thanks to an increase of over 50,000 spectators. Halifax increased their gate takings by 50 per cent, and even bottom club Rochdale Hornets made a profit of £96, despite winning only four of their forty-two games. This was an important vindication for the NU. The sketchy evidence available suggests that the senior Northern clubs had seen a decline in profitability in the period up to 1895; although crowds appear to have remained stable, the expense of ground refurbishments and covert player payments had taken a heavy toll. Without the qualitative leap in attendances that soccer was experiencing, many clubs found themselves on shaky financial foundations. This applied most particularly at the extreme ends of the spectrum: Bradford and Leeds, with large capital investments in their grounds, faced a constant battle for financial success, while clubs based on small towns, such as Brighouse Rangers and Tyldesley, found it difficult to generate enough revenue to justify their places among the elite. Even at the height of their success, winning their respective county leagues in 1895, both clubs made a loss. These economic realities did not excuse even the most pristine custodians of the amateur cause: Manchester FC voted to wind the club up in March 1895 after it was revealed that they had accrued liabilities of £409, although the decision was later rescinded.[24]

The success of the NU's first season was crucial in attracting the second wave of splits from the RFU. For Salford and Swinton, the North's most successful clubs to remain aloof from the splitters, the lack of quality opposition in the reconstituted Lancashire Club Championship and the potential financial boost of joining the NU were overwhelming arguments to jump ship. Both had been involved in the initial discussions about a new rugby body but had dropped out because of a combination of personal antagonism and organisational jealousy. In April 1896 Salford held a special general meeting at the request of members to discuss joining the NU. J. Daniels moved the motion to join the NU, pointing out that the club had lost £713 over the last four years:

> [As] Salford was a working class club and didn't contain any so-called gentlemen, he considered that it would be very nice for the players to have a present of six shillings worth of silver every week. If they continued on amateur lines they would go to smash. They all knew that working class clubs were better supported than clubs such as Liverpool or Manchester.

Out of a gathering of 400 people, only three opposed the switch.[25] Following a season in which they had lost £450, Swinton's move to the new body received similar acclamation at their general meeting, at which it was pointed out that over the previous four seasons, annual gate money had slumped from £1,016 to £383 and the number of season ticket holders had halved. Vindication of their decision was quick in coming: in their first two seasons in the NU they made record profits of £450 and £529.[26] Over the summer of 1896 a steady stream of Lancashire's junior and local clubs followed into the NU; Rochdale St Clements,

Radcliffe, Werneth, Morecambe and others tearing the heart out of an already emaciated Lancashire Club Championship. At a local level, the effect was no less cataclysmic – that summer saw most of Warrington's local clubs go over to the NU, as did around fifty clubs that formed the Oldham Junior Rugby League.[27] In July, at its first annual general meeting, Platt announced that the NU now had forty-eight members and fully expected that number to increase substantially.

In contrast, by the following summer the Lancashire Rugby Union had only thirteen member clubs, focused on the traditional ex-public school boy sides.[28] Their last base of popular rugby, in the northwest of the county, had evaporated when promises of fixtures with Manchester, Liverpool and Liverpool Old Boys made to Barrow and Ulverston, the leading clubs in the area, failed to materialise. By April of 1897 Barrow had voted unanimously to join the NU and a petition was circulating in Ulverston calling on the club to make the switch. At the beginning of July, Ulverston, Millom and the rest of the North West League voted to join the NU. Ulverston's general meeting was told that James Higson, who had become the LRU secretary after Salford's departure to the NU and who was one of the NU's most vociferous critics, had secretly told an Ulverston committee member that 'the best thing they could do was to join the NU' because middle-class clubs would not play them.[29] The loss of the northwest Lancashire clubs had a knock-on effect on Cumberland and Westmoreland clubs, who generally looked south for their better fixtures. The success of Millom's first season in the NU – after seeing gate money slump to just £107 in their last rugby union season, they had taken almost £300 at the gate and made a record profit of £81 – had given the impetus to other clubs in the region to abandon the RFU. At the start of the 1898–99 season *Athletic News* commented that rugby union in Cumberland had been reduced 'to an almost vanishing quality' and by January 1899 there was not a single rugby union club left in west Cumberland, a former hot bed of the game.[30]

The effect in Yorkshire was no less devastating. Regardless of earlier pledges of loyalty to the YRU, the majority of the county's Number One Competition, the Yorkshire leagues' first division, went over to the NU in the summer of 1896. Holbeck's chairman, George Chapman, summed up their plight when he stated bluntly, 'when it came to be a serious question of finance, they should follow the example of the majority of leading clubs'. Leeds Parish Church, that year's champions, recorded only five votes against their switch of allegiance.[31] Unfortunately for the YRU, the spectacle of their senior league members decamping at the end of the season was something to which they would grow accustomed. In June 1897 Hull Kingston Rovers, that year's Yorkshire cup and league champions, went over and the following summer most of what remained of the Number One and Number Two Competitions resigned en bloc to reconstitute themselves as the NU's Yorkshire Number Two Competition. In 1899 Hebden Bridge, Ossett, Kirkstall and Alverthorpe flew the nest and in the summer of 1900 Keighley, Otley and Bingley decided that 'the interest has gone out of rugby union' and joined the NU.[32] This pattern was repeated locally as one by one the existing local leagues and unions lined up with the NU. By June 1897 there was not a single rugby union club in the Halifax district, which was described by a Sowerby Bridge rugby union supporter as being 'a hot bed of Northern Unionism and bigotry'. At the start of the following season the *Yorkshire Post* reported that 'in Leeds, rugby union football is practically non-existent', while the NU 'is at the height of its popularity'.[33] The Bradford and Huddersfield district rugby unions simply voted to disaffiliate from the YRU and affiliate to the NU. At its opening round in 1901, the Yorkshire Cup, once one of the biggest football competitions of any type, a symbol of rugby union's domination of Yorkshire winter sport and capable of attracting at its height 132 entrants, could boast a mere eleven clubs. The mighty had been felled.

Although the NU undoubtedly presented a highly attractive alternative for many clubs, it was not solely responsible for the collapse of Yorkshire rugby union. The YRU and the RFU also played a critical role in the destruction of their own power base. The RFU's September 1895 general meeting had attempted to cast out the NU evil by declaring that any contact with an NU club or player on the football field was an act of professionalism, punishable by a life ban from the Rugby Union. Initially, loyal clubs had asked Rowland Hill if it were pos-sible for them or their reserve sides to play their NU equivalents, believing the situation to be analogous to Football League sides playing the Corinthians, who were members of the RFU as well as the FA. Hill replied by saying that any RFU club that played a NU side would professionalise itself and be expelled.[34] This immediately posed problems at a local level: for example, Beverley FC were left with virtually no fixtures after clubs in the Hull District Union, with whom they played most of their matches, voted to support the NU. Eventually they admitted defeat and played matches with NU-supporting clubs, whereupon the YRU expelled them for professionalism. More corrosively, the RFU's insistence that any contact with NU football automatically contaminated a player, and the zeal with which this edict was pursued, meant that any player who had any contact with the NU was thrown out of the Rugby Union. In February 1896, the YRU banned a Wyke player who travelled with Brighouse Rangers to a match at Leigh. He did not play in the game but the fact that Rangers paid his third-class rail fare was enough to condemn him. The following month the Horbury club were suspended because one of their players had earlier played for a Wakefield junior side against a team that contained a NU player. Elland had two players banned for the same offence and Primrose Hill's G. A. Cliffe was banned for playing in a game staged at Huddersfield's Fartown ground. The YRU was faced with numerous requests for reinstatement as amateurs from players who had played occasional games with NU sides, the vast majority of which had to be refused. Most bizarrely of all, in January 1898 the YRU ordered Goole FC not to play a charity rugby match against a touring Little Red Riding Hood pantomime troupe; this was deemed to be an act of professionalism because earlier on its tour the troupe had played in a charity match with the NU's Batley! Clearly, no-one was safe from the contagion – one unnamed RFU official allegedly even being of the opinion that anyone who *watched* a NU game, let alone played it, should be barred from taking part in rugby union.[35]

Such antics seemed arbitrary and irrational to most clubs, even those loyal to the RFU. However, there was method in this apparent madness. The RFU truly believed that the danger of working-class professionalism was, in Arthur Budd's words, a hydra and that a policy of Laudian 'Thorough' had to be pursued in order to root it out. In response to those who said that the RFU's action would leave only a remnant of their game in the North, A. W. Pullin, who by now had become a generally accurate guide to RFU thinking, said 'possibly the Rugby Union would like to see that result, believing that the "fit but few" principle is conducive to a cheerful and settled state of mind'.[36] From its own vantage point, the RFU leadership's belief that a continued purge of the game in Yorkshire was necessary was not hard to substantiate. It was common knowledge that players in Yorkshire still received payment for play – indeed, immediately after the split some of the clubs remaining in the YRU boasted of how they would pay more than the NU clubs' six shillings a day – and problems with overly boisterous working-class crowds remained, despite the declining interest in the Union game.[37] In the four years following 1895 the YRU suspended ten grounds and reprimanded six other clubs for crowd trouble, most notoriously at Sharlston, near Wakefield, when on Christmas Eve 1898 a fight broke out between two players:

> The referee intervened and a general melee ensued. The spectators broke into the field and joined in the fighting. The Kippax players had to be guarded by the police from the field. Some of them could not get dressed and two of them had to run two miles to escape their assailants.[38]

In fact, the central core of the YRU leadership – James Miller, now a virulent opponent of broken-time, Mark Newsome, Harry Garnett, Barron Kilner and Arthur Hartley – had a conscious strategy of reconstructing Yorkshire rugby union on the same public-school basis as it had been in the 1860s and 1870s, but this time freed from the danger of contamination by the working classes. The YRU's actions were part of the general growth of exclusive middle-class leisure activities that was taking place in late Victorian society. As John Lowerson has highlighted, the growth of golf and tennis clubs in particular were among the most visible examples of the development of discrete leisure spheres for the middle classes. Eric Hobsbawm has also pointed to the fact that, while only two golf courses were built in Yorkshire before 1890, twenty-nine courses were built in the county between 1890 and 1895. The 1895 split was seen as an opportunity:

> [for] clubs to be formed on the same lines as the clubs of fifteen to twenty years ago, when members played for the pure love of the game, found their own clothing and paid all their own expenses (except, perhaps, third-class railway fares), besides paying the annual sub to the club.[39]

Thus nostalgia for a lost golden age intersected the generalised growth of an exclusive middle-class sporting culture. By 1900, when it had been abandoned by the great majority of its working-class-based clubs, the YRU was confidently predicting 'a turn of events caused by the public school boys and others taking part in the game' as it sought to 'encourage the class of players who hitherto have been elbowed out in the evolution of professionalism'.[40] Clubs began to be formed by ex-public and grammar school boys. Old Dewsburians was formed 'by some of the better class Dewsbury and Batley residents', the creation of the Hull and East Riding club was 'taken in hand by the sons of Hull and district's leading citizens' and Wakefield RFC was founded by 'Grammar School old boys and others'.[41] In Lancashire, the Furness, Oldham, Leigh and Vale of Lune rugby union clubs were formed in a similar fashion during the same period. The most prominent of this new wave of clubs in Yorkshire was Headingley FC in Leeds, which had been formed in 1892 on strictly amateur lines and was to dominate Yorkshire rugby union from the early 1900s onwards, thanks to its ability to attract the county's best Oxbridge and ex-public school players and its uncannily close relationship with the YRU committee – the latter most notoriously demonstrated at the 1909 Yorkshire Cup final, when Skipton walked off after a controversial Headingley try. It was later revealed that the referee was a member of the Headingley club.[42] By 1907, when the YRU formed the Yorkshire Wanderers side to promote the game in public schools, it was estimated that over 180 of those currently playing rugby union in the county were former public school boys, which, considering that the YRU had barely twenty clubs, accounted for at least half the players in the county.[43]

This drive towards middle-class exclusivity was not a linear process. Many in the YRU sought to preserve the all-encompassing basis of the YRU that existed from the mid-1880s. There was consequently a running battle with the RFU and its supporters in the YRU over the question of reinstatement of those who had played Northern Union football, with the majority of the YRU continuously appealing for a more lenient attitude: 'the English Union, instead of assisting us when they know we are fighting their battle in the face of great odds, do all they can to thwart and hinder us,' complained YRU committee member Harry Brown in 1897. Requests for flexibility from the RFU were met with a brick wall of indifference: an RFU report on the situation in Yorkshire in January 1898 stated unequivocally that 'no help can be given to the Northern clubs without sacrificing all the principles of amateur football'.[44] As well as the reinstatement issue, the suspension of Hull KR in 1897 and the RFU's compromise over the Arthur Gould case in Wales in the same year animated the disillusionment of YRU loyalists with the RFU. Hull KR had been found not guilty of professionalism by a YRU investigative committee but this had been overturned by the RFU and a secret hearing had suspended the club for a month. This was viewed as a serious slight on the YRU committee. Just as damaging was the RFU climbdown in 1897 over the Gould case (which is discussed in Chapter 6) in which the RFU cynically abandoned it zealous pursuit of amateurism in order to avoid a split with

Welsh rugby. The RFU's behavior seemed so blatantly hypocritical that even Harry Garnett was moved to complain that 'the Rugby Union should not cause a feeling that they had one mode of dealing with a working man professional and another method where the person indicated happened to belong to another class'.[45] Unfortunately, this was exactly the way the RFU did operate, a fact not lost on many embattled YRU loyalists. Indeed, such was the anger and frustration that the YRU committee discussed joining the NU or forming an independent Northern Amateur Union several times in the late 1890s. Neither proposal amounted to much as clubs simply voted with their feet and went over to the NU.

Those seeking a third way between the burgeoning professionalism of the NU and contracting exclusivity of the RFU could not succeed. The social conditions that had led to the rise of rugby in the 1880s no longer existed. Between middle-class exclusivity and mass, working-class-based forms of entertainment there was no middle ground. In fact, it was the NU that kept alive the community-based, populist traditions of the mass-supported rugby of the 1880s, recreating the network of locally based cup and league competitions and continuing the intense discussions about the direction of the sport, which had characterised Lancashire and Yorkshire rugby union. The NU immediately revived the debate on the need to make rugby more attractive, although the evolution of NU rules into an entirely separate and distinct sport to that of rugby union was to take another ten years. Most notably, the inauguration of the Northern Union Challenge Cup in 1897 was a conscious decision to emulate, on a grander scale, the success of the Yorkshire Cup. With fifty-two entries in its first year and an average crowd of around 6,000 per game, the cup fulfilled all expectations, not least for the eventual winners Batley, for whom it helped to return a record profit on the season of £879. The return of the victors to their home town recalled the triumphant home-comings of Yorkshire Cup winners in years past:

> The first notification of their arrival in Batley was the discharge of no fewer than 160 fog signals, the deafening racks of which were ably seconded by thousands of hoarse-voiced, lusty-lunged enthusiasts, who crowded all available space along Station Road and Hick Lane; these two, and in fact all other principal thoroughfares, presenting to the lookers-on nothing but a heaving, restless sea of animated faces. A procession was formed and headed by the Batley Old Band, and as it paraded along the thickly-populated streets, coloured lights, torches, and numerous other methods of illumination were employed in order to manifest the enthusiasm of the delighted followers of the successful team.[46]

Throughout the next few years the Challenge Cup presented ample evidence of the health of the new organisation. While not on the scale of the monster attendances that now marked FA Cup ties, crowds between ten and twenty thousand were commonplace, with over 20,000 for semi-finals in 1897 and 1899, and for the 1900 quarter-final at Leeds Parish Church. The 1898, 1901 and

1903 finals, held at Headingley, set records for English club rugby crowds, with 27,941, 29,569 and 32,507 spectators respectively.

Despite the confident assertions of failure by its opponents, the NU's first years were unequivocally successful. By 1899 the former northern strongholds of rugby union had gone over wholesale to the new body, leaving a small rump of largely exclusive clubs based on former public school boys. The NU's senior clubs were, to a large extent, profitable and their crowds were the equal of, if not larger than, those of northern rugby union's heyday in the late 1880s and early 1890s. In the working-class communities of the northern towns on which the split was based, NU had retained and possibly increased its popularity. The NU even appeared to have held back the challenge of soccer. No greater witness to its success could be found than F. E. Smith, later Lord Birkenhead, the future Conservative cabinet minister and avowed supporter of amateur sport, who wrote in late 1897:

> We who live in the North of England see clearly that at least in Lancashire, Yorkshire and Cheshire, the success of the movement is now assured. Undoubtedly there have been and there will be financial difficulties in individual cases – such difficulties are not unknown in association football, but they have not, I am sorry to say, placed professionalism in danger. There is a *verve* about the game as it is now played in the disaffected districts, there is a degree of public interest about the competitions, and there is a keenness among the players themselves, which teach those who have eyes to see that the revolt will be both permanent and successful. (emphasis in original)[47]

Professionalism and players

Although the NU initially disavowed any intention of introducing professionalism, it was clear to all that this state of affairs could not last. From the initial announcement of the six shillings per day limit on broken-time payments, widespread doubt was expressed as to how players would be attracted to play for such a small amount, especially from Wales, when covert payments in rugby union were known to be higher. The simple answer was, of course, that many clubs paid more than the maximum allowed – and with no effective means of policing broken-time payments the Union could do little to stop it. Stockport were widely rumoured to be offering players £2 a week during the season and a job at thirty shillings a week during the summer just three weeks after the split.[48] The payments entered in club accounts varied widely: in the 1896–97 season, Challenge Cup winners Batley recorded payments of just £59, while Leeds, who had a mediocre season, paid out £553 in broken-time.[49] At a maximum payment of £4/10s per match and thirty-five games in the season, Leeds's first team total should not have exceeded £160, especially when four of that season's away games were with other clubs in Leeds. As a disgruntled Leeds member had pointed out at the previous year's annual general meeting, the figures did not add up.[50] Presumably in an attempt to deflect such criticism, the club actually understated players' expenses by two-thirds in 1898, recording a more acceptable £193 when the actual total was £579.[51] As this, and club officials' experience in covering their tracks under the RFU regime, proved, even those clubs returning low broken-time figures were not necessarily telling the whole truth.

As we saw in Chapter 4, one of the underlying reasons for the call for broken-time was to improve the control of payments to players. In the first few weeks after the split, many clubs had tried to implement the broken-time regulations rigorously and only pay a proportion of the six shillings maximum – one club paying its men just four shillings for three games. However, this met with widespread opposition from the players and payment of the six shillings became seen as, at the very least, the minimum payment.[52] The steady flow of Welsh players into the game and the need to provide them with wages and jobs was also a key factor in the undermining of broken-time. By 1897 it was clear that, as a system for controlling wages, it was not working and that widespread abuses were taking place. The London-based *Mascot*, commented:

> it does not seem likely that the Northern Union officials will long be able to shut their eyes to the existing state of things in their own clubs. Either they must constitute searching enquiry and *punish* clubs that have practised professionalism or openly embrace the payment of players.[53]

In November of that year, the NU appointed a seven-man committee to look into this state of affairs and examine the options in a move towards open professionalism. Two months later it presented a majority and a minority (of one) report, the former supporting the introduction of professionalism, albeit with residential and occupational restrictions, and the latter opposing profession-alism.[54] The debate flourished throughout the next six months, with Bradford proposing the introduction of a maximum wage of £1 a week. This was rejected as being both impossible to police and, as had happened with the six shillings broken-time payment, likely to become a standard wage which few clubs could afford.[55]

When the new regulations were unveiled in the summer of 1898, they began with the fateful words 'Professionalism is legal' but proceeded to detail such stringent conditions as to make its operation unique. Defining a professional as anyone in receipt of remuneration over and above travelling expenses, the 'work clauses' of the rules specified that every professional player must be in 'bona-fide employment' and that any change or loss of employment, including any caused by fire, strike or lock-out, must be notified to the NU secretary, who would decide if a player was eligible to play. Examples of employment not regarded as 'bona-fide' were given as 'billiard markers, waiters in licensed houses, or any employment in connection with a club'. Players could register with a club for one season at a time but, unless they had special permission, could not transfer during a season. No professional was allowed to receive wages during the close season and no professional could serve on a club or Union committee. In any case of alleged contravention of the new rules, the burden of proof was to lie with the accused player or club. Those found guilty would be suspended.[56]

To a great extent, the rules were a quite conscious amalgam of the experience of soccer, rugby union and the labour relations' codes of the factory. From soccer, the lessons learned were largely negative, hence the outlawing of payments to players during the close season and, albeit overlaid with a large dose of paternalism, the insistence that players have work outside of football. These measures were felt to be vital in keeping down wages. From rugby union was taken the definition of professionalism, the objection to professionals playing any part in the governance of the game (which was also an FA rule) and the placing of the burden of proof on the accused rather than the accuser. From the factory was taken the complex registration and reporting systems designed to control the activities of the players and the paternalistic rationale that the rules had been introduced for the welfare of the players. Harry Waller justified the new regulations with the argument that:

> the Northern Union was anxious to make football the means of improving the positions of players. They would do what they could to find positions for players as they were able to under the rules. He did not think that anyone would like to join a football club for the sake of playing the game on Saturdays only and idling during the remainder of the week.[57]

Because of such statements it has been argued that the central motivation for the introduction of the work-clause regulations was to impose a form of 'social control' on players and to transmit bourgeois values to the working class.[58] While it is true that the regulations did tighten control over players and exclude some forms of pub-based employment, the underlying reasons for this were to regulate the economic conditions in which the NU operated. For example, working as a pub waiter or billiard marker was specifically outlawed because it was a common method used by clubs to give virtually work-free employment to players. Although declining in importance since the early 1890s, the drinks industry had a close relationship with football and the NU was no exception. During this time many leading NU officials were publicans, the 1895–96 Hull and District RFU *Official Guide* carried a one-line advertisement for Hull Brewery products at the head of every page and the chairman of the Leeds club was C. F. Tetley, a member of the famous Leeds brewing family. Similarly, although the insistence on players having 'real' jobs may have been based on a concern for the long-term prospects of the players, it had been a particular criticism made by rugby followers of soccer's professionalism that the latter's economic difficulties were caused in part by paying players a full week's wages for only a few afternoons' work of training and playing.[59]

" Saints " at the Cardigan Arms. The Consolation of Defeat.

Figure 12 As this cartoon of the Leeds St John's side illustrates, alcohol, public houses and rugby had been inseparable since the late 1870s (from *Toby, the Yorkshire Tyke*).

Although not a true cartel, many of the NU's concerns resembled those of a cartel and, until the turn of the century at least, much of its regulatory work was aimed at establishing equality of competition. Thus the minutiae of the work clauses were drawn up in order to stop clubs finding ways around the rules and gaining an unfair advantage. This even extended to the employment of private investigators to check the veracity of a player's story.[60] There were therefore numerous additions and caveats added to the regulations over time, which sought to restrict even further the actions of players. By 1903, it had been decided that a player who was ill and off work on the Thursday, Friday or Saturday morning could not play in that Saturday's match; he must work three days after being off work before being allowed to play again. Players who had as much as a half-day holiday during the week had to apply to the NU for permission to play. Eventually, any absence from work during the season meant that a player had to apply for permission to play.[61]

In justifying the new rules the leaders of the NU found themselves repeating many of the concerns about professionalism expressed by the leaders of the RFU a few years earlier. 'The Northern Union,' said Waller in 1899, 'although it had adopted professionalism, could congratulate itself that its management was in the hands of amateurs.'[62] Budd and Hill's arguments that the professional footballer was a man who was sacrificing his future for short-term gain were alluded to by Hull chairman Charles Brewer when he argued that the work clauses would prevent that from happening:

> The clause was provided solely for the benefit of the players themselves. While the men are playing football they are receiving a certain return for it, and if they followed their ordinary occupation, as the committee expected them to do, they were making a nest egg for future years. The committee put the working clause before the players in the latters' own interests, and asked for their loyal co-operation in carrying out the rule.[63]

It is impossible to say whether the work clauses succeeded in their professed goal of raising the long-term prospects of the players. One must doubt it, if only because of the silence of the architects of the policy on the question. As with pre-1895 working-class rugby union players, the tenancy of a pub was probably the best a player could hope for, although the availability of these sinecures had diminished sharply since the early 1890s. Even then, a pub was far from a passport to a supposed life of indolence: in 1897 Dicky Lockwood, now playing for Wakefield Trinity, was declared bankrupt after accumulating debts of £300 in running the Queen's Hotel at Heckmondwike, and later that year Oldham and Lancashire stand-off Harry Varley disappeared from his pub because of financial difficulties.[64] In general, players continued the occupations they already had outside of football, partly because the work clauses forced them to stay in regular employment and forbade club payments outside of the season, but mainly because the low level of remuneration available in the NU could do little more than supplement their non-football wages. Although a critic of the work clauses claimed that most NU players were unskilled labourers, this seems to have been an exaggeration and there appears, as in pre-split times, to be no particular pattern to the occupations followed by the players, with the geographically dominant industries of mining and textiles heading the table of employment (see Table A.6 of the Appendix).[65]

In reality, the paternalism expressed by the NU's Waller and Brewer towards working-class players was no different from that of the RFU's Rowland Hill – their differences were about *how* to protect players from themselves. As Waller himself said: 'The English Rugby union legislated for clubs as they would like them to be; and the Northern Union for the clubs and the players as they were today. The Northern Union, in a word, went with the times.'[66]

The exclusion of professionals from NU committees was ample demonstration of their determination not to let working-class players gain too much influence over the game. And when it came to implementing the work clauses, the trials of players accused of infractions brought forth eerie echoes of the 1880s rugby union trials, as the following extracts from the cross-examination of J. Trowell, a player from Beverley FC accused of playing in a game against Bridlington while not working, make clear:

J. Clifford
(Chair):   It is reported to us that Trowell had not worked for two weeks previous to playing in this match.

Trowell: I was working under the same stevedore all that time. This week I started to work on Monday morning and finished on Wednesday night.

Welsh: The stevedore is really your employer?

Trowell: Yes.

Lister: What did you draw last week?

Trowell: Fifteen shillings

Clifford: And what the week before?

Trowell: Twenty-seven shillings and sixpence

Clifford: And what the week before that?

Trowell: Sixteen or seventeen shillings.

Clifford: And what this week?

Trowell: Fourteen shillings.

Platt: And have you had a permit from this committee when you have lost any time?

Trowell: Yes.
. . .

Evidence was then presented from a private investigator, employed by the NU, who said that he had gone to see Robert Middleton, Trowell's stevedore, but found that he did not live at the address given by Trowell. Trowell introduced the investigator to Middleton who could show him neither a wages book nor when Trowell last worked for him:

Clifford: When did you last work for Middleton?

Trowell: This week.

Clifford: Did you work for him last week too?

Trowell: Yes. Monday, Tuesday and Wednesday.

Clifford: What was the ship you took our representative to?

Trowell: It was a fresh one we were going to start working on the Friday. We did not work on the Thursday.

Clifford: What ship did you work on the Monday, Tuesday and Wednesday?

Trowell: The Bouradina.
. . .

Platt: Why did you not wire your secretary (Mr Simpson) [about not working on Thursday]?

Trowell: I can't afford to send wires to Beverley.

Platt:	You can afford to get your club into trouble.
Houghton:	Where does Middleton live?
Trowell:	I don't know.
Lister:	You say Holland's, the stevedores, pay your wages?
Trowell:	Yes, and Middleton bullies us.
Lister:	I suppose Holland's will keep an account of the time? Are you paid by the hour?
Trowell:	Yes, Middleton has a book which he gives in after every ship.[67]

As can be seen, the work clauses signalled the NU's determination to institute an iron rule over its players. In the first few months of the new regulations' operation, Swinton had two league points deducted because their star Welsh player, Owen Badger, took time off work to visit his sick child in Wales but did not receive NU permission to play in the following Saturday's match. A Hull player was banned for a month for not telling the NU that he had changed jobs. Most famously, Dai Fitzgerald, Batley's Welsh international three-quarter, was banned for eighteen months in 1898 when a private detective working for the NU discovered that his job as a coal agent did not actually involve any work. The following season Hull KR full-back H. Sinclair received a similar suspension when the sub-committee found that he was not 'following regular employment'. In 1902 Hunslet had two league points deducted after one of their players accidentally submitted the wrong form to the NU. That same year the NU General Committee refused to allow Broughton Rangers' Willie and Sam James, younger brothers of the famous James brothers, to open a tobacco shop together and ordered them to find alternative employment within two weeks.

The activities of the NU leadership were accompanied by ever-tightening control over players by their clubs. In November 1895 Bradford captain Jack Toothill was forced to resign from the club committee after he had declared himself unfit to play in a game owing to his job in a dye house. Wigan summarily transferred John and Joe Winstanley to Leigh after they had argued with club selection policy. Alf Mann was forced to miss playing for England against Wales in 1908 after his club suspended him for 'insubordination and using bad language to members of the committee'. Bradford even refused to agree to a player's transfer to Batley until he had repaid the insurance money they had given him after he had broken his leg playing for them.[68] Little wonder that one commentator was moved to remark that 'we are unable to discriminate between the mailed fist of the Rugby Union and the knuckle-duster of the younger body. Each is equally bent on having its own rule obeyed'.[69]

The response of the players to the discipline imposed on them veered between acceptance, resignation and resistance. In the first month after the split, Warrington players had gone on strike for two matches against the club committee not paying them the full six shillings per day broken-time and disputes on this matter were common in many clubs. In December Leigh forwards refused to play unless they received a higher rate of broken-time. The following January Huddersfield suspended four players who had objected to receiving their usual two shillings and sixpence tea money in kind rather than in cash. These strikes and other actions by players were important factors in making the maximum payment of six shillings broken-time the standard, and indeed the minimum, payment. It appears to be the case that, as with the introduction of covert payments into northern rugby union, the pressure to increase wages came directly from the activities and expectations of the players themselves. Of the fifteen strikes taking place in the NU in the first decade of its existence, all were over issues of wages, as Table A.7 of the Appendix shows. Although they tended to be short-lived, with none lasting more than one or two games, the incidence of strikes indicates a relatively high level of unrest among players. There is other evidence of concern among NU leaders about the state of player relations: a few weeks before the introduction of the work clauses, Waller called for a reduction in 'friction' between players and club officials. In 1899 Wigan officials blamed their poor run of results on the 'considerable trouble with some of the players' that they had been having. At Leeds's AGM in 1903, club chairman Joshua Sheldon asked that players 'consider some of the difficulties the management of clubs laboured under, instead of putting obstacles in the way of committees by making great demands'.[70] It is difficult to gauge how successful strike actions were, although players in the early years of the NU were more likely to succeed in demands for higher payments simply because there was more money in the game at that time. In 1898 the Lancashire and Cheshire county organisations agreed to players' demands for wages of £1 for playing in county games, even though Yorkshire only paid six shillings broken-time.

Others were not so fortunate. D. Rogan, the leader of the Leeds strikers, was banned from the game for life for 'insubordination'. The five leaders of the Castleford strike suffered a similar fate, although all were reinstated within two years.[71] Paradoxically, the NU's insistence on having work outside the sport probably meant that players were more willing to take action than the full-time professionals of the Football League, who ran the risk of losing their livelihoods if they went on strike. Conversely, this was also probably the reason that NU players did not develop any form of trade union organisation until after World War One, because, aside from the obvious problem of sportsmen recognising that they had a commonality of interest, they had a sense that their real economic interests lay at the workplace rather than at the football club. In fact, there were a number of instances of players accepting pay cuts because of the parlous economic state of their clubs: for example, Keighley, Batley and Leigh players did so in 1905 and 1907, and Lancaster players voted to continue at their club after the committee had resigned, saying they were unable to pay players, in June 1905.[72]

Although it is difficult to assess general wage levels because of the paucity of club records, a general indication can be gained from newspaper reports. At the highest echelons of the game, wages were comparable with those in the Football League; one unnamed Lancashire club being reported in 1898 as paying its players between thirty shillings and £4 per week, with bonuses of 50 per cent for a win and 25 per cent for a draw, which would put the top earning players comfortably above the Football League's £4 a week maximum wage. Dai Fitzgerald was paid £2 a week by Batley before he was suspended. In 1903 Leeds said that their players were paid an average of thirty shillings per match, although this is on the low side for the first team because the figures also included 'A' (reserve grade) team players. At the same time, Halifax were paying £1/10s a win to the backs but five shillings less per win to their forwards. By 1908 Wigan paid their backs £2/10s a win and £2 for a loss. In common with Halifax and many other clubs, they also paid less to their forwards, who had to make do with £1/7s/6d a win and £1/2s/6d a loss. Justified on the basis that backs deserved more because they attracted spectators, this differential unsurprisingly caused much resentment and, as can be seen from the Table A.7, was the direct cause of at least three strikes by forwards.

But, as the NU was forced to come to terms with its economic difficulties at the turn of the century, few clubs could afford such high wages. Even by 1899, Manningham were claiming to pay players only between ten shillings and twelve shillings and sixpence a match, while a local rival was offering Elland players sixteen shillings a win, twelve shillings a draw and eight shillings a loss. The Rochdale Hornets strike in 1902 was caused by the committee's non-payment of the team's wages of seven shillings and sixpence for an away game at Millom. In 1904 Swinton, one of the game's leading sides, were forced to reduce wages to ten shillings for a win and five shillings a loss. In dire financial straits, Castleford were only paying players five shillings a match in 1906, less than the previously scorned broken-time limit. For the lucky few, a good run in the Challenge Cup usually meant bonuses for winning teams – when they won the cup in 1900 Swinton players received ten shillings extra for winning their first round game, £1 for winning subsequent rounds and £5 for winning the cup, as did Halifax when they lifted the trophy in 1904.[73]

Of course, star players were normally able to demand higher wages than the team average. Halifax full-back Billy Little commanded £4/11s a game in 1905 and at least two other players received at least twice the average pay of their team mates. Warrington's legendary winger Jack Fish was the only man in his side to receive £1 a week in the early 1900s. New Zealander Lance Todd received a straight £250 per season when he signed for Wigan in 1908, and, at the outer reaches of the NU's wages' universe, Hull's centre three-quarter Billy Batten, a future founding member of the Rugby League Hall of Fame, was reputedly earning £14 a week shortly before World War One, which probably made him the highest paid professional footballer in Britain, if not the world.[74] Curiously enough, there is no evidence of resentment towards such players by their team mates, presumably because they were seen as benefiting other players owing to their ability to win matches and draw crowds.

Welsh players also regularly received more than their native team mates, although this was often because of the large cash sums they were paid when signing for NU clubs. Many, like Llanelli captain and Wales three-quarter Owen Badger, found themselves in a position to negotiate significant amounts from suitor clubs:

> The bidding started at £20 and a weekly salary, which sum daily increased, and on Tuesday Badger's price had reached £75. The brilliant three-quarter back held out for £100 and two pounds, ten shillings per week standing wages, until the end of the season, and at these figures he was invited to meet a deputation of Swintonians at Shrewsbury.[75]

When Cardiff and Wales scrum-half Dicky Davies signed for Wigan in 1907 he received £200 down, £2/10s weekly wages and another thirty shillings per win. The highest signing-on fee paid to a Welsh player was the £300 received by Swansea's Dan Rees from Hull KR in 1905, although the £155 paid in 1913 to George Hayward, also of Swansea, was the highest received by a Welsh forward, demonstrating again the difference in the commercial potential of forwards as perceived by NU clubs. Gwyn Nicholls, future Welsh captain in the historic defeat of the 1905 All Blacks, felt sufficiently confident of his future that he turned down Hull's offer of £500 and 'a substantial weekly salary' to stay with Cardiff in October 1901.[76] The signing-on fee was particularly important in tempting players to 'Go North', not only because it was probably the largest amount of cash a working-class player would ever see, but also because many players in the Principality were already in receipt of regular monies from their ostensibly amateur Welsh clubs. Indeed, some may even have been earning more in the 'amateur' game than many 'professionals' in the NU – Treherbert were accused of offering Pontypridd's Dawson £1 a week to play for them in 1901 and in 1907 allegations were made that players were commonly paid between a sovereign and six shillings per match.[77]

The fortunes of Welsh players in the NU varied widely. Many were undoubted successes, like Wigan's Johnny Thomas and Bert Jenkins, who became the fulcrum of the club's successes in the late 1900s, Thomas eventually becoming a director of the club. Others were not: a year after signing for Swinton, Badger had left for Wales after being disciplined under the NU's work-clause rules. Dicky Davies played just sixteen games for his £200 and Gwyn Nicholls' brother Garnett signed for Wigan but never played for them. Such behaviour gained Welsh players the reputation of being both work-shy and overly expensive for the standard of play they provided: 'It appears that a man has only to say he comes from Wales to be put into some Northern Union team straight away, sometimes to the detriment of promising local young players,' complained *The Yorkshireman* as early as 1895.[78] The introduction of the work clauses was widely perceived as an attempt to stop Welsh players from taking advantage of easy jobs on offer from clubs and make them work in real jobs. At its extreme, this resulted in Hull and Wigan taking legal proceedings against players who had received signing-on fees but never showed up at their new clubs, Wigan receiving £65 compensation from the courts for the £120 they paid to Aberavon's Tommy Thomas.[79]

This growing self-confidence of the clubs in dealing with their players and in controlling wages reduced the need for the work clauses. The static attendances and economic decline of the sport in the early 1900s drastically reduced inflationary pressures, leaving little leeway for clubs to emulate their spendthrift soccer cousins of the 1890s. And, as can be seen, apart from star performers, players could not earn enough playing the game to allow them not to have a full-time job. Indeed, within the first few months of the introduction of the new rules, complaints were being raised that they were heavy-handed and counterproductive. This was partly due to the large administrative burden placed on clubs and the NU in regulating the system. On one Friday in January 1900 the Professional Sub-Committee dealt with 167 cases, a total exceeded by the work of the committee on 4 October 1901, when they looked at 203 applications, including the entire Brighouse Rangers' team and thirteen of the Leigh side. The sum total of their deliberations was to refuse permission to play to just four players.[80] Many of the decisions of the committee appeared to be both bureaucratic and arbitrary: Hunslet had requested exemption from the need to receive permission to play after a half-day holiday for the eleven miners in their side, whose working patterns gave them a mid-week half-day, but the committee refused. Leeds's T. D. Davies was barred from playing after being sacked as a pub landlord on a Thursday and being unable to find new employment on the Friday. R. Petrie of Seaton found himself investigated for missing work despite the fact he did not receive any wages from his club. Most egregious was Broughton Rangers' fine for a number of their players not working on the morning of the 1902 Challenge Cup final.[81]

The severity of the punishments handed down to clubs for breaches of the work clauses also caused much resentment. Swinton lost two league points over the Owen Badger affair and the following season both Broughton Rangers and Rochdale Hornets received the same sanction. In the 1901–02 season six of the clubs in the fourteen-team Northern Rugby League had points deducted for transgressing the clauses. In order to maintain strict adherence to the rules, the NU had little choice but to adopt such measures. Fines could simply be regarded as trading losses but the deduction of points struck at the heart of a club's existence. Unsurprisingly, most of the leading clubs resented not only the interference in their affairs but also the undermining of the league competition that points' deduction caused. As with the YRU's attempts to stifle professionalism in the late 1880s and the Lancashire suspensions for professionalism in 1894, such harsh discipline meant that, ultimately, a side was being judged by off-field criteria rather than on-field performances and posed a threat to the integrity of competition, which would consequently affect spectator interest. This had happened in the 1901–02 season when Swinton's playing record would have made them runners-up in the championship but the deduction of four points placed them in fourth position.

By 1901 there was significant opposition to the work clauses, and support for outright professionalism was expressed by a large minority of the senior clubs that formed the elite Northern Rugby League that year. They were able to exert enough pressure in 1902 to force the ending of punishment by points deduction but attempts to introduce open professionalism at the 1904 NU Annual General Meeting, backed by Broughton Rangers, Salford, Swinton, Oldham, Hull and Hull KR, failed, largely due to the residual fear of poorer clubs that it would mean that their players would be easy prey for the richer clubs. Opposition was also voiced by those who maintained that the work clauses fulfilled a wider social role by discouraging work-shy attitudes among players: the Hunslet committee supported the clauses because 'open professionalism would be detrimental to the players by encouraging loafing', as did Leeds and Bradford, whose chairman, Fred Lister, threatened to refuse his turn as NU president for the 1904–05 season if the clauses were abolished.[82] It is notable that these latter two clubs were also those that looked most hopefully for some form of rapprochement with the RFU, suggesting again that the paternalistic attitudes embodied in the work clauses were not so far removed from those of the RFU. A majority for their abolition was only gained for the start of the 1905–06 season, after they had been fatally discredited by the events surrounding the Leigh versus Wigan Challenge Cup tie. Two weeks after Leigh had beaten Wigan and the day before they were due to play Halifax in the next round, Wigan complained that one of the Leigh players had played without a permit. The NU ordered the game to be replayed; Wigan won the replay, and were then faced with a Leigh complaint that a Wigan player had taken part in the match in contravention of the work clauses. Faced with the postponement of yet another cup tie the NU allowed Wigan to play Halifax but ordered them to forfeit their share of the gate money, thus admitting Leigh's charge.[83] The affair managed to encapsulate both the administrative nightmare of the system and the threat to the credibility of the NU's competitions posed by the work clauses. It therefore came as no surprise when the regulations were finally struck from the rule book at the 1905 general meeting. Finally, open professionalism had been introduced by the Northern Union, yet the poor financial state of the sport meant that the momentous decision had little, if any, impact on the game.

The rise of soccer and the decline of the Northern Union

The chief reason for the NU's change in fortune from the late 1890s to the middle of the 1900s could be summed up in two words: association football. As early as 1893 the Manchester FA was arguing that it should have its own seat on the FA council because of its success in popularising soccer in 'the stronghold of Rugbyism' and the 50,000 attendance at Fallowfield in Manchester for that year's FA Cup final had shocked rugby supporters.[84] By the mid-1890s, soccer leagues had been established in most traditionally rugby towns and in Lancashire by 1897 professional sides had been formed in Oldham, Rochdale and Wigan. None of these clubs lasted more than three years as financial difficulties quickly overcame what were essentially speculative ventures, yet the growth of the game in schools and communities was rapidly undermining the bedrock of rugby support.

In Lancashire's northwest, the rise and decline of the two sports was such that rugby had completely disappeared from Ulverston by 1906 and neighbouring Barrow could boast only nine local rugby sides as opposed to twenty-three soccer clubs. As the *Athletic News* pointed out, 'for all practical purposes that famous recruiting area for Northern Union football [from Lancaster to Barrow] in the North West may be considered wholly "soccerised" '.[85] In Yorkshire, the former rugby town of Barnsley had been completely swamped by association, so much so that in December 1898 the Beckett Cup, the district rugby knock-out competition trophy, was handed over to the local FA because there were no longer any rugby teams left to play for it. The two Bradford clubs found themselves outflanked by soccer enthusiasts who had persuaded the local board schools to take up the 'dribbling code' after a boy had broken his leg in a rugby game and Leeds also developed a thriving schools' competition. In Hull, the decade following the split saw the number of local soccer sides grow from just seven to ninety-six. Despite continual organisational problems, soccer leagues in the East and West Ridings of Yorkshire continued to attract new sides and by 1904 there were 436 clubs affiliated to the West Yorkshire FA.[86]

As many of the leaders of pre-1895 Lancashire and Yorkshire rugby had recognised, soccer had more appeal to spectators because of its more open style of play. The administrators of the NU were also exceptionally conscious of this, as could be seen from the debates on the rules of the game throughout the union's early history. But soccer's attraction was not simply due to its mode of play: in an era of national culture and national consciousness, soccer was a truly national sport. By 1906, it could claim over 7,500 affiliated clubs, approximately fifteen times the number of clubs claimed by the NU and the RFU combined.[87] The superseding of old regional ties by growing centralisation, the popularity of national newspapers and the importance of national events to localities previously untouched by them, all of these factors gave soccer's national pre-eminence an unassailable advantage in the struggle for football dominance. As the *Leeds Mercury* pointed out in 1905:

> the public want a national game rather than a code peculiar to a circumscribed area. . . . Thus, while the Northern Union has too limited an area to be really a great force, and the Rugby Union is to some extent discredited as a purely amateur combination and is weakened through the loss of the cream of the clubs of the North, the Association game is national in scope and influence, and is yearly becoming more powerful and more popular.[88]

Soccer was also a national sport in more than just a geographical sense. Despite the dominance of the working-class professional player and spectator, it still remained a game of all the classes, even if they rarely played it together. Soccer was widely played in the public schools and by teams of ex-public school boys. In the armed forces, it enjoyed total domination, the FA in 1906 recording 578 teams in the army, where it was the only recognised football code until 1907, and 180 navy sides.[89] It therefore suffered none of the social disadvantages that the NU faced, despite the apparently similar proletarian base of the two sports. Indeed, the attitude of many northern RFU supporters to soccer's untrammelled professionalism was in very marked contrast to that which they displayed towards the NU. James Higson, Lancashire rugby union secretary following the split, became a director of Newton Heath AFC (later to become Manchester United) in 1897. Mark Newsome, who despite his advocacy of broken-time payments in 1893 remained a loyal supporter of the RFU and became its president in 1906, saw no contradiction between his support for amateurism and his club, Dewsbury, abandoning rugby union and concentrating on soccer in 1897. A. W. Pullin, journalistic scourge of the Northern Union and intransigent defender of the RFU, became the founding vice-chairman of Leeds City AFC. This double-think was no better demonstrated than by the response of a rugby union supporter to the NU's establishment of a schools competition who stated that:

> it will be a great pity to introduce NU ideas into the minds of school-lads beyond what they know already. I consider it unhealthy for boys to grow up with the idea that they are going to play a game for which in the future they are going to receive wages.

He went on to call on schools to play soccer![90] Unlike the Northern Union game, soccer was not perceived as being aberrant or at odds with English national identity – in fact, its hierarchical pyramid of upper-class national administrators, middle-class controlled clubs and working-class players and supporters fitted the nationalist framework of late Victorian and Edwardian society perfectly.[91]

The NU was therefore at a structural disadvantage about which it could do very little when faced with the soccer threat. Its clubs had initially responded to the round ball game's popularity in its strongholds by co-opting it. At the time of the split, Bradford, Halifax, Huddersfield and Leeds had formed soccer sections of their clubs and in 1896 eight of the West Yorkshire FA's twenty-seven members were NU clubs; Huddersfield's secretary, William Hirst, even became its president. The initial success of the NU's competitions however led most of the clubs to abandon soccer by the late 1890s, especially as the soccer sections almost invariably made a loss, in some cases quite substantially, and attracted poor attendances.[92] There was another reason for their abandonment. In the period up to the split, when the clubs were menaced by the RFU's professionalism rules, the existence of a soccer section was regarded as an insurance policy: if a club was expelled from the RFU on its own, the association game offered a way in which it could continue its footballing activities. The consolidation of the NU removed this need.[93] The shock of the soccer explosion in their own backyards also stimulated many clubs to form new local competitions or sponsor existing ones. Warrington had begun a rugby competition for local factory sides in 1895, from which they both recruited players and made a profit by staging the finals at their ground, and in 1899 Halifax had reinvigorated their local rugby league by providing financial backing of £5 to each club and offering a cup to be competed for, albeit with the proviso that all 350 players in the league were to be registered as Halifax players.[94] Both initiatives were copied by other clubs as they attempted to recreate the thicket of local league and cup competitions that northern rugby had established in the late 1880s. Stung by the strides made by soccer in local schools, in 1902 the Yorkshire NU committee started a schools' competition which embraced schools across the county, all of them board or council schools. In Leeds, twenty-four schools participated in the local schools' league and the final of their knock-out competition attracted crowds of up to 3,000 people.[95]

But the major initiative to secure the NU dam against the tidal wave of soccer was to prove more controversial. In April 1901 Halifax called a meeting of twelve of the leading clubs in Lancashire and Yorkshire – themselves plus Batley, Bradford, Broughton Rangers, Huddersfield, Hull, Hunslet, Oldham, Rochdale Hornets, Runcorn, Salford and Swinton – to consider the formation of an elite Northern Rugby League. They felt that the prevailing fixture system whereby each club played opponents from its own county provided too few top-class fixtures and sought to establish a fixture system whereby the best clubs would play each other regardless of county location. The NU had tried such an arrangement in its inaugural year, with each club playing every other club, but the volume of fixtures – each club played forty-two matches that season – coupled with the costs of travelling, forced them to switch to a county-based system. The twelve NRL clubs felt that the original system could be reconstituted but with fewer clubs. There was also a strong minority of the clubs, led by Broughton Rangers and Hull, who favoured open professionalism. Most revolutionary, the twelve sought to expand their number to include rugby union teams from the North East and the Midlands. South Shields rugby union club joined in June, after having sounded out the NU about joining the previous year, but Leicester, which had been approached because of their notoriety for covertly paying players, declined, largely because, it was commented, 'they have been extensively patronised by the English Rugby Union, as well as by the crack southern clubs, and really do not need any attraction in the way of the Northern Union'.[96] The new league was forced to expand its numbers anyway, but for reasons of constitutional politics. In order to get a majority on the NU committee to sanction the formation of the Northern Rugby League (NRL), Brighouse Rangers and Leigh were offered places in the new venture. Such horse-trading won the new league no friends among those excluded from its plans and the non-NRL clubs in Yorkshire voted to boycott all matches with them. The rancour continued until the beginning of the 1902–03 season when the thirty-six leading clubs were incorporated into a two-division structure. Three seasons later this was abandoned in favour of a return to a single league with a county-based fixture system after clubs in the second division complained about high travelling costs and declining gates due to unattractive fixtures. The entire exercise had proved to be 'an unqualified failure', in the words of the Hull committee, and had seen the disbanding of the NU's only outpost in the North East, after the clubs had voted against South Shields's inclusion in the NRL at the end of the 1903–04 season because of the costs involved in travelling to Tyneside.[97]

The failure of the NRL and the continued erosion of its base by soccer only served to deepen demoralisation within the sport. The cross-class composition of soccer and the overt appeal of middle-class exclusivity from the RFU had helped to 'proletarianise' the NU, making it difficult for clubs to attract business-men to the game and serving to increase the disillusionment of many of its exist-ing middle-class patrons. As early as 1898 A. D. Penny, the chairman of Leeds, had complained about the lack of support the club was receiving from the city's employers and the same concern was expressed by Hull, Hull KR and Hunslet officials over coming years.[98] This disillusionment with the NU was also accom-panied by a desire in some quarters to abandon professional rugby and return to amateurism and the RFU. Significantly, although for reasons not apparent at the time, Manningham's outgoing chairman, James Freeman, had called in 1900 for his club to 'go back to that free and independent style of amateur play' and in 1902 Leeds's president, Joshua Sheldon, declared 'I don't appreciate a sport for which men have to be paid for its promotion, and I wish that Leeds had stayed a strong amateur club'. In the same year, and most damaging of all, Herbert Hutchinson, Wakefield Trinity's leading committee member and a former NU president, resigned from his club to rejoin the RFU, calling on the leading clubs of the NU to do the same.[99]

Another symptom of the haemorrhage of middle-class support for the NU was the abandonment of the sport by the Church of England, signified by the abrupt closure of the Leeds Parish Church club in 1901. Even before the split, the church's belief in the evangelising power of rugby was waning and the Leeds Parish Church side in particular, with its reputation for rough play, covert payments to players and violent crowds, was an acute embarrassment to the church with which it was nominally attached. The fact that the club was also heavily supported by members of Leeds's immigrant Jewish community, which was situated near the club's ground, also confirmed to the church that rugby was no longer a useful means of extending its influence among the lower classes.[100] Nevertheless, at the turn of the century, the club was, after Hunslet, the leading force in Leeds rugby, and certainly put its richer rival at Headingley, to the north of the city, in the shade. In 1900, 20,000 packed into its ground to see the Challenge Cup quarter-final with Runcorn, one of two quarter-final appearances it made, and crowds of ten thousand were not uncommon for important games. The club finished above Leeds in the league four out of its five years in the NU, including being fourth in its penultimate season. But its death knell was sounded with the appointment of Sidney Gedge as a curate at the church in 1900. All curates were automatically made vice-presidents of the club, but rarely concerned themselves with its activities. Gedge, however, was a Scottish rugby union international, a personal friend of Rowland Hill and an active RFU referee. He played a role in the financial management of the club and was a key member of the committee that decided to shut it down. The ostensible reason was that the lease on their ground could not be renewed but as even A. W. Pullin admitted, the club had had ample time to relocate and had even been offered a ground nearby, but had done nothing. Within eight weeks of voting to disband in July 1901, the club had disappeared without trace, its effects being auctioned off in early September.[101] Other than through local Sunday schools, this ended the church's involvement with the NU at a national level, with future links being limited to the referee, the Reverend Frank Chambers, and a handful of appearances for St Helens by the Reverend Christopher Chevasse, the son of the Bishop of Liverpool who was a curate at the local church.[102] In another example of the relationship between rugby union and soccer in the North, Leeds Parish Church became a bastion of local soccer.

But the biggest blow came two years later, when Manningham, winners of the NU's first championship in 1896, voted to go over to soccer and joined the second division of the Football League. As we saw above, the leadership of the Manningham club had expressed their disquiet at the direction of the NU before the turn of the century, and this had continued as their playing fortunes declined. In 1901, when Bradford, Halifax and Leeds were winding up their soccer sections, Manningham had told the West Yorkshire FA that 'we are doing all we possibly can to help the Association game' and that they would look again later at the question.[103] This was something of an understatement and may well have been deliberately so: rumours had circulated in West Yorkshire since about 1900 that the Football League was keen to establish a side in Leeds or Bradford, if possible without links to an NU club. At some point towards the end of 1902 it appears that the Manningham committee approached the Football League and formed a relationship with Bradford's leading soccer evangelists, James Whyte, a Scotsman who was a sub-editor on the *Bradford Observer*, and Charles Brunt, a headmaster prominent in the promotion of soccer in Bradford schools. A series of semi-official meetings took place in the early months of 1903 and in May the club was sensationally accepted into division two of the Football League, by 30 out of 35 votes, without ever having played a game of soccer. In hindsight, it seems unlikely that such a coup could have been carried off so smoothly without guarantees having been made by the Football League. Having been accepted into soccer's elite, the club committee then moved to sever all links with the NU. At the general meeting that endorsed the committee's decision to switch to soccer and abandon rugby, committee member and textiles manufacturer Alfred Ayrton summed up the mood by expressing a dissatisfaction that managed to combine nostalgia for rugby union and support for soccer:

> I will never be a member once more, in any shape or form, of the Northern Union. As at present constituted, it is badly managed. The game has been

tampered with, tinkered with and spoilt, and we are trying to substitute for it a game which will be attractive.[104]

As can be seen, there was more to Manningham's decision than to simply find a game which would pay.[105] In fact, the club had made profits in four of its eight years in the NU but in its first three years as Bradford City AFC it made an aggregate loss of £1,638, almost its total NU losses, £1,687. But the difference was in the crowds attracted to the new club – in its first season under association rules it took £4,546 at the gate, easily doubling Manningham's best ever receipts in a season. Manningham had become a middling club in a regional competition of a declining sport; Bradford City were the most talked-about club in the national competition of a sport that was conquering the nation. The civic mission that had inspired the formation of northern rugby clubs in the 1870s was being repeated, but this time on a national scale with a different sport. The centralised and unified nation that England had become by the turn of the century meant that civic ambition could no longer be fully satisfied within a regional framework. Even Manningham's dropping of their district's name in favour of their city's seemed to signify the entrance of the club on to a new, national stage.

The success of Manningham's switch quite naturally led other NU clubs to investigate their options. Throughout 1903 and 1904 rumours abounded of other clubs following their example: Hull held meetings with Bradford City to discuss a possible switch, but this only resulted in them sharing their ground with the newly formed Hull City.[106] Salford and Swinton were also rumoured to be considering taking the plunge, although again the only outcome was in Salford sharing their ground with Salford United AFC.[107] At the end of the 1903–04 season the Leeds-based Holbeck club disbanded after losing their promotion play-off game to determine if they were to be promoted to division one of the NRL. Six days later, the newly formed Leeds City AFC rented their Elland Road ground and announced their intention to buy it for £5,000.[108] The NU General Committee sought to flush out any remaining soccer sympathies among clubs in June 1905, when its annual general meeting decided 'that no club shall be represented on the Union committee whose interest in football is not solely devoted to the Northern Union game'. Although this appeared to steady the ship, the alarm bells started ringing once again three months later when the *Yorkshire Post* reported that 'indications are that before very long we shall have an association club in opposition to the one at Valley Parade'.[109]

That club was Bradford, the self-proclaimed flagship of Yorkshire rugby's power in the 1880s and 1890s. Again, it appears that much covert planning went on behind the scenes, but whatever the final mechanics of the rupture, the forces underlying it had been at work since before the 1895 split. These centred on the debts that had been incurred in the purchase and development of the club's Park Avenue ground, itself a symbol of civic pride and of the competition between the county's senior clubs to have the most prestigious sporting amenities in Yorkshire. Even in the NU's first season the club reported an outstanding debt of £10,300 on the ground and had defaulted on the 1895 and 1896 instalments of their £1,000 annual payments. Despite making a profit every year in the NU except their last, including one of £1,319 in 1900, by 1904 they were still £7,000 in debt.[110] It is also probable that those who lent the club the money to buy the ground – three knights of the realm, a local MP, a colonel who was also a companion of the order of Bath, and two local firms – no longer felt the same attachment to a club that had ceased to be the embodiment of the town's leadership and their civic values, as it had been when they first lent the money. Public subscriptions and bazaars were held to reduce the debt, but they only made a small dent. In an example of how profit maximisation did not operate as the driving principle of the NU, the club never considered selling off the adjoining cricket pitch, despite the fact that cricket invariably made a loss and attracted generally woeful gates; in 1904 only £70 was taken during the entire cricket season. To have sold off the cricket pitch would have deprived Bradford of its county cricket ground, an unthinkable option that would have been a disastrous blow to the prestige and civic standing of the town throughout Yorkshire.[111]

Indeed, it was the desire for social prestige combined with the club's long-term economic problems that underpinned the eventual split. The success of Manningham's switch to soccer and the national attention it brought to the town was felt deeply by the Bradford committee, accustomed to being the city's premier sporting club. When viewed in the context of the NU's increasing marginalisation and its image as a purely working-class sport, the pressure to act became intolerable, regardless of the club's winning of the Challenge Cup in 1906. This sense of thwarted social superiority was captured by Mr H. Geldard of the club committee when he stated that 'the downfall of the Northern Union game had been brought about by the election of men from small unknown places to represent the Union'.[112] But the club itself was deeply split about the course it should take. Led by former player Laurie Hickson and the Reverend J. E. Leighton, the club committee voted in December 1906 to leave the NU unless it reverted to RFU rules – which was clearly impossible – and Hickson received assurances from the RFU that the club would be welcomed back with open arms, although not the players because they were professionals.[113] Three months later, it was reported that the committee were in favour of applying to join the Football League and a special meeting of members was called to vote on the future of the club. After acrimonious debate the meeting ignored the committee's vote for soccer and voted to return to the RFU by 'a good majority'. Unimpressed by the decision of the meeting, the committee sent out voting papers to members, which resulted in a majority for soccer, and a week later had the members' meeting declared illegal and contrary to the club's articles of association. On 7 May the Finance and Property Committee, the club's ultimate decision-making body, voted 18–2 to switch to soccer, 'recognising that association is the best paying game from a financial point of view'. The die was now cast, despite a rearguard action by NU supporters, who three weeks later founded Bradford Northern at a meeting of 300 people. Bradford's difficulties were not over however; their application to join the Football League was rejected and, to prevent their venture being stillborn, they successfully applied to join the Southern League, along with the newly formed Oldham Athletic. Ironically, in view of the club's quest to recapture its social standing of the 1880s, throughout its life as a soccer club it was destined to play second fiddle to Bradford City until its eventual demise in 1974.[114]

Because it was expected, Bradford's breakaway came as something of a relief to the NU. Indeed, it had come out of the episode relatively well, with a new club, a committed layer of supporters and the district league unscathed by the machinations of the senior clubs. Just as important, Bradford had not been joined by other clubs, despite the prevalent rumours that Leeds, who shared many of the same aspirations and dissatisfactions with the NU's direction, would follow them. Despite club president Joshua Sheldon's desire to return to the RFU fold, economic reality and the election of Leeds City AFC to the Football League in 1905 dictated that Leeds would remain a NU club, because, as Sheldon himself admitted: 'something more than the game as played by rugby union clubs was required.'[115] In short, the Headingley grounds could only remain open through the regular cash flow provided by the NU club: without it, the grounds, and in particular the nationally renowned cricket pitch, would close.

Other signs of demoralisation within the NU seemed to have dissipated too. Hull and Barrow had raised the question of opening discussions with the RFU in 1905 but had received no support – indeed, by mid-decade the NU probably had more adult clubs affiliated to it than the RFU.[116] As the first decade of the twentieth century passed its mid-point, the NU, buffeted by a world that was forcing it to change and abandon its old certainties, stood at a crossroads.

Chapter 6

A revolution in rugby: 1905–1910

Late Victorian and Edwardian working-class life was, it has often been argued, a 'life apart'.[1] The rapid expansion of trade unionism and the concomitant anti-trade union measures of the early 1900s led to social and political tensions unparalleled since the age of the Chartists in the 1840s. The formation of the Labour Party in 1900 marked the organisational break of the trade union movement from its long-standing political alliance with the Liberal Party. As the middle classes moved out of the towns and cities and into the suburbs, the working classes found themselves segregated by geography. Exclusive middle-class leisure activities, such as golf and tennis, grew in popularity and served to further increase the division between the classes in the social sphere. In a sense, the turn of the century was marked by a return to the harsher, more adversarial social climate of the mid-nineteenth century, when the lack of contact between the classes had been one of the spurs to the creation of the rational recreation movement. But unlike earlier times, there was no movement of sections of the middle classes attempting to bridge that gulf. Despite differences of degree and regional variations, the working class increasingly occupied a sphere of existence outside of the knowledge and experience of the middle classes. Not only were the classes segregated, they were also alienated from each other. As Ross McKibbin has argued:

> the British ideology, for in effect that is what it was, ensured a high degree of social cohesion but not social integration. Associations, groups and classes lived and let live; they knew there were certain boundaries that could not be crossed and rights which could not be infringed.[2]

The chasm between the classes was brilliantly illuminated by the consequences of the split in rugby. In the decade following the rift, the social nature of rugby in the North changed dramatically. Public and grammar school old boys took refuge in the exclusivity of the rugby union, many of the civic worthies formerly associated with rugby transferred their patronage to soccer and by 1905 the Northern Union itself had been almost entirely deserted by the manufacturing and professional middle classes that were the backbone of northern rugby in the 1880s and 1890s. As we saw earlier in the discussion on the North/South divide in rugby, the 1895 split was not about southern gentry and northern industrialists: the supporters of the RFU had as many, and probably more, industrialists and textiles manufacturers in their camp as the splitters. In fact, the NU found it extremely difficult to stem the haemorrhage of the middle classes, and especially the employing classes, from the game. As Table A.8 of the Appendix demonstrates, factory owners actually made up a very small percentage of the leadership of the NU. The handful of manufacturers who joined the NU, with the exception of Huddersfield's William Hirst, had not played prominent leadership roles in rugby union previously and the four included in Table A.8 – Hirst, John Clifford, Richard Collinge and Harry Waller – had all left the NU General Committee by 1906, although Clifford was appointed joint manager of the first NU tour to Australia in 1910.[3] The majority of the leaders of the NU were in fact drawn from the lower middle classes, especially smaller retailers such as publicans and shop owners, and, to a lesser extent, the 'respectable' upper working classes.

A similar pattern can be found in Table A.9 of the Appendix, which gives details of shareholders in NU clubs – although the Leeds club, formed at the height of rugby's cross-class popularity in 1890, unsurprisingly shows a significant variation – and in Greenhalgh's analysis of Northern Union club directors, where he found almost two-thirds could be classified as proprietors, publicans or skilled proletarians. As if to underline the NU leadership's confinement to the less socially prestigious sections of the middle classes, the two schoolmasters who were members of the NU committee were teachers at board and church schools, rather than middle-class private schools. Indeed, most of the listed occupations entailed continuous contact with the working classes through shops, pubs and schools, not to mention foremen and managers, and were part of the daily structure of working–class life. As Robert Roberts pointed out in his description of working-class life in Edwardian Salford, publicans and shopkeepers were commonly viewed as members of the highest echelons of the working class, rather than belonging to the middle classes.[4] But even if not of working-class origin themselves, the day-to-day economic interests of the proprietors and retailers who led the NU meant that they were less liable to join the flight from the sport of the more socially illustrious members of the middle classes.

The social composition of the NU leadership also helps to explain the development of a distinct and separate ideology of the sport, with its emphasis on the supposed rights of players and its self-proclaimed democracy, which was to prove as deep-going and durable, and almost as capable of international diffusion, as the RFU's commitment to amateurism. In part, this was a reflection in microcosm of a broader social shift affecting the northern middle classes at the turn of the century, which, as John Walton describes in the case of Lancashire:

> left Liberalism and Dissent increasingly, though never exclusively, the preserve
> of the smaller and newer employers, the shopkeepers, traders and artisans, and
> the politically articulate segments of the working class, [and] was matched by

a growing tendency to cultural homogeneity among late Victorian and Edwardian urban elites.[5]

Much of the NU's ideology had been carried over from the rhetoric of the campaign for broken-time, which sought to place the working man on an equal footing with middle-class players. The NU was also forced to accept the way its opponents portrayed it as a sport fit only for the working classes, a view most graphically expressed in 1903 by Crawford Finlay, the Scottish rugby union referee, who 'was surprised that Wales selected miners, steelworkers and policemen for their international teams and suggested that these players should join the Northern Union'.[6] The NU's attempts at expansion in the latter half of the Edwardian period were explicitly based on forming clubs that would appeal to the working class – the initiators of the Coventry NU club in 1909 were said to 'propose catering for the working class population with the offer of single shares of one pound'.[7] This ideology was acceptable to the leaders of the NU because of the position they occupied in society – as members of the lower middle classes, they desired opportunities for themselves greater than their economic power could provide (hence, in many cases, their involvement in the sport), and were frustrated by the power exerted over their lives by those with greater access to privilege and power.

But despite its emphasis on equality, the NU's ideological framework had nothing to do with socialist, or even trade union-based, ideas. Indeed, it was oppositional only to the extent that the stance of others, and in particular the RFU, forced it to oppose the status quo. Unlike that of amateurism, the NU's ideology was inclusive, in that it sought to include all sections of society in the sporting life of the nation. In this, to expand on Walton's observation, it followed Gladstonian Liberalism, with its belief in the removal of all barriers that affected political, liberal or economic life. Gladstone's rallying cry of 1865, 'the interest of every class is to have justice done to all' would have served equally well as the NU's motto.[8] This was no accident. While it would be an exaggeration to say that the 1895 split divided the leadership of northern rugby into Tory supporters of the RFU and Liberal supporters of the NU, there is some truth in this statement. Harry Waller, the NU's founding president, was a prominent member of the Liberal Party in West Yorkshire. Waller's successor as president, Warrington's James Warren, was also a member of the Liberal Party, as was the president for the 1904–05 season, Rochdale's Richard Collinge, who, like Waller, was a textile manufacturer. By contrast, the NU's most vigorous opponents in the RFU were Tories: James Higson, Harry Garnett, Barron Kilner and Mark Newsome (the latter three being personifications of the gruff northern businessman stereotype), as well as Rowland Hill and Arthur Budd in the South, were all leading members of their local Conservative Parties.[9] This scenario was played out on a local level in 1897 at Wakefield Trinity, where club secretary and Liberal councillor J. H. Fallas no doubt took great pleasure in informing the club's former chairman, and future Tory town mayor, Barron Kilner that his name was to be 'struck from the list of vice-presidents and that he be asked to return his membership ticket'. A similar split took place in Manchester in 1895 when Broughton Rangers, with strong links to their local Liberal Party, joined the NU, while Salford, with equally strong connections to the Conservative Party, initially stayed loyal to the RFU.[10]

The socialist movement took little interest in rugby or in the NU, with the exception of A. A. Sutherland's football column in Robert Blatchford's *Clarion*, despite the fact that the Independent Labour Party's birthplace was the Bradford and Keighley area of West Yorkshire and that Salford was one of the strongholds of H. M. Hyndman's Social Democratic Federation. To a large extent this was due to the fact that the majority of British socialists viewed professional sport through the same spectacles as the supporters of amateurism, seeing it as a commercially inspired corruption of play.[11] In contrast, it was not unknown for players to organise benefit matches for striking workers. Dicky Lockwood was involved, along with Castleford's Harry Speed and Halifax's Fred Firth, in organising games to raise funds during the 1897–98 engineering employers' lock-out, and Speed, a surface worker at Glasshoughton Colliery and a local independent councillor of Liberal sympathies, also organised games for striking miners. Even so, there is no evidence that the NU game or its ideology became seen as a component of broader working-class political activity. While there was an overwhelming consciousness of class within the culture of the sport, there was no class consciousness that saw the working class having interests fundamentally opposed to capitalism – at best there was a belief that rugby demonstrated how society was divided into 'us and them'.

To take as a point of departure the work of Patrick Joyce, the culture and customs of the NU became a component of the 'master narrative' of the working classes, a confirmation in sporting terms of how the 'true people' of England had been excluded from their birthright. It is striking how, in the discourses of almost all of those connected with the game, the dominant theme is the identification of themselves as ordinary people or decent Englishmen who, to borrow Joyce's words, 'showed respect and [were] respected but who were yet refused their proper place in the scheme of things'.[12] For the supporters of the NU that feeling was especially acute, for they had almost taken their proper place at the high table of rugby union, only to be driven from it by those who were, in their eyes, less worthy than themselves – hence the overwhelming desire of the NU to stress their honesty as opposed to the RFU's hypocrisy. This, in turn, intersected the NU's confinement to the northern counties of England and fed into what Joyce has called 'a radical populism conceiving of the true England as the industrial north in struggle with Privilege'.[13] Thus the NU combined a parochialist pride in its 'Northernness' with a belief that the wider world was not as it should be. It was through these processes that the NU became to its players and supporters one of the many elements of working-class cultural activity that were largely sealed off from the rest of society but whose uniqueness and underlying values were an important factor in the development and articulation of working-class identity in the communities where the game was played.

The game and its supporters

Throughout the early 1890s, Lancashire and Yorkshire rugby union crowds were drawn from all sections of the local community, from the gentry to factory workers. 'It was very agreeable,' said one correspondent about the 1891 Yorkshire Cup final 'to notice doctors, lawyers, parsons and even the magistracy swelling the immense crowd by their presence'.[14] But the 1895 secession was the catalyst for the flight of much of the middle class from mass spectator rugby. Although available evidence makes this impossible to quantify, contemporary commentators were agreed on the growing absence of the middle classes from rugby grounds. Just a year after the split, it was noted that:

> the 'tone' of football is being gradually but perceptibly lowered. . . . The repeated scenes of rowdyism, the hooting and coarse language that also too often disgrace the public part of football enclosures are likewise driving away self-respecting patrons of the game week by week.

By 1899 *Yorkshire Chat* could argue that:

> I doubt if anyone will venture to deny that the tone of Yorkshire football has lowered distinctly during the past decade. 'Gentlemen Players'. . . are very few at the present time, and so are spectators from the ranks of the middle and upper classes. It is a pity.[15]

This contraction of its social base of support does not appear to have led to a long-term decline in attendances compared to pre-1895 levels. In fact, the NU's problem was that, overall, average crowd sizes remained relatively static and did not expand in the dramatic fashion of soccer. This point was captured by the chairman of Leigh in 1906 when he remarked that the population of the town had increased by 50 per cent since 1890 yet his club's attendances had not grown at all – indeed, in their championship-winning season of 1905–06, the side had an average attendance of just 3,176.[16] However, for important matches, especially those in the latter stages of the Challenge Cup or the Championship race, the drawing power of NU clubs easily exceeded what they had experienced before the split. Before 1895, attendances of twenty thousand or more were extremely rare, but the NU recorded at least thirty-one instances before 1910, 70 per cent of them in the Challenge Cup.[17] The realisation that cup competitions generated large crowds was instrumental in the NU's decision to begin Yorkshire and Lancashire Cup competitions in 1905. With the exception of Leeds, all the major NU clubs also established new record attendances during this period. Bradford, formerly the best supported club in the rugby union, recorded their highest ever attendance of 27,000 in March 1906, ironically just a year before they abandoned the game. In November 1909, 28,600 broke the Huddersfield ground record by cramming into Fartown to see the Yorkshire Cup semi-final with Halifax. Nor had the new sport any difficulty in easily drawing in more crowds than local rugby union, most notably on one Saturday in March 1903 when 22,000 spectators watched a Hunslet versus Leeds cup tie but just 3,000 showed up to see England play The Rest in the city. Occasionally, NU games even drew larger gates than major soccer matches; for example, in 1909 22,000 people watched that year's NU Yorkshire Cup final, almost three times as many as those at the previous week's England versus Ireland soccer international at Elland Road. But these large crowds were the exception rather than the rule, and average club attendances rarely exceeded ten thousand.

Like the playing personnel of the Northern Union, the game's spectators were drawn very largely from the working class. Again, lack of data makes this impossible to quantify, although there is some evidence that can give an insight into the composition of crowds. For example, of the 800 people who attended Whitehaven's replayed Challenge Cup tie with Idle in 1902, 582 of them were miners, fully 72.75 per cent of the entire crowd. In 1901, season ticket holders at Hull FC fell from 1454 to 992, a fall blamed by the club on the closure of the nearby Earle's shipyard works, 'amongst whose employees the club had a large number of supporters'.[18] Speaking at a reception for the Batley side after it had won the Challenge Cup for the second time running, the town's mayor noted that the club's supporters were predominantly working class. And from a more jaundiced perspective in 1897, James Miller denounced Northern Union spectators as 'the same crowd which formerly followed rabbit coursing, dog fighting and matters of that description'.[19] The only other statistics relating to club support are those to be found in the shareholder records of those clubs that became limited companies. While these are useful in highlighting the dominance of shopkeepers, publicans and minor employers in the control of clubs, it is impossible to gauge the relationship of such figures to the composition of crowds. Certainly, paying £1 or ten shillings for no tangible return was a luxury few working-class households could afford, and would therefore probably militate against all but the most deeply committed working-class supporter becoming a shareholder. Indeed, if a working-class family did have any spare money to spend on football, it is probably more likely that the cash would go on a season ticket, as implied by the impact of the shipyard closure on Hull FC, and which was invariably cheaper than buying a company share – for example, a Leeds season ticket for the 1896–97 season cost five shillings to stand in the uncovered terraces, reduced to three shillings and sixpence for women and boys.[20]

There is even less information on the gender breakdown of crowds. Although women made up a sizeable proportion of Lancashire and Yorkshire rugby crowds in the 1880s and early 1890s, very little reporting of their presence at matches is evident towards the end of the century. *Yorkshire Chat* in 1898 thought that there had been a decline in women spectators since the 1880s, largely because 'women will not mix amongst men who use such foul language as one hears so repeatedly at football matches'.[21] Shareholders' lists reveal a bare handful of women shareholders, most of them listed as 'married women'. Whilst the apparent decline in female attendance may well be related to the NU's lack of 'respectability', the 1890s were also a period in which women's interest in football, of whatever code, was frowned upon and mocked by football's administrators, as they sought to assert football's masculinity in a society increasingly preoccupied with preparations for, and actual participation in, war. The fact that by the turn of the century most clubs now charged women for attending games, reversing the old practice of allowing them in free, also probably had an adverse impact on their attendance. A little more can be said about the proportion of boys under fourteen who attended games, mainly thanks to Hull FC's diligent record keeping. Between 1895 and 1910, boys attending Hull FC home games amounted to between 12 and 7 per cent of the total paid admission.[22] Throughout the game, boys were commonly charged threepence, half the sixpence admission price for adults, although in 1897 the NU had ordered Rochdale Hornets to charge boys the full admission price after a referee had complained about rowdy behaviour by young spectators at the ground.

Northern Union crowds differed from soccer crowds most obviously in one key aspect. Soccer attendances were bigger. Much bigger. As can be seen from Table A.10 of the Appendix, both Bradford City and Bradford Park Avenue recorded average attendances far in excess of those in the NU, and both Hull City and Leeds City consistently exceeded those recorded for Hull FC and Leeds, although Leeds NU edged ahead slightly in their Challenge Cup-winning 1909–10 season. These latter two examples are, however, not so straightforward because both cities had more than one senior NU side, and given the success of both Hunslet and Hull KR during the mid-1900s the total number of people attending NU matches in these cities still surpassed those going to Football League games. Indeed, Hunslet, the nearest NU club to Leeds City, actually saw a rise in gate receipts in the soccer side's inaugural season.

It would therefore be too simplistic to assume that the new soccer clubs merely siphoned away supporters from their NU rivals, although this did happen to some extent. A fuller explanation of soccer clubs' larger crowds lies in the fact that they were able to tap into broader sections of the local population than their NU rivals. Although it is probably impossible to gain an accurate picture or comparison of the structure of the crowds of the two sports, we can gain an insight into their supporters by comparing the shareholders' registers of Leeds City and Holbeck NU, the original owners of City's Elland Road stadium, as detailed in Table A.11 of the Appendix. Holbeck had joined the Northern Union in 1896 and, despite being overshadowed by its rivals in the city, rapidly established itself as a middle-ranking NU side, forming a limited company in 1897 to facilitate the purchase of Elland Road. In 1904, they were runners-up in the second division but lost to St Helens in the play-off game to decide who should be promoted to the first division. They promptly resigned from the NU, whereupon Leeds City immediately acquired their ground. Although not remarked upon at the time, it cannot have been coincidence that the major shareholder in Holbeck, local foundry owner and future Lord Mayor of Leeds, Joseph Henry, also became the key director of the new soccer club. The following year, Leeds City were elected to the Football League's second division.[23]

In comparison to Holbeck, Leeds City drew far greater numbers of shareholders from the upper and professional classes, but significantly lower levels from manual workers. Holbeck, a fairly typical NU side, drew its shareholders largely from the working class and the publican/shopkeeper strata of the middle classes. Leeds City, being the only professional soccer club in the city, also had a wider catchment area than any of the local rugby clubs, each having a limited area from which to draw spectators. There is too little information to speculate with profit about possible differences between working-class NU supporters and working-class soccer supporters but, in Leeds at least, there may have been occupational differences, soccer traditionally being strong in the iron and steel industries to the south of the city. On a more general level, it is more probably a reflection of the diversity of working-class culture at the time; as others have pointed out, Hobsbawm's picture of the emergence of a unified working-class culture emerging in 1870–1914 is somewhat simplistic and, taken literally, would certainly exclude the variety of sporting affiliations that this work has sought to explore.[24] City's wealthier supporters came from similar sections of society to those that had set up rugby sides in the 1870s and 1880s – reinforcing the fact that the civic pride of the upper middle classes, such as Leeds City director N. R. Hepworth, of the mass production clothing company Hepworths, was now being expressed through the national forum of soccer. The soccer club could therefore be seen as representative of the entire city and able to command support from virtually all sections of the local community.

In general, it seems that crowd disturbances increased under the Northern Union. Certainly in comparison to Yorkshire rugby union in the decade prior to the split, disturbances were more frequent, greater in intensity and took place at more senior levels of the game. As Table A.12 of the Appendix demonstrates, in the fifteen years following the split the NU General Committee investigated no less than thirty incidents at the grounds of senior clubs, ordering disciplinary action in all but two cases. Of these disturbances, sixteen were directed at referees, eight at opposing teams and two at both, with four categorised as general 'rowdiness'. The variety of the offences against referees ranged from the largely innocuous, such as the referee who was snowballed by Bradford supporters, to the positively menacing, as experienced by Mr Slevin, the referee at the 1896 Rochdale Hornets versus Brighouse Rangers match:

> At the conclusion of the game the spectators rushed on the ground and mobbed the referee, and but for the presence of some of the players and the police and private detectives he would have been very roughly handled. He was struck several times with sticks and umbrellas, and at length hustled into the dressing room. An attempt was made to get him out of the ground by a private entrance but he was intercepted by the crowd. At last he was got into a cab, and was driven off with a detective and one of the Hornets' players.

The cab was followed by the mob and stopped, and another route had to be taken. The detective fell out of the hansom, but fortunately was not seriously hurt. The referee was afterwards driven to Heywood, a distance of three miles. In anticipation of the referee returning by train a large crowd had assembled at the railway station at Rochdale, but after waiting some time they dispersed.[25]

The throwing of stones and mud was an occupational hazard for NU referees, and many of them also had to face being punched and kicked by home supporters as they left the pitch. Nor was the experience of the unfortunate Mr Slevin unique – in March 1899 a policeman had to drive a decoy cab away from Swinton's ground in order to fool a large crowd waiting to remonstrate with the match referee. Mr Farrar, refereeing at Keighley in 1903, found himself denuded of even police protection when a certain Sergeant Dickinson took it upon himself to encourage a disgruntled crowd to exact its own justice on the official.[26] Violence directed against opposing teams usually took the form of stone throwing, either directly at the end of the match or later as they made their way from the ground. This too could range from the relatively harmless, such as the throwing of sods of earth at departing buses, to the frighteningly intimidating: leaving the Leeds Parish Church ground in 1900 Brighouse Rangers' Charlie Denham was struck by a one and a half inch steel nut and his team mate Eli Robinson was hit between the eyes by a heavy cinder. The fact that many grounds did not have dressing rooms on them, forcing teams to walk from the ground to the changing facilities (more often than not to be found in a nearby pub), unfortunately gave spectators an opportunity to harry their side's opponents at will. To counter this, the NU sought to encourage clubs to build dressing rooms on their grounds, in 1909 going so far as to order Keighley to do so as soon as possible following an assault on a visiting team. Although there are no instances of fighting between players and spectators at the senior level of the sport, such incidents were not unknown during reserve team games. In 1906, a fight broke out between players in the match between Sharlston and Wakefield Trinity 'A' team, whereupon a large number of spectators invaded the pitch, knocking one Trinity player unconscious and severely biting the hand of another. Similar scenes were witnessed the following year during a game between Huddersfield 'A' team and Stanningley.[27]

Mann and Pearce, supported by Vamplew, have identified five specific causes of crowd disorders in soccer: *frustration*, when the crowd perceives a grievance related to access to the game or the way it was played or refereed; *outlawry*, when anti-social or criminal elements are violent to property or rival supporters; *remonstration*, when disorder results from political causes; *confrontation*, those due to ethnic, religious or nationalist differences; and *expressive*, where disturbances are caused by the emotional intensity of victory or defeat.[28] Most NU crowd disturbances in the above list are directly attributable to frustration or emotion following a home side's loss, which was then directed against the referee, the opposing team or both. Whether one can distinguish precisely between the frustration and expressive categories of disorder is largely a matter of semantics. What is noticeable is the almost complete absence of attacks on rival supporters or simple acts of criminality. Unlike in the pre-1895 period, I have been unable to locate a single assault on a group of opposing supporters in the first fifteen years of the NU. This could not be through lack of opportunity. Large numbers of supporters regularly travelled to their team's away games, especially for cup ties and Christmas and Easter 'derby' games between local sides. For example, at the 1905 Challenge Cup final between Warrington and Hull KR, 10,000 people had travelled from Hull and another 5,000 from Warrington.[29] Similarly, the only recorded instance of criminal damage taking place outside of the immediate aftermath of a game took place in 1905. Leeds supporters travelling back by train from a game at Hull KR broke windows, straps and communication cords, and somehow managed to uncouple half of the carriages during a stop at Selby. Nevertheless, the local police made no arrests.[30]

The NU sought to curb crowd disorders through the closure of grounds and the fining of clubs. When they felt an offence warranted it, they would also encourage a club to take out prosecutions against spectators identified as causing trouble. As one might expect from a body keen to enhance its respectability, it paid great attention to attempts to stamp out bad language at grounds. In January 1897 the General Committee circularised all clubs with instructions to eject spectators who were being rowdy or using bad language.[31] In 1900, Mr Oakland, who was refereeing a game at Leeds Parish Church (by now a byword for the most disorderly of spectators, much to the chagrin of the institution whose name it bore), stopped play in the second half and asked the police to remove from the ground a man 'using filthy and abusive language'.[32] When a club was ordered to post notices at its ground or in its town, they invariably warned spectators to mind their language. As part of this desire to be seen as respectable, assaults on referees by spectators were treated far more harshly than similar attacks on players. For the former, as can be seen from Table A.12, the usual punishment was the closure of a club's ground for a specified period, whereas for the latter, a fine or an order to post warning notices was more likely to be handed down. But despite their best efforts, the rate at which crowd disorders were investigated by the General Committee stayed constant throughout the first fifteen years of the sport.

Why was there such an increase in crowd disorder? Other than pre-season training matches, all NU games were competitive, being played either for league points or knock-out cup advancement. This contrasted sharply with games under the rugby union regime, where until 1892 at least the majority of games were 'friendlies', and this competitiveness may well have contributed to higher levels of tension and volatility among spectators, as mistakes by referees or advantages taken by opponents could result in the loss of important matches. But this is only a partial reason, and does not explain why disorder was directed primarily at referees, less so at opposing players and rarely at rival supporters. A broader explanation may be that the referee was seen as a symbol of authority and that more generalised feelings of frustration were being vented at him.[33] The NU's claims to represent the interests of working-class players must also have had a resonance among supporters, increasing their self-confidence about their ability to influence the game – which was, in fact, no greater than it was before 1895. This contradiction between perception and reality was most readily expressed through anger towards the referee. The crowd's distrust of authority can also be seen in the alacrity with which supporters backed their clubs when the latter were faced with sanctions from the NU's ruling bodies. After being fined £60 and £50 respectively for breaches of the professional rules, both Batley and Hull KR appealed to their supporters to raise the money through public appeals. In contrast to other appeals for monetary support from clubs in times of financial difficulties, which rarely met their targets, both clubs found their appeals oversubscribed, with Hull KR supporters raising over £30 in just two days.[34] The common view of the NU game as a working-class, democratic sport would also explain the lack of violence between rival supporters, who perhaps felt a greater affinity with each other because of the sport's ideological underpinnings, as well as its emerging status as a minority taste. And, as we shall see when discussing the changing pattern of violence in the game, working-class conceptions of masculinity often involved a view of 'fairness' that was based on openness and honesty amongst each other, coupled with indifference or hostility to those in authority. Thus the culture of the game became infused with the attitudes of its working-class players and spectators, regardless of the craving for respectability of its administrators.

'A game without monotony'

The transformation of the Northern Union game from a professionalised version of rugby union into a separate and distinct sport with its own rules and playing style was a long process. The foundations for the change had been laid in the early 1890s when northern rugby clubs debated calls for a move to thirteen-a-side and consequently the 1895 split was accompanied by expectations of radical rule changes to the game. Within two weeks of its birth, the NU engaged in a deep-going discussion about the future direction of the game as the Halifax and Leeds committees proposed moving to thirteen-a-side, with Leeds also calling for the abolition of the line-out and the replacement of the oval ball with a soccer-style round ball. The rationale, explained Leeds committee member Harry Sewell, was that:

> we want to do away with that scrummaging, pushing and thrusting game, which is not football, and that is why I propose to abolish the line-out and reduce the number of forwards to six. The football public does not pay to see a lot of scrummaging.[35]

Initially, the thirteen-a-side proposal was greeted with almost unanimous support, including from Yorkshire rugby union loyalists Mark Newsome and Barron Kilner, the latter claiming that former RFU president William Cail had also supported such a move in the past. The abolition of the line-out received a more mixed response, especially from the players. Dicky Lockwood wanted it replaced by a soccer-style throw-in, but many others worried that without line-outs the game would become too fast and, as Liversedge captain Ben Sharpe put it, would mean that 'the great and almost only qualification required to make an effective player would be speed'. The introduction of the round ball was opposed by almost all because of the difficulty in passing or drop-kicking it. The only advantage to the round ball was that it was easier to dribble, a skill that was then highly prized by forwards, who would attempt to break away from a scrum with the ball at their feet and dribble towards the opposition's line, gaining such momentum that only an extremely brave or foolhardy opponent would dare to recover the ball with his hands. The round ball proposal was therefore somewhat at odds with the general feeling that more should be done to give the backs greater scope, a view that was confirmed at the two experimental matches sanctioned by the NU in October and November 1895. Although they suffered because of the players' unfamiliarity with the new rules, both matches tended to give support to the thirteen-a-side proposal and underlined the possibilities for back play opened up by the abolition of the line-out, as one observer pointed out: 'The line-out must be sacrificed, not merely because it is as a rule an unattractive incident succeeded by a scrimmage, but also because it is a piece of play which is undesirable in a scientific and sportsmanlike sense.'[36]

Despite the groundswell of support for change, the NU's special general meeting in December 1895 voted decisively against any major alterations to the rules. Anticipating the future of the game by eleven years, Halifax's Joe Nicholl proposed that: 'The Rugby game of football as played by the Northern Rugby Football Union should be played by thirteen players on each side, and to consist of six forwards, two half backs, four three-quarters and one full back,' only to see his motion lost by eighteen votes to nine. In his speech, Nicholl made much of the financial savings that the reduction in players would bring but, given the self-confidence of the new organisation and its desire not to appear radical, even this appeal to monetary self-interest failed. Indeed, the Hunslet representative spoke against the motion because he felt that it would 'make a difficulty with the players,' presumably a reference to players' fears that the game would become too fast.[37] The one rule change to which the meeting agreed was the introduction of 'the half back rule', which forced scrum-halves to stay behind their forwards until after the ball came out the scrum, in order to stop the constant obstruction by the scrum-halves that was a feature of rugby union scrums.

With hindsight, it is clear that the NU's failure to grasp the nettle cost them dearly over the coming years. At the end of the first season, concern was expressed at the lack of tries scored by clubs, no side averaging more than nine points per game, and the following year saw the reduction in value of all goals to two points, regardless of how they were scored. This placed the emphasis firmly on the scoring of tries, which brought three points, and, unlike in the rugby union game, were now more valuable than any form of goal. Nevertheless, the problems caused by the domination of the game by forward play continued to haunt the sport. At the same time as the value of goals was reduced, the line-out was abolished and replaced by a punt-out from touch, whereby a ball going over the touchline would be kicked back into play. Although this was felt to open up greater possibilities for attractive play, it more often than not produced speculative high kicks into opposition territory, increasing the possibilities of illegal charging and rough play, which, because of the difficulty in gathering such a ball, resulted in either a scrum or a penalty – exactly the same criticism made of the line-out.[38] Just two years after its introduction, the NU general meeting discussed replacing the punt-out with a scrum, a proposal which was finally introduced in 1902. While the replacement of the punt-out by the scrum removed the scrappy play that the former had brought, it also drastically increased the amount of scrummaging in the game, a problem that had been exacerbated even further by an 1899 rule change, which decreed that if a tackled player could not release the ball, a scrum had to be formed. The combination of these rules led to matches like Hunslet's 1902 encounter with Halifax, in which there were 110 scrums.[39] It was even claimed that the excessive amount of scrummaging in the game was turning young players towards soccer.[40] Indeed, the same criticisms of the game were being made as had been of rugby union in the 1890s, one spectator claiming that the 1905 Challenge Cup semi-finals and final:

> were between clubs which are supposed to play the most attractive style of football and yet they were simply one succession of scrummages from beginning to end, with very few redeeming features to break the monotony. If it had not been that the results of theses matches were important I can scarcely imagine people remaining to see the finish.... Northern Union football is being completely ruined by the almost incessant scrummaging, which under present rules not only takes place, but is to a large extent unavoidable.[41]

Although they do not appear to have been aware of it, the NU was wrestling with the same problem as had been faced by American football after it had discarded rugby union rules in the 1870s – how to get the ball back into action after play had broken down. In the US the solution had been found in the invention of the 'snap' at the line of scrimmage, itself a sort of ersatz scrum, but NU thinking was at that time based on traditional rugby union beliefs, which saw the struggle for possession of the ball as being as of equal importance as the use of the ball once possession had been gained.[42] Many in the NU therefore thought that the way to decrease the number of scrums was simply to reduce the number of forwards on the field, which would allow backs more room to use the ball. In December 1900, Halifax and Oldham played an experimental twelve-a-side game and, gradually, twelve-a-side became the norm for schools and workshop competitions. In 1901 a twelve-a-side England versus Wales match was played as a testimonial for Broughton Rangers' Evan James and in June 1903 the

NU General Committee voted in favour of teams of twelve, made up of six forwards, two half-backs, three three-quarters and a full-back. 'The essence of our existence is a game without monotony', said Hull chairman C. E. Simpson in support of the changes.[43] At that year's annual general meeting, Widnes's J. H. Smith moved the motion for change, noting that forwards had become scrummaging machines and that defences were so well organised that 'it was almost impossible to break through,' ending with the observation that 'a reduction in players was imperative as long as they wished to hold their own with the association code'.[44] Despite a majority of fifty-four votes to twenty-four, the motion failed by just five votes to gain the requisite three-quarters majority to enter the rule book. Even so, it was agreed to allow county and junior league games to play twelve-a-side and by the beginning of the 1904–05 season, virtually every NU competition except the Northern Rugby League and the Yorkshire Senior Competition played under twelve-a-side rules.[45]

The decision not to radically change the playing of the game left the NU in limbo: it was neither satisfied with what it had nor prepared to initiate radical change. Into this vacuum came suggestions that the NU should revert to rugby union rules. This had been reflected in Barrow and Hull's 1905 desultory call to open discussions with the RFU but was pursued in earnest by Bradford in 1906 when they proposed a complete return to RFU rules, with the sole exception of the NU's half-back rule. Largely motivated by the club's disenchantment with the NU, it was also partly inspired by the impact of that season's historic rugby union tour of the British Isles by the New Zealand All Blacks, who, claimed Bradford's Fred Lister, had demonstrated 'what fine football could be produced with fifteen-a-side'.[46] When it convened in June 1906 the NU AGM was therefore confronted with four different motions to determine its future direction: Bradford's embrace of RFU rules, Whitehaven Recreation's call for twelve-a-side, Warrington and Leigh's advocacy of thirteen-a-side and St Helens' previously unheard of proposal for fourteen-a-side. Indicatively, no-one called for a continuation of the status quo. After a decade of indecision, thirteen-a-side was adopted by forty-three votes to eighteen with very little controversy – in moving the motion Harry Ashton of Warrington stated that the change would introduce a better, faster game and 'in addition, it would mean a saving of fully £100 a year to many clubs'.[47]

In order to solve the problem of endless scrummaging, the meeting also voted to introduce a new rule for playing the ball after a tackle. Now, instead of a scrum being formed, the tackled player was allowed to get to his feet, put the ball down in front of him and play it with his foot, usually to a team mate standing behind him. Although this was seen as a reversion to an old rugby union rule, whereby the tackled player had to use his feet when releasing the ball while still on the ground, it actually marked a revolution in the game as profound as the switch to thirteen-a-side.[48] As with American football, the NU had accepted that the struggle for possession of the ball was secondary to the use of the ball in open play. The new 'play-the-ball' rule meant that the skills of scrummaging, although still important, were now subordinated to those of passing and running with the ball. In 1908, as if in afterthought, the break with the past was formalised when Law One was changed from that of rugby union, 'the object of the game shall be to kick the ball over the crossbar and between the posts' to 'the object of the game shall be to cross an opponents goal-line to score tries and kick the ball over the crossbar and between the posts'.[49] The adoption of the thirteen-a-side and play-the-ball rules, combined with the earlier elevation of tries above goals, marked a decisive rupture with the old rugby game and created the distinct and separate sport of Northern Union football. The impact of this revolution became obvious as soon as the 1906–07 season began – over 800 points were scored in the first two weeks of the season, far and away a NU record, and an *Athletic News* headline was able to proclaim boldly: 'The New Rules Completely Vindicated.'[50]

The fundamental nature of the change that had taken place was widely recognised, not least by the 1906 South African rugby union tourists, whose officials gracelessly took the opportunity of the post-match meal after their game against Yorkshire at Headingley to attack the sport of their hosts, calling it 'the revised version of Rugby football – which, it cannot be too often insisted upon, is not Rugby football at all'. *The Times* claimed that Northern Union football was 'an incoherent parody of rugby football'.[51] In this, they echoed earlier critics of the NU's rule innovations, such as Arthur Budd and Frank Mitchell who had seen such changes as departures from the traditional playing philosophy of rugby. Budd had denounced the NU's diminution of the value of goals in 1897, reasoning that:

> the very fact that try-getters are plentiful while goal-droppers are scarce shows that the latter art is very much more difficult of acquirement. Now this being so, why, I should like to ask, ought the more skilful piece of play to be depreciated, while a premium is placed on mere speed of foot?[52]

Frank Mitchell felt that line-outs had been discarded simply because Northern working-class players were not up to them: 'the Northern players are so bad out of touch that the law was infringed in every instance and scrummages were constantly necessary,' and went on to dismiss the NU's other changes by saying that 'the play of the working classes has not, on the whole, gained one whit in the finer points which distinguish the intelligent player from him who relies on his stamina and physique'.[53]

Other rugby union supporters were not so condemnatory. The Reverend E. H. Dykes, the founder of Leeds Parish Church FC and committed advocate of muscular Christian amateurism, expressed his admiration of the NU style of rugby; of the four reasons given by Elland rugby union club as to why they were switching codes the first was that the new 'game was more open and pleasant to watch'. In 1909, the secretary and committee of the Coventry rugby union club, recently suspended by the RFU amidst allegations of professionalism, saw their first Northern Union game and were amazed: 'The swiftness of the play quite carried them away; nothing like it had ever before been seen... it was in fact, regarded as a more scientific game than is seen under ordinary rugby rules, except on rare occasions.'[54] A similarly effusive reaction was also experienced by a reporter on the London *Daily Graphic*, who travelled 'up North' to watch the 1910 Challenge Cup final.

> The spirit of Rugby is not dead, nor does it sleep. The true spirit of Rugby is as alive as ever in England, and the ancient glamour of a glorious old sport has not yet departed from the hearts of the people. A journey to Huddersfield on Saturday, where Hull and Leeds fought out a gallant struggle for the much coveted honour of the Northern Union Cup, would have been sufficient to convince any reasonable person of this fact. . . . It was a thrilling and delightful spectacle.[55]

For the NU leadership, the 1906 rule changes were also recognised as being a watershed and, once initial scepticism had died down, they celebrated their innovation. 'The game as now played,' said Hunslet's T. V. Harrison, 'was the best that had ever been played by either the Northern Union or the Rugby Union.' Leeds vice-president J. W. Wood echoed this, declaring that 'the rules of the Northern Union were the best ever seen in the rugby game', while NU president J. B. Cooke cast aside modesty and congratulated 'the men who had been connected with the NU. Through many bitter criticisms, they had brought forward the finest game of Rugby football that had ever been conceived.'[56]

The new game was certainly faster, more open and greatly exciting, but had it become 'more dangerous and less enjoyable to the players' in order to be 'brisker and more enjoyable to the man behind the ropes' as was claimed by its amateur critics?[57] The little evidence we have from players would suggest not. The concerns of many players in 1895 that the game would become too fast seem to have disappeared by the 1906 reduction in team size, although the introduction of the punt-out in 1898 led to some disquiet about the amount of off-the-ball charging that accompanied it.[58] But it seems that most players welcomed the opportunities to run with the ball in their hands that had been opened up by the NU rule changes: Albert Goldthorpe, Yorkshire county representative at both games felt that:

> the alteration of the rules has made accidents to players less liable, especially so when the referee rules with a stern hand; and, so far as I am concerned, I can assure you that I prefer the Northern Union in every way to the fast declining old Yorkshire rugby union.[59]

Hull captain C. C. Lempriere, one of the few public-school-educated players to welcome the formation of the NU, compared the new game with the developments in soccer: 'In four years [the Northern Union] has made rapid strides; she is becoming scientific and skilful too.'[60]

Certainly deaths in Northern Union matches were less frequent than in rugby union games in Yorkshire before the split. As can be seen from Table A.13 of the Appendix, of the twelve deaths recorded between 1895 and 1910, only three took place at senior level, the remainder occurring in junior leagues. Two of those deaths, of Green and Hanson, were not directly attributable to the playing of the game: Green died of lockjaw that set in after he had been injured in a match and the unfortunate Hanson became possibly the only man ever to die of drowning during a football match when he tried to rescue the ball from a nearby canal and fell in. The most famous death was that of Cumberland county full-back John Richardson, who died playing against Yorkshire at Headingley. According to match reports, the fatal injuries were sustained when Richardson ran into one of his own players when trying to field a high ball. Discounting these latter three incidents, the aggregate nine deaths in fifteen years represents a significant decrease from the period of rugby union rules examined in Chapter 4.

What of non-fatal injuries and players subjected to disciplinary measures because of rough play? As with the rugby union period, there is no way of discovering the number or extent of injuries to players. Harry Waller certainly tried to make capital out of the lack of rough play in the NU compared to Yorkshire rugby union. Speaking after the first Challenge Cup final in 1897, he claimed that in 900 games that season, the NU had only forty-five players (thirty in Yorkshire and fifteen in Lancashire) reported by referees for rough play, whereas the YRU had 150 players reported for roughness during the same season. 'Not bad for uneducated working-man players,' he was moved to say sarcastically.[61] The following season he presented a more detailed breakdown of players reported by referees in the NU version of the Yorkshire Senior Competition. In 480 games thirty-four players had been reported, of which seven were acquitted, twelve found guilty of rough play and fifteen of 'foul charging', most of which were probably committed during the rushes to catch the ball following a punt-out.[62] However, figures from 1903–04, the first season for which reliable Northern Union General Committee minutes can be found relating to disciplinary offences, paint a less rosy picture. In 647 senior games played, 111 players were reported by referees for a variety of offences, the majority of which, eighty-seven, were for kicking, striking, fighting or wrestling with an opponent. As can be seen from Table A.14 of the Appendix, ten were for acts of rough play, six were for arguing or insulting the referee and four were for tripping. Compared with broadly equivalent figures for Yorkshire rugby union in the 1890–91 season (see Chapter 4), these figures indicate a steep decline in incidences of rough play and dissenting from referee's decisions. Whereas in the 1890–91 season these offences constituted almost 65 per cent of the total reported, by 1904 they had plummeted to just over 16 per cent. In contrast, individual acts of violence between players had increased dramatically. Why this should be so is unclear. It may be the case that definitions of offences altered over time and that what was once rough play was now defined as, for example, wrestling, but it is unlikely that such a change would have led to such a dramatic shift. More likely, the growth of individual violence was perhaps linked to the increased effectiveness of tackling and defensive tactics of NU teams, giving more scope for individual clashes. The rise may also have been due to the 'proletarianisation' of the sport and the emergence of working-class conceptions of masculinity within it. Certainly, within rugby league up to the 1970s, it was common for games to start with a 'softening up period' during which the opposing forwards would seek to physically intimidate their opposite numbers through fair and, more often than not, foul means. One-to-one confrontations to establish physical domination in a particular position were expected. Striking an opponent, although illegal, was seen as semi-legitimate because it was done in the open and no subterfuge was involved, yet tripping was viewed as being beyond the pale because of the danger to a man running with the ball. Punching was not necessarily an offence for which the culprit would be sent off, tripping inevitably resulted in dismissal. The rise in individual violence in 1903–04, coupled with the disproportionately small percentage of tripping offences, may well indicate that traditional rugby league conceptions of masculinity and violence held sway less than a decade after the birth of the game.[63] The revolution in rugby had taken place not only in the NU's rule book, but also in its culture.

What does this tell us about the application of Norbert Elias's theory of the 'civilising process' to the development of rugby?[64] In *Barbarians, Gentlemen and Players*, his followers Eric Dunning and Ken Sheard claim that the NU leadership believed 'the roughness of rugby league to be one of its most problematic aspects'.[65] But as we have seen in Chapter 4, rugby in the north of England under union or league rules was no more and no less violent than in any other region. Nor was violence confined to the lower classes. The 'half-back rule', the playing rule to be changed by the NU in 1895, which Dunning and Sheard claim was introduced to reduce the high levels of violence in the game, was actually brought in to open up play by giving the scrum-half the opportunity to pass the ball quickly away from the scrum without interference from his opposite number, in some ways anticipating the measures taken by the RFU in the inter-war years to eradicate 'wing-forward' play at the scrum. Indeed, William Cail proposed in 1902 that the RFU should adopt the rule in order to 'popularise' its game and make it more attractive in the face of threats from soccer and the NU.[66]

Dunning and Sheard also claim that evidence 'that rugby league remained physically dangerous comes from the fact that, in 1910, the Essex and Suffolk Insurance Company refused to continue insuring players'. In fact this had nothing to do with violence in the game but was brought about by the 1906 Workmen's Compensation Act. The act, which among other things extended compensation for injuries sustained at work to professional soccer and rugby footballers, significantly increased the potential benefits payable to employees injured at work. The small pool of professional football clubs of both codes meant that insurance companies put themselves at considerable risk if faced with paying compensation out on an extensive scale, thus making them wary of underwriting football insurance. To counter the difficulties of finding affordable insurance, the Football League, along with the Southern League and the Scottish Football League, formed the Football Mutual Insurance Federation (FMIF) in 1907. The reluctance of the insurance companies to insure footballers was confirmed to some extent by the fact that in the 1910–11 season the FMIF made a loss of £200, leading to the Football League starting a new insurance federation in 1912.[67]

The minutes of the Northern Union meeting at which the insurance problem was discussed, which are cited in *Barbarians, Gentlemen and Players*, note the similar experiences of the soccer authorities:

> The Secretary reported that the Essex & Suffolk Insurance Company refuse to continue Football Insurance, and that he could not get any of the strong offices to take it up. The question of forming a Mutual Insurance Company to take over the risks was suggested, and it was decided to leave the matter in the hands of the Emergency Committee, the Secretary in the meantime to get in touch with Mr J. Bentley [a president of the Football League and vice-president of the FA], with respect to the Mutual Insurance Company formed by the Association League.[68]

This is indeed what happened and a mutual insurance scheme was set up by the NU later that month. As an indication of the levels of payments made to injured players, it is worth examining how much was actually paid out in insurance claims at this time. In the three years before Essex and Suffolk stopped insuring rugby league players, total sums of £17, £12/6s and £18/8s/4d were paid to injured players, amounts which hardly suggest huge numbers of players being laid low by on-field acts of violence.[69]

In fact, when examined properly, none of the examples used by Dunning and Sheard indicate an unusually large amount of violence in rugby league. While it is undoubtedly true that the game could be violent, there is no evidence to suggest that it was more violent than any other code of football. Indeed, using Dunning and Sheard's theory of the 'civilising process', one could easily argue that the NU authorities' rule changes were aimed at civilising rugby *union*. The move to thirteen players per side and the abolition of the dangerous rucks and mauls in favour of the more orderly play-the-ball after a tackle, suggests a very strong case in favour of the argument that the abandonment of rugby union rules and the evolution of the distinctive rugby league rules represented the creation of a more civilised form of rugby. But the theory of the 'civilising process' prevents its followers from making this argument, because in the Eliasian worldview the 'civilising process' always flows downwards from the upper classes, leading to the automatic assumption that the predominantly working-class Northern Union form of rugby is more violent than rugby union.

And of course, the definition of 'civilised' modes of behaviour also depends on a set of value judgements that differ from era to era, country to country, class to class, and so on. Not to mention the fact that, to the historian, the thesis appears to suggest a teleological 'Whig interpretation of sports history' in which sports gradually evolve to a plateau of peaceful competition. So when applied to rugby, the evidence hardly seems to fit neatly into the theory, even if one leaves aside the virtual impossibility of quantifying incidents of injury and violence. While deaths decreased in the NU, individual violence between players increased. And, as referees of the time could testify, crowd behaviour also appeared to become less 'civilised'. Yet, paradoxically, the players believed that the game was less dangerous than under rugby union rules. Individual violence between players was not viewed as 'uncivilised' by the NU's supporters; the fact that it was controlled, in the open and confined to the playing arena demonstrated that it was merely part of a game. In fact, it was the rucking and mauling of rugby union, with its opportunities for stamping anonymously on one's opponents – acts that were anathema in the league game – that came to be seen as gratuitously violent by rugby league people. The concept of the 'civilising process' also ignores changes in modes of play and the impact of medical improvements in treating injuries and their effects. Rather than being part of an historic process, violence within rugby, as we have constantly seen throughout this work, was to a large degree defined by the cultural context of those who were doing the defining.

1907: The world turns upside down

If the rule changes of 1906 had set the Northern Union on a new course, the events of 1907 saw it discover a new continent, both literally and metaphorically. Ironically, much of the impulse for the expansion of the sport into the southern hemisphere lay with the 1905 New Zealand rugby union tour of the British Isles. The All Blacks lost just one game, conceded only 39 points and racked up 830, vanquishing all the English, Scottish and Irish teams by huge margins. By laying waste to the cream of rugby union in the mother country, they had caused much soul searching among those who saw rugby as a measure of British national fitness – although the fact that the drubbings were at the hands of colonial subjects steeped in British imperial ideology helped to sweeten the pill.[70] In the southern hemisphere, the tour helped to cement the national identity of white, or *pakeha*, New Zealand, seemingly confirming the youthful vigour and optimism of the colony. The return of the side was greeted with a patriotic fervour normally associated with the return of a conquering army and the All Blacks became synonymous with the manly spirit of the furthest reaches of the British Empire.

But beneath the surface, the knots of social cohesion by which Antipodean rugby was bound were fraying. The tour had been an incredible financial success, recording a profit of £8,908.[71] Yet the players, lauded as national heroes and pioneers of a new era in rugby union, received only three shillings per day expenses. An 'Original All Black', writing in 1908, highlighted the dissatisfaction abroad.

> That they, the All Blacks, could scarcely raise £10 in the whole team on their return passage home to New Zealand is well known, and the fact made a great

impression in colonial circles. This brought the question before the colonial public and it was generally admitted that the team were not well treated. Several were men of means, and could well afford the loss of time, but the majority were working men.[72]

Not only that, but the levels of disquiet among the players were matched by the tour's confirmation that rugby could be a profitable business. The New Zealanders had also witnessed at first hand that the Northern Union not only paid players but attracted much larger crowds than the vast majority of rugby union clubs in Britain. They had seen that there was an alternative way for rugby, something that was also true on the field as well as off it. It had been widely noted that the All Blacks' style of play focused on running and passing the ball in order to score tries. The traditional English rugby union style, which relied on forward play and kicking for touch to set up scrums, found little favour in New Zealand. Despite being honoured visitors from 'Home', the 1904 British tourists to New Zealand and Australia had been criticised for their negative tactics and overly rough play.[73] The Northern Union game, even before the decisive rule changes of 1906, emphasised the primacy of try-scoring, matching the instincts of wide sections of New Zealand rugby.

Similar rumblings of discontent were also being heard across the Tasman Sea in Australia, where a more ethnically diverse and urbanised working class had come to dominate the playing and watching of rugby in a way similar to that in northern England. Indeed, the development of rugby in Australia in many ways mirrored that in the north. The first recorded games of Rugby football in Sydney took place in 1865, although the earliest games of organised football in Melbourne can be traced back to 1858. Ironically, given the gulf that now separates the rugby codes from Australian rules football, it is probable that these games were played under a variation of the rules of Rugby school football, not least because Tom Wills, the man traditionally portrayed as the 'father' of Australian rules and the instigator of the codification of football in Melbourne, had been a pupil at Rugby school in the 1850s. Until the 1890s rugby in New South Wales (NSW) and Queensland, the two eastern states of Australia where the game had come to dominate, was primarily a sport for the sons of the middle classes, highlighted by the preeminence in NSW of the Sydney University club and the private schools. It was also deeply loyal to Britain and the Empire, as illustrated by the formation by ten Sydney clubs in 1874 of the Southern Rugby Football Union as the governing body for the sport, the choice of name emphasizing the Australians' belief that they were merely the most 'southern' outpost of Britain. But, as with cup competitions in Yorkshire in the 1880s, inter-colonial matches between NSW, Queensland and New Zealand stimulated public interest in the sport and were by the early 1890s attracting large crowds and increasing the numbers playing and watching rugby. In 1892 over 50,000 spectators had seen a three-match series between NSW and New Zealand in Sydney and in 1896 the NSW Rugby Union (as the Southern RFU had renamed itself in 1892) could boast seventy-five clubs in membership, many of them composed of the industrial and manual labourers of the NSW working class.[74]

As in Britain, this development had started to cause tension within the NSWRU. In order to protect its power, not to mention the large amounts of money that now flowed into its coffers from the inter-colonial matches, the NSWRU had handed over control of the Sydney club competition to a subordinate Metropolitan Rugby Union in 1897. The following year the first rumours of men paid to play rugby began to circulate and by the dawn of the new century the sport was awash with rumours of the poaching of players by clubs, violent play and social discrimination by the leading clubs against working-class players. The re-organisation of clubs into geographically defined district clubs in 1900 did little to quell the storms – indeed, by tying teams so closely to a locality the new system exacerbated the intense competition between clubs. The following year many of the more socially elite clubs opted out and formed their own City and Suburban Association, playing only friendly matches against each other and strictly safeguarding their amateur status.

To anyone with knowledge of the origins of the Northern Union, the situation in Sydney was not unfamiliar. Moreover, Australian society at the end of the Victorian era also bore similarities to the North of England, not least in the growing sense of working-class self-confidence and assertiveness. The 1880s and 1890s had seen major strikes by miners, dockers and shearers, leading a substantial growth in trade union membership. In 1899 a short-lived Labour government had been formed in Queensland. Following the depression of the late 1890s, resurgent industrial and social unrest in the 1900s had led to the establishment of a system of industrial arbitration to try and rein in working-class militancy, a process highlighted by the election of the first Australian Labour government in 1904. By 1912 almost a third of the working population was organised in trade unions.[75] Much more so than in England, where the sport's working-class roots were rarely expressed in an openly political fashion, the origins of rugby league in Australia were overtly linked to the rise of the labour movement. As Andrew Moore has pointed out, the sport was from the outset 'strongly circumscribed within a labour universe, a reflection of the self-confidence and sense of separate identity of a working-class movement recovering from the defeats of the 1890s'.[76] Harry Hoyle, who was to become the first president of the New South Wales Rugby Football League (NSWRFL), was a prominent activist in the railway workers' union and an Australian Labour Party (ALP) election candidate. Ted Larkin, the league's first full-time secretary, was elected ALP representative for Willoughby in North Sydney in 1913. Many of the founding clubs of the NSWRFL had prominent ALP or trade union leaders as committee members or patrons. Future Labour prime minister Billy Hughes was the patron of Glebe, while John Storey, who became Labour's NSW premier in 1920, was a founder of the Balmain club. In Queensland, the central figure in the split from rugby union was Jack Fihelly, a future deputy leader of the Queensland ALP and prominent Irish nationalist. By the 1930s these links with the labour movement had been deepened and extended, to the extent that between 1934 and 1950 the trophy for the winners of the Sydney club competition was provided by the *Labor Daily*, a newspaper founded by the Miners' Federation.

In the early years of the new century it became an open secret that leading players had received payment for play: for example, in 1904 Harry Hamill of the Newtown club was paid fifteen shillings by the NSW Rugby Union to play against the British touring side after he told them that he could not afford to take time off work.[77] In the same year, there had been widespread dissatisfaction in Sydney over the treatment of Alec Burdon, who had broken a shoulder playing against England but had received no insurance or compensation payments from the NSWRU, causing him significant financial hardship. Indeed, the question of compensation for injury became one of the catalysts that was to precipitate the cleavage of 1907. Just before the start of the season the Metropolitan Rugby Union voted to end its medical insurance scheme for injured players, placing the burden on the clubs. This effectively meant that the players themselves had to pay for their own insurance premiums and consequently the annual club membership fee, which had to be paid by all registered club players, rose from five to ten shillings. What made this even more galling for players was the fact that the MRU's income from matches had almost trebled between 1902 and 1906 to £3,724, owing to the growing interest in club games in Sydney, some of which could now attract gates of up to 20,000.[78] Players' resentment of their treatment at the hands of the rugby union leadership was now at breaking point. Blair Swannell, a tourist to Australia with the 1899 and 1904 British sides now living in Sydney, warned of the danger that 'the players will take the matter into their own hands, and go from one extreme to another, electing to office officials pledged to what every lover of Rugby football should strive to prevent – professionalism'.[79]

Again in contrast to Britain, there does not appear to have been any explicit attempt by rugby's leadership to drive out the predominantly working-class clubs.[80] Rather, it was the NSWRU's high-handed arrogance and indifference to the needs of players that brought about the conflict. The fact that the Northern Union existed, which paralleled the class-composition of the discontents and shared their concerns about payments and playing styles, meant that there was an alternative course that could be followed by the rebels. And at a cultural level, the meritocratic NU had more in common with the self-image of the majority of Australians than the stiff-necked amateurism of the RFU; the lower levels of social deference and the ostensibly more democratic norms of Australian society (at least for whites) meant that the rigid imposition of the amateur ethos was not possible.

However, player discontent alone was not enough to force a rupture. The satisfaction of their demands for compensation and welfare were dependent on the financial success of rugby. Indeed, as was the case in Britain, the full participation of working-class players at the highest levels of rugby was only possible through professionalism and the commercialisation of the sport. The role, therefore, of sporting entrepreneurs in the break from union to league was crucial to facilitating the commercial framework for the new venture. Indeed, the dialectic of sport, business and the working class was neatly encapsulated in the fact that the New South Wales Rugby Football League was founded in August 1907 by legendary Australian test cricketer Victor Trumper, Sydney businessman James Giltinan and Labor Party politician Harry Hoyle.

This combination of player discontent and commercial initiative also found its expression in the moves to organise a professional All Blacks' tour to Britain. Although there is no hard evidence, it appears that George Smith, the All Black winger and champion all-round athlete, stopped off in Sydney in the Spring of 1906 on his way back home from the tour and discussed the situation in Antipodean rugby and the Northern Union with his Australian rugby contacts. According to a 1928 account. Smith had actually met with the NU while on the 1905 tour and that the 1907 venture 'had really been suggested by the N.U. officials at Home [sic]'. Smith had also had the opportunity to study the NU during a visit to Britain for an athletics' meeting in 1902 and George Stephenson, a native of Otago, had played for Manningham both before and after 1895, highlighting that the new form of rugby was not an unknown quantity down under.[81] Certainly the All Blacks' return home in 1906 must have been quickly followed by discussions about the Northern Union, because barely twelve months later, in March 1907, Canterbury postal clerk Albert Baskerville blew apart the national euphoria by announcing that a professional All Black side would tour England to play Northern Union clubs. No mean player himself, Baskerville was known in New Zealand rugby for his book *Modern Rugby Football*.[82] Rugby league folklore has him picking up a stray copy of the *Athletic News* and being inspired by reports of the new union's success, but it seems that he was the public face of a significant movement of New Zealand players dissatisfied with their position and seeking to make the most of their football talents.

The response in English and New Zealand rugby circles to Baskerville's announcement could not have been greater if the Kaiser had declared himself the rightful claimant of the British crown. The New Zealand Rugby Union (NZRU) banned Baskerville from all rugby grounds in New Zealand and demanded that players nominated for that year's North Island versus South Island game sign a declaration stating that they were amateurs and had not been approached to tour. Those who actually played in the match had to affirm a further five clauses saying that they would help the rugby union authorities to identify tourists and stop the tour taking place. The Anglican Bishop of Auckland denounced the tour from the pulpit and the New Zealand Athletic Association called on the country's parliament to outlaw professional sport. In England, C. Wray Palliser, the Agent General of New Zealand in the UK, assured the RFU that any touring player would be banned from the sport and ludicrously called the tour 'some kind of sensation to save the Northern Union' which he portrayed as under threat from 'the renewal of the spirit of real Rugby'. 'It is a phantom side,' he stated with a conviction borne of ignorance and hope. For its part, the RFU announced that if there was the slightest hint of support for the tourists from the NZRU, all relations would be broken.[83]

Despite this barrage of opposition, Baskerville gained significant support from New Zealand players. Duncan MacGregor, a railway worker who had become a national hero by scoring four tries against England in the 1905 international, was one of the first players to refuse to sign the authorities' ultimatum. Twelve Auckland representative players refused to sign and Baskerville claimed to have received requests to join the tour from 160 players, including eighteen of the 1905 tourists.[84] Even the *New Zealand Post* was moved to concede that 'the promoter of the scheme in this colony has met with even more success than he anticipated'.[85] Of the twenty-eight strong party, nine were All Blacks, including four of the 1905 side, and eleven other players had gained representative honours. H. R. 'Bumper' Wright, the captain of the side – whose registered title was 'The New Zealand All Black Rugby Football Team' – was confident that his team had been picked on merit and that it was 'thoroughly representative and consists of the cream of New Zealand football'.[86]

The tourists' first stop was Sydney where, with a degree of precision that the circumstantial evidence gathered by Sean Fagan makes it difficult to imagine was not pre-planned, they became a lightning rod through which the pent-up frustration with the NSWRU was channelled.[87] In anticipation of their arrival, on 8 August 1907 the New South Wales Rugby Football League was founded, claiming the support of over 130 prominent NSW players, including Dally Messenger, the most famous rugby player in Australia. It quickly announced a three-match test series against the professional All Blacks to be played over the following two weeks. Although staged under rugby union rules because the Northern Union rule books failed to arrive in time, the test series proved to be a financial success and provided sufficient impetus for a huge swathe of Sydney's leading players to abandon rugby union for the new league at the start of the following season.[88] A new era had dawned.

One can only imagine the reaction of the marginalised and embattled Northern Union to the seismic shifts in rugby that were unfolding on the other side of the world. Much to their surprise, they now found themselves at the head of a worldwide rugby revolution. When Baskerville's proposal arrived, the NU General Committee cautiously polled clubs to see if they accepted his tour terms of £3,000 or 70 per cent of the gate receipts, whichever was higher. Of course, the enthusiasm was boundless, so much so that in May the General Committee felt compelled to warn clubs against signing any of the players while the tour was in progress.[89] When the All Blacks finally arrived in Leeds at 8pm on October 1, their reception was overwhelming. In scenes reminiscent of victorious cup winners returning home, thousands of people turned out to greet them at the city's Midland Station:

> When the players appeared the crowd burst into tremendous cheering, which continued until the men had got into their charabanc. Then Wright, the

New Zealand captain, called for 'three cheers for the people of Leeds', which were followed by the stirring Maori war-cry and further cheering. The players were escorted to the Grand Central Hotel by the Hunslet charabanc and the Northern Union officials in carriages, together with the still cheering crowd. The crush was so dense in Boar Lane and Briggate as to cause the stoppage of traffic.[90]

As the scale of the reception indicated, the tour was about much more than a team of overseas rugby players: the crowd was celebrating a triumph over the forces of the establishment. After months of disparagement and denunciations from the press, the RFU and New Zealand government officials, the tourists had arrived. The Northern Union, for years semi-pariahs in their own nation, had turned the tables on its enemies and scored a stunning victory.

The New Zealanders more than fulfilled the hopes of their hosts. Playing a sport that they had never before seen, let alone played, they were unbeaten in their first eight matches, including a famous victory over Broughton in front of 24,000 people, eventually losing at Wigan before an even bigger crowd of 30,000. They won the test series against the Northern Union but lost against both Wales and England. Despite dips in performance owing to the sheer length of their tour – it lasted five months and comprised thirty-four games – well over 300,000 people watched their matches, including 14,000 at the second test match at Chelsea's soccer ground in London.[91] When they finally began their journey back to New Zealand in February 1908, gate receipts in Britain totalled £12,625 and the tourists had a profit of £5,641 to distribute between themselves.[92]

How good were the professional All Blacks? Unfortunately, it is impossible to compare them with their 1905 forerunners, not least because the standard of opposition facing the 1907 side was far greater than anything the 1905 side encountered outside of Wales. Looking back in 1929, William 'Massa' Johnston, who toured with both sides, wrote

> Mackrell, MacGregor and [my]self, had a good idea in 1905–06 what the union players were like, but not for one moment did we think we would meet such continuous opposition as we did in 1907–08. I tell them here Jack [Wilson, the RFL secretary to whom he was writing], every match played in England is a test match . . . No place for weaklings or one who has a habit of looking for the easy or flash stuff on a football field.[93]

The 1907 side also found it difficult to adjust to NU rules, as the *Yorkshire Post* commented during the first month of the tour: 'it is the fashion to say that the difference between the Northern Union rules and the RFU rules is so slight that it can be easily overcome, but this is very far from being the case'.[94] Initially, the tourists tried to use classical New Zealand wing-forward play, only to find it useless against the wily NU forwards, and their attempts to play two five-eighths and

Figure 13 The 1907 New Zealand tourists conquer Huddersfield. Note that they are called All Blacks (from *Athletic News*, 14 October 1907).

three three-quarters suffered a similar fate. Bumper Wright, one of the most experienced of the tourists, was amazed at the defensive and scrummaging qualities of NU players. Not only that, 'for pace and cleverness, the professionals were much superior to the amateurs; in fact, as regards bustling play and determined methods there was no comparison between the two'.[95] Wright's comments were echoed by Fred Bonsor, the former Bradford half back, a stalwart of Yorkshire rugby union and no friend of the NU: unlike the 1905 side, the professional All Blacks were:

> meeting their equals at all parts of the game, and that instead of facing untrained and half-hearted amateurs, they have to tackle the cream of northern athletes … men of great physique, speed and stamina, full of resource, and up to every move on the football board.[96]

Underlining the fact that the NU was now an international force, the following season saw the first visit of an Australian touring side, inevitably nicknamed 'the Kangaroos' after they arrived at Tilbury docks with a silver grey kangaroo in tow. The tour was a victim of its own ambition – lasting six months and taking in forty-five matches, the tourists lost half their matches and made a financial loss of £418.[97] James Giltinan, tour manager and promoter, found himself declared bankrupt when he returned home. To some extent circumstances got the better of them as their tour coincided with one of the worst industrial slumps to hit the north of England in a generation, although their insistence on charging a minimum one shilling admission to all games, double the normal price, did them no favours in communities wracked by sudden unemployment. But even the hostile *Yorkshire Post* was sympathetic to their plight:

> No-one will deny that they are the unluckiest football team who have yet visited the British Isles. One match after another has been ruined by adverse weather. Rain, frost and fog have all united to make the financial success of their tour more questionable.

At just over 6,000 spectators per match, attendances averaged only two-thirds of those for the New Zealand tour, although 22,000 attended the second test match, held with expansionary zeal at Newcastle.[98] Nevertheless, by proving that the All Black tour was not a flash in the pan, the Australian tour helped to cement the NU's new found international credibility.

The defining moment of the Northern Union came in 1907. The arrival of the All Blacks, the creation of the NSW Rugby League in Australia and the formation of NU clubs in Wales, as outlined below, at last confirmed to the NU and its supporters the correctness of the course they had taken. Not only had the new rebels accepted the professionalism and playing rules of the NU, they had also accepted its ideological underpinning of equal rights for working-class players. At the welcoming dinner for the All Blacks, their spokesman, Jim Gleeson, denounced the 'pseudo-amateurs, who received their bonuses and obtained what they called in New Zealand "billets" ' and said that the tourists 'by coming into the limelight as professionals, were doing what any honest man should do'.[99] Indeed, the side itself was organised as a players' co-operative with each player contributing between £50 and £200 towards the cost of the tour and receiving an equal share of the profits, regardless of how many matches they played in. In Australia, the links between the new game and the rights of the working-class player were even more explicit: Harry Hoyle even likened the movement to the campaign for the eight-hour day.[100]

And herein lay a critical factor in the sport's success in Australia. A growing, self-confident industrialised working class in a society that lacked the caste-like social restrictions of Britain meant that the rigours of amateurism were largely incompatible with the organisation of daily life, as Harry Hoyle argued in 1907: 'the set of conditions controlling the football union are not suitable to the democracy and social conditions of the Australian people.' Although there was a rhetorical flourish to this statement, the ideology of the NU therefore fitted well with Australian society's ostensibly more egalitarian and urbanised culture and helped the new sport grow rapidly.[101] Moreover, in a society that still saw itself very strongly as British and a loyal member of the Empire, rugby league also provided an imperial link that appeared to be more meritocratic than that of the traditional British elite, as seen in cricket for example. In many ways, rugby league could be described as the most 'Australian' of sports because, unlike the geographically limited Australian rules football and the unashamedly exclusive rugby union, it bound together the two seemingly contradictory attitudes of imperial loyalty and hostility to social privilege.

However, despite its promising beginnings, rugby league in New Zealand was never to emulate Australia and eclipse rugby union. It would take another three years following the formation of the professional All Blacks for the New Zealand Rugby League to be formed and the sport remained entirely amateur until the 1980s. Partly this marginalisation was due to the 1905 All Blacks, whose success in making the country the foremost exponent of the winter game of the Empire tied rugby union closely to New Zealand national identity. This can be overstressed however; as Greg Ryan and Geoff Vincent have highlighted, rugby union was wracked with calls for reform up until the outbreak of World War One and in Auckland union's hegemony was strongly contested, and occasionally overshadowed, by league.[102] In November 1911 the RFU-loyal *Rugby Football and Cricket* confessed that it feared that New Zealand would break with the RFU, following reports that the Otago and Wanganui unions were calling for radical reform of the game. It was only in the aftermath of World War One that such fears were finally allayed. As union consolidated its position, league became an urban game of sections of industrial workers and of Maori and Polynesian people. At a deeper level, its failure to overtake rugby union was also a consequence of the essentially rural nature of New Zealand society and the country's lack of a large industrialised and urban working class, which in Britain and Australia provided both the basis of league's support and also the source of the hostility of rugby union's leadership.[103] Without the social weight of a large working class, the scales of New Zealand rugby could not be tilted decisively in favour of rugby league.

Why was there no rugby league in Wales?

Closer to home, the prospect of a professional All Blacks' tour to Britain had also exacerbated the cracks that had begun to appear within Welsh rugby union. Shortly before the arrival in Wales of the 1905 All Blacks, the Welsh authorities had asked all of its member clubs to submit their financial records for inspection for possible breaches of the amateur regulations. Although jubilation over Wales' defeat of the New Zealanders and the narrow losses to the tourists by the Welsh club sides temporarily relegated to the sidelines the concerns over 'veiled professionalism', the creaking foundations of amateurism continued to give cause for concern about its long-term survival in South Wales. The announcement of the New Zealanders' tour in March 1907 seems to have been crucial in stimulating interest in the NU, reviving as it did memories of the commercial success of the 1905 All Black tour, and in May E. H. Rees, a former secretary of Aberdare RUFC, placed an advertisement in the *South Wales Daily News* asking for players to join a new NU club at Aberdare. Rees had accused the Merthyr Alexandra club of paying its players, provoking an official inquiry into professionalism, but, more fundamentally, he believed that the tide was turning against the union game. His confident declaration that 'the days of sham-amateurism are over' clearly touched a chord and rumours of the formation of other Welsh NU teams circulated throughout the summer.[104] Despite being under investigation, at its AGM Merthyr Alexandra members voted against a motion calling on it to join the NU but within a week of the meeting the press reported that a NU club was being formed in the town. In contrast, over in Ebbw Vale the existing rugby union club voted 63–20 in July to go over to the NU. E. H. Rees was not so successful himself, as his Aberdare NU club was thwarted in its attempts to rent a ground in the town and its participation was postponed until the following season.

Despite both Merthyr and Ebbw Vale finishing in the bottom five of the league in their first season of NU rugby, the appeal of the new game and the commercial opportunities it appeared to offer, not least the visit of the first Australian touring side in 1908, led to another four Welsh clubs – Aberdare, Barry, Mid-Rhondda and Treherbert – joining the rebels in 1908. The men who formed these clubs were generally not from the professional middle-classes that controlled Welsh rugby union. They had more in common with the men in the north of England who ran the NU. Aberdare's board of directors included a brewer, a fruit merchant, two innkeepers, a fish merchant, a grocer and a builders' merchant. The first subscribers of shares in the Barry NU club were an auctioneer, an engineer, a foreman, two joiners, a clerk and a cycle maker. As with the NU leadership, they were men from the lower sections of the middle class or members of the upper sections of the working class, such as skilled tradesmen, all of whom had daily contact with working-class people in the course of their business.[105] They had neither the status nor the national social networks of the university and public school-educated leaders of rugby union.

Figure 14 The Northern Union breaks out of northern England: September 1907 sees Ebbw Vale play their first game in Lancashire (from *Athletic News*).

Unfortunately, the four new clubs fared little better than the two pioneers. Although Merthyr and Ebbw Vale finished eighth and fourteenth in the league in 1908–09, the others struggled to stay off the foot of the table. Demoralised by the enormous disparity in playing strength between themselves and the northern clubs, which inevitably meant that crowds rarely rose above a few thousand, Aberdare, Barry and Mid-Rhondda folded after one season, followed by Treherbert the next. Methyr struggled on until 1911 and Ebbw Vale, who reached the quarter-finals of the Challenge Cup in 1910, finally admitted defeat just before the start of the 1912–13 season. Thus ended the first of many attempts to establish the thirteen-a-side game in the Principality.

But from the start of the venture, the problems faced by the Welsh NU clubs meant that their long-term survival was going to be more of a hope than an achievable goal. The most obvious of these difficulties was geography. Northern clubs, used to shuttling back and forth over the Pennines for matches, were not keen to travel such great distances to play matches that did not attract large crowds. Conversely, the trek north for the Welsh sides was even more of an ordeal when the prospect of an inevitable drubbing was waiting at the end of it. For their second game in the NU, Barry undertook a nine and a half hour journey to Keighley, leaving home at five o'clock in the morning, only to return later that same day on the wrong end of a 31–0 scoreline. The NU tried to lessen the financial burden of travel by making a grant for each journey north of £10, which was reduced to £5 following the admission of the four other Welsh sides in 1908, but this did little to sweeten the pill.[106]

Conversely, if Welsh clubs found the journey north arduous, the best Welsh players certainly did not. Sixteen Welsh union internationals switched to league during the lifetime of the Welsh clubs, 1907–1912, but only Dai 'Tarw' Jones, a forward who had played in the Welsh victory over the All Blacks, joined a Welsh NU side. He had already been suspended for professionalism by the Welsh authorities during their investigation into Merthyr Alexandra. Bridgend forward Ben Gronow turned down the offer of £25 and a job to join Ebbw Vale NU club in 1909 but the following year signed for Huddersfield for £125, eventually becoming one of their greatest players.[107] Despite the NU leadership warning northern clubs about taking players from underneath the noses of the new Welsh sides, when it came to attracting the best Welsh talent, local clubs could not hope to compete financially with the big sides in the north. Even lower down the scale, there was little that could be done to stop northern scouts scooping up players with either the potential or the experience to make a name for themselves in the NU game, thus depriving the Welsh clubs of players who would never be stars but who could provide a backbone for a team. Even Merthyr's attempts to circumvent the problem by signing the dual All Black Duncan MacGregor in 1908, the man who had scored four tries against England in 1905 and had been instrumental in the 1907 tour, came to naught when he was badly injured after only a few games.

Then there was the problem of soccer. As in the rugby heartlands of the north of England, soccer had begun to make major headway in South Wales by the mid-1900s.[108] Between 1906 and 1910 the number of clubs affiliated in the region to the Welsh FA more than tripled from 74 to 262. Much of the popularity of the round-ball game was concentrated in the Cynon, Taff and Rhondda Valleys, areas which also encompassed most of the Welsh NU clubs. In Tonypandy, where the Mid-Rhonnda club was based, the collapse of the NU side in 1909 was immediately followed by the Mid-Rhonnda soccer club taking over their ground. The chairman of the NU club echoed his counterparts at Manningham and Bradford when he stated at the end of the club's first and last season that:

> they were going to have a soccer team at Tonypandy next season. He had been a great supporter of amateur rugby and Northern Unionism but the financial position had not realised expectations. They were going to fall away from Northern Unionism as they could see that Soccer was the coming game.[109]

In Merthyr, where by 1909 there was no senior rugby union side, there developed a straight fight between the NU club and Merthyr Town AFC. The collapse of the union club was followed by the soccer club gaining sole tenancy of its old ground Penydarren Park and turning down an offer from the NU side to share the ground. Again, in echo of events in the north, the formation of the soccer side had included 'several gentlemen formerly connected with the amateur rugby club ... though the soccer club is to be run on professional lines', which may have explained why the ground-sharing proposal was turned down. In the spring of 1909 Manchester City made an evangelical visit to play a friendly against Merthyr Town and at the start of the following season the side joined soccer's Southern League, now the most important league outside of the Football League's two divisions. As in the north, soccer enabled the town to be represented on a national stage, whereas the Northern Union was still a regional sport, and, combined with the poor performances of the NU side, the soccer side consistently won the battle for spectators in the town.

Of course, the problems faced by Welsh NU sides were exacerbated by their lack of success on the playing field. The Welsh public were prepared to turn out for top-class Northern Union matches – 15,000 watched Wales defeat New Zealand 9–8 at Aberdare in 1908 – but the average fare served up by the local clubs every week would not attract enough spectators to keep a professional side financially afloat indefinitely. And unlike the clubs in the north, most of which had deep roots in the social and cultural life of their localities stretching back thirty or forty years, the Welsh clubs had no similar local support or social resonance on which to draw during difficult times. Indeed, in many cases they were simply speculative ventures whose officials, as in the case of Mid-Rhonnda, had no deep allegiance to the sport. It was thus easy for enemies of the NU to portray the clubs as outsiders, alien to Welsh national culture.

In the 1900s rugby union was becoming increasingly important to Welsh national identity. With the exception of a draw at Leicester in 1904, Wales had won every match against England from 1899 to 1909, and the 3–0 success against the otherwise unbeaten 1905 All Blacks, who had easily vanquished all the other home nations, was the high point of the decade. Ironically, much of this success would not have been possible had the RFU not driven the northern working classes out of the game, leading to the devastation of the England national side. Nevertheless, the acclaim and publicity that Wales' run of success brought had enabled the game's supporters to claim that rugby union was one of the most well-known symbols of Welsh nationhood and identity. Although the relationship between the union game and Welsh national identity can be exaggerated – for example the 1905 victory did nothing to halt the growth of soccer in the region and the All Blacks tour actually stimulated the formation of the Welsh NU sides – the international success of Wales gave rugby union a national importance unrivalled by any other sport.

Moreover, despite the fact that it sought to position itself as an integral component of Welsh national culture, the leadership of Welsh rugby union was neither separatist nor fundamentally opposed to the English RFU's control of the game. Its national feeling was part of its loyalty to the monarch, the British state and the Empire, as Gareth Elwyn Jones has pointed out about much of Welshness of the time.[110] Indeed, throughout the Empire, rugby union was part of an integrative imperial culture, one of a multitude of social, economic and cultural networks for the white upper and middle classes. Not for nothing did the Welsh national side's jerseys sport the three feathers emblem of the Prince of Wales and the motto 'Ich dien' or 'I serve'. Indeed, many Welsh nationalists had little time for rugby: Lloyd George complained in the mid-1890s that the grip of 'morbid footballism' was one of the factors stopping South Wales supporting his projected Welsh Liberal Party. And, as Gareth Williams has pointed out, 'The WFU itself was guided by men like Sir John Llewellyn, Bart., H. S. Lyne and W. E. Rees, all three privately educated in England, Conservative in politics, Anglican in religion...',[111] who shared the same background, outlook and prejudices of the English rugby union leadership.

It was not surprising therefore that the launch of the Northern Union in Wales was portrayed by the Welsh rugby union authorities as an affront to the nation. One Welsh official claimed that:

> the quarters affected are not those in which the Welsh national sentiment is fairly reflected. The mining districts of the Principality are the natural quarters for the development of the professional element, but these are not the localities whence the strength of Welsh international football is derived.[112]

As this quote demonstrates, much of the hostility to the NU was, as in England, also based on anti-working class prejudice. Despite the wishes of its leadership, the NU was widely identified as a sport of the working class that was outside of the control of the respectable middle classes. The relationship between the NU and the working classes was noted by others too. The *Western Mail* commented that 'to the colliers especially, the Northern Union code, with its faster play, undoubtedly appeals', while another Welsh newspaper, writing about Mid-Rhondda's 1908 game against Australia commented approvingly that the home team 'consists of miners and workmen engaged in the collieries. Democracy is more strongly represented among the Kangaroos than among any previous touring teams. The total absence of the 'swank' ... makes them appear a cut above the ordinary.'[113] This was not merely a sociological observation. The latter half of the first decade of the century had seen a rising level of industrial conflict and social unrest in South Wales. As Kenneth Morgan has pointed out, 'South Wales showed an entirely different industrial climate from that prevalent ten years earlier. It was already a cauldron for new doctrines of social and economic revolution, already in the militant vanguard of the working class in Britain generally.'[114] The Welsh NU clubs were based in areas at the centre of this upsurge: Aberdare had been a centre of working-class militancy since the days of the Chartists, and Tonypandy, home to Mid-Rhondda NU, was to become notorious in 1910 when Winston Churchill sent in troops to quell protesting miners. The NU seemed to symbolise the separation of the classes, and the Welsh middle classes who promoted rugby as a vehicle for social harmony between the classes were at best indifferent and at worst extremely hostile to the sport. Unlike the NU, Welsh rugby union was never identified as 'working-class sport', support for the sport stretching right across society, as illustrated by the response to the Welsh national side's victory over the 1935 New Zealand tourists: 'Wales ... is particularly proud of the fact that Welsh peers and Welsh labourers – with all the intervening strata of society – were united in acclaiming and cheering the Welsh team,' said the *Western Mail*, a statement of cross-class social solidarity that it would be inconceivable to apply to any activity of the NU.[115] It was therefore always highly unlikely that, deprived of social status, deep-rooted support and playing success, the Welsh NU clubs could have survived.

This is not to say that the Northern Union could not have found a place in Wales. But the establishment of anything more than a marginal existence for the game would have only been possible on the basis of a split within Welsh rugby union, a division that would have led to senior Welsh clubs and officials going over to the side of the Northern Union. Only with a Cardiff, a Swansea or a Newport in its ranks could a Welsh Northern Union be taken seriously. But by 1907, the prospects of such a development were remote to say the least, with rugby union entrenched as the national sport of Wales and the NU having been marginalised as a socially and geographically isolated sport.

With the benefit of hindsight, however, it is clear that the historic 'moment' of opportunity for the NU in Wales occurred ten years previously, during the controversy over the Arthur Gould affair in 1896. Gould, the most famous and talented Welsh player of his generation, had been the recipient of a hugely successful testimonial, the proceeds of which, it was decided by the Welsh Football Union (as the WRU was then known), were to be used to present him with the deeds to his house in Newport. Perhaps unsurprisingly, this had been denounced by the RFU in April of that year as an act of professionalism. In February 1897 the rugby union International Board endorsed the RFU position and, in protest, the Welsh had withdrawn from the Board. A split appeared to be looming, although heated controversies between the home nations were not unusual. In 1888 and 1889 England had not played against the other sides owing to a dispute over the formation of the International Board and Scotland's participation in the 1909 home internationals had been in doubt up until the last minute due to a dispute over professionalism. The Welsh withdrawal was not so much an expression of 'home rule' by the WFU as a part of an established negotiating quadrille. And so it proved.

At its annual general meeting in September 1897, the RFU backtracked and declared that, although Gould had committed an act of professionalism, 'the exceptional circumstances' of the case meant that he would not face a ban. Rowland Hill admitted openly that the decision 'was a question of expediency', arguing that it would be 'a serious strain on the loyalty of the West Country clubs of England if those fixtures [against Welsh sides] were prohibited'. F. E. Smith candidly admitted in *The Times* that a compromise had been reached to 'prevent the great accession of strength to the Northern Union which would have followed had the Welsh Union been driven into their arms'. Philip Trevor, writing in the *Badminton Magazine* called the whole affair 'squalid'.[116] Coming merely two years after the English split, a definitive break with the Welsh, which would have inevitably resulted in the NU and the WFU joining together in a semi-professional British rugby union, would have been a body blow to the RFU's prestige and authority from which it may have been difficult to recover. Faced with a choice between enforcing its principles or maintaining its authority, the RFU, as always, chose the latter. And given the opportunity to compromise with the RFU, the leadership of Welsh rugby was more than happy to fall back into line behind the English, regardless of its rhetoric about Welsh independence and despite the fact that Gould remained banned from playing international rugby and from playing or refereeing outside of Wales.[117]

On a broader level, the Gould compromise set the template for Welsh rugby union and its relations with the RFU for the next century. First and foremost, it helped to legitimise the undercover payments made to working-class players by the Welsh clubs: if the WFU was willing to endorse Gould's emoluments, it would also turn a blind eye to those of the sport's lesser lights, provided a reasonable amount of discretion was maintained. Of course, in demonstration of the truth of Oscar Wilde's dictum that hypocrisy is the homage that vice pays to virtue, the Welsh authorities periodically carried out investigations into professionalism, but these were of minor players and clubs whose monetary dealings had become too obvious and threatened to embarrass the code of silence over payments. It was the WFU's refusal to pursue amateurism with the vigour of the RFU that was crucial in maintaining rugby union as a sport for all classes in Wales and thus maintaining it as the country's national game.

This was not the only safety valve that helped to release the pressure from players for payments. Working-class players looking to benefit from their rugby skills could express their dissatisfaction simply by going north to join an NU club. And for those at the elite levels of the sport, as was demonstrated by Gould himself, union's cross-class support meant that there were significant opportunities for social advancement through the provision of jobs, social networks and educational opportunities, none of which were available to players in the largely mono-class NU. Most importantly, the Gould compromise signalled that the RFU would not adopt the same degree of amateur zealotry west of Offa's Dyke as it would at home. As long as the Welsh clubs pretended not to pay their players, the RFU would pretend to believe them. The WFU had demonstrated that it posed no threat to the RFU and would therefore not be subjected to the 'iron rigour' of English amateurism. Thus was the NU locked out of Wales – although not from Welsh life, as attested to by the hundreds of Welsh players who continued to go north to earn the just and open rewards to which their rugby talents entitled them.

The post-partum RFU: Agony and exorcism

The RFU was fully aware of the impact on English rugby that its driving out of the northern clubs would have. As the *Yorkshire Owl* had predicted in 1893, the RFU was quite prepared to sacrifice many fine proponents of the game and lose a good many international matches in order to rid itself of the incubus.[118] And in the aftermath of the split, its sacrifices in pursuit of amateur purity became legion.

Between 1890 and 1895 England won eleven of eighteen matches against Ireland, Scotland and Wales. With the exception of the 1895 matches, when pre-split manoeuvrings led the RFU to select only two players from future NU clubs, there were never less than four players in the England side from clubs that would break away in 1895. Indeed, the 1892 team, which did the 'Grand Slam' to win the international championship for the first time since 1884, never had less than eight such players in the side, with the team that defeated Scotland in the final match of the championship having ten. In all, almost 43 per cent of the players who played for England between 1890 and 1894 came from clubs or would join clubs that would go on to form the NU.

But in the five seasons following the split, England won just four, and drew two, out of fifteen matches, as the number of future NU players declined as their clubs left the RFU. Writing in 1898 Philip Trevor noted that 'amateur rugby football has fallen upon evil times; a state of affairs that is rendered the more humiliating by the fact that the Northern Union ... flourishes even as a green bay tree'.[119] Even worse was to come. Between 1901 and 1909 England won just six, and drew one, of twenty-seven matches with the three home nations. The continual defeats suffered by England in the 1900s became a testimony to the RFU's sacrifice and steel in upholding the amateur banner: the comment of New Zealand's Dave Gallaher and Billy Stead, that 'it is better that a game should be played badly, and that none should go to see it, than that the price should have to be paid for professionalism' encapsulated the attitude of the RFU, if not necessarily their own.[120]

These problems were compounded by financial difficulties and the impact of soccer on the game. Although the RFU believed that its amateurism made it immune from the pressure of commercial forces, this was not the case. As we have already seen, the patrician Manchester club had been on the verge of disbanding in 1895 owing to financial difficulties. In 1898 the Broughton club, also in Manchester and one of the oldest in Lancashire, disbanded because in the words of its president, it was 'not in a position to pay its way'.[121] In 1897 the Durham union sought to form a league to stimulate public interest in the face of soccer's runaway popularity in the region. When the RFU committee discussed the proposal the following year, they unsurprisingly refused to sanction the idea, and also refused to support a similar league that had been formed in Cornwall. Durham's neighbours in the Northumberland union also opposed the idea, believing that it would 'mean the extinction of rugby north of the Tyne', despite the fact that, with only five clubs in membership, the Northumberland union was not too far from extinction itself.[122] It was perhaps a belated sense of self-awareness that led the Northumbrians in 1902 to propose the introduction of a national rugby cup competition – as A. W. Pullin noted:

> the popularity of the Association game in and around Newcastle and Sunderland, and the encroachment of the Northern Union, with its threatened developments, appear to have raised in certain Rugby unionists the necessity of attempting something in the direction of popularising their own game in the North East.[123]

The RFU's studied indifference to the fate of clubs in the region led to a steady stream of clubs disbanding. In 1904 Tudhoe, one of the few remaining clubs with a working-class following in Durham, folded after a 'financially disastrous' season, followed in 1906 by Blaydon Wanderers, one of the county's oldest clubs. At the 1904 RFU AGM Northumberland's Rockcliff club had proposed adjusting the scoring system to make the scoring of tries more important than goals, similar to the NU system, to make the game more attractive, but it fell by the wayside owing to a lack of interest among other clubs.[124] This steady contraction of the game in the North East culminated in 1908 when West Hartlepool, which had been losing money since at least 1902 despite being arguably the region's best side, disbanded and reformed itself as Hartlepools United AFC.[125] Writing in the same year, the collapse of the union game in the North was captured by a returning member of the 1905 All Black side:

> In the Northern counties I find nearly a total abolition [of rugby union]. All round it seems retrogression. The causes are too various to mention. The masses have never been catered for and the game is not to their liking.

They have been ignored and prejudiced and their support dwindled. Only the upper classes, colleges, universities etc have been studied and so the game remains with them.[126]

This retrogression was not just confined to the North. In all of the remaining areas in which rugby union retained a modicum of a working-class support it struggled to retain its popularity in the face of the soccer behemoth. At the 1900 RFU AGM Bristol District RFU asked permission to form a local league to counter the growth of soccer in the city. Rugby 'was being killed by the competition of the association game' declared one of the Bristol delegates, adding that 'if the resolution was not carried, the younger portion of players would go over to the association code'. Despite this heartfelt plea, the resolution was lost. In Devon the need to counteract the sudden popularity of soccer led to the formation of a league structure in defiance of the RFU.[127] Such was the enthusiasm for the round-ball code that it had even begun to threaten rugby union in its more middle-class strongholds. In 1904 Frank Potter-Irwin of the Ilford Wanderers club, a future vice-president of the RFU, described how 'the Rugby Union included something like 250 clubs, whereas in his own district there were 247 association clubs, He appealed to the Union to give up its antiquated methods and do something to popularise the game.'[128]

Of course, this was the very opposite of what the central leadership of the RFU wanted to do. But the rapid decline of the sport's fortunes in England both on and off the pitch presented the RFU with a dilemma. Its ferocity in pursuing the evil of professionalism was threatening to undermine its credibility as a major national sport, yet no matter how hard it tried, it could not finally cast out the incubus. As the 1900s progressed, the RFU became increasingly divided between purifiers, who would stop at nothing in their pursuit of spotless amateurism, and pragmatists, whose amateur ideals were tempered by the need to maintain the organisational strength of the RFU. Nowhere was this tension more apparent than in the ongoing controversies over allegations of professionalism among Midlands clubs.

Aside from the socially prestigious clubs of London and the working-class rugby strongholds of Lancashire and Yorkshire, Leicester was the biggest club in English rugby. But since the mid-1890s at least, it had been constantly suspected of paying players and offering them inducements to join the club. The club itself, with its well-appointed ground, large crowds and rigorous team selection policies at the expense of the 'clubability' displayed by southern sides, seemed to resemble an NU club more than it did its allies in the RFU. In February 1896 the team had been subject to an RFU inquiry about the transfer of A. C. Butlin to the club from Rugby. Although they were found not guilty, William Cail told the press that 'Leicester had had a bad name for poaching and using undue influence but they had come out of the inquiry clean'.[129] Nevertheless, suspicions remained, not least among NU clubs who suspected that the RFU turned a blind eye to Leicester's indiscretions in order not to force them into the arms of the NU. By the mid-1900s similar fears were also being expressed by those who favoured a more aggressive 'purification' policy by the RFU.

In an attempt to put an end to the professional miasma that hung over Leicester and the other leading Midlands sides, the RFU announced in January 1907 the formation of a 'Commission on Veiled Professionalism', and invited any interested party to submit evidence to it. The Commission took over a year to report, apparently visiting Bristol, Hartlepool, Hull, Leicester, Manchester, Plymouth and York to take evidence, during which time Coventry, Leicester and Northampton had been openly accused of paying players by Moseley club secretary James Byrne. When the report was published, it presented a litany of abuses of the RFU's amateur regulations, including unaudited accounts, vague balance sheets, expenses being paid without receipts, 'unnecessary refreshments' for players and one case of a player actually being offered money to remain at a club. Despite this, the report concluded by incongruously stating that 'so far as they could ascertain . . . veiled professionalism did not now exist in the Rugby Union game'![130]

The somewhat startling disjuncture between the findings of the report and its conclusion enraged the supporters of absolute purification. Byrne, supported by fellow Birmingham club Old Edwardians, submitted a motion to that year's RFU AGM declaring themselves 'not satisfied that "veiled professionalism" does not exist in the Rugby Union,' and viewing 'with alarm the attitude of the Rugby Union towards the whole question'. At the AGM itself Byrne tore into the RFU, pointedly asking that if there was no veiled professionalism why were Leicester and Northampton asked to refund payments that had apparently been made to players. Supporting Byrne, Sam Tattersall of the YRU asked why Leicester had not been suspended for fielding a former NU player, an offence that had led to the expulsion of clubs in Yorkshire. Byrne's motion was lost by just nine votes.[131]

Stung by its narrow escape, the RFU committee sought to appease the purifiers and appointed a sub-committee to look into the work of the Commission on Veiled Professionalism. Almost buckling under pressure, it then announced another inquiry into accusations of professionalism against Leicester, voting down a counterposed motion calling for Leicester to be summarily expelled. Four players were suspended for allegedly having played NU football. When the inquiry reported back in January 1909, it amazingly cleared Leicester of all charges of veiled professionalism. This was too much for the purifiers, among them the RFU president Charles Crane who promptly resigned his post, complaining that the RFU's stance was 'rather an encouragement of professionalism rather than an effort to eradicate it'. Byrne responded by sending a circular to clubs claiming that the RFU was refusing to act against any case of professionalism unless the evidence was overwhelming and calling on it to implement the letter of its own laws.

At this point, although probably more through coincidence than design, the RFU found their amateur fealty being questioned from over the border by the leaders of Scottish rugby union. The Scots had traditionally seen themselves as the upholders of the true spirit of rugby, whether in the playing of the game or in their devotion to amateurism, and they had been deeply troubled by the 1905 All Blacks tour, which seemed to them to be professional in all but name. Their failure to grasp the commercial appeal of touring sides had stupidly led them to agree to pay the whole of the gate money from the Scotland versus New Zealand match to the All Blacks, which may have jaundiced their view of the tour, but they argued that the regular payment of touring expenses (which in the All Blacks' case was three shillings per day) was a form of wage and therefore professionalism.[132] In 1907 they had asked to see the accounts of the 1905 tour, which seem not to have been forthcoming, and in March 1908 they had even suspended a player, Tom Wilson, for accepting a place on the 1908 Anglo-Welsh tour of New Zealand on the grounds that he had professionalised himself by accepting a place on a tour that would pay regular expenses, although he subsequently withdrew from the tour. As with the English purifiers, their discontent had smouldered for some time and it was the one guinea (twenty-one shillings) a week payment to Australian players on the 1908–09 tour of the UK that brought things to a head. Unable to persuade the RFU to act, the Scots abruptly announced on 12 January 1909 that they would not play their scheduled match against England in March. When it came to amateurism, 'there can be no halfway house in Rugby football,' Scottish secretary James Smith sternly instructed the RFU.[133]

As many commentators pointed out, the three shillings per day payment was the same as had been paid on the 1904 British rugby union tour of Australasia, which had been captained by a Scotsman, David Bedell-Sivright. Some even pointed out that a guinea a week was considerably less than the six shillings per week broken-time allowance that the Northern Union had sanctioned in 1895. RFU secretary C. J. B. Marriott claimed in a letter to the Scots that the three shillings a day was merely an allowance to cover drinks taken with meals, perhaps giving an insight into the sobriety of touring teams, but less than a fortnight later the RFU backtracked slightly and decided that, although three shillings per day was not an unreasonable amount, in the future it should not be paid directly to players. This concession seems to have placated the Scots somewhat and in February an International Board resolution declaring that 'the making of any allowance to players in cash is contrary to the principles of amateur Rugby football, and in future no such allowance be made to any player' ended the dispute in time for the England–Scotland match to take place and the Calcutta Cup to be carried home by a victorious Scots team.[134]

The compromise with Scotland, who nevertheless still insisted that the 1905 All Blacks should be declared professionals, took some of the wind out the sails of the purifiers, not least because it demonstrated the ability of the RFU to manoeuvre and hold together the varying shades of amateurism. At that year's RFU AGM, a motion from Byrne calling on the RFU to expel the guilty Midlands clubs was overwhelmingly defeated by 189 to 11 votes on the recommendation of Rowland Hill who, as he done during the Gould affair in 1897, urged pragmatism and a policy of expediency. To pass such a motion, he warned, 'would be to practically break up the union'.[135]

This pragmatism had become the guiding principle of the RFU following the split of 1895. Once the threat to its own power, which it identified as the working-class players and spectators in the north of England, had been removed, it no longer saw the need to pursue uncompromisingly the pristine amateurism it espoused in principle. Hence its compromise over the Gould affair, its leniency towards Leicester and its apparent double standards when dealing with player payments. As the somewhat facetiously named 'Young Ebor' (as if to highlight the hypocrisy of 'Old Ebor', the pen name of the RFU-supporting A. W. Pullin) pointed out in 1909:

> [the RFU] turn out bag and baggage all players who wish to be recompensed for loss of working time and consequent loss of wages, and the next they are willing to 'allow' sums of 12s or 21s a week for what are euphoniously described as 'personal and petty expenses' ... what is professionalism in a working man is evidently something very different in a player of slightly superior social status.[136]

This was indeed the point. The RFU's goal was to re-establish rugby on the same basis on which it had been played in the 1860s and 1870s: as a sport that was part of the male middle-class social network, untroubled by the threat of working-class domination, professionalism or commercialism. The fanatical zeal with which it pursued any traces of Northern Unionism (in contrast to its equivocal stance towards player payments that were not connected with the NU) was the means by which it defined and protected its boundaries. The NU was the 'Other', the existence of which could be used to cajole, threaten and intimidate those who criticised the RFU leadership. The demonisation of the NU – and the language used by RFU supporters to describe the rival body was steeped in the rhetoric of good versus evil – meant that it was effectively impossible within the RFU to express sympathy or propose compromise with it. It was not accidental that the creation of Northern Union clubs in Coventry in late 1909 and in Devon in 1912 resulted from splits within rugby union clubs in areas that still had significant working-class participation in rugby union or that both ventures ultimately failed owing to a combination of economic factors and the fanatical hostility of local rugby union authorities.

What working-class participation remained in English rugby union by 1910 was deferential, non-threatening and strictly controlled, and confined to limited parts of the Midlands and the South West. The leadership of the sport was, and would remain so for the rest of the century, unshakably in the hands of the southern-based, public-school- and university-educated middle classes. This it had sought to ensure from the mid-1900s by encouraging wider sections of the middle-classes to take up the game, most notably among the public schools and the Army. In 1906 it launched a concerted campaign to persuade public schools to take up the sport, issuing a circular that urged them to try the game rather than soccer and warning, to the public annoyance of the Football Association, of 'the danger of young men being driven to look on at games between paid-for men'. The circular further spelt out the RFU's philosophy: 'the game of Rugby football has always been at its best when good players were available from our Public Schools, and the more Public School men get to play our game, the better we are certain it is for it.'[137]

The years that followed seemed to offer ample evidence for such an assertion. From 1910 the transformation of the national side's fortunes could not have been more marked. After a generation of failure, in the five years from 1910 England won sixteen matches and lost just three, finishing top of the Five Nations table four times, and completed successive 'Grand Slams' in 1913 and 1914. This success was based firmly on players from the public schools and the exclusive London clubs and founded on the attacking three-quarter play that had been introduced by England and Harlequins' captain Adrian Stoop. Following Stoop's retirement from the international side in 1912 the system continued with even greater success, embodied in his successor as captain, Ronald Poulton-Palmer, whose pace and elusiveness had first come to public notice in the 1909 Oxford versus Cambridge Varsity match when he had scored an unprecedented five tries for Oxford.[138] With England resurrecting the image of the dashing public-school three-quarter who could score tries at will, the mythic appeal of the game to the middle classes was re-established. The fact that both Stoop and Poulton-Palmer were former pupils of Rugby school seemed to offer historical justification for the correctness of the path that the RFU had followed since 1895.

No longer a northern Union

The gap between the Northern Union and the RFU had never been wider. By 1910, no-one seriously discussed a re-unification of the two bodies. The disdain of the RFU for the NU was matched by the latter's increasing self-confidence. The rule changes of 1906, the New Zealand and Australian tours in the following years, and the reciprocal visit by the NU to the Antipodes in 1910 were crucial in giving NU football a legitimacy it had hitherto lacked. International matches against Australia and New Zealand meant that it too could now lay claim to be a representative of the British nation. Regular international competition, and the importation of players from down under, freed the game from the geographical constraints of the north of England and allowed it to express on the international football field its distinct ideology, which was, to quote Patrick Joyce's phrase, 'the idea of the true unadorned England of the north [which] was a variant of the broader mythology of the true political nation of the excluded English'.[139]

This allowed the NU to create its own niche in the British sporting pantheon, acknowledging its working-class base yet accepting a socially deferential position. As with many other aspects of working-class culture, it was part of the working classes' 'life apart'. It may have been proudly proletarian in composition but it was most definitely not oppositional: 'We have as loyal a body of sportsman in the NU as they have in the rugby union,' said Harry Ashton when attacking the lack of press coverage of the NU in comparison to that of their rivals. The sense of deference was also expressed by Joe Platt, speaking at a farewell dinner for the 1910 tourists:

> They were sending out men who represented a democratic union for the first time. There had been many teams sent out to Australia and New Zealand from this country, but they had generally been composed of men of high social standing. The Northern Union team had been chiefly selected from the artisan class. He hoped the players making the tour would do honour to the occasion.[140]

This sentiment was most vividly encapsulated by a poem written for the departing tourists, which attempted to render the public school imperative of the *Vitai Lampada* into a form appropriate to the 'artisan class'.

> You're not of the bluest blood, boys,
> Not aristocrats, what then?
> You're something that's quite as good, boys,
> You're honest young Englishmen.
> And what does it matter the rank, boys,
> 'Tis better that you should claim
> That you are straightforward and frank, boys,
> And keen upon 'Playing the Game'.[141]

To ensure that the message was not missed, the other two verses ended with the couplets 'So ever be true to the core lads/To the principle "Playing the Game"' and 'We'll put it in the form of a toast lads/"The NU" and "Playing the Game"'. The NU's discovery of a national role for itself also gave it the confidence to seek royal approval. Proposing a toast to the new king George V in May 1910, J. B. Cooke told his audience that he 'thoroughly believed that if [the king] saw one or two Northern Union games he would be a convert to the game,' and in April 1911 the king acceded to the NU's request that he become patron of their sport. Despite a well-known fondness for rugby union, the new patron never bothered to watch a game of NU football.[142] Like Kipling's 'Tommy', the NU may have been looked down upon, but it believed that it was just as responsible for upholding British honour whatever its social superiors might think of it. Put crudely, it saw itself as the sporting equivalent of the NCO, in contrast to the RFU's officer class.

The international dimension added by the events of 1907 was as vital to the development of the NU as the rule changes of the previous year. As well as increased influence and credibility from international matches, the NU's competitions gained a cosmopolitan flavour unknown in British sport – ten of the Australian tourists stayed behind to join English clubs, as had a handful of 1907 tourists, and they started a pattern of international movement by rugby league players that exists to this day. Indeed, two of these early imports, New Zealander

Lance Todd and Australian Albert Rosenfeld, etched their mark so deeply on the game that they are still household names in rugby league circles. With regular international competition and the constant importation of overseas players into the game, the NU now had its alternative to the glamour of soccer's nationwide competitions and the national kudos of rugby union. Out of necessity and while retaining its northern insularity, the NU had become one of the most international of domestic sports.

Conclusion: The Northern Union and working-class culture

In April 1910, a new journey began for the Northern Union when twenty-six of the NU's finest players left England for the Union's first ever tour of Australia and New Zealand. Flushed with the self-confidence of a successful new code of rules, firmly established in the southern hemisphere and buoyant in its heartlands, for the NU the Australasian tour was the final piece in the jigsaw that became the pattern of rugby league for almost sixty years. A new era had begun – and although the NU was not to change its name until 1922, the setting out of the tourists on the high seas marked the beginning of modern rugby league.

Symbolically, the tourists' departure marked the end of the odyssey that working-class rugby had made since the miners and millworkers of the north of England first ran with an oval ball in their hands. From now on, the northern working classes' relationship to rugby was based entirely on a different sport and a different culture to that which the rugby union had provided. It was the culmination of a process that had begun in the 1870s as the working-class brought their numbers and culture to the public school boys' game. Neither simple class expression nor mere passive diffusion, working-class culture contained strong elements of commercialism and sought to utilise existing leisure outlets for its own purposes. The ultimate outcome was by no means inevitable – given the advantages the sport had over soccer at the time, the possibility existed for it to become the dominant football code – but fear of working-class domination saw the development of an amateur ideology that was ultimately incompatible with either mass working-class participation or the growth of a commercial, mass-based leisure industry. This was the rock that split asunder the consensus of rugby's leaders. But the desertion of most of rugby's middle-class supporters to rugby union and soccer and its exclusion from the pantheon of national sport left the NU an almost exclusively working-class game, albeit with a fringe of administrators from the marginal sections of the middle classes. The road to the formation of the NU was as much a case history in the formation of middle-class culture as it was of working-class culture. And, in a sense, the wheel had turned full circle: the working classes' leisure activities of the pre-football mid-Victorian period had been largely unknown and unknowable by the middle classes; now the NU occupied a position in society that was similarly beyond the pale of middle-class comprehension and experience.

Given the varying levels of conflict in rugby, how useful is the concept of hegemony in understanding its development? John Hargreaves, a leading proponent of the theory of hegemony, has argued that the development of mass spectator sports in the late nineteenth century 'signified also a degree of depoliticization within the working class which commercial interests were quick to exploit'.[1] But the question of commercialism is much more complex and contradictory than the hegemony theorists allow. Far from being counterposed to it or 'accommodated' by it, working-class participation in rugby both spurred on and was facilitated by commercialisation. Working-class players' demands for remuneration were the motor force for the professionalisation of the sport. Indeed, in the debate leading up to the split, the most vociferous champions of open professionalisation of the game were the supporters of players' rights, not the industrialists who occupied leading positions in the game. As Eileen and Stephen Yeo have argued, 'there was a formidable working class, even socialist, case for the professionalisation and capitalization of sport'.[2] A similar point could be made about soccer: those who were most in favour of the operation of the laws of supply and demand in the sport were the players. By and large, it was the working-class participants in both codes of football who were the most committed to 'pure' bourgeois values.

This is not so contradictory as it may appear. To survive in daily life, working-class men and women were forced to sell their labour power to the highest bidder. And in a market where a premium was on football talent, it was inevitable that players would desire the freest operation of that market, shorn of the restrictions of amateurism, enforced semi-professionalism or professionalism bounded by a maximum wage. 'Freedom' for working-class males to play sport at the highest levels in a capitalist society could only be achieved by the commercialisation of football. And herein lies the problem posed by rugby for the hegemony theory: all of the demands of working-class players in the 1880s were eventually met by the Northern Union, yet the working-class exerted no greater control over the new body than it did over the avowedly anti-working-class RFU.

Was this because they were defeated ideologically by the commercially minded middle classes or because they 'consented' to such an arrangement? Neither solution provides a satisfactory answer in my opinion. Society is not a blank page upon which differing ideologies or value systems compete for dominance. Any struggle for hegemony is unequal from the start – consciousness, of whatever class, is formed in an environment in which the necessity of day-to-day economic survival under capitalism is accepted as the 'natural order'. Leisure activity is necessarily shaped by the economic imperatives of capitalism that seep into every corner of life. Thus working-class players were prepared to accept the leadership of the Northern Union because it provided the most equitable solution available under capitalism to the problems they faced from the RFU and its amateur ethos. This does not imply an endorsement of a crude base/superstructure theory, but it does stress the importance of economics to the relationship between rugby and the working class – indeed, from the earliest pressures for covert payments in the 1870s to the players' strikes of the 1900s, the wage relationship played a critical role in the sport. Into this were woven varying degrees of civic pride, regional patriotism, consciousness of class, feelings of injustice and political ideology, from which was woven the fabric of the Northern Union.

Central to the culture of the Northern Union game and its claim to national importance were the regular test match series with Australia for which the 1910 tour set the pattern. As could be expected, preparations for the tour had been fraught with difficulty, Negotiations with the Australians over the share of the gate takings had been long and arduous, and at one point the entire venture had been in jeopardy. In order to reach Australia in good time, the tourists had to set sail before the end of the season, forcing the NU to play the two championship semi-finals on the same day as the NU Cup Final - fortunately none of the cup finalists were championship contenders, although, as if beset by fate, the cup final was drawn for the first time in its history and had to be replayed two days later – and five members of the touring party left a week late because of their clubs' appearance in the championship final. The five were joined at the last minute by Hunslet's star centre three-quarter Billy Batten, who had been selected in the touring party but had aggravated a knee injury received in the tour trial match at Headingley. Despite the NU committee announcing that he had withdrawn, Batten was determined to prove his fitness and, three days before the final party was to leave, turned out for Hemsworth in a Wakefield district league match. Perhaps inevitably, given his renowned drive to succeed, he scored three tries and was passed fit to tour on the spot by watching NU officials. Amazingly, the tour proceeded as planned and went on to be an outstanding success, both on and off the pitch.

Billy Batten himself had a meaning for the Northern Union that extended far beyond his outstanding prowess on the field. He was symbolic of what the new game had become. Unlike earlier stars, he had played no other code. His character and playing style were entirely shaped by the demands of the NU game. As if to emphasise the centrality of physicality to the sport, his strength, speed and power as a centre three-quarter were unprecedented. He became famous for leaping over, or more often than not through, opponents. His determination and will to win – nearly ninety years on, one only has to look at the intensity of his expression in photographs and film footage to realise that 'mental focus' is nothing new – encapsulated the attitude of the new generation of professional rugby players.

Off the field, he embodied all of those traits that were to characterise generations of rugby league players. A man who was still part of the community that had raised him – he gave £350 of his testimonial fund to mining families in his home village of Kinsley near Wakefield during the 1921 miners' strike – he was also acutely aware of his own value and saw to it that he squeezed the last drop of cash out of those who employed him to play rugby. When Hunslet failed to meet his demands in 1912 he was transferred to Hull FC for £600, doubling the previous NU transfer record, and received an astronomical £14 per match. His relationship with the sport's administrators was similarly tense. In 1920 he refused to play in a trial match and so sacrificed the chance to join that year's touring party to Australia, arguing that if the selectors did not know whether he was good enough to tour after fifteen years in the game, one trial match would not make a difference. In contrast to contemporaries in other sports, such as soccer's Billy Meredith and cricket's Sydney Barnes, who shared both Batten's brilliance and hostility to authority, Batten was not marginalised or viewed as a maverick. He was accepted by supporters, fellow-players and, albeit grudgingly, officials, as a phenomenon: Hull FC would stick strips reading 'Batten Certain To Play' over posters advertising their matches, guaranteeing a large attendance at games in which he played.[3]

Although not specifically referring to him, it was in unconscious recognition of the achievements of players such as Batten that the saying 'T'best in t'Northern Union' came into being across the north of England in the period around World War One.[4] Used to denote that something was of the highest quality, the phrase carried with it the unspoken assumption that if whatever was referred to was the best in the Northern Union, it was the best in Britain. It therefore carried into popular parlance – of both men and women, it must be stressed – the belief of the NU and its supporters that their players and their game were superior to those of the RFU, binding this up with the broader assumption of the superiority of the northern way of life. It also expressed the different relationship to their communities of soccer and NU rugby. Logically, it would have made greater sense to say 'the best in the Football League' given the national spread of soccer, yet that would have been to lose that sense of apartness and regional pride that the NU gave the phrase. Other phrases relating to the game also slipped into regional language: 'to nip around the blind side', referring to a movement where the ball was passed to the side of a scrum furthest from the referee, became used to denote a shortcut to avoid a queue or an obstruction; 'to sell a dummy', whereby a pass was faked to fool an opponent, became a synonym for a dodge or ruse.

The way in which the terminology of the game slipped into everyday use demonstrates the role of the NU in the construction of a 'Northern' regional identity. Despite the fact that the NU was initially forged from national forces in which regionalism played a subordinate role, as the NU sought to develop its own identity it naturally assimilated the customs and culture of its location. In doing so, it largely transcended the county-based regionalism of the pre-1895 days – unlike in the rugby union era, when the sport in the North identified itself as 'Lancashire rugby' or 'Yorkshire football', the new game prided itself on being 'Northern'. This decline in county patriotism can also be seen in the fall in attendances at county matches from the early 1900s and the lack of importance attached to them; less than ten years after the split there were even calls to abandon them completely. And while working-class civic pride in town or city, of which support for a rugby or soccer team had been an integral part since the 1870s, remained a potent force, this too had merged at some points, but not completely, with a sense of corporate

'Northernness'. In an era of increasingly national culture and identity, the development and meaning of the NU demonstrated not only that regionalism survived but also how it changed and reformulated itself in new circumstances. Equally, the NU itself became part of northern identity. Not only did it become part of everyday language, but it became part of the symbolism of northern working-class history and identity. Supporter or not, everyone knew that, like their own communities, the NU was the best at what it did, that it suffered from discrimination by the establishment and that it was one of 'us' against 'them'. It took its place 'in the realm of everyday practice', to quote Patrick Joyce, in which its sayings, personalities and culture came to symbolise northern life.[5]

However, a note of caution must be sounded about placing too much emphasis on cultural meaning. Commercial exigencies were central to the origins and development of the game and the relationship between the players and club officials was inevitably that of employee and employer. While significant elements of working-class practices were reflected in the overall culture of the game, especially in relation to physicality, crowd behaviour and the meaning assigned to the sport in cultural life, other elements of working-class life, such as distrust of employers and the desire to secure the highest level of wages, were a constant source of tension. The stance of Billy Batten and many other players to the clubs for which they played was often portrayed as disloyal or mercenary but their attitudes were simply those of working-class people seeking to secure the best possible return for their labour power. As the not uncommon occurrence of player's strikes demonstrated, far from being an island of northern working-class unity, the NU was subject to the same conflicts between employers and employees as any other branch of industry.

For the supporter, identification with the NU allowed him or her to stand both inside and outside of society. It was a confirmation of what Richard Hoggart has called a feeling 'in their bones that the public and the generalised life is wrong'.[6] Part of its appeal was the fact it was almost entirely separate from the middle and upper classes, and, because of its marginalised position in wider society, not wholly part of national public life.[7] In this, it was a cultural expression of what Tom Nairn has described as the working classes' sense of being 'something of an exile inside the society which [they] supported'.[8] The NU was a self-contained world in which the participants could demonstrate to themselves that their code of football rules and players were better than those of the establishment RFU. In the Northern Union, there was no need to prove themselves in the techniques of social advancement or the niceties of etiquette: as in life, what counted was how you performed on the field. This emphasis on ability and merit, partially drawn from working-class attitudes to life but also based on the fact that the sport was an entertainment business, would allow the game to develop a higher level of racial integration than most other sports in Britain, giving rise to a cosmopolitanism that saw white English working men playing with and against black Welshmen, Maoris, Aboriginals and Fijians, not to mention white working-class Australians, New Zealanders and Welshmen.[9]

It was this combination of working-class alienation from society, Gladstonian Liberalism, persecution by the rugby union authorities and geographic restriction that moulded the NU. The game's appeal of brilliant handling and running skills and hard physicality was combined with a sense of injustice and righteousness to produce a potency of sporting ideology equal to that of any fuelled by national or racial pride. For working men and women who thought that the order of society was not how it should be, the Northern Union was living confirmation of their suspicions. Like the English populists' vision of Merrie England before the imposition of the Norman Yolk, they had seen justice snatched from their hands by the RFU.[10] But, like socialists, they knew that the future lay with them, that ultimately right would prevail and that their game would be recognised in all its superiority for what they believed it truly was: the greatest game of all.

Appendix

Table A.1 Occupational backgrounds of rugby football club secretaries 1877–1884

Private resident	6
Beer retailer/Publican	4
Factory owner	2
Textile merchant	2
Overseer	1
Commission agent	1
Wholesale grocer	1
Grocer	1
Commercial traveller	1
Furniture dealer	1

Sources: *Football Annual*, 1877–1884. *Kelly's Directory of the West Riding* 1877–1884.

Note: This represents twenty individuals I have been able to trace out of a total of fifty-seven named secretaries of Yorkshire sides.

Table A.2 Occupational analysis of Wakefield Trinity supporters 1887

Private resident	30	Barber	1
Publican	20	Beer retailer	1
Butcher	8	Builder	1
Clerk	6	Cab owner	1
Joiner	6	Carting agent	1
Draper	5	Cattle dealer	1
Solicitor	5	China dealer	1
Blacksmith	4	Clerk of corn exchange	1
Maltster	4	Eating house owner	1
Manager	4	Engraver	1
Chemist	3	Farmer	1
Coal agent	3	Fish dealer	1
Glass manufacturer	3	Flyposting proprietor	1

(Continued)

Table A.2 Continued

Rates collector	3	Furniture dealer	I
Shopkeeper	3	Hatter	I
Tailor	3	Horse dealer	I
Tobacconist	3	Hosier	I
Wholesale grocer	3	House agent	I
Baker	2	Insurance agent	I
Building company owner	2	Insurance superintendent	I
Civil engineer	2	Ironmonger	I
Confectioner	2	Journalist	I
Corn merchant	2	Leather worker	I
District registrar	2	Livery stable keeper	I
Dyer	2	Lodging house owner	I
Grocer	2	Member of Parliament	I
House painter	2	Music teacher	I
Iron foundry partner	2	Music warehouse owner	I
Married woman	2	Newspaper publisher	I
Painter	2	Organ builder	I
Photographer	2	Outfitter	I
Print worker	2	Plasterer	I
Shoemaker	2	Railway inspector	I
Surgeon	2	School inspector	I
Wine & spirits merchant	2	Servant	I
Woollen manufacturer	2	Smallware dealer	I
Accountant	I	Stationer's assistant	I
Aerated water mfctr	I	Stonemason	I
Architect	I	Tin plate worker	I
Assistant overseer	I	Toy dealer	I
Auctioneer	I	Upholsterer	I

Breakdown according to occupational category

Category		Number	Percentage
A.	Aristocracy and gentry	42	21
B.	Upper professional	13	7
C.	Lower professional	6	3
D.	Proprietors and employers associated with the drinks trade	27	14
E.	Other proprietors and employers	58	29
F.	Managers and higher administrators	4	2
G.	Clerical	9	5
H.	Foremen, supervisors and inspectors	4	2
I.	Skilled manual workers	26	13
J.	Semi-skilled manual workers	7	3

Table A.2 Continued

K.	Unskilled manual workers	–	–
L.	Unspecified (Married women)	2	I

Sources: *Wakefield Express*, 9 April and 9 July 1887. *Slater's Directory of the West Riding of Yorkshire, 1887*, London 1887. *Kelly's West Riding Directory 1889*, London 1889. *White's General and Commercial Directory of Wakefield 1888*, Wakefield 1888. J. C. Lindley, *100 Years of Rugby*, Wakefield, 1973.

Note: Of the 277 subscribers' names I have been able to trace 198, 71 per cent of the total. Occupational categories are those used by Vamplew in *Pay Up and Play the Game*, Cambridge, 1988.

Table A.3 Crowd disturbances at Yorkshire rugby union matches 1887–1895

Club	Date	Offence	Punishment
Leeds St John's	Nov. 1887	Crowd attacked opponents after game	Unknown
Shipley	Sept. 1888	Crowd 'jostled and hustled' referee after game	Unknown
Liversedge	Sept. 1888	Visiting fans invaded pitch after players' fight	Unknown
Mytholmroyd	Nov. 1888	Crowd attacked referee after game	Ground closed
Bradford Rgrs	Nov. 1889	Spectators and players fight during game	Unknown
Castleford	March 1889	'Spectator violence'	Ground closed – four weeks
York	Nov. 1889	Crowd threw mud at referee after game	Ground closed – four weeks
Normanton	Jan. 1890	Crowd mobbed referee after players walk-off	Ground closed – four weeks
Mirfield	Jan. 1890	Crowd 'abused referee'	Ground closed – two weeks
Ingrow	March 1890	Crowd subjected referee to 'ill-treatment'	Ground closed – two weeks
Leeds PC	Sept. 1890	Crowd attacked referee after game	Ground closed – four weeks
Otley	Feb. 1891	Crowd abused referee and touch judge	Ground closed – one week
Yeadon	Oct. 1891	Crowd invaded pitch after spectator punched player	Ground closed – six weeks
Wortley	Jan. 1892	Spectator attacked opposing player during game	Ground closed – three weeks
Mirfield	Oct. 1892	Crowd attacked referee after game	Ground closed – one week

(Continued)

Table A.3 Continued

Club	Date	Offence	Punishment
Ingrow	Oct. 1892	Crowd attacked referee after game	Ground closed – one week
Featherstone	Nov. 1892	Referee beaten up by twenty youths after leaving ground	No action taken
Hull	Feb. 1893	Crowd attacks referee after game	Severe reprimand
Dewsbury	March 1893	Spectators seize referee by throat after game	Reprimand
Saltaire	Jan. 1894	'Hostile demonstration' against referee after game	No action taken
Bailiffe Bridge	March 1894	Three fights between players and spectators	Match replayed
Leeds	Nov. 1894	Crowd jostle referee after game	Club censured
Beeston	Dec. 1894	Crowd threw stones at referee after game	Ground closed – one week
Hunslet	April 1895	300-strong crowd attempts to assault referee after game	Ground closed – twelve weeks

Sources: These are the incidents reported to the committee of the Yorkshire Rugby Union from its foundation to the year of rugby's split. The primary source is the *Yorkshire Post*, supported by *Athletic News*. Incidents not brought to the attention of the YRU have not been included. Unfortunately, the minutes of the Lancashire County Football Committee do not record crowd disturbances and the *Athletic News* is not comprehensive enough to be used as an accurate guide.

Table A.4 Occupations of working class rugby players 1886–1895

Textile worker	8	Draper	1
Miner	6	Iron dresser	1
Cricket professional	4	Iron moulder	1
Labourer	4	Machine foreman	1
Unemployed	3	Painter	1
Boilermaker	2	Plumber	1
Cabinet maker	2	Printing worker	1
Shopkeeper	2	Railwayman	1
Apprentice joiner	1	Stone breaker	1
Boilermaker	1	Telegraphic operator	1
Bricklayer	1	Tailor	1
Brushmaker	1	Travelling salesman	1
Builder	1	Weaver	1

Sources: *Athletic News, Clarion, Salford Reporter, Oldham Evening Chronicle, Yorkshire Post, Yorkshire Evening Post, Leeds Daily News, Bradford Observer, The Yorkshireman, The Yorkshire Owl* and U. A. Titley and R. McWhirter, *The Centenary History of the RFU*, London, 1971.

Notes: These figures have been taken from forty-nine players whose occupations I have been able to identify. I have deliberately excluded from the sample some twenty players who were publicans or waiters on the grounds that, more often than not, these positions were gained as a result of their footballing prowess and would not shed any light on their backgrounds.

Table A.5 Deaths in Yorkshire rugby 1886–1895

Date	Name	Club	Cause of death
Jan. 1888	A. Mann	Manningham Rgrs	Injured kidneys
Sept. 1888	A. Dougherty	Huddersfield	Pelvic abscesses
Feb. 1889	T. Greenwood	Primrose	Damaged spinal cord
March 1889	L. Wade	Shipley	Severe concussion
Sept. 1890	J. Walker-Smith	Lockwood	Abdominal injuries
Nov. 1890	W. Armitage	St Albans (Leeds)	Ruptured liver
Nov. 1890	W. Scoley	Buslingthorpe (Leeds)	Blood poisoning
Dec. 1890	W. Middleton	Harrogate	Internal injuries
March 1891	J. Featherstone	Hull Britannia	Unknown
Sept. 1892	M. Hutchinson	Harrogate	Unknown
Feb. 1893	J. Kirk	Shepley	Broken neck
March 1894	J. W. Speight	Kirkstall	Unknown
Sept. 1894	B. Hudson	Idle	Spinal injuries

Sources: These figures have been obtained through a reading of *The Yorkshireman's* rugby column from 1882, in which the first reported death at a Yorkshire football match occurred in 1886 (at soccer in Keighley), the *Yorkshire Post's* reports of YRU executive committee meetings and the *Pall Mall Gazette's* lists of injuries. I have excluded one death reported in the *Pall Mall Gazette* – in Keighley in 1891–as I have found no other record of it.

Table A.6 Occupations of Northern Union players 1895–1910

Miner	8	Engineer	1
Textile worker	4	Gas stove fitter	1
Docker	3	School master	1
Brass moulder	2	Steel shearer	1
Glass bottle maker	2	Stone mason	1
Labourer	2	Tailor	1
Blacksmith's striker	1	Tobacconist	1
Boiler maker	1	Wagonette driver	1
Boot maker	1	Waiter	1
Clerk	1	Window cleaner	1
Colliery engine winder	1		

Sources: *Athletic News, Salford Reporter, Oldham Evening Chronicle, Yorkshire Post, Yorkshire Evening Post, Yorkshire Chat, Bradford Observer, Wigan Observer, Pontefract and Castleford Express, Hull Daily Mail* and minutes of the Northern Union Professionalism Sub-Committee.

Notes: These figures have been taken from thirty-six players whose occupations I have been able to identify. As before, I have not included occupations that were the result of footballing largesse, such as publicans. To avoid skewing the details, I have also excluded the eleven miners who played for Hunslet and another eleven who played for Normanton. Interestingly, the one schoolmaster was a Welshman from Swansea playing for Hull KR.

Table A.7 Strikes by Northern Union players 1895–1905

Date	Club	Reason
Sept. 1895	Warrington	Unpaid broken-time
Dec. 1895	Leigh (forwards only)	Wanted nine shillings broken-time
Oct. 1896	St Helens (forwards only)	Wanted more broken-time
Dec. 1896	Wakefield Trinity 'A'	Non-payment of broken-time
Dec. 1898	Ulverston	Low pay
May 1899	Oldham	Dispute over bonuses
Jan. 1900	Leeds (5 players)	Dispute over terms
May 1901	Swinton	Non-payment of bonuses
Feb. 1902	Oldham (4 Welsh players)	Wanted extra pay for mid-week game
March 1902	Rochdale	Non-payment of wages
April 1902	Castleford	Wanted increased wages for cup tie
Nov. 1902	Runcorn	Wanted higher pay
Feb. 1904	Cleckheaton	Non-payment of wages
Oct. 1904	Pontefract (forwards only)	Reduction in terms
Sept. 1905	Wakefield Trinity (3 players)	Reduction in terms

Source: *Athletic News, Warrington Guardian, The Yorkshireman, Yorkshire Post, St Helens Lantern, Barrow News, Oldham Evening Chronicle, Salford Reporter*, NU General Committee minutes.

Note: I have defined a strike as being a refusal to play by three or more players for reasons other than on-pitch activities.

Table A.8 Occupations of Northern Union General Committee members 1895–1910

Licensee/Hotel keeper	6	Oil importer	1
Textile manufacturer	3	Paper tube manufacturer	1
Foreman	2	Pawnbroker	1
Salesman	2	Private resident	1
Schoolmaster	2	Railway booking clerk	1
Builder	1	Solicitor	1
Builder's merchant	1	Surveyor/Music hall proprietor	1
Clerk	1	Travelling draper	1
Coal merchant	1	Wholesale jeweller	1
Furniture shop owner	1	Wood engraver	1
Hosier and hat shop owner	1	Works manager	1
Jeweller	1		

Source: Extant Northern Union *Official Guides* list forty-seven members of the General Committee, the Union's ruling body, during this period, of which I have been able to trace the occupations of thirty-three.

Table A.9 Occupational analysis of Northern Union club shareholders and directors 1895–1910

	Leeds (1889) £25,000 x £1				Holbeck (1897) £2,500 x £1			
	Shareholders		Shareholdings		Shareholders		Shareholdings	
	No.	%	No.	%	No.	%	No.	%
A	7	2.5	555	5.3	5	6.0	215	14.1
B	49	17.6	4247	40.9	2	2.4	85	5.6
C	6	2.2	96	0.9	3	3.6	40	2.6
D	10	3.6	925	8.9	10	12.0	176	11.6
E	68	24.4	2176	20.9	26	31.3	761	50.0
F	28	10.0	720	6.9	4	4.8	45	3.0
G	52	18.6	452	4.3	2	2.4	20	1.3
H	1	0.4	5	–	3	3.6	33	2.2
I	47	16.8	1102	10.6	21	25.3	121	8.0
J	9	3.2	96	0.9	6	7.2	25	1.6
K	2	0.7	35	.03	1	1.2	1	–
Total traced	279	100	10419	100	83	100	1522	100
L	49	–	3324	–	–	–	–	–

	Castleford (1899) £1,500 x 10s				Salford (1901) £2,500 x £1			
	Shareholders		Shareholdings		Shareholders		Shareholdings	
	No.	%	No.	%	No.	%	No.	%
A	1	2.1	60	5.3	6	1.3	119	8.6
B	3	6.4	130	11.4	6	1.3	16	1.2
C	3	6.4	50	4.4	36	7.9	138	10.0
D	17	36.2	465	40.8	21	4.6	165	12.0
E	14	29.8	245	21.5	81	17.8	291	21.1
F	2	4.3	60	5.3	15	3.3	37	2.1
G	2	4.3	30	2.6	85	18.7	260	18.9
H	2	4.3	25	2.2	13	2.9	44	3.2
I	3	6.4	75	6.6	131	28.7	216	15.7
J	–	–	–	–	47	10.3	68	4.9
K	–	–	–	–	15	3.3	25	1.8
Total traced	47	100	1140	100	456	100	1379	100
L	–	–	–	–	146	–	305	–

(Continued)

Table A.9 Continued

	Rochdale (1906) £1,000 x 10s				Ebbw Vale (1907) £250 x 10s			
	Shareholders		Shareholdings		Shareholders		Shareholdings	
	No.	%	No.	%	No.	%	No.	%
A	I	0.7	10	0.9	–	–	–	–
B	10	6.8	131	11.4	I	1.0	5	1.4
C	7	4.8	60	5.2	3	3.1	10	2.7
D	9	6.2	117	10.2	10	10.2	67	18.3
E	49	33.6	499	43.5	21	21.4	67	18.3
F	12	8.2	74	6.5	6	6.1	28	7.7
G	12	8.2	98	8.5	4	4.1	24	6.6
H	I	0.7	10	0.9	7	7.1	20	5.5
I	43	29.9	139	12.1	18	18.4	35	9.6
J	I	0.7	5	0.4	28	28.8	75	20.5
K	I	0.7	4	0.3	–	–	–	–
Total traced	146	100	1147	100	98	100	366	100
L	–	–	–	–	–	–	–	–

	Aberdare (1908) £500 x £1				Barry (1908) £250 x 10s			
	Shareholders		Shareholdings		Shareholders		Shareholdings	
	No.	%	No.	%	No.	%	No.	%
A	–	–	–	–	–	–	–	–
B	–	–	–	–	–	–	–	–
C	–	–	–	–	2	8.7	II	7.5
D	9	25.7	40	25.5	–	–	–	–
E	16	45.7	75	47.8	8	34.6	58	39.5
F	2	5.7	8	5.1	I	4.3	10	6.8
G	I	1.9	5	3.2	2	8.7	6	4.1
H	–	–	–	–	I	4.3	10	6.8
I	2	5.7	8	5.1	7	30.4	40	27.2
J	4	11.3	12	7.6	2	8.7	12	8.2
K	I	2.9	9	5.7	–	–	–	–
Total traced	35	100	157	100	23	100	147	100
L	–	–	–	–	–	–	5	–

Table A.9 Continued

	Coventry (1909) £2,000 x £1				Broughton Rangers (1910) £2,000 x 10s			
	Shareholders		Shareholdings		Shareholders		Shareholdings	
	No.	%	No.	%	No.	%	No.	%
A	2	2.2	20	1.4	–	–	–	–
B	2	2.2	60	4.3	2	2.5	14	2.3
C	15	18.3	102	7.4	6	7.6	39	6.5
D	11	13.4	201	14.5	5	6.4	67	11.2
E	30	36.6	647	46.8	21	26.9	255	42.8
F	9	11.0	287	20.8	10	12.8	61	10.2
G	5	6.1	31	2.2	8	10.2	44	7.3
H	1	0.1	5	0.4	3	3.8	41	6.9
I	5	6.1	23	1.7	16	20.5	46	7.7
J	2	2.2	6	0.4	6	7.6	27	4.5
K	–	–	–	–	1	1.2	1	0.1
Total traced	82	100	1382	100	78	100	595	100
L	1	–	1	–	2	–	3	–

Directors of NU clubs – Breakdown of 124 directors of seven clubs by occupational category – Percentages only

Category	%
A	3.2
B	4.0
C	8.9
D	14.5
E	37.1
F	4.0
G	7.3
H	4.0
I	12.9
J	4.0
K	–

Source: Wray Vamplew Pay Up and Play the Game, Cambridge, 1988. Paul Greenhalgh The History of the Northern Rugby Football Union 1895–1915, unpublished PhD thesis, University of Lancaster 1992 – see page 198 for breakdown of directors' occupations. Public Record Office BT 31 32073/111081; BT 31 7363/52183; BT 31 9364/69546; BT 12142/95202.

Key: Year in brackets is date of incorporation. The figure below is authorised share capital and cost of a single share.

A: Aristocracy and gentry. B: Upper professional. C: Lower professional. D: Proprietors and employers associated with the drink trade. E: Other proprietors and employers. F: Managers and higher administrators. G: Clerical. H: Foremen, supervisors and inspectors. I: Skilled manual workers. J: Semi-skilled manual workers. K: Unskilled manual. L: Occupations untraced.

Table A.10 Northern Union and soccer crowds − a comparison

Season	Hull FC	Hull City	Leeds NU	Leeds City	Bradford	Bradford City	Bradford Park Avenue
1902−03	5,181	−	5,774	−	7,026	−	−
1903−04	5,025	−	7,593	−	8,333	9,941	−
1904−05	5,628	−	9,022	−	n/a	10,700	−
1905−06	4,041	6,500	5,632	9,978	n/a	9,531	−
1906−07	3,000	7,833	4,735	10,131	4,166	10,789	−
1907−08	4,904	8,305	5,476	11,210	−	16,317	9,342
1908−09	4,809	7,368	6,334	11,315	−	22,684	11,157
1909−10	5,119	9,342	7,071	7,026	−	21,052	10,778

Source: Hull FC annual reports and accounts. Leeds Cricket, Football and Athletic Club annual reports and accounts. J. Goldthorpe, *Twenty Years' Records of Leeds FC*, Leeds, 1910. *Yorkshire Post. Athletic News. Bradford Observer.* Chris Elton, *Hull City − A Complete Record*, Derby, 1989. Martin Jarred and Malcolm Macdonald, *Leeds United − A Complete Record*, Derby, 1986. Terry Frost, *Bradford City − A Complete Record*, Derby, 1988. Malcolm Hartley and Tim Clapham, *The Avenue*, Nottingham, 1987.

Note: n/a = not available

Table A.11 A comparison of shareholders in rival Northern Union and soccer clubs

	Holbeck (66 x £1)	Leeds City (61 x £1)		Holbeck (66 x £1)	Leeds City (61 x £1)
Gentleman/scholar	3	1	Foreman	1	1
Surgeon/Physician	2	−	Mechanic	9	−
Manufacturer	1	6	Engineer	7	1
Company director	−	2	Joiner	6	1
Manager	1	4	Slater	3	−
Woollen merchant	1	−	Contractor	3	2
Timber merchant	1	−	Printer	1	1
			Decorator	1	−
Auctioneer	−	1	Coach builder	1	−
Schoolmaster	−	7	Brick maker	1	−
Tax officer	−	2	Mill hand	1	−
Manufacturing Warehouseman	1	−			
Chemist	−	1	Wheelwright	−	1
General agent	−	1	Blacksmith	−	1
Commission agent	−	1	Gardener	−	1
			Boat attendant	−	1
Publican	10	5	Steel worker	−	1
Shopkeepers	5	8			
Tailors/drapers	3	4	Married woman	−	1
Salesman	3	3			
Landlady	−	1			
Clerk	−	2			
Cashier	1	−			

Source: Shareholders registers. Public Record Office BT31 7363 52138 (Holbeck) and BT 31 17428 84163 (Leeds City).

Table A.12 Crowd disturbances at Northern Union senior matches 1895–1910

Club	Date	Offence	Punishment
Rochdale	Feb. 1896	Referee attacked after match	Ground closed – six weeks
Wakefield	March 1896	Referee attacked after match	Ground closed – eight weeks
Rochdale	Nov. 1896	Opponents attacked after match	Ground closed – five weeks
Bradford	Jan. 1897	Referee snowballed after game	No action taken
Rochdale	Dec. 1897	'Rowdy conduct' by boys	200 notices put up in town/boys' prices raised to 6d
Swinton	April 1898	'Rowdyism'	Ground closed – four weeks
Castleford	Oct. 1898	Stones thrown at opponents	Fined £5
Swinton	March 1899	Referee opponents attacked after match	Ground closed
Salford	Nov. 1899	Opponents stoned after match	Notices put up
Castleford	Feb. 1900	'Rowdyism'	Fined £25
Batley	March 1900	Referee 'mobbed' after match	Fined £25
Leeds PC	Oct. 1900	Opponents stoned after match	Fined £20
Huddersfield	Jan. 1902	Referee opponents attacked after match	Not recorded
Hull KR	Jan. 1902	'Rowdyism'	Notices put up
Sowerby	March 1902	Stones thrown at referee and police	Fined £10
Rochdale	March 1902	Referee attacked after match	Ground closed – two weeks
Dewsbury	March 1902	Referee attacked after match	Ground closed – four weeks
Runcorn	Nov. 1902	Referee punched by spectator	Ground closed – three weeks
Huddersfield	Feb. 1903	Referee attacked after match	Ground closed – two weeks
Keighley	Dec. 1903	Referee kicked by spectators	No action taken
Batley	Sept. 1904	Referee stoned after match	Ground closed – four weeks
Hull	March 1905	Opponents stoned after match	Ground closed – four weeks
Merthyr	March 1908	Mud thrown at referee after game	Ground closed – two weeks
Hunslet	March 1908	Referee kicked by spectator after game	Notices put up
Bramley	April 1908	Referee stoned after match	Ground closed – four weeks
Hull	April 1908	Opponents 'barracked' and attacked	Notices put up
Widnes	Sept. 1908	Referee 'shouted and hooted' at	Notices put up
Keighley	Feb. 1909	Opposing player punched after match	Notices put up
Keighley	Dec. 1909	Crowd kicked opponents after game	Club ordered to provide dressing rooms on ground
Merthyr	Jan. 1910	Referee stoned after match	Ground closed – four weeks

Source: NU General Committee minutes, *Yorkshire Post* and *Athletic News*.

Table A.13 Deaths in the Northern Union 1895–1910

Date	Name	Club	Cause of death
Nov. 1897	Robert Cuss	Ripon	Fractured spine
Aug. 1898	Joe Gerrard	St Helens (practice game)	Unknown
Oct. 1900	Harry Lovell	Half Acre Trinity	Unknown
Dec. 1900	Fred Croft	Brighouse Rangers	Unknown
Jan. 1902	Thomas Leather	Tyldesley Shamrock	Unknown
Nov. 1902	John Richardson	Cumberland	Abdominal injuries
Nov. 1902	William Long	Barrow Primrose	Concussion
Dec. 1902	G. Harwood	North West Manchester	Unknown
April 1904	F. Green	Fairburn	Lockjaw
Feb. 1906	A. Hanson	Warmfield	Drowning
Dec. 1906	Harry Myers	Keighley	Damaged spinal cord
Oct. 1909	Albert Barraclough	Lane End United	Unknown

Source: *Yorkshire Post*, *Athletic News*, Northern Union General Committee minutes.

Table A.14 Foul play in the Northern Union in the 1903–04 season

Offence	Number of incidents	Average suspension
Striking	42	1.6 weeks
Kicking	30	2.1 weeks
Rough play	10	3.1 weeks
Fighting	6	2.0 weeks
Arguing with referee/ using bad language	6	2.2 weeks
Wrestling	6	None – sending off deemed to be sufficient punishment
Tripping	4	2.2 weeks
Kicking and striking	3	5.6 weeks
Foul charging	2	2.0 weeks
Retaliation	2	2.0 weeks

Source: Northern Union General Committee minutes, 25 August 1903 to 17 May 1904.

Notes

Preface to the second edition

1 Ernest Renan, *Qu'est-ce qu'une Nation?*, quoted in Eric Hobsbawm, *Nations and Nationalism Since 1870*, Cambridge, 1990, p. 12.
2 LeRoy Angel at http://www.rfu.com/index.cfm/fuseaction/RFUHome.News_Detail/ StoryID/11196, accessed on 23 July 2005.
3 Richard Beard, *Muddied Oafs: The Soul of Rugby*, London, 2004, p. 203.
4 Trevor Gibbons, 'Why Are There Two Forms of Rugby?', *Open Rugby*, May 1998.
5 Andrew Moore, *The Mighty Bears. A Social History of North Sydney RLFC, Sydney, 1996; Jimmy Devereux's Yorkshire Pudding. Reflections on the Origins of Rugby League in New South Wales and Queensland*, Sydney, 1996; and 'Opera of the Proletariat: Rugby League, the Labour Movement and Working-Class Culture in New South Wales and Queensland', *Labour History*, No. 79 (November 2000), pp. 57–70. Sean Fagan, *The Rugby Rebellion: The Divide of League and Union*, Sydney, 2005. Greg Ryan, *The Contest for Rugby Supremacy: Accounting for the 1905 All Blacks*, Christchurch, 2005; and as editor *Tackling Rugby Myths: Rugby and New Zealand Society 1854–2004*, Dunedin, 2005.

Introduction

1 Richard Holt, *Sport and the British*, Oxford, 1989.
2 Tony Mason, *Association Football and English Society 1863–1915*, Brighton, 1980. Keith Sandiford *Cricket and the Victorians*, Aldershot, 1994.
3 While I do not necessarily agree with their overall approach, Eileen and Stephen Yeo make a powerful case for the importance of understanding change in the cultural context in their essay 'Ways of Seeing' in E. Yeo and S. Yeo (eds), *Popular Culture and Class Conflict 1590–1914*, Brighton, 1981.
4 Rev. Frank Marshall, *Football – the Rugby Union Game*, London, 1892.
5 For example, see Eric Dunning and Kenneth Sheard, *Barbarians, Gentlemen and Players*, New York, 1979 or Gareth Williams, 'Rugby Union' in Tony Mason (ed.), *Sport in Britain, A Social History*, Cambridge, 1989.

I From folk football to civic pride: Origins to 1879

1 I have chosen the description 'folk football' to describe all the variants of the pre-industrial game because it best captures the traditional, rural-based cross-class popularity of these games. 'Mob' football is a term laden with the value judgements of the nineteenth-century fear of the crowd, whilst mass football does not necessarily

apply to all forms of pre-industrial football – for example, the Dorking form of camp ball seems to have involved only fifteen men per side. The sometimes used 'rough football' is not only value-laden but reeks of the drawing rooms of genteel maiden aunts.

2 Montague Shearman, *Athletics and Football*, London, 1887, p. 260. For recent summaries of the history of folk football, see Robert Malcolmson, *Popular Recreations in English Society 1770–1850*, London, 1975 and Derek Birley, *Sport and the Making of Britain*, Manchester, 1993. Other sources are referred to throughout this chapter.

3 Joseph Lawson, *Letters to the Young on Progress in Pudsey During the Last Sixty Years*, Stanningley, 1887, p. 58.

4 Horatio Smith, *Festivals, Games and Amusements*, London, 1831, p. 122.

5 *Derby and Chesterfield Reporter*, 23 February 1832, quoted in Malcolmson, p. 113.

6 For more on the debate on the decline of folk football see D. A. Reid, 'Folk-Football, the Aristocracy and Cultural Change: A Critique of Dunning and Sheard', *The International Journal of the History of Sport*, Vol. 5, No. 2, September 1988.

7 *Stow's Survey* of 1720, quoted in Horatio Smith, *Festivals, Games and Amusements*, London, 1831, p. 121.

8 Joseph Strutt, *The Sports and Pastimes of the People of England*, London 1801, p. 100.

9 The White Roding episode is outlined in Birley, p. 115. For the Kettering incident see E. P. Thompson's *Customs in Common*, London, 1991, p. 234. Malcolmson lists another three examples.

10 *Derby and Chesterfield Reporter*, 7 February 1845, quoted in Anthony Delves, 'Popular Recreation and Social Conflict in Derby, 1800–1850' in Eileen and Stephen Yeo (eds), *Popular Culture and Class Conflict 1590–1914*, Brighton, 1981, p. 94.

11 Delves, ibid., p. 91.

12 Strutt, p. 100. The claim is echoed in Jemoshaphat Aspin's *A Picture of the Manners, Customs, Sports and Pastimes of the Inhabitants of England*, London, 1825, p. 242. Malcolmson lists sixteen local games still being played in the nineteenth century.

13 *Dewsbury Reporter*, 1 March 1884.

14 See for example Stanley Chadwick, *Claret and Gold*, Huddersfield, 1945.

15 *Hull and East Riding Athlete*, 27 November 1889. The question of cultural continuity between pre-industrial and industrial periods is dealt with in Hugh Cunningham, *Leisure in the Industrial Revolution*, London, 1980.

16 Jennifer Macrory, *Running with the Ball*, London, 1991.

17 Despite the impression created by *Tom Brown's Schooldays*, football may not have been as popular as its supporters wished – the 1845 rules note 'the great abuse' of notes to be excused football.

18 Philip Mason, *The English Gentleman: The Rise and Fall of an Ideal*, London, 1993, p. 170. The definitive account of the role of games in the English public school system is in J. A. Mangan's *Athleticism in the Victorian and Edwardian Public School*, Cambridge, 1981.

19 Interview with H. W. T. Garnett in *Yorkshire Evening Post*, 12 January, 1901.

20 Interview with Rev. E. H. Dykes in *Yorkshire Evening Post*, 9 February 1902.

21 See William Baker, 'William Webb Ellis and the Origins of Rugby Football: The Life and Death of a Victorian Myth', *Albion*, Vol. 13, 1981. Jennifer Macrory, op. cit., is the only serious modern defence of Webb Ellis's claim to posterity. The report of the Old Rugbeian Society can be found in *The Origin of Rugby Football*, Rugby, 1897. The Webb Ellis myth is rivalled for its inventiveness only by the story of Abner Doubleday's 'invention' of baseball, for which see Stephen Jay Gould's 'Creation Myths of Cooperstown' in his *Bully for Brontosaurus*, London, 1991.

22 See John Lowerson *Sport and the English Middle Classes 1870–1914*, Manchester, 1993. The re-creation of rugby as an exclusive pastime is dealt with in Ch. 5.

23 Rev. Frank Marshall, *Football – the Rugby Union Game*, London, 1892, p. 2.

24 A healthy mind in a healthy body.

25 An Old Rugbeian in *Bell's Life*, 22 November 1863.

26 The phrase is Peter Bailey's, from *Leisure and Class in Victorian England*, Second Edition, London, 1987, p. 68. For more on middle-class culture in the north of England during this period, see A. Kidd and M. Roberts (eds), *City, Class and Culture*, Manchester, 1985 and R. J. Morris, 'Middle Class Culture' in Derek Fraser (ed.), *A History of Modern Leeds*, Manchester, 1980.

27 Letter to *Leeds Mercury*, 31 March 1864.

28 For the Volunteer movement in general, see Hugh Cunningham, *The Volunteers*, London, 1975. For demands that the Volunteers take up sporting activities see the *Leeds Mercury*, 7 April 1864.

29 Montague Shearman *Athletics and Football*, London, 1887, and Peter Lovesey, *The Official Centenary History of the Amateur Athletics Association*, London, 1979.

30 See *Leeds Mercury* 30 April 1864 and Stanley Chadwick *Claret and Gold*. In reversal of usual practice, Leeds Athletic Club was formed out of Leeds FC.

31 See J. R. A. Dalglish, *Red, Black and Blue, The First 125 Years of Liverpool Football Club*, Swinton, 1983. There appears to be little hard evidence about when the club itself was formed however.

32 The three founders were Sykes, Major Tom Brown, a Rugbeian, and Howard Aston, formerly of Cheltenham College. See letter from Sykes to Roger Walker, 14 February 1907, quoted in Len Balaam, *Manchester Football Club 1860–1985*, Manchester, 1985, p. 5.

33 William Hutchinson in *Yorkshire Evening Post*, 1 December 1900.

34 For Leeds Grammar School, see *Football Annual*, London, 1868. No copy of the St Peter's rules appears to have survived, although extracts are quoted in the *Oxford English Dictionary*, Second Edition on CD-Rom, Oxford 1993, and a summary can be found in A. Raine, *History of St Peter's School, York*, London, 1926, p. 134.

35 See A. M. Crooks, 'County Football – Lancashire' in Marshall op. cit., Ch. 19.

36 For Garnett see *Yorkshire Evening Post*, 12 January 1901. The pupils of the other schools are respectively Tom Scarborough, a leading light in the Halifax club, C. Hutton Coates, a founder of Yorkshire Wanderers and E. H. Dykes, the instigator of the Leeds Parish Church club.

37 'Referee' *A History of Barrow Football Club*, Barrow, 1914, p. 14.

38 *Yorkshire Evening Post*, 22 February 1901.

39 *Yorkshire Evening Post*, 15 November 1902.

40 Source: *Football Annual*, 1868.

41 Interview with J. G. Hudson, *Yorkshire Evening Post*, 8 December 1900.

42 Hull FC Rule book of 1870, quoted in *Yorkshire Evening Post*, 20 February 1904. Huddersfield also decided that it be compulsory for players to wear the team uniform in October 1870.

43 *Yorkshire Post*, 24 November 1874.

44 Details of the school, which folded after an outbreak of fever in 1869, can be found in *Some Account of Bramham College* by 'An Oxford Graduate', London 1854; the *Yorkshire Weekly Post* of 8 June 1904; and in the *Bramham College Magazine*. The school is listed as a member of the FA in the *Football Annual* of 1870.

45 For a discussion on the varying rules of the metropolitan clubs, see Marshall, op. cit., p. 73.

46 Interview with J. G. Hudson, *Yorkshire Evening Post*, 8 December 1900.

47 *Yorkshire Evening Post*, 22 February 1901. Halifax were even said to oppose tackling below the knee according to the *Athletic News*, 18 November 1876.

48 For Rochdale, see *Football Annual* for 1868. For Sale see M. Barak, *A Century of Rugby At Sale*, Sale, 1962. For Preston, see A. Marsden, *Preston Grasshoppers' Centenary*

Brochure, Preston, 1969. For Bradford, see *Yorkshire Evening Post*, 15 November 1902. For St Peter's, see Raine, op. cit. For Hull see *Yorkshire Evening Post*, 1 December 1900 and 20 February 1904. The explanation for the strange rule would appear to be that Hull's Beevor Lambert had been a pupil at St Peter's where he had presumably been convinced of its efficacy.

49 *Yorkshire Evening Post*, 1 December 1900.

50 Bradford FC 1873/74 Fixture Card, reprinted in *Yorkshire Evening Post*, 5 January 1901.

51 For more on the Sheffield Association, see Percy Young, *Football in Sheffield*, London, 1964.

52 The full text of both the Cambridge and Football Association rules, plus the transcript of the FA's discussion on the rules is in Jennifer Macrory, *They Ran with the Ball*, London, 1991.

53 For reports on Hull FC's soccer adventures, see *Athletic News*, 11 October 1876.

54 *Yorkshire Evening Post*, 15 December 1900.

55 *Yorkshire Evening Post*, 21 February 1903.

56 *Yorkshire Evening Post*, 8 December 1900.

57 Interview with Harry Beardsell, *Yorkshire Evening Post*, 15 December 1900.

58 Letter of Richard Sykes to Willie Parlane, 8 January 1913, quoted in Len Balaam's *Manchester Football Club 1860–1985*, p. 6. Manchester were still playing the occasional game under hacking rules as late 1879.

59 'The YRU' by A Wag in *The Yorkshireman Football Number*, March 1890.

60 Robert Christison in *Yorkshire Evening Post*, 22 February 1901.

61 *Yorkshire Evening Post*, 22 February 1901.

62 Richard Holt, *Sport and the British*, Oxford, 1989, p. 174.

63 *The Times*, 30 October 1896. Valuable background to this section can be found in Patrick Joyce, *Work, Society and Politics*, Brighton, 1980.

64 The key text is obviously Asa Briggs *Victorian Cities*, London, 1963, but see also C. Arscott, and J. Wolff, 'Cultivated Capital', *History Today*, Vol. 37, 1987.

65 In 1895, Brighouse Rangers, a team founded by sons of two of the town's leading textile manufacturers, held a dinner at which the toast was made to 'the town and trade of Brighouse', *Yorkshire Post*, 16 May 1895.

66 See *Halifax Guardian*, 1 November 1873 and *Yorkshire Evening Post*, 9 February 1901.

67 *Wigan Observer*, 29 November 1872 and 24 January 1873.

68 *Oldham Evening Chronicle*, 1 November 1876.

69 James Higson, *History of Salford Football Club*, Salford, 1892.

70 Source: *Football Annual*, 1868–1876.

71 K. A. P. Sandiford, *Cricket and the Victorians*, Aldershot, 1994, which is also the definitive account of nineteenth-century cricket.

72 S. R. Platt at Werneth CC AGM, *Oldham Evening Chronicle*, 1 November 1876.

73 For more on the organised churches' relationship to the working classes, see K. S. Inglis, *The Churches and the Working Class in Victorian England*, London, 1963 and Brian Harrison, 'Religion and Recreation in Nineteenth Century England', *Past and Present*, No. 38, 1967.

74 Reprinted in *Yorkshire Evening Post*, 12 December 1903.

75 See the *Wakefield Express*, 2 and 23 November, and 14 December 1872.

76 The phrase is A.W. Pullin's, otherwise known as 'Old Ebor', the self-appointed doyen of Yorkshire cricket and football writing and, as the son of a clergyman, a vigorous advocate of muscular Christianity. A summary of Leeds Parish Church clergy's views on the importance of games can be found in a sermon of the Reverend Maurice Ponsonby in *The Leeds Parish Church Magazine*, December 1879, pp. 311–12.

77 *Yorkshire Post*, 11 March 1876.

78 See G. H. Cooper, *Spen Valley Rugby Football Reminiscences*, Cleckheaton, 1920.

79 *Yorkshire Evening Post*, 9 February 1902.

80 Wakefield Trinity FC cash book, quoted in *Yorkshire Evening Post*, 1 November 1903. See also *Athletic News*, 23 March 1877.

81 A. G. Guillemard, 'The Past Season', *Football Annual*, 1877.

82 For accounts of the formation of the YCFC see Ch. 20 in Marshall, op. cit. and *Yorkshire Evening Post*, 12 January 1901.

83 *Yorkshire Evening Post*, 12 January 1901.

84 *Athletic News*, 22 December 1876 and *Yorkshire Evening Post*, 1 December 1900.

85 *Yorkshire Post*, 26 December 1877.

86 *Yorkshire Post*, 31 December 1877. For an account of Halifax's winning season, see *The Yorkshireman Football Number*, 1890.

87 *Yorkshire Post*, 14 April 1879.

88 Sam Duckitt reminiscencing in *Yorkshire Evening Post*, 9 February 1901.

89 *Yorkshire Evening Post*, 12 January 1901 and 16 November 1901.

90 'An Old Trinity Stager', *The Yorkshireman Football Number*, March 1891. A rough translation of this would be: 'Rufus had started to develop nicely as a player when he fell out with some of the Trinity chaps and became friendly with Halifax. Don't go jumping to conclusions. I didn't say the Cup started the kidnapping business. Only this is the first case I know of and it was just to help Halifax win the Cup for the first time. Two and two, you know, make four.' For alternative explanations of Ward's move, see *Yorkshire Evening Post*, 9 July 1901 and 1 November 1902.

91 *The Yorkshireman Football Number*, 1890.

92 'An Old Trinity Stager', *The Yorkshireman Football Number*, March 1891. This translates as 'I copped [caught] football fever at the same time as many hundreds more did – when the Yorkshire Cup was first played for thirteen years ago, and what's more – or less if anything – I've had it ever since.'

2   The coming of the working classes: 1879–1886

1   The failure of Bradford hardware store owners to agree to 2pm Saturday closing in 1881 led to a minor protest by young counter clerks who were therefore unable to watch football. *The Yorkshireman*, 2 April 1881.

2   Useful summaries of the development of working-class leisure time can be found in Hugh Cunningham, 'Leisure and Culture' in Vol. 2 of *The Cambridge Social History of Britain 1750–1950*, Cambridge, 1990, and Wray Vamplew's *Pay Up and Play the Game*, Cambridge, 1988. The classic text on Saint Monday remains D. A. Reid, 'The Decline of Saint Monday 1766–1876', *Past and Present*, No. 71, May 1976.

3   Moses Heap, diary manuscript in Rawtenstall Library, Lancashire.

4   *Yorkshire Evening Post*, 1 November 1902.

5   A. G. Guillemard, 'The Past Season' in *Football Annual*, London, 1880.

6   This is the term used in Dunning and Sheard's *Barbarians, Gentlemen and Players*.

7   The 'slumbers' quote is from Engels' article 'May 4 in London' of 23 May 1890 in Marx and Engels, *On Britain*, Moscow, 1971, p. 401. The quote which follows is from 'England in 1845 and 1885' of February 1885, pp. 387–8.

8   See Michael Latham, *Buff Berry and the Mighty Bongers*, Chorley, 1995, p. 71.

9   Interview in *North West Daily Mail*, 15 November 1919.

10 *Yorkshire Post*, 10 October 1883.

11 Stuart Barlow, 'The Diffusion of "Rugby" Football in the Industrialised Context of Rochdale 1868–90', *The International Journal of the History of Sport*, Vol 10, No. 1, April 1993.

12 W. Corlyon manuscript notebooks in Hull City Archives.

13 *Yorkshire Post*, 15 October 1887.

14 *The Yorkshireman*, 16 February 1884.
15 *Yorkshire Post*, 11 November 1893. For a broader perspective on the relationship between working-class participants and the clerical sponsors of recreation clubs, see Peter Bailey, *Leisure and Class in Victorian England*, Second Edition, London, 1987.
16 *The Lantern* (St Helens), 13 September 1889. See also *Clarion*, 24 December 1892 and *Athletic News*, 9 March 1896. See also J. Arnold, *The Influence of Pilkington Brothers (Glass Manufacturers) on the Growth of Sport and Community Recreation in St Helens*, unpublished MEd thesis, University of Liverpool, 1977. For the paternalism of the company, see John Walton, *Lancashire: A Social History* 1558–1939, Manchester, 1987, p. 321.
17 *The Yorkshireman*, 11 October 1885.
18 For more on this see S. Bradley, *Leisure and Society in Huddersfield 1868–95*, BA thesis, University of Bristol, 1989.
19 *The Yorkshireman*, 8 April 1882 and *Yorkshire Evening Post* 21 November 1903.
20 *Yorkshire Football Handbook*, 1881–82 and 1885–86.
21 *The Yorkshireman*, 29 November 1884. For an insight into the importance of the pub to recreation in the working-class communities of the English North East, see Alan Metcalfe, 'Organised Sport in the Mining Communities of South Northumberland', *Victorian Studies*, No. 25, Summer 1982.
22 *Yorkshire Evening Post*, 16 January 1904.
23 *Yorkshire Post*, 21 December 1893.
24 For this and many other examples, see the *Yorkshire Post*, 11, 12 and 13 December 1879.
25 *Yorkshire Post*, 12 December 1879.
26 See Bryn Trescatheric, *Sport and Leisure in Victorian Barrow*, Barrow, 1983.
27 *Wigan Observer*, 8 November 1879.
28 *Yorkshire Post*, 10 February 1880.
29 *The Yorkshireman*, 1 December 1887.
30 *Yorkshire Post*, 2 December 1879.
31 A Londoner, 'Metropolitan Football' in Marshall (ed.), *Football – the Rugby Union Game*, p. 329. The Goole quote is from a letter of 9 May 1882 in the papers of Munby & Scott, Solicitors, in York City Archives.
32 For the story of the declined cup offer, see Marshall, op. cit., p. 86. Hill's comments can be found in 'The Past Season' in *Football Annual*, London 1882.
33 A. G. Guillemard, 'The Past Season' in *Football Annual*, London, 1880. See also *The Field*, 12 January 1884 for southern-based calls for a national rugby cup contest.
34 For information on the Hull amalgamation, see *Yorkshire Evening Post*, 1 December 1900 and 20 February 1904 (in which the resolution is reprinted) and the *Yorkshire Post*, 11 March and 1 April 1879.
35 *Yorkshire Evening Post*, 21 February 1903.
36 In this they reflected many of the same concerns as the leadership of the RFU who urged an end to all cup competitions. See G. Rowland Hill, 'The Past Season' in *Football Annual* for both 1882 and 1883.
37 *Yorkshire Post*, 20 February 1883. Bradford did eventually boycott the cup in the late 1880s.
38 For an account of the formation of the Lancashire County club, see A. M. Crook 'County Football: Lancashire', Ch. 19 of Marshall, op. cit., and Lancashire County Football Club minutes, 22 December 1881.
39 *Athletic News*, 4 November 1876, 1 September 1877 and 8 February 1882.
40 *Manchester Guardian*, 12 October 1882.
41 *Burnley Express and Advertiser*, 21 October 1882. *Football Field and Sports Telegram*, 17 January 1885 for further details. Key texts are Rob Lewis's, *The Development of Professional Football in Lancashire, 1870–1914*, unpublished PhD thesis,

University of Lancaster, 1993; Anon. *History of the Lancashire Football Association*, Blackburn, 1928; Graham Williams, *The Code War*, Harefield, 1994; Dave Russell, ' "Sporadic and Curious": The Emergence of Rugby and Soccer Zones in Yorkshire and Lancashire c1860–1914', *The International Journal of the History of Sport*, Vol. 5, No. 2, 1988; and, more generally, John Bale, *Sport and Place*, London, 1982.

42 For Suter, see Tony Mason, *Association Football and English Society 1863–1915*, Brighton, 1980, p. 69 and *Football Field and Sports Telegram*, 10 October 1885. Details of the others can be found in *History of the Lancashire Football Association* above.

43 The Free Critic, 'The Past and the Future', *Athletic News Football Annual, 1892–93*, London, 1892, p. 107.

44 *Wigan Observer*, 6 October 1886.

45 LCFC committee minutes 15 February 1887 and *Yorkshire Post*, 16 February 1887.

46 An Old Player, 'The Rugby Union Game in 1888–89' in *Football Annual*, London, 1889.

47 *Dewsbury Reporter*, 8 March 1884. The preceding figures are taken from the *Yorkshire Post*. It must be stressed that all figures are newspaper estimates, as no accurate records of attendances were kept at this time.

48 *Dewsbury Reporter*, 5 April 1884.

49 'The Rugby Game in Yorkshire' in *Football Annual*, London, 1882.

50 *Yorkshire Post*, 4 April 1887 and 31 October 1887.

51 The Salford figures are taken from the financial summaries in James Higson's *History of Salford FC*, Salford, 1892. For Warrington, see the *Warrington Guardian*, 8 June 1887.

52 *Warrington Guardian*, 14 April 1886. The club's president was a Tory and two committee members were Liberals.

53 Tony Mason in *Association Football and English Society 1863–1915*, is able to give a partial picture of the class and occupational backgrounds of spectators by an analysis of the casualties at the 1902 Ibrox disaster. Fortunately, rugby never suffered such tragedy.

54 *The Yorkshireman*, 15 March 1884.

55 *The Yorkshireman*, 26 March 1881.

56 *Wakefield Express*, 9 July 1887.

57 *Wigan Observer*, 22 November 1886.

58 *Yorkshire Post*, 16 January 1880.

59 *The Yorkshireman*, 8 September 1887.

60 *Yorkshire Post*, 21 January 1880.

61 *Huddersfield Daily Examiner*, 20 September 1886.

62 For details see *The Yorkshireman*, 18 October 1884 and 16 October 1886.

63 *The Lantern* (St Helens), 9 May 1890. The formation of pub-based clubs to pay for excursions was a common phenomenon in working-class communities. See, for example, the 'Going-Off' clubs described in John Walton's 'The Demand for Working Class Seaside Holidays in Victorian England', *Economic History Review*, Vol. 34, 1982.

64 See *The Yorkshireman*, 17 January and 7 March 1885, 30 January and 18 September 1886.

65 *The Yorkshireman*, 11 April 1885.

66 *Yorkshire Post*, 22 September 1884 and *The Yorkshireman*, 27 September 1884.

67 *The Yorkshireman*, 3 March 1883.

68 *The Yorkshireman*, 14 March 1885.

69 *The Yorkshireman*, 20 April 1892.

70 *The Yorkshireman*, 15 April 1891.

71 *The Yorkshireman*, 2 December 1891.

72 *Salford Reporter*, 2 June 1888. *Yorkshire Evening Post*, 29 November 1902.

73 *The Yorkshireman*, 26 September 1886 and 11 April 1888.

74 *Yorkshire Post*, 7 November 1888.

75 Higson, op. cit. p. 137.

76 *The Yorkshireman*, 28 April 1887.

77 *The Yorkshireman*, 24 February 1883.

78 *Yorkshire Post*, 27 May 1889 and 28 April 1892.

79 *Clarion*, 10 February 1894.

80 *The Yorkshireman*, 27 September 1884 and *Yorkshire Post*, 8 November 1886.

81 The dialogue comes from *The Yorkshireman*, 21 November 1885. More information on the charges of referees, which were soon to be outlawed by the RFU, can be found in the issue for 10 October 1885.

82 *The Yorkshireman*, 21 October 1882.

83 Higson, op. cit.

84 For Batley, see C. F. Shaw *The Gallant Youths*, Batley, 1899, p. 22. For Pudsey, see *The Yorkshireman*, 6 March 1884.

85 Unfortunately, the lone custodian was not able to prevent several hundred spectators entering the ground for free. *The Yorkshireman*, 5 January 1885.

86 Robert D. Storch, 'The Policeman as "Domestic Missionary": Urban Discipline and Popular Culture in Northern England 1850–1880', *Journal of Social History*, Vol. 9, 1976. The broadest historical overview of the behaviour of sports crowds can be found in Allen Guttman, *Sports Spectators*, New York, 1986.

87 *The Yorkshireman*, 14 March 1885. A more extended discussion of rugby crowd behaviour can be found in Chapter 6.

88 *Yorkshire Post*, 8 November 1886.

89 *Yorkshire Post*, 2 December 1879.

90 *Yorkshire Post*, 17 February 1880. *The Yorkshireman*, 9 December 1882. Wakefield Trinity committee minutes 4 November 1878 and 1 June 1880, quoted in *Yorkshire Evening Post*, 1 November 1902. The word 'induced' was deliberately used by former Wakefield Trinity and Yorkshire RFU president Barron Kilner in an interview describing Teddy's signing in the *Yorkshire Evening Post*, 23 November 1901, in which he admitted that 'in the light of more recent legislation the move would have been taken as one of professionalism by the Rugby Union'. This evidence contradicts the assumption of Dunning and Sheard in *Barbarians, Gentlemen and Players*, that the professional question only emerged as an issue in rugby in the early 1890s.

91 *Yorkshire Post*, 25 November 1879.

92 *Yorkshire Post*, 2 December 1879. For more on the question of professionalism in cricket, see Ric Sissons, *The Professionals: A Social History of the Professional Cricketer*, London, 1988.

93 Quoted in P. Lovesey, *The Official Centenary History of the Amateur Athletic Association*, London, 1979, p. 22.

94 Ibid., p. 24.

95 *Yorkshire Post*, 11 October 1886.

96 *Bradford Observer*, 26 January 1886.

97 See *The Yorkshireman*, 9 May 1888. For details of W. W. Read's expense payments on tour see David Montefiore, *Cricket in the Doldrums*, Campbelltown, 1992.

98 Lovesey, op. cit., p. 22.

99 *Yorkshire Post*, 6 March 1880.

100 *Yorkshire Post*, 20 December 1879.

101 *Yorkshire Post*, 2 December 1879.

102 *Leeds Intelligencer*, 2 March 1773.

103 William Whellan, *The History and Topography of the Counties of Cumberland and Westmoreland*, Pontefract, 1860.

104 *Northampton Mercury*, 29 July 1765.

105 Stanley Chadwick *Claret and Gold*, Huddersfield, 1945.

106 Eric Hobsbawm and Terence Ranger, *The Invention of Tradition*, Cambridge, 1983, p. 9.

107 *Leeds Mercury*, 9 December 1884.

108 *Leeds Mercury*, 2 October 1886, and *Yorkshire Post*, 27 September 1886.

109 Wakefield Trinity Committee minutes, 28 November 1881, quoted in J. C. Lindley, *100 Years Of Rugby – The History of Wakefield Trinity 1873–1973*, Wakefield, 1973, p. 34.

110 Hull FC *Report and Accounts 1883–84* and committee minutes, 10 March 1884, 17 March 1884 and 1 April 1884.

111 York FC committee minutes 5 December 1885, quoted in *Yorkshire Evening Post*, 21 February 1903.

112 Yorkshire County Challenge Cup rules, point six, quoted in the *Yorkshire Post*, 28 September 1885.

113 *The Yorkshireman*, 10 January 1885.

114 *The Yorkshireman*, 15 May 1886.

115 *The Yorkshireman*, 1 May 1886.

116 *Yorkshire Post*, 28 April 1883.

117 *The Yorkshireman*, 14 May 1885.

118 *The Yorkshireman*, 28 February 1885.

119 *The Yorkshireman*, 1 March 1884.

120 *Toby, the Yorkshire Tyke*, 22 March 1884.

121 *Leeds Mercury*, 2 October 1886.

122 *The Yorkshireman*, 9 February 1884. 'They want no more than a leg of mutton and two bottles of wine each and then they'll play.' 'Yes, and if I had the money they would have it.' To appreciate the importance of such 'presents' to working class players' diets, see D. J. Oddy, 'Working Class Diets', *Economic History Review*, Vol. 23, 1970, and J. R. Roberts, 'Working Class Standards of Living in Barrow and Lancaster, 1890–1914', *Economic History Review*, Vol. 30, 1977.

123 *The Yorkshireman*, 30 September 1882.

124 *The Yorkshireman*, 13 September 1884.

125 *The Yorkshireman*, 12 and 26 September 1885 and 14 November 1885.

126 *Wigan Observer*, 9 October 1886.

127 *Leeds Mercury*, 2 October 1886.

128 *Dewsbury Reporter*, 22 February 1884.

129 *Dewsbury Reporter*, 20 September 1884.

130 *Bradford Observer*, 21 and 28 September 1885, *Bradford Daily Telegraph*, 22 September 1885, *The Yorkshireman*, 12 September and 3 October 1885.

131 *The Yorkshireman*, 3 March 1885.

132 For details of the Stadden and Stuart affair, see *The Yorkshireman*, 25 September 1886 and *Leeds Mercury*, 12 October 1886. Both diplomatically did not name Stadden's and Stuart's employer. Only the *Evening Express*, 11 October 1886, felt compelled to reveal the most pertinent fact in the case.

133 *Yorkshire Post*, 25 January 1886.

134 Details of the hearing are taken from the *Yorkshire Post*, *Leeds Mercury* and *Bradford Observer*, 2 and 3 March 1886.

135 *Yorkshire Post*, 20 September 1886.

136 *Bradford Observer*, 28 September 1886. A. E. T. Watson (ed.), *The Year's Sport: A Review of British Sports and Pastimes for the Year 1885*, London, 1886, p. 246.

137 A. Budd, 'The Rugby Union Game' in *Football Annual*, London, 1886, p. 52.

138 *Yorkshire Post*, 27 September 1886.

139 Minutes of the Rugby Football Union committee, 15 January 1880.

140 G. Rowland Hill, 'The Past Season' in *Football Annual*, London, 1885.

141 *Pastime*, 7 October 1885. Details of expenses paid to southern teams are difficult to ascertain. In the 1887–88 season, Bradford paid a total of £244/15 s to visiting teams from southern England and Scotland, made up as follows: Blackheath £57/15 s; Richmond £42/10 s; Guy's Hospital £30; Oxford University £20; Edinburgh Institution £30; Fettes-Loretto combined schools side £37/10 s; London Scottish £27/10 s. See *The Yorkshireman*, 2 May 1888.

142 For a fuller exposition of Budd's views on the probable need of the middle-class clubs to separate themselves from working class-based clubs, see his article in Marshall, op. cit.

143 *Yorkshire Post*, 27 September 1886.

144 *Yorkshire Post*, 11 October 1886.

145 See Minutes of the RFU, 4 October 1886, *Leeds Mercury* and *Yorkshire Post*, both 5 October 1886, and the *Bradford Observer*, 12 October 1886. Garnett's words later became immortalised by Budd, who used almost exactly the same formulation six years later in his article in Marshall, op. cit., p. 132. By that time, Garnett, like most of the Yorkshire leadership, had abandoned this position.

146 As above. Ironically both Horace Lyne and Mark Newsome became presidents of their respective Rugby Unions and members of the rugby union International Board after the Northern Union split of 1895.

147 For the wording of the Lancashire amendment see the LCFC committee minutes of 1 October 1886. Unfortunately the RFU minutes of the meeting are incomplete and do not record individual votes. The details about the votes cast against come from the *Leeds Daily News*, 11 October 1886. The names of the other two clubs which voted against the motion do not appear to have been recorded.

148 *The Yorkshireman*, 29 October 1886. 'Who is going to provide the mutton? Because no mutton, no playing.'

3 'King Football': 1886–1893

1 This is the title of a celebratory anonymous poem that appeared on the front page of *The Yorkshireman*, 8 October 1890.

2 *The Times*, 30 October 1896.

3 For the observation on Bede, see H. M. Jewell, *The North–South Divide: The Origins of Northern Consciousness in England*, Manchester, 1994, p. 4.

4 Elizabeth Gaskell, *North and South*, London, 1855. Penguin edition, p. 398.

5 Talbot Baines, *The Industrial North in the Last Decade of the Nineteenth Century*, Leeds, 1928, p. 17.

6 Donald Horne, *God is an Englishman*, Sydney, 1969. Quoted in Martin Wiener *'English Culture and the Decline of the Industrial Spirit 1850–1980'*, Cambridge, 1981, p. 41.

7 For an exploration of the cultural activities of the northern Victorian bourgeoisie, see Janet Wolff and Caroline Arscott, 'Cultivated Capital', *History Today*, Vol. 37, 1987, and R. J. Morris, 'Middle Class Culture 1700–1914' in Derek Fraser (ed.), *A History of Modern Leeds*, Manchester, 1980. For factory culture, see Patrick Joyce, *Work, Society and Politics*, Brighton, 1980.

8 Talbot Baines, op.cit., p. 18.

9 It must, however, be pointed out that the idea of the North versus South game was proposed by Hull's William Beevor-Lambert in 1873.

10 Yorkshire County Football Club circular of 10 October 1881. For more on the YRU and RFU at this time see the *Yorkshire Post* throughout January 1888.

11 Hostilities were increased by the exclusion of sixteen Yorkshire clubs from the 1891 AGM for irregularities over their payments of subscriptions. Rochdale Hornets were one of the few Lancashire clubs to vote with Yorkshire.

12 *Yorkshire Post*, 16 September 1891.

13 For an interesting discussion of this point see Charles Dellheim 'Imagining England: Victorian Views of the North', *Northern History*, Vol. 22, 1986.

14 Frank Musgrove, *The North of England. A History from Roman Times to the Present*, Oxford, 1990, p. 310. For a rejoinder, see J. Walton, 'Professor Musgrove's North of England: A Critique', *Journal of Regional and Local Studies*, Vol. 12, No. 2, 1992.

15 The quote is from *The Yorkshireman*, 14 April 1887. The Huddersfield Holliday Cup, founded in 1885, is still played for by local rugby league teams.

16 *The Yorkshireman*, 2 May 1893.

17 *Yorkshire Post*, 3 June 1890. In December 1894 the LCFC had forty-three member clubs, see *Salford Reporter*, 1 December 1894.

18 *Wigan Observer*, 6 October 1886.

19 For full details, see *Athletic News*, 8 October 1889.

20 *Wigan Observer*, 22 April 1886. *Rochdale Observer*, 11 April 1888.

21 *Warrington Guardian*, 5 June 1886.

22 Clowes was later badly injured in an industrial accident that almost ended his career. *The Yorkshireman*, 6 November 1889.

23 A. W. Pullin, *Alfred Shaw: Cricketer. His Career and Reminiscences*, London, 1902, p. 102. See also David Firth, *My Dear Victorious Stod*, London, 1977 and Peter Wynne-Thomas, *Give Me Arthur*, London, 1985.

24 See *Yorkshire Post*, 3 April 1883 and subsequent issues for the full story. It was one of the few disputed cases in Yorkshire rugby in the 1880s that had nothing to do with accusations of professionalism – Halifax claimed Jones was not eligible to play for Dewsbury because he had previously been a reserve for the Lancashire county side.

25 Rev. Frank Marshall, 'Foreign Tours', in *Football – the Rugby Union Game*, London, 1892.

26 *Halifax Guardian*, 17 and 24 March 1888.

27 Letter of Arthur Shrewsbury to Alfred Shaw 14 March 1888: 'We sent [Stoddart] a cheque for £50 only a few days since which should bind him.' I am grateful to Peter Wynne-Thomas at Nottinghamshire CCC archive, Trent Bridge and Trevor Delaney for making available copies of Shrewsbury's correspondence.

28 Shrewsbury to Shaw, 14 March 1888.

29 Shrewsbury to Shaw, 22 June 1888.

30 Shrewsbury to Shaw, 29 February 1888 and 5 June 1888.

31 Shrewsbury to Shaw, 22 June 1888 and 5 June 1888.

32 Shrewsbury to Shaw, 18 January 1888.

33 *Yorkshire Post*, 26 November 1888.

34 *Yorkshire Post*, 18, 20, 22, 24 and 30 October 1888.

35 *Yorkshire Post*, 13 November 1888.

36 *Yorkshire Post*, 20 February 1889.

37 An Old Player, 'The Rugby Union Game in 1888–89' in the *Football Annual*, London, 1889 and *The Yorkshireman*, 27 November 1889.

38 *Yorkshire Post*, 8 March and 16 and 20 July 1889.

39 This was confirmed some years later by former Leeds Grammar School and Heckmondwike player Aulay MacAulay in the *Yorkshire Evening Post*, 9 March 1901.

40 *The Yorkshireman*, 29 January 1890.

41 *Yorkshire Post*, 8 and 15 May and 4 June 1889.

42 *Clarion*, 1 October 1892.

43 *Yorkshire Post* 19 May 1892.

44 A. W. Pullin, 'Competition Football in Yorkshire: Has it proved a success?' in *The Yorkshireman Football Number*, March 1893.

45 The phrase 'social zoning' is from John Walton, 'Residential Amenity, Respectable Morality and the Rise of the Entertainment Industry: The Case of Blackpool 1860–1914', *Literature and History*, Vol. 1, 1975, and many other works, in which he describes the social segregation of Blackpool holiday sites.

46 *Oldham Evening Chronicle*, 13 October 1890.

47 *Oldham Evening Chronicle*, 26 and 29 September and 15 November 1890. Two years later, while playing for Werneth's neighbours Oldham, Ashworth played for England.

48 This is confirmed in an article in the Manchester *Umpire*, quoted in the *Oldham Evening Chronicle*, 30 October 1890.

49 McCutcheon later became a leading Northern Union referee and president of the Oldham club.

50 The description of Marshall is from RFU committee member G. F. Berney in Rev. Frank Marshall and L. R. Tosswill, *Football – the Rugby Union Game*, Second Edition, London, 1925, p. 58.

51 *Oldham Evening Chronicle*, 13 and 30 October 1890. *Yorkshire Post*, 23 October 1890.

52 *Manchester Guardian*, 27 October 1890.

53 *Yorkshire Post*, 17 January 1891.

54 *Clarion*, 29 October and 5 November. It is interesting to compare the similarity of the words used by the Broughton Rangers secretary and those used by Dewsbury in 1886 in explanation of Stadden's and Stuart's move from Cardiff.

55 *The Yorkshireman*, 1 November 1892.

56 For more details on the RFU's volte-face see the *Yorkshire Post*, 3 December 1892 and 27 January 1893 and *The Yorkshireman*, 31 January 1893. They were reinstated as amateurs in 1896 before signing for Broughton again in 1899, by which time Rangers had become founding members of the Northern Union.

57 *Clarion*, 2 April 1892.

58 *Salford Reporter*, 24 September 1892.

59 *Yorkshire Post*, 3 June, 15 September and 4 October 1892.

60 *Clarion*, 22 December 1894.

61 *Yorkshire Evening Post*, 9 February 1901.

62 *Yorkshire Post*, 18 September 1894.

63 *The Yorkshireman*, 12 January 1889.

64 *The Yorkshireman*, 25 March 1891.

65 *Hull and East Riding Athlete*, 8 October 1890.

66 *The Yorkshireman*, 11 November 1891.

67 *The Yorkshireman*, 27 November 1889.

68 *Yorkshire Post*, 13, 16 and 17 March 1894.

69 Mason, op. cit., Ch. 4.

70 Interestingly, Ross McKibbin, in his 'Work and Hobbies in Britain, 1880–1950' in *The Ideologies of Class*, Oxford, 1990, p. 161, suggests that 'the principal hobby of the unskilled labourer was certainly sport', which seems to add further weight to undermine the case for footballers being predominantly skilled men.

71 *Yorkshire Post*, 16 July 1889.

72 *Yorkshire Post*, 22 November 1892.

73 *Yorkshire Post*, 23 March 1892.

74 *Yorkshire Post*, 14 and 25 October 1890.

75 *Yorkshire Post*, 24 October 1890.

76 *Yorkshire Football*, 24 January 1888.

77 *Yorkshire Post*, 16 September 1889.

78 *Yorkshire Post*, 14 October 1889.

79 *Yorkshire Post*, 20 and 28 December 1890.

80 *Yorkshire Post*, 7 February 1893.

81 *Yorkshire Post*, 20 July 1889.

82 *Yorkshire Post*, 2 October 1888.

83 *The Yorkshireman*, 21 October and 2 December 1891. *Yorkshire Post*, 28 November 1891.

84 'The YRU' by A Wag, in *The Yorkshireman Football Number*, March 1890.

85 *Salford Reporter*, 17 November 1894.

86 *Hull and East Riding Athlete*, 29 January 1890.

87 On the Armley strike, see *The Yorkshireman*, 16 December 1891. On Wakefield, see *Yorkshire Post*, 6 February 1893 and *The Yorkshireman*, 14 February 1893. For Harrogate, see *Yorkshire Post*, 3 January and 1 February 1894.

88 *Yorkshire Post*, 21 October 1891.

89 *The Yorkshireman*, 29 January 1890. 'If I'm not good enough to play football with them without a collar and tie, I'm not going to play at all.'

90 *Yorkshire Post*, 28 September 1889. Sutcliffe's unique career encompassed a try-scoring debut for England in their 1889 match against the Maori tourists, a professional soccer debut for Bolton Wanderers eight months later and an England soccer debut against Wales in 1893. He subsequently played for Millwall, Manchester United, Plymouth Argyle and Southend United before returning to his native West Yorkshire in 1919 as the trainer to Bradford City, the club that as Manningham had made the same switch of codes in 1903.

91 *Yorkshire Chat*, 25 November 1899.

92 *The Yorkshireman*, 1 April 1891 and 13 September 1893 and *Clarion*, 22 October 1892.

93 *Yorkshire Post*, 9 September 1889.

94 *Yorkshire Post*, 20 September 1889.

95 *The Yorkshireman*, 6 November 1889.

96 *Yorkshire Post*, 2 March 1886.

97 *Yorkshire Post*, 13 December 1889.

98 *Salford Reporter*, 10 November 1894.

99 *The Yorkshireman*, 18 September 1889 and the *Yorkshire Post*, 20 September 1889.

100 *Yorkshire Post*, 10 November 1891 and *The Yorkshireman*, 31 January 1893. The three Welshmen had initially gone North to play for Holbeck but on arrival in Leeds had been 'kidnapped' by the Church club's officials.

101 *Oldham Evening Chronicle*, 27 October 1890.

102 *Yorkshire Post*, 6 October 1893. Unfortunately, we have no way of knowing the identity of this enterprising Welshman – nor if he was successful in finding a situation.

103 *Yorkshire Post*, 9 October 1894.

104 *Yorkshire Post*, 16 March 1893.

105 *Yorkshire Post*, 17 January 1887.

106 *The Yorkshireman*, 29 November 1892 and 11 April 1893.

107 *The Yorkshireman*, 23 August 1893.

108 Figures taken from Trevor Delaney, *Rugby Disunion*, Keighley, 1993, p. 71.

109 *Yorkshire Owl*, 23 January 1895.

110 *Yorkshire Post*, 6 December 1892. *The Yorkshireman*, 29 October 1890.

111 *The Yorkshireman*, 30 May 1888.

112 *Yorkshire Post*, 20 September 1889.

113 *Yorkshire Post*, 2 March 1886.

114 *Yorkshire Post*, 13 December 1889.

115 *Yorkshire Post*, 20 September 1889.

116 These figures come from the chapter on players in Tony Mason, op. cit., p. 95.

117 *Salford Reporter*, 17 November 1894 and *Yorkshire Post*, 8 September 1894.

118 Quoted in C. F. Shaw, *The Gallant Youths*, Batley, 1899.

119 See for example O. L. Owen, *The History of the Rugby Football Union*, London, 1955.

120 *Yorkshire Evening Post*, 21 and 28 November 1903. *The Yorkshireman*, 8 April 1882.

121 *The Yorkshireman*, 11 October 1893.

122 *The Yorkshireman*, 5 March 1889.

123 *The Yorkshireman*, 17 February 1887.

124 *The Yorkshireman*, 6 and 27 September 1892.

125 *The Yorkshireman*, 15 January 1890 and *Yorkshire Post*, 28 April 1892.

126 William 'Monsey' Parr, St Helens Recreation captain in 1889. *The Lantern* (St Helens), 13 September 1889.

127 A Londoner, 'Metropolitan Football' in Rev. Frank Marshall, *Football – the Rugby Union Game*, London, 1892.

128 See Marshall, *Football – the Rugby Union Game*, London, 1892. *Yorkshire Post*, 10 February 1880 and *The Yorkshireman*, 9 December 1882.

129 *Athletic News*, 7 April 1890.

130 *Yorkshire Post*, 7 January 1888.

131 *The Yorkshireman*, 18 February and 25 March 1891.

132 *Halifax Guardian*, 2 February 1889. The West Riding club played the three half-back system, albeit unsuccessfully, in their 1894 Yorkshire Cup semi-final.

133 Advocacy of two full-backs and eight forwards can be found in the *Yorkshire Post*, 24 November 1892. For the development of the four three-quarter system see Gareth Willliams and David Smith, *Fields of Praise*, Cardiff, 1980. p. 61.

134 *Athletic News*, 23 April 1906. *The Yorkshireman*, 3 March 1887.

135 *Yorkshire Post*, 26 November 1891.

136 *Yorkshire Post*, 30 April 1894.

137 *Yorkshire Post*, as above. *Manchester Guardian*, 28 November 1892.

138 H. H. Almond, 'Football as a Moral Agent', *Nineteenth Century*, Vol. 34, 1893.

139 *The Yorkshireman*, 15 March 1884.

140 *Yorkshire Post*, 22 March 1887. For details of the Inland Revenue, see *Yorkshire Post*, 2 March 1893.

141 *Bradford Observer*, 9 March 1886.

142 For details see *The Yorkshireman*, 8 December 1894.

143 *The Yorkshireman*, 26 September 1886 and 1 September 1887. *Yorkshire Post*, 10 February 1891. Some of this material is taken from Trevor Delaney's excellent and exhaustive *The Grounds of Rugby League*, Keighley, 1991.

144 *Warrington Guardian*, 4 June 1892.

145 *Yorkshire Post*, 30 April 1891, 14 and 19 May 1892, 13 April 1893. Hull FC annual reports and accounts 1883–84 and 1887–88. James Higson, *The History of Salford FC*, Salford, 1892. *The Yorkshireman*, 2 January 1886.

146 *Yorkshire Post*, 16 September 1890.

147 *Yorkshire Post*, 10 June 1889.

148 *Warrington Examiner*, 25 November 1895.

149 *Yorkshire Post*, 10 January 1887 and *Huddersfield Daily Examiner*, 13 October 1886.

150 *Warrington Examiner*, 4 June 1890.

151 *The Yorkshireman*, 12 September 1885 and 24 April 1887.

152 *Wigan Observer*, 22 November 1886.

153 *The Yorkshireman*, 30 October 1886.

154 *Athletic News*, 11 October 1887.

155 *Yorkshire Post*, 22 January 1887 and 17 April 1890.

156 *Yorkshire Post*, 3 June 1890 and 9 May 1891.

157 Higson, op. cit.

158 See, for example, the *Yorkshire Post*, 10 September 1894.
159 *Yorkshire Post*, 21 January 1891.
160 *The Yorkshireman*, 2 May 1888.
161 *Bradford Illustrated Weekly Telegraph*, 25 September 1886.
162 *Yorkshire Post*, 10 February 1891.
163 *Yorkshire Post*, 26 January 1891.
164 An excellent account of Leeds's road to cityhood can be found in Arthur Elton, 'Becoming a City: Leeds, 1893', *Publications of the Thoresby Society, Miscellany*, Second Series, Vol. 3, 1993.
165 *The Yorkshireman*, 4 September 1886 and *Yorkshire Post*, 10 March 1887.
166 Leeds Cricket, Football and Athletic Company Limited, *Annual Report and Accounts*, year ending 30 April 1891.
167 *Slater's Directory of Leeds and District*, London, 1890.
168 *Yorkshire Post*, 14 May 1892.
169 *Warrington Guardian*, 8 June 1887. For more on this debate regarding soccer clubs, see Stephen Tischler, *Footballers and Businessmen*, New York, 1981; Wray Vamplew, *Pay Up and Play the Game: Professional Sport in Britain 1875–1914*, Cambridge, 1988; and also his 'The Economics of a Sports Industry, Scottish Gate Money Football 1890–1914', *Economic History Review*, November 1982, Vol. 35.

4 Schism: 1893–1895

1 H. Hendrick, 'The Leeds Gas Strike', *Publications of the Thoresby Society, Miscellany*, Vol. 16, Part 2, 1993. Cyril Pearce, *The Manningham Mills Strike*, Hull, 1975.
2 For detailed statistics on strike activity for this period see the Board of Trade's *Report of the Chief Labour Correspondent on the Strikes and Lockouts of 1896*, London, 1896. For the shooting of Featherstone miners see J. J. Terrett, *H. H. Asquith and the Featherstone Massacre*, London, 1906. For Hull dockers see E. Gillett and K. A. MacMahon, *A History of Hull*, Hull, 1980.
3 Matthew Arnold, 'Culture and Anarchy' in Gordon Haight (ed.), *A Victorian Reader*, New York, 1972, p. 209.
4 *The Yorkshireman*, 21 January 1891 and Pearce, op. cit.
5 *Yorkshire Post*, 20 April 1893.
6 *Yorkshire Post*, 7 and 14 November 1893.
7 See Bradford's Jack Toothill in *Clarion*, 26 November 1892.
8 *Yorkshire Post*, 14 October 1889.
9 *The Yorkshireman*, 8 May 1886.
10 *The Yorkshireman*, 28 April 1887 and 9 May 1888. 'Put their hands in their pockets for the players.'
11 *Yorkshire Post*, 15 and 19 December 1888.
12 *The Yorkshireman*, 11 November 1891.
13 *Clarion*, 7 October 1893.
14 Arthur Budd, 'The Past and Future of the Game' in Marshall (ed.), *Football – The Rugby Union Game*, London, 1892, pp. 132–3.
15 *Clarion*, 6 October 1894.
16 Marshall (ed.) *Football – The Rugby Union Game*, 1892, p. 135. This view was also propounded by H. H. Almond, Headmaster of Loretto school in Scotland. See his two articles, 'Rugby Football in Scottish Schools' in Marshall, op. cit., and 'Football as a Moral Agent', *Nineteenth Century*, Vol. 34, 1893.
17 Montague Shearman, *Athletics and Football*, London, 1887.
18 *The Yorkshireman*, 28 March 1893.
19 G. Rowland Hill, 'The RFU 1880–81 to the Present', in Marshall, op. cit., p. 106.

20 Speech at the 1895 AGM of the RFU, *Yorkshire Post*, 20 September 1895.

21 John Stuart Mill 'Principles of Political Economy' (1865 edition), quoted in John Golby (ed.), *Culture and Society in Britain 1850–1890*, London, 1986, p. 134. Similar attitudes could also be seen among the southern slave holders in the United States in the nineteenth century; see Eugene Genovese, *Roll, Jordan, Roll: The World the Slaves Made*, London, 1974.

22 Rev. Frank Marshall, 'Payment for Broken Time at Rugby Football' in *Athletic News Football Annual, 1892*, Manchester, 1893, p. 149.

23 The Past Season' in *The Rugby Union Football Handbook 1894–95*, London, 1894.

24 Hill's devotion is attested to in *The Times*, 25 April 1929.

25 *Yorkshire Post*, 5 December 1887 and 18 July 1888.

26 *Yorkshire Post*, 30 September 1890 and 9 March 1892.

27 *Yorkshire Post*, 27 October 1890 and 14 April 1891.

28 *Yorkshire Post*, 22 March 1893.

29 *Clarion*, 20 October 1894.

30 The Anglican church's troubles with the working class in this period are detailed in Keith Inglis, *The Churches and the Working Classes in Victorian England*, London, 1963. On Marshall's troubles with the locals, see Gerald Hinchliffe, *A History of King James's Grammar School in Almondbury*, Huddersfield, 1963, p. 183.

31 *Yorkshire Post*, 21 February 1893.

32 B. F. Robinson, *Rugby Football*, London, 1896.

33 Mark Rutherford, *Deliverance*, London, 1885, p. 85, quoted in W. E. Houghton, *The Victorian Frame of Mind*, London, 1957, p. 58.

34 Frank Mitchell, 'A Crisis in Rugby Football', *St James's Gazette*, 24 September 1897.

35 Creston, 'Football', *Fortnightly Review*, Vol. 55, 1894.

36 Letter from 'An Old Player' to the *Yorkshire Evening Post*, 30 September 1893.

37 *Salford Reporter*, 27 October 1894. *Clarion*, 7 October 1893.

38 Arthur Budd, 'The Past and Future of the Game' in Marshall (ed.), *Football – the Rugby Union Game*, 1892, p. 137.

39 Creston, op. cit. The Mohocks were aristocratic ruffians who terrorised the night-time streets of eighteenth-century London.

40 *Manchester Guardian*, 18 September 1893.

41 'The Rugby Game in Yorkshire' in the *Football Annual*, London, 1881.

42 *Yorkshire Post*, 27 February 1883.

43 *The Yorkshireman*, 27 December 1884 and 3 October 1885. Middle-class hostility to miners in a sporting context can also be seen in Alan Metcalfe's 'Organised Sport in the Mining Communities of South Northumberland', *Victorian Studies*, No. 25, Summer 1982.

44 Nomad, 'The Future of Rugby Football: Professionalism and the League', *The Yorkshireman Football Number*, March 1892.

45 Old Ebor (A. W. Pullin), 'Competition Football in Yorkshire: Has It Proved a Success?', *The Yorkshireman Football Number*, March 1893.

46 *Clarion*, 7 October 1893. 'Purring' was an informal test of strength that involved kicking an adversary's shins and was common around the Merseyside area. See John Walton, *Lancashire, A Social History*, Manchester, 1987.

47 C. B. Grundy, quoted in John Lowerson, *Sport and the English Middle Classes*, Manchester, 1993, p. 84.

48 *The Yorkshireman*, 7 November 1885 and *The Scotsman*, 8 November 1885.

49 'The YRU' by A Wag in *The Yorkshireman Football Number*, March 1890.

50 *Athletic News*, 30 November 1876.

51 *Yorkshire Post*, 29 November 1886. For the same reasons, the paper also opposed the RFU's introduction of sending-off for foul play in 1888.

52 'Referee', *History of Barrow FC*, Barrow, 1914, p. 5.

53 *Athletic News*, 23 October 1888.

54 *Yorkshire Post*, 2 April 1886.

55 These figures are taken from the reports of the YRU executive committee appearing in the *Yorkshire Post* for the 1890–91 season.

56 See *The Yorkshireman*, 21 October 1882 and 3 November 1883. James Higson, *History of Salford Football Club*, Salford, 1892. *Yorkshire Evening Post*, 21 February 1893. *Warrington Guardian*, 8 June 1886.

57 *Yorkshire Post*, 10 October 1890.

58 Sir Henry Seton-Karr quoted in Alex Service, *Saints in Their Glory*, St Helens, 1985, p. 15.

59 B. F. Robinson, op. cit., pp. 49–50.

60 Quoted in Kenneth Pelmear, *Rugby Football, An Anthology*, London, 1958, p. 344.

61 Gerald Hinchliffe, op. cit., p. 231.

62 *Pendleton Reporter*, 28 November 1891.

63 The latter quote can be found in H. H. Almond, 'Football as a Moral Agent', *Nineteenth Century*, Vol 34, 1893 (emphasis in original). The other two phrases are from his chapter in Marshall (ed.), *Football – the Rugby Union Game*, 1892, p. 55. For a broader perspective on women's participation in sport during this period see J. A. Mangan and Roberta J. Park (eds), *From 'Fair Sex' to Feminism: Sport and the Socialisation of Women in the Industrial and Post-Industrial Eras*, London, 1987.

64 Eric Dunning and Kenneth Sheard, *Barbarians, Gentlemen and Players*, New York, 1979, p. 220. These figures are also quoted by A. J. Arnold, *A Game That Would Pay*, London, 1988, Greg Ryan, *Forerunners of the All Blacks*, Canterbury NZ, 1993, and, implicitly, in John Walton, op. cit., pp. 319–20. Dunning and Sheard found the clipping from the *Wakefield Express* in scrapbooks, sadly now lost, formerly belonging to founding Northern Union president Harry Waller at the Rugby League headquarters in Leeds (conversation with Kenneth Sheard, July 1995).

65 *Pall Mall Gazette*, 23 March 1892. For criticism of the figures see the *Yorkshire Post*, 6 April 1891 – 'the list is inaccurate in more than one instance' – and H. H. Almond, a stern opponent of professionalism and leagues and someone who could have been expected to point to such figures as proof of the correctness (and safety!) of amateur values, in 'Football as a Moral Agent', *Nineteenth Century*, Vol. 34, 1893.

66 *Pall Mall Gazette*, 30 March 1891 and 23 March 1892. In the 2005 edition of *Barbarians, Gentlemen and Players* Dunning and Sheard admit that these figures were 'a serious mistake' (p. 248) but argue that 'they were not too wide of the mark' and cite the *Lancet* as 'supportive' of their argument that 'in late nineteenth century Britain, football, especially the Rugby form, was viewed as a hazardous activity' (p. 249). In fact, the *Lancet* drew precisely the opposite conclusion. In 1894 it argued that 'Association, at first sight a tame game compared with the other, is possibly more perilous than Rugby Union' (24 March 1894, p. 766) and in 1907, following the split in rugby and the huge expansion of soccer, it stated that 'everything seems to show that the degree of danger incurred by players is greater in the dribbling than in the carrying game' (16 November 1907, p. 1402).

67 *Wigan Observer*, 2 October 1886.

68 *Pendleton Reporter*, 28 November 1891.

69 Speech at the first AGM of Leeds Cricket, Football and Athletic Club, *Yorkshire Post*, 2 May 1891.

70 *The Yorkshireman Football Number*, March 1891.

71 *Yorkshire Post*, 6 March 1893.

72 XYZ in *The Yorkshireman*, 4 October 1893. Nomad, 'The Future of Rugby Football: Professionalism and the League', *The Yorkshireman Football Number*, March 1892.

73 *Oldham Evening Chronicle*, 13 October 1890. *The Yorkshireman*, 1 April 1891.

74 A Professional in Mufti, 'A Plea for Legitimate Concessions', *The Yorkshireman Football Number*, March 1891.

75 See *The Yorkshireman* and the *Yorkshire Post* throughout April, May and June of 1891.

76 *Yorkshire Post*, 11 April 1891.

77 *Yorkshire Post*, 2 November 1891.

78 *Bradford Observer*, 18 September 1893.

79 Old Ebor (A. W. Pullin), 'Competition Football in Yorkshire: Has It Proved a Success?', *The Yorkshireman Football Number*, March 1893.

80 Charles Edwardes, 'The New Football Mania', *Nineteenth Century*, Vol. 32, 1892.

81 *The Times*, 25 September 1893.

82 *The Yorkshireman*, 28 March 1893.

83 OPQ, 'Professionalism in Football', *The Yorkshireman*, 6 September 1893.

84 A letter from 'Straightforward' in *The Yorkshireman*, 4 October 1893.

85 Nomad, 'The Future of Rugby Football: Professionalism and the League', *The Yorkshireman Football Number*, March 1892.

86 Nomad, ibid.

87 *Yorkshire Owl*, 27 September 1893.

88 *Clarion*, 24 November 1894.

89 Minutes of the RFU, 16 September 1891. Marshall's comments are in *Pastime*, 23 September 1891.

90 An unsubstantiated rumour circulated that Cail had originally supported the broken-time motion but turned his back on it when offered Rowland Hill's support to continue as president for a second year. See *Yorkshire Post*, 6 February 1909.

91 *The Yorkshireman*, 20 September 1893.

92 *Leeds Mercury*, 16 September 1893.

93 *Leeds Mercury*, 19 September 1893.

94 *Yorkshire Evening Post*, 20 September 1893.

95 Minutes of the RFU, 20 September 1893. No full transcript of the meeting exists and the minutes only list the clubs present. I have therefore reconstructed the debate with the help of the daily papers of the time.

96 *Leeds Mercury*, 21 September 1893.

97 Ibid.

98 *Yorkshire Post*, 21 September 1893.

99 All quotes are from *Leeds Mercury*, 21 September 1893.

100 *Yorkshire Evening Post*, 21 September 1893.

101 *Leeds Mercury*, 21 September 1893.

102 G. F. Berney, 'Progress of the RFU from the season 1892–93 to the present time' in Rev. Frank Marshall and Leonard R. Tosswill (eds), *Football – the Rugby Union Game*, London, 1925 (2nd edition).

103 *Pastime*, 6 September 1893.

104 *Leeds Daily News*, 21 and 25 September 1893. Trevor Delaney in his *Rugby Disunion*, Keighley, 1993 estimates that at least 22 Yorkshire clubs voted against the broken-time motion.

105 *Leeds Mercury*, 23 September 1893.

106 Indeed, the meeting attracted little attention in the Lancashire press, and the local newspapers in Barrow and Oldham, at least, did not even mention the momentous events.

107 The text of H. E. Steed's circular of 1894 can be found in the *Yorkshire Post*, 8 December 1894.

108 *Clarion*, 23 September 1893.

109 Ibid.

110 *Yorkshire Evening Post*, 25 September 1893.

111 OPQ, 'Payment for Broken Time', *The Yorkshireman*, 27 September 1893.

112 *Manchester Guardian*, 25 September 1893, *Pastime*, 27 September 1893, Creston, 'Football', *Fortnightly Review*, Vol. 55, 1894 and *Yorkshire Post*, 14 October 1893.

113 *Yorkshire Owl*, 4 October 1893.

114 *Huddersfield Daily Examiner*, 5, 9 and 27 October, 15 November and 4 December 1893. Not only were Forsyth and Boak banned from playing by the RFU but they were also fined £3 and £1 respectively by Carlisle Magistrates Court for leaving their jobs at Cummerdale Print Works without giving notice.

115 Lancashire Rugby Union minutes 28 August 1894 and *Yorkshire Post*, 8, 12 and 28 September 1894.

116 *Salford Reporter*, 20 October and 10 November 1894. Lancashire Rugby Union minutes 17 October 1894.

117 Lancashire Rugby Union minutes 13 November 1894 and *Wigan Observer*, 17 November 1894.

118 *Yorkshire Post*, 5 and 17 November 1894. The *Bradford Observer* speculated that the manifesto had been written by Frank Marshall, 3 December 1894.

119 *Yorkshire Evening Post*, 29 December 1894.

120 *Yorkshire Post*, 31 December 1894.

121 *Clarion*, 8 December 1894.

122 *Yorkshire Post*, 21 and 31 January 1895.

123 *Yorkshire Evening Post*, 19 February 1895.

124 *Pastime*, 8 February 1895.

125 *Yorkshire Post*, 28 and 29 March 1895.

126 *Yorkshire Post*, 19 July 1895.

127 This view has been expressed most notably in Michael Latham and Tom Mather's *The Rugby League Myth*, Adlington, 1993. The *Yorkshire Post*, 9 September 1895, effectively answered it when it said that 'questions of promotion and relegation in the Yorkshire Union have been shown to be but the outward and visible methods of offering resistance to the rigid amateurism that the authorities desired to enforce, and it has been made clear that the real wish of the Senior clubs was to control the county organisation so as to find shelter for themselves in the time of the Rugby Union's visitation.'

128 *Bradford Daily Argus*, 26 August 1895 and *Yorkshire Post*, 27 August 1895.

129 *Yorkshire Post*, 29 August 1895.

130 Letter from Rowland Hill, published in the *Yorkshire Post*, 27 August 1895.

131 *Yorkshire Post*, 30 August 1895.

5 The rise and decline of the Northern Union: 1895–1905

1 This is particularly true of the weekly and monthly journals dedicated to regional interests, such as *The Yorkshireman*, *Yorkshire Owl*, the *Manchester Monthly* and Manchester's *Ben Brierley's Journal*, all of which failed in the 1890s. See Margaret Beetham, 'Healthy Reading: The Periodical Press in Late Victorian Manchester' in A. J. Kidd and K. W. Roberts (eds), *City, Class and Culture: Studies of Cultural Production and Social Policy in Victorian Manchester*, Manchester, 1985 and C. B. Phillips and J. H. Smith, *Lancashire and Cheshire From AD 1540*, London, 1994. On the impact of the contrary effect of national newspapers being printed in the provinces, see Donald Read, *The English Provinces*, London, 1964, p. 272.

2 Holbrook Jackson, *The Eighteen Nineties*, London, 1913, p. 28. For more on the centralisation of British society during the 1890s, see Asa Briggs, *Victorian Cities*, London, 1963; Raymond Williams, *The Long Revolution*, London, 1961;

and Eric Hobsbawm, 'The Making of the Working Class 1870–1914' in his *Worlds of Labour*, London, 1984.

3 The Vesta Tilley quote is from Gareth Stedman-Jones, 'Working Class Culture and Working Class Politics in London 1870–1900: Notes on the Remaking of a Working Class', *Journal of Social History*, Vol. 7, No. 4, Summer 1974. Useful commentary on this period can also be found in Penelope Summerfield's 'The Effingham Arms and Empire' in Eileen and Stephen Yeo (eds), *Popular Culture and Class Conflict 1590–1914*, Brighton, 1981. For the warrior-patriot see J. A. Mangan, *The Games Ethic and Imperialism*, London, 1986, p. 60. See also J. A. Mangan, 'Duty unto Death: English Masculinity and Militarism in the Age of the New Imperialism', *International Journal of the History of Sport*, Vol. 12, No. 2, August 1995. David Cannadine's 'The Context, Performance and Meaning of Ritual: The British Monarchy and the "Invention of Tradition", c. 1820–1977' in Eric Hobsbawm and T. Ranger (eds), *The Invention of Tradition*, London, 1983, also makes relevant points about the importance of this period to the growth of nationalist symbolism and ritual.

4 P. A. Vaile writing to *The Times*, 10 October 1905. For Cecil Rhodes, see Rev. Frank Marshall and Leonard R. Tosswill (eds), *Football – the Rugby Union Game*, London, 1925, Ch. 23.

5 Arthur Budd, 'The Northern Union', in *Football*, 1897, p. 32.

6 Old Ebor, 'The Northern Union in Yorkshire', *Athletic News Football Annual 1896*, London, 1896, p. 187.

7 Ernest Ensor, 'The Football Madness', *Contemporary Review*, Vol. 74, November 1898, p. 756.

8 *Yorkshire Post*, 29 May and 26 October 1896.

9 *Yorkshire Post*, 3 November 1896.

10 After much controversy, the AAA passed the motion 'No professional footballer can be allowed to compete under AAA rules' in May 1899. *Yorkshire Post*, 15 May 1899.

11 *Athletic News*, 5 December 1898. Technically the ban was on policemen playing any form of professional football but as the vast majority of soccer professionals were full-time and unlikely to indulge in part-time policing, the ban was actually directed at the semi-professionals of the Northern Union. In 1907 the same regulation was used to discipline Police Constable Arch, an Aberdare player who had been suspended by the Welsh Rugby Union for receiving payments. See *Yorkshire Post*, 14 September 1907. It may simply have been coincidental that this suspension was handed down in precisely the same month in which the new Welsh NU clubs were launched.

12 In a pre-emptive strike the RFU reached an agreement with the FA in November 1894 to honour each others suspensions, including those for breaches of the professionalism rules; see *Yorkshire Post*, 5 November 1894. Discussions continued after the split but the FA decided not to implement the RFU's ban on players with NU clubs, because of the opposition of the Football League and the adverse impact such a ban would have on the prospects for the growth of soccer in West Yorkshire. See the *Yorkshire Evening Post*, 25 September 1895, *Yorkshire Post*, 21 November and 18 December 1895 and the *Bradford Illustrated Weekly Telegraph*, 31 August 1895. However, H. Milnes was prevented from playing for Hunslet AFC by the FA in 1898 because he had previously been found guilty by the RFU of signing for Holbeck Northern Union club. See *Yorkshire Post*, 28 January 1898.

13 *Yorkshire Post*, 12 September 1907. In Australia, rugby league was also for many years accused of being unpatriotic in rugby union circles for its allegedly ambiguous attitude to the outbreak of World War One – see Murray Phillips, 'Football, Class and War: The Rugby Codes in NSW 1907–1918' in John Nauright and T. J. L. Chandler, *Making Men*, London, 1996. For a slightly more modern comment

on the exclusion of rugby league from the English national sporting pantheon, see Angus Calder, *The Myth of the Blitz*, London, 1991.

14 'The Case for the Belligerents', *Hull Daily Mail*, 4 September 1895.

15 *Wigan Observer*, 7 September 1895 and *Yorkshire Post*, 21 September 1895.

16 *Yorkshire Evening Post*, 6 September 1895.

17 Harry Waller speaking at a dinner for the NU's first champions, Manningham. *Yorkshire Post*, 29 April 1896.

18 *Salford Reporter*, 7 September 1895. *Yorkshire Chat*, 4 September 1895. *Bradford Daily Argus*, 31 August 1895. *Leeds Evening Express*, 30 August 1895. *Bradford Observer*, 29 August 1895.

19 *Leeds Daily News*, 27 August 1895.

20 *Hull Daily Mail*, 20 September 1895.

21 *The Yorkshireman*, 14 September 1895.

22 *Salford Reporter*, 7 September 1895. *Yorkshire Post*, 31 August 1895.

23 *Yorkshire Post*, 7 September 1895.

24 See L. Balaam, *Manchester FC 1860–1985*, Manchester, 1985.

25 *Athletic News*, 20 April 1896. *Salford Reporter*, 18 April 1896.

26 *Salford Reporter*, 2 May 1896. *Swinton FC: Souvenir History of the Club*, Swinton, 1929.

27 *Yorkshire Post*, 17 April 1896.

28 *Yorkshire Post*, 31 May 1897. The clubs were: Manchester, Manchester Free Wanderers, Liverpool, Liverpool Old Boys, Waterloo, Sale, Broughton Park, Broughton, New Brighton, Birkenhead Park, Blackley, Little Borough and Castleton Moor. The following year Castleton Moor joined the NU and Broughton disbanded.

29 *Barrow News*, 10, 4 and 24 April, and 1 and 3 July 1897.

30 *Athletic News*, 14 and 21 March and 24 October 1898. Millom's figures are in the *Yorkshire Post*, 25 May 1898.

31 *Yorkshire Post*, 20 and 21 May 1896.

32 Keighley president W. R. Elgie in the *Yorkshire Post*, 13 April 1900.

33 *Yorkshire Post*, 10 July 1897, 3 and 13 September 1898.

34 *Salford Reporter*, 7 September 1895.

35 *Yorkshire Post*, 18 February 1896, 10 and 31 March 1896. Somewhat unsurprisingly, later that month Horbury voted to join the NU. The pantomime story is in the *Yorkshire Post*, 25 January 1898. The story about the RFU official is told in a letter from A. R. Meek, a RFU supporter, in the *Yorkshire Post* 21 January 1901. A history of rugby league in London alleges that the RFU did indeed threaten to ban rugby union players who attended matches of the London Highfield club in 1933: see D. Farrar, P. Lush and M. O'Hare, *Touch and Go*, London, 1995, p. 77.

36 *Athletic News*, 7 February 1898.

37 *Bradford Daily Argus*, 31 August 1895.

38 *Yorkshire Post*, 4 January 1899. Sharlston, the ground and twelve players were expelled from the YRU.

39 Letter to the *Yorkshire Post*, 5 November 1895.

40 YRU president James Hall in the *Yorkshire Post*, 26 June 1899. *Yorkshire Post*, 1 January 1900.

41 *Yorkshire Post*, 24 October 1900 and 2 July 1901. *Hull Daily Mail*, 15 January 1901.

42 The Headingley club published a centenary brochure in 1978, claiming descendency from various clubs that had called themselves Headingley in the 1870s and 1880s. In fact, the club itself originally dated its foundation as 1892, as attested to by their celebration of fifteen years existence in 1907. See 'The Headingley Club – Fine Fifteen Years' Record' in the *Yorkshire Post*, 18 September 1907. For complaints about YRU favouritism towards the club, see especially the *Yorkshire Post*, 19–24 April 1909.

43 *Yorkshire Post*, 10 December 1907.

44 *Yorkshire Evening Post*, 4 March 1897 and *Yorkshire Post*, 11 January 1898.

45 For details of the RFU discussion, see *Yorkshire Post*, 17 September 1897. For a full background to the Gould case, see Gareth Williams, 'How Amateur Was My Valley: Professional Sport and National Identity in Wales 1890–1914', *The British Journal of Sports History*, Vol. 2, No. 2, September 1985. Ironically, Gould was from a working-class family but his fame and the channels of social advancement available in Welsh rugby union had given him a respectability unattainable to northern rugby stars. I am grateful to John Jenkins and Gareth Williams for letting me see their research into Gould's background.

46 Figures from the *Yorkshire Post*, 30 April 1897. Description from C. F. Shaw *The Gallant Youths*, Batley, 1899, p. 77.

47 *The Times*, 18 October 1897.

48 *Yorkshire Evening Post*, 16 September 1895.

49 *Yorkshire Post*, 30 April 1897.

50 *Yorkshire Post*, 30 June 1896.

51 See *Yorkshire Post*, 27 May 1898 for the incorrect figure and *Yorkshire Post*, 26 May 1899 for its correction. No explanation was offered for this action.

52 For an example of this see *Yorkshire Evening Post*, 30 September 1895.

53 *The Mascot*, 26 December 1896.

54 I have been unable to confirm the identity of the author of the minority report, but the available evidence suggests that it could have been NU secretary Joe Platt of the Oldham club.

55 *Yorkshire Post*, 14 January 1898.

56 The full text of the regulations can be found in *Athletic News Football Annual 1898*, Manchester, 1898, pp. 198–9.

57 Harry Waller speech at presentation of Yorkshire county medals in the *Yorkshire Post*, 23 May 1898.

58 See, for example, Eric Dunning and Kenneth Sheard, *Barbarians, Gentlemen and Players*, New York, 1979, p. 205, and Paul Greenhalgh, ' "The Work and Play Principle": The Professional Regulations of the Northern Rugby Football Union 1898–1905', *The International Journal of the History of Sport*, Vol, 9, No. 3, December 1992. For a critique of the use of the term 'social control' in the context of leisure, see Gareth Stedman-Jones, 'Class Expression versus Social Control?', *History Workshop*, No. 4, Autumn 1977.

59 On the latter point, see particularly *Clarion*, 5 January 1895.

60 On the notion that the NU was an economic cartel, see Brian Davies, 'Bifurcation in Sport: Some Preliminary Thoughts on the Case of Rugby League', *The Journal of Regional and Local Studies*, Vol. 8, No. 1, Spring 1988 and Wray Vamplew, *Pay Up, Pay Up and Play The Game: Professional Sport in Britain 1875–1914*, Cambridge, 1988. Paul Greenhalgh makes a convincing case that the NU was not a genuine cartel in his *The History of the Northern Rugby Football Union 1895–1910*, unpublished PhD thesis, University of Lancaster, 1992.

61 See 'Rulings of the Professional Sub-Committee' in the NU's *Official Guide 1903–04*.

62 Waller speech at Batley in the *Yorkshire Post*, 24 April 1899.

63 Charles Brewer after the Yorkshire versus Lancashire match in the *Yorkshire Post*, 6 November 1899.

64 *Yorkshire Post*, 7 January and 21 November 1897. Harry Varley later reappeared to captain Leeds for a season. An anonymous contributor to *Pastime* (4 October 1893), who may well have been the Rev. Frank Marshall, argued that players were often given poorly performing pubs with little support from the breweries concerned.

65 *Hull Daily Mail*, 25 January 1899.

66 *Yorkshire Post*, 24 April 1899.

67 Northern Union Professional Sub-Committee minutes, 20 February 1903 and 13 March 1903. Unfortunately, there is no record of whether Trowell was found guilty.

68 *Athletic News*, 25 April 1898. *Yorkshire Post*, 28 December 1908.

69 For Badger, see *Athletic News*, 7 November 1898. For the Yorkshire cases, see *Yorkshire Post*, 3 November and 8 December 1898, 7 October 1899 and 22 February 1902. For the James brothers see NU General Committee minutes, 7 December 1902. The quote is from the *Yorkshire Post*, 2 January 1899.

70 *Yorkshire Post*, 23 May 1898, 19 January 1899 and 28 May 1903.

71 *Yorkshire Post*, 5 December 1898 and 9 March 1900. NU General Committee minutes 11 June 1902, 8 September 1902 and 8 November 1904.

72 *Yorkshire Post*, 11 January and 10 June 1905, and 9 January 1907.

73 *Athletic News*, 26 September 1898, *Yorkshire Post*, 23 January 1899, 31 May 1899, 28 May 1903, 27 February 1906 and 29 July 1908. The Halifax details are in Andrew Hardcastle, *The Thrum Hall Story*, Halifax 1986. For a comparison with soccer wages, see Mason, *Association Football and English Society 1863–1915*, Brighton, 1980, pp. 96–104.

74 Billy Batten's wages were attested to by his son Eric, himself a rugby league great, in an interview in 1988 for the video *Rugby League Tours*, Micron Video, Wigan, 1988. For independent confirmation see *Yorkshire Evening Post*, 9 February 1928.

75 *Yorkshire Post*, 3 December 1897.

76 *Yorkshire Post*, 7 October 1901. For more details about Welsh players' journeys to the Northern Union, see Robert Gate's superb *Gone North*, Ripponden, 1985.

77 *Yorkshire Post*, 31 January 1901 and 13 June 1907. See also Gareth Williams, op. cit. For confirmation that some Welsh clubs paid wages comparable to NU clubs up until the 1920s, at the very least, see Dai Davies' biography in Phil Melling, *Man of Amman*, Llandysul, 1993.

78 *The Yorkshireman*, 2 November 1895.

79 *Yorkshire Post*, 21 January 1900 and 19 July 1908. On the impact of the work clauses on Welsh players, see *Athletic News*, 12 December 1898.

80 Northern Union Professional Sub-Committee minutes, 4 October 1901 and *Yorkshire Post*, 6 January 1900.

81 Northern Union General Committee minutes, 14 May 1902. Cumberland Professional Sub-Committee minutes March 1903. *Yorkshire Post*, 4 January 1904.

82 *Yorkshire Post*, 3 and 11 June 1904.

83 *Yorkshire Post*, 18, 24 and 25 March 1905.

84 The quote is from Graham Williams' fascinating *The Code War*, Harefield, 1994, p. 123.

85 *Barrow and District Yearbook*, compiled by E. Foster, Barrow, 1906. *Athletic News*, 6 August 1906.

86 *Yorkshire Post*, 15 May 1904 and 30 May 1905.

87 See the minutes of the FA Council meeting of 12 March 1906.

88 *Leeds Mercury*, 2 October 1905.

89 FA Council minutes, 12 March 1906. Neither the army nor the navy affiliated to the Amateur Football Association, which was formed in 1906.

90 *Yorkshire Post*, 6 December 1902.

91 The question of the social composition of the leadership of the NU and its supporters is examined at the beginning of Chapter 6.

92 Both the Leeds and Bradford soccer sections lost over £180 in 1896 and 1897 respectively. See *Yorkshire Post*, 24 June 1896 and 28 May 1897.

93 Although this was not explicitly stated by the clubs for obvious reasons, circumstantial evidence suggests that soccer was viewed as a get-out option. See *Huddersfield Daily*

Examiner, 14 October 1893, *The Yorkshireman*, 7 September 1895 and *Athletic News*, 20 April 1896.

94   Such mass signings of junior players was outlawed in November 1899 by the NU, which placed a limit of seventy-five registered players on each club and laid down that they pay two shillings and sixpence to the junior club from which the player was signed.

95   Minutes of the Leeds Schools (Northern) RFU, various dates. The creation of a schools' Northern Union competition was the direct stimulus for the formation of the English Schools Rugby Union, which was proposed to the RFU committee in 1904 by Mark Newsome in order to counter the threat of the NU.

96   *Yorkshire Post*, 22 May 1901.

97   Hull FC, *Annual Report and Accounts* 1905–06.

98   *Yorkshire Post*, 23 April 1898, 31 May 1902 and 21 May 1908. Hull Kingston Rovers, *Annual Report and Accounts 1903–04*.

99   *Yorkshire Post*, 24 May 1900, 31 May and 3 July 1902. Hutchinson became a member of the Headingley club, for which his son, a future England international, played.

100   The high level of Jewish support for the Leeds Parish Church side had been noted in the early 1890s, so much so that *The Yorkshireman* uniformly referred to the club's supporters by the anti-Semitic epithet 'sheenies'. See *The Yorkshireman*, 29 September 1894.

101   *Athletic News*, 22 July 1901. *Yorkshire Post*, 10 September 1901. Gedge's position as a vice-president of a NU club was an expellable offence under the RFU's professionalism laws but, as he explained, Rowland Hill had confirmed that the rules 'were not intended to apply to cases' such as his. *Yorkshire Post*, 6 December 1900.

102   For Frank Chambers and his own brand of muscular Christianity, which was not above punching rowdy spectators, see Gerald Hinchliffe, *A History of King James's Grammar School in Almondbury*, Huddersfield, 1963. For Chevasse, see Alex Service, *Saints in Their Glory*, St Helens, 1985, and J. R. A. Dalgleish, *Red, Black and Blue, The First 125 Years of Liverpool Football Club*, Swinton, 1983.

103   Letter from Manningham's S. S. Naylor to the West Yorkshire FA committee, *Yorkshire Post*, 12 December 1901.

104   See *Bradford Observer* and the *Yorkshire Post* throughout May 1903. The quote is from the *Yorkshire Post*, 30 May 1903. Background information can also be found in A. J. Arnold's 'Shall it be Bradford or Leeds? The Origins of Professional Football in the West Riding Textile District', *Publications of the Thoresby Society – Miscellany*, Vol. 19, 1990.

105   For the argument that it was the quest for profitability that took both Manningham and Bradford from rugby to soccer, see A. J. Arnold, *A Game That Would Pay*, London, 1988.

106   *Yorkshire Post*, 3 and 9 December 1903.

107   *Yorkshire Post*, 13 June 1904.

108   *Yorkshire Post*, 14 September 1904.

109   Minutes of NU AGM, 14 June 1905. *Yorkshire Post*, 6 September 1905.

110   *Yorkshire Post*, 9 June 1904.

111   For details of the 'benefactors' see *Yorkshire Post*, 20 March 1896. For cricket losses see *Yorkshire Post*, 22 October 1904. The same point about cricket income can be made about all NU clubs that also had a cricket ground. Halifax lost over £1,000 in the 1898 and 1899 cricket seasons and even Headingley struggled to make a cricket profit: in 1901 cricket made a loss of £455.

112   *Bradford Observer*, 16 April 1907.

113   How the players could be guilty of professionalism but not the club that paid them was a riddle that remained unanswered by the Rugby Union.

114 For details of the club's switch see the *Bradford Observer* throughout April, May and early June 1907. The quotes are from *Bradford Observer*, 16 and 17 April 1907. The club's discomfort at being denied membership of the Football League was increased when Oldham Athletic were offered Burslem Port Vale's second division Football League place two weeks after their acceptance into the Southern League. Bradford were eventually accepted into division two of the Football League in 1908. In yet another example of the links between rugby union and soccer in the North, Bradford's chief spokesman at the meeting that accepted them into the Southern League was the RFU-supporting Rev. J. E. Leighton.

115 *Yorkshire Post*, 15 October 1906.

116 For moves to begin a rapprochement with the RFU, see NU General Committee minutes, October 1905. For the respective sizes of the two rugby organisations, see the *Northern Union Official Guide 1904–05*, Manchester, 1904 and O. L. Owen, *The History of the Rugby Football Union*, London, 1955. In 1906 Widnes's J. H. Smith claimed a figure of 420 clubs, including juniors and schoolboys, for the NU, see *Athletic News*, 19 February 1906.

6   A revolution in rugby: 1905–1910

1 See, for example, Standish Meacham, *A Life Apart: The English Working Class 1890–1914*, London, 1977, and Eric Hobsbawm's 'The Making of the Working Class 1870–1914' in *Worlds of Labour*, London, 1984.

2 Ross McKibbin, *The Ideologies of Class*, Oxford, 1990, p. 166.

3 To be fair, William Hirst's departure from the NU was caused by his committing suicide in 1899 (as his father had done previously).

4 Robert Roberts *The Classic Slum*, Manchester, 1971, p. 18.

5 J. K. Walton, *Lancashire: A Social History 1558–1939*, Manchester, 1987, p. 233.

6 David Smith and Gareth Williams *Fields of Praise*, Cardiff, 1980, p. 124.

7 *Athletic News*, 22 November 1909.

8 Quoted in Patrick Joyce, *Visions of the People*, Cambridge, 1991, p. 56.

9 There were exceptions to this: the YRU's Arthur Hartley, president of the RFU in 1913, was a Liberal and the leadership of the Leeds and Bradford clubs were predominantly Tories. Hartley's allegiances may be explained by his freemasonry links and we have already seen how Leeds and Bradford were the most reluctant of the clubs forming the NU but were forced to join by economic exigencies.

10 The correspondence between Fallas and Kilner is reprinted in the *Yorkshire Post*, 4 February 1897.

11 See Chris Waters, *British Socialists and the Politics of Popular Culture*, Manchester, 1990, especially Ch. 6.

12 The final chapter of Joyce's *Visions of the People* is especially relevant to the study of the development of the Northern Union and its culture. The quotes are from p. 332. Intriguingly, despite his concern for popular culture and the meanings given to it by the working class in Lancashire and Yorkshire, Joyce has almost nothing to say about rugby or soccer.

13 Joyce, ibid., p. 329.

14 *Yorkshire Post*, 17 April 1891.

15 *Yorkshire Post*, 26 December 1896. *Yorkshire Chat*, 18 November 1898.

16 *Athletic News*, 9 July 1906.

17 This is the number I have been able to trace but there may well have been more – even at the end of the Edwardian period, rugby crowds were not accurately reported. A sense of perspective of comparative crowd sizes can be gained by the fact that

in their first two seasons in Football League Division One in 1908–09 and 1908–1910, Bradford City had twenty-three crowds in excess of 20,000.

18 For Whitehaven, see Northern Union General Committee minutes, 4 April 1902. For Hull, see the club's annual report for 1900–1901.

19 Alderman Nettleton quoted in C. F. Shaw, *The Gallant Youths*, Batley, 1899, p. 88. The James Miller quote is from the *Yorkshire Post*, 18 January 1897.

20 See advertisement in *Yorkshire Owl Cricket Annual*, for 1896.

21 *Yorkshire Chat*, 18 November 1898.

22 Figures taken from Hull FC annual reports, 1895–96 to 1909–1910.

23 As with Bradford, Leeds Parish Church and Manningham, one does not have to be a conspiracy theorist to recognise powerful coincidences involved in the demise of Holbeck NU club, not least the fact that the club's 1897 lease on Elland Road specified that rugby had to be played on the ground for seven years; that is, until 1904.

24 For a relevant discussion of the diversity of working-class culture in Manchester during this period see Andrew Davies and Steven Fielding (eds), *Workers' Worlds: Cultures and Communities in Manchester and Salford 1880–1939*, Manchester, 1992. There is also evidence that, certainly during the inter-war period, some people watched both games regularly; see, for example, W. R. Mitchell, *By Gum, Life Were Sparse!*, London, 1981, p. 181.

25 *Yorkshire Post*, 15 February 1896.

26 *Yorkshire Post*, 28 March 1899. NU General Committee minutes, 8 and 29 December 1903.

27 *Yorkshire Post*, 22 October 1906 and 5 October 1907.

28 See L. Mann and D. Pearce, 'Social Psychology of Sports Spectators', in D. Glencross (ed.), *Psychology and Sport*, Sydney, 1979; Wray Vamplew, 'Sports Crowd Disorder in Britain 1870–1914', *Journal of Sport History*, Vol. 7, No. 1, 1980; N. L. Tranter, 'The Cappielow Riot and the Composition and Behaviour of Soccer Crowds in Late Victorian Scotland', *The International Journal of the History of Sport*, Vol. 12, No. 3, December 1995.

29 *Yorkshire Post*, 1 May 1905.

30 *Yorkshire Post*, 4 April 1905.

31 *Yorkshire Post*, 14 January 1897.

32 *Yorkshire Post*, 3 December 1900.

33 Such a view is supported by Richard Hoggart in *The Uses of Literacy*, London, 1957, p. 109.

34 *Yorkshire Post*, 24 September and 3 November 1898. *Athletic News*, 8 December 1898 and 1 May 1900.

35 *Yorkshire Evening Post*, 13 September 1895.

36 *Yorkshire Evening Post*, 16 and 17 September 1895. *The Yorkshireman*, 19 October 1895.

37 The report of the NU SGM can be found in the *Yorkshire Post*, 10 December 1895.

38 For confirmation of this, see the letter from the unnamed Northern Union player in the *Yorkshire Post*, 21 September 1897.

39 Hunslet president T.V. Harrison speaking at his club's 1903 AGM. *Yorkshire Post*, 16 June 1903.

40 *Athletic News*, 23 April 1906.

41 *Yorkshire Post*, 18 May 1905.

42 The centrality of the snap at the line of scrimmage to the development of American football as a distinct sport from rugby union is attested to by Michael Oriard, *Reading Football: How the Popular Press Created an American Spectacle*, Chapel Hill, 1993, p. 27.

43 *Yorkshire Post*, 30 May 1903.

44 Report of 1903 Northern Union AGM, *Yorkshire Post*, 15 July 1903.

45 The Lancashire Northern Union Combination league played twelve-a-side with five forwards and four three-quarters.

46 Report of 1906 NU AGM, *Yorkshire Post*, 13 June 1906. The NU's J. H. Smith was also an admirer of the 1905 tourists, *Athletic News*, 15 January 1906.

47 Smith, ibid.

48 For a discussion on the play-the-ball rule, see *Athletic News*, 18 June and 3 September 1906.

49 'Rules of the Game', *Northern Union Official Guide 1908–9*. The similarity with American football was noted, uniquely, by *The Times*, 3 December 1907.

50 *Athletic News*, 16 September 1906.

51 *Yorkshire Post*, 22 October 1906. *The Times*, 3 December 1907.

52 Arthur Budd, 'The Northern Union' in *Football*, London, 1897, p. 34. See also his comments in *Athletic News*, 7 March 1898.

53 Frank Mitchell, 'Forward Play' in Montague Shearman, *Football*, London, 1899, pp. 210 and 276.

54 *Athletic News*, 28 November 1898. *Yorkshire Post*, 6 May 1898 and 10 November 1909.

55 *Daily Graphic*, 18 April 1910.

56 *Yorkshire Post*, 24 January 1907, 30 May 1908 and 6 May 1910.

57 H. Graves, 'A Philosophy of Sport', *The Contemporary Review*, December 1900. Ernest Ensor also made the same point in 'The Football Madness' in the same journal's November 1898 issue.

58 See the *Yorkshire Post*, 21–27 September 1897 for the punt-out debate.

59 *Yorkshire Chat*, 1 November 1899.

60 *Yorkshire Chat*, 7 October 1899.

61 *Yorkshire Post*, 22 April 1897.

62 *Yorkshire Post*, 2 May 1898.

63 Little work on the rugby league and masculinity has been carried out and much of the knowledge of the game's traditions is retained as oral culture. Much of the latter section of this paragraph is drawn from anecdotal experience. For a decidedly non-academic view of violence in Australian rugby league see Tony Adams, *The Hit Men*, Sydney, 1994.

64 Norbert Elias, *The Civilising Process*, Oxford, 1978. The theory is developed in the context of rugby by Eric Dunning and Kenneth Sheard in *Barbarians, Gentlemen and Players*, New York, 1979. For a critical examination of the thesis, see my 'History, Theory and the "Civilising Process"', *Sport in History*, Vol. 25, No. 2, August 2005 and Daryl Adair's 'Competing or Complementary Forces? The "Civilising" Process and the Commitment to Winning in Nineteenth Century English Rugby and Association Football', *Canadian Journal of the History of Sport*, Vol. 24, No. 2, December 1993.

65 This and the following quote are from the 2005 Routledge edition of *Barbarians, Gentlemen and Players*, p. 187.

66 For Cail, see the *Yorkshire Post*, 10 February 1902. The Yorkshire Rugby Union also made the same proposal in 1898, *Yorkshire Post*, 10 October 1898.

67 On the insurance difficulties of soccer, see *Athletic News*, 25 September 1911 and Matthew Taylor, *'Proud Preston' A History of the Football League 1900–39*, unpublished PhD thesis, De Montfort University, 1997, pp. 229–30.

68 NU General Committee minutes, 9 August 1910. The insurance scheme was set up on 29 August.

69 Figures taken from Northern Rugby Football Union, *Report and Balance Sheet*, years ending 1 June 1908, 1 June 1909 and 1 June 1910.

70 For the impact and wider implications of the 1905 tour see John Nauright's 'Colonial Manhood and Imperial Race Virility' in John Nauright and T. J. L. Chandler,

Making Men, London, 1996 and his 'Sport, Manhood and Empire', *The International Journal of the History of Sport*, Vol. 8, No. 2, September 1991. *The Complete Rugby Footballer*, written by tour captain David Gallaher and W. J. Stead, London, 1906, gives the official New Zealand view of the tour.

71 Figures in the original version of *Rugby's Great Split* concerning the finances of the tour, culled from contemporary newspaper reports, have been corrected in line with the new research presented by Greg Ryan in his definitive account of the 1905 tour, *The Contest for Rugby Supremacy: Accounting for the 1905 All-Blacks*, Christchurch, 2005, which reprints the official tour balance sheet on p. 201. My assertion in the original edition that the New Zealand government subsidised the tour, taken from the *Yorkshire Post*, 30 June 1906, was also incorrect.

72 'Rugby Football in the Colonies' by 'An Original All Black' in the *Yorkshire Post* 13 November 1908.

73 For example, see the report of the New Zealand versus Great Britain test match at Wellington in the *Wanganui Chronicle*, 15 August 1904.

74 For the origins and early development of rugby in Australia see Thomas V. Hickie, *They Ran with the Ball: How Rugby Football Began in Australia*, Sydney, 1993; Thomas V. Hickie and Anthony Hughes, *The Game for the Game Itself. The History of Sub-District Rugby in Sydney*, Sydney, 2004; Sean Fagan, *The Rugby Rebellion: The Divide of League and Union*, Sydney, 2005.

75 See, for example, Ray Markey, 'Explaining Union Mobilisation in the 1880s and Early 1900s', *Labour History* No. 83, November 2002.

76 For more on the links between rugby league and the Australian labour movement see Andrew Moore, 'Opera of the Proletariat: Rugby League, the Labour Movement and Working-Class Culture in New South Wales and Queensland', *Labour History*, No. 79, November 2000, pp. 57–70.

77 See Ian Heads, *True Blue*, Sydney, 1992, p. 17.

78 Sean Fagan, *The Rugby Rebellion*, Sydney, 2005, p. 125.

79 *Australian Star*, 8 October 1907.

80 For a fascinating discussion on the differences in the formation of rugby league in Britain and Australia, see Andrew Moore, *Jimmy Devereux's Yorkshire Pudding. Reflections on the Origins of Rugby League in New South Wales and Queensland*, Sydney, 1996.

81 Ian Heads (op. cit.) provides convincing circumstantial evidence of Smith's visit. Claims of Smith meeting the NU in 1905 are in J. F. O'Loghlen (ed.), *Rugby League Annual and Souvenir 1928*, Sydney 1928, p. 23. For Stephenson, see Charles Little, *Travelling Away to Play at 'Home': New Zealand Footballers in Britain*, unpublished paper presented to the All Blacks and the 'Mother Country' 1905–2005 conference held at Twickenham, 12 September 2005.

82 A. H. Baskerville, *Modern Rugby Football: New Zealand Methods; Points for the Beginner, the Player, the Spectator*, London, 1907.

83 For the response to Baskerville see *Athletic News*, 14 September 1907, *Yorkshire Post*, 10 April and 12 September 1907, and John Coffey, *Canterbury XIII*, Christchurch, 1987.

84 Although this claim was dismissed by the NZRU, Fred Marsh, 'Forward' the *Athletic News* rugby correspondent, claimed that the 1907 tourists' captain, H. R. Wright, had shown him letters from fourteen of the 1905 touring party and that another four had enquired verbally. *Athletic News*, 7 October 1907.

85 Quoted in *Yorkshire Post*, 5 September 1907.

86 *Athletic News*, 7 October 1907. The disparaging title 'All Golds', as the 1907 side has become known to history, appears to have not been used at the time of the tour, at least in Britain. When not called the All Blacks, NU circles referred to them as the 'Phantoms', an ironic reference to C. Wray Palliser's comment.

87 Sean Fagan, *The Rugby Rebellion*, pp. 180–7. The 1907 tour is covered in depth in John Haynes, *From All Blacks to All Golds*, Christchurch, 1996.

88 For accounts of the formation of the NSWRFL see Ian Heads, op. cit.; Chris Cuneen, 'The Rugby War: The Early History of Rugby League in NSW 1907–1915' in Richard Cashman and Michael McKernan (eds), *Sport in History*, Queensland, 1979; and Murray Phillips, 'Football, Class and War: The Rugby Codes in NSW 1907–1918' in J. Nauright and T. Chandler, *Making Men*, London, 1996. The text of letters from Baskerville and Giltinan describing the NSWRFL's foundation can be found in the *Yorkshire Post*, 24 September and 2 October 1907.

89 NU General Committee minutes, 25 March and 30 May 1907.

90 *Yorkshire Post*, 2 October 1907.

91 The England versus Ireland rugby union international held on the same day attracted between 15,000 and 18,000. The success of the Chelsea game gave rise to moves to form a London NU club. See *Yorkshire Post*, 25 February and 7 and 27 March 1908.

92 For the figures, see *Yorkshire Post*, 12 June 1908. This does not include the takings from their games in Australia or their one game in Ceylon.

93 William 'Massa' Johnston to John Wilson, 1 Aug, 1929 (RFL Archives, Leeds).

94 *Yorkshire Post*, 10 October 1907. *The Times*, 3 December 1907, unsympathetically compared the tourists to a reasonable home internal side.

95 *Athletic News*, 14 September 1907.

96 *Athletic News*, 23 December 1907. It is often forgotten that the 1905 All Blacks struggled on the Welsh leg of their tour, losing to Wales and beating Swansea by only one point and Cardiff by just two, scoring a mere twenty-nine points in five games.

97 Ian Heads, *True Blue*, p. 83.

98 *Yorkshire Post*, 5 February 1909. For fuller accounts of the 1908–09 tour see Robert Gate, *The Struggle For The Ashes*, Ripponden, 1986 and Ian Heads, *The Kangaroos*, Sydney, 1990. The Australian national rugby union side, 'the Wallabies' toured England and Wales at the same time as the Kangaroos and proved to be an even greater financial disaster, losing £1,500, although their playing record, on a shorter tour, was better. *Yorkshire Post*, 6 April 1909.

99 *Yorkshire Post*, 7 October 1907.

100 Quoted in Ian Heads, *True Blue*, p. 38.

101 Ibid., p. 49.

102 See in particular, G. T. Vincent, 'Practical Imperialism: The Anglo-Welsh Rugby tour of New Zealand 1908', *The International Journal of the History of Sport*, Vol. 15, No. 1, April 1998, pp. 123–40.

103 *Rugby Football and Cricket*, 4 November 1911.

104 For the background to Rees's move, see 'How Amateur was my Valley' in Gareth Williams's *1905 And All That*, Llandysul, 1991, and the *Yorkshire Post*, 27 May 1907, from which the Rees quote is taken. Full details of the Welsh NU clubs can be found in Dave Farrar and Peter Lush (eds), *Tries in the Valleys*, London, 1998, upon which this section draws heavily. The WRU's official 1907 report into professionalism is reprinted in *Athletic News*, 9 September 1907.

105 For data on the Barry founders, see Farrar and Lush, op. cit., p. 27.

106 NU General Committee minutes, 13 August 1907 and 14 July 1908.

107 Robert Gate, *Gone North*, Vol. 2, Ripponden, 1987, p. 3.

108 The definitive history of soccer in South Wales is Martin Johnes' outstanding *Soccer and Society, South Wales, 1900–1939*, Cardiff, 2002.

109 Farrar and Lush, op. cit., p. 35.

110 Gareth Elwyn Jones, *Modern Wales: A Concise History*, Cambridge, 1984, p. 209.

111 Gareth Williams, *1905 And All That*, Llandysul, 1991, p. 169.

112 *Yorkshire Post*, 20 January 1908.

113 Quoted in David James, 'The First Ever Northern Union International', *Code 13*, September 1989. D. M. Messenger, *The Master*, Sydney, 1982, p. 50.

114 Kenneth O. Morgan, *Rebirth of a Nation: Wales 1880–1980*, Oxford, 1981, p. 80.

115 *Western Mail*, 23 December 1935, quoted in David Smith, 'Focal Heroes: A Welsh Fighting Class' in Richard Holt (ed.), *Sport and the Working Class in Modern Britain*, Manchester, 1990, p. 201.

116 *The Times*, 18 October 1897. Philip Trevor, 'Football during the Season', *The Badminton Magazine*, April 1898, p. 431.

117 The definitive account of the Gould affair can be found in David Smith and Gareth Williams *Fields of Praise*, Cardiff, 1980, pp. 92–9 and pp. 108–112. Full details of the RFU and International Board deliberations can be found in the *Yorkshire Post*, 12 January, 7 February and 3 March 1898.

118 *Yorkshire Owl*, 4 October 1893.

119 Philip Trevor, op. cit., p. 431.

120 David Gallaher and W. T. Stead, *The Complete Rugby Footballer*, London, 1906, p. 222.

121 *Yorkshire Post*, 13 May 1898.

122 *Yorkshire Post*, 19 November 1897 and 18 December 1898.

123 *Yorkshire Post*, 8 February 1902 and 1 September 1902.

124 *Yorkshire Post*, 30 June and 26 September 1904, 9 January 1905, 31 March 1906.

125 For West Hartlepool's financial troubles, see the *Yorkshire Post*, 14 June 1902.

126 'An Original All Black' writing in the *Yorkshire Post*, 13 November 1908.

127 *Yorkshire Post*, 21 September 1900.

128 RFU AGM minutes, 21 September 1900 and 30 September 1904.

129 *Yorkshire Post*, 20 February 1896.

130 A detailed account of the report can be found in the *Yorkshire Post*, 3 March 1908.

131 RFU AGM minutes, 28 May 1908.

132 See Greg Ryan, *The Contest for Rugby Supremacy: Accounting for the 1905 All Blacks*, Christchurch, 2005.

133 *Yorkshire Post*, 13 January 1909.

134 Marriott letter reprinted in the *Yorkshire Post*, 19 January 1909, RFU and International Board decisions in the *Yorkshire Post*, 1 and 20 February 1909.

135 Crane letter of resignation is in the *Yorkshire Post*, 1 February 1909. RFU AGM minutes, 28 May 1909.

136 *Yorkshire Post*, 3 February 1909.

137 The circular is reprinted in the *Yorkshire Post*, 3 March 1906.

138 The best analysis of English rugby union in this period is James Martens, 'They Stooped to Conquer: Rugby Union Football 1895–1914', *Journal of Sport History*, Vol. 20, No. 1, Spring 1993. Poulton changed his name to Poulton-Palmer in 1913 in order to meet the terms of his inheritance from his uncle, G. W. Palmer.

139 Joyce, *Visions of the People*, p. 329.

140 *Yorkshire Post*, 15 April 1910.

141 *Athletic News*, 28 February 1910.

142 *Yorkshire Post*, 26 May 1910. It was thirty-seven years before a reigning monarch actually went to a match, the first being the 1948 Cup Final.

Conclusion: The Northern Union and working-class culture

1 John Hargreaves, *Sport, Power and Culture*, London, 1986, p. 83.

2 Eileen and Stephen Yeo, 'Perceived Patterns: Competition and Licence versus Class and Struggle' in their edited collection, *Popular Culture and Class Conflict 1590–1914*, Brighton, 1981, p. 278.

3 Sadly, like his predecessor Dicky Lockwood, Billy was also declared bankrupt after running into difficulties running a pub shortly after his retirement from the game – see *Yorkshire Evening Post*, 9 February 1928. His contribution to rugby league was heightened by the fact he was the first of a family dynasty. His son Eric was a record-breaking try scorer and his great-nephew Ray was an international loose-forward. For more on Meredith, see John Harding, *Billy Meredith*, Derby, 1985. For Barnes, see Derek Birley, *The Willow Wand*, London 1979. Richard Holt has made a number of relevant and suggestive comments about the lack of English soccer national heroes in the pre-World War One period: see his 'Contrasting Nationalisms', *International Journal of the History of Sport*, Vol. 12, No. 2, August 1995.

4 As with many other examples of oral culture, the specific origins of the saying are impossible to pin down. Despite the fact that the Northern Union became the Rugby Football League in 1922, the phrase continued to be used and can very occasionally still be heard today. For example, in the Salford-based soap opera *Coronation Street*, in an episode broadcast on 17 June 1996.

5 Patrick Joyce, *Visions of the People*, Manchester, 1991, p. 170.

6 The phrase is from Richard Hoggart's *The Uses of Literacy*, London, 1957, p. 94. Hunslet, the community about which Hoggart writes and in which he was brought up, was of course home to one of rugby league's most successful clubs.

7 Alan Metcalfe makes a similar point about the appeal of soccer to Northumberland miners in his 'Football in the Mining Communities of East Northumberland', *International Journal of the History of Sport*, Vol. 5, No. 3, December 1988.

8 Tom Nairn, 'The English Working Class' in Robin Blackburn (ed.), *Ideology in Social Science*, London, 1972, p. 198.

9 It appears that the first black rugby league player was Hunslet's Lucius Banks, a black American serviceman signed in 1912.

10 See Christopher Hill, 'The Norman Yoke' in his *Puritanism and Revolution*, London, 1958. Curiously enough, the Norman Yoke theory survived during this period primarily thanks to Robert Blatchford's *Britain for the British*, published in 1902. Blatchford's *Clarion* was, of course, the most outspoken advocate of a split with the RFU in the 1890s. The phrase 'the greatest game of all' was first used in Australia in the 1920s. Its encapsulation of the self-esteem of the game and its supporters meant that it rapidly became rugby league's unofficial motto – and, indeed, the title of a rugby league magazine founded in the 1990s.

Bibliography

Manuscript sources and official publications

British Playing Fields Society: Committee minutes 1909–1910

W. Corlyon: MSS notebook on Southcoates FC 1881–89

Hull Football Club: Committee minutes 1883/84. Report and Accounts 1881–1910

Lancashire County Football Club (Lancashire Rugby Union): Committee minutes 1881–1895

Leeds Athletic Club: Annual Report 1871

Leeds Cricket, Football and Athletic Club Ltd: Reports and Accounts, 1890–1911

Leeds Grammar School: Admission Books 1820–1900

Leeds Schools Rugby Football Union (Northern Union): Minutes of General Committee 1903–1914

Rugby Football Union: Minutes 1871–1895. Handbooks: 1874/75–1910/1911

Northern Rugby Football Union: Minutes of General Committee 1899–1914. Minutes of Professionalism Sub-Committee 1899–1905. Minutes of Cup Committee 1899–1914. Official Guide: 1898/99, 1899/1900, 1903/04, 1904/05, 1907/08, 1908/09, 1909/10, 1910/11. Report and Balance Sheet: 1899/1900, 1900/01, 1902/03, 1903/04, 1904/05, 1905/06, 1906/07, 1907/08, 1908/09, 1909/1910. Players' Register 1906–1909

Northern Rugby League: Minutes of General Committee 1903–1905. Report and Balance Sheet 1903/04, 1905/06, 1907/08, 1908/1909, 1910/1911

West Riding of Yorkshire Rifle Volunteer Corps: Scrapbooks 1859–1938

Yorkshire County (Northern) Football Union: Committee minutes 1905–1908

Hull Kingston Rovers FC: Report and Accounts 1897–1910

York FC: Correspondence and general documents 1881–83 (Munby & Scott, Solicitors, papers)

Yorkshire Rugby Football Union: Commemoration Book 1914–1919 and Official Handbook 1919–1920

Rules and Bye Laws

Batley and District Junior Football Vase Competition: Rules 1902/03

Bradford and District Junior Football League (NRU): Bye Laws 1899/1900, 1902/03, 1905/06

Cheshire Junior Rugby Football League: Rules 1905/05

Cumberland Junior Rugby Football Union: Rules 1903/04

Cumberland Northern Football Union Shield Competition: Rules 1899/1900

East Riding Rugby League: Bye Laws 1907/08
Furness and District Junior Rugby Football League: Rules 1901/02
Halifax and District Junior Football League (NU): Bye Laws 1900/01
Halifax Charity Cup: Rules 1899/1900
Heavy Woollen District Football League (NU): Rules 1900/01, 1903/04
Keighley and District Football Charity Cup (NU): Rules 1902/03
Leeds and District NRU Junior Football League: Rules 1899/1900
Leeds and District Rugby Football League Challenge Cup: Rules 1905/06
Manchester and District Rugby Football League: Rules 1901/02, 1902/03
North Lancashire District Northern Union Football League: Rules 1900/01
North West Junior Rugby Football League: Rules 1899/1900
South West Lancashire and Border Towns Cup: Rules 1899/1900, 1900/01
St Helens and District Intermediate Rugby Football League: Rules 1908/09
Swinton FC Junior Challenge Cup: Rules 1899/1900
Wakefield and District Junior Football League: Bye Laws 1904/05, 1905/06
Welsh Rugby Football League: Bye Laws 1907/08
Wigan and District Junior Rugby Football League: Rules 1903/04, 1908/09

Contemporary publications

Newspapers and Periodicals

The Almondburian
Athletic News
Barrow Herald and Dalton Advertiser
Barrow News
Barrow Times
Bradford Daily Argus
Bradford Daily Telegraph
Bradford Observer
Bramham College magazine
Bell's Life
Brighouse and Elland Echo
Burnley Express and Advertiser
Burnley Gazette
Clarion
Cleckheaton Advertiser
Dewsbury Reporter
The Field
Football Field and Sports Telegram (Bolton)
Football Programme and Weekly Calendar (Manchester)
Green Final (Oldham)
Halifax Daily Courier
Halifax Guardian
Heckmondwike Herald

Huddersfield Daily Chronicle
Huddersfield Daily Examiner
Hull and East Riding Athlete
Hull Critic
Hull Daily Mail
Hull Times
The Illustrated Weekly Telegraph (Bradford)
Justice
Keighley News
Lancashire Evening Post
The Lantern (St Helens)
Llanelli and County Guardian
Leeds Daily News
Leeds Evening Express
Leeds Intelligencer
T'Leeds Loiners' Comic Olmenac
Leeds Mercury
Leeds Parish Church Magazine
The Leodiensian
The Magazine of Sport
C. B. Fry's Magazine of Sports and Outdoor Life
Manchester Evening News
Manchester Examiner and Times

Manchester Guardian
The Mascot
New Wortley Almanack
North West Daily Mail
Oldham Evening Chronicle
Oldham Standard
Pall Mall Gazette
Pastime
Pendleton Reporter
Pontefract and Castleford Express
Preston Herald
Rochdale Observer
Salford Chronicle
Salford Reporter
Saturday Review
Sheffield Telegraph
Sporting Chronicle
The Sportsman
St Helens Newspaper
St Helens Standard
St James's Gazette
The Times

Toby, The Yorkshire Tyke
To-Day
Ulverston Advertiser
The Umpire (Manchester)
Wakefield Express
Wakefield Free Press
Wakefield and West Riding Herald
Warrington Examiner
Warrington Guardian
The Weever's Awn Comic Olmenack
Widnes Weekly News
Wigan Examiner
Wigan Observer
Yorkshire Busy Bee
Yorkshire Chat
Yorkshire Evening Post
Yorkshire Factory Times
Yorkshire Football
Yorkshire Weekly Post
The Yorkshireman
The Yorkshire Owl
Yorkshire Post

Articles and contributions to books

Almond, H. H., 'Football as a Moral Agent', *Nineteenth Century*, Vol. 34, 1893
Anonymous, 'Sport and Decadence', *The Quarterly Review*, Vol. 211, October 1909
Creston, 'Football', *The Fortnightly Review*, Vol. 55, 1894
Edwardes, C., 'The New Football Mania', *Nineteenth Century*, Vol. 32, 1892
Ensor, E., 'The Football Madness', *The Contemporary Review*, Vol. 74, November 1898
Graves, H., 'A Philosophy of Sport', *The Contemporary Review*, Vol. 78, December 1900
Jackson, N. L., 'Professionalism and Sport', *The Fortnightly Review*, Vol. 67, 1900
Sewell, E. H. D., 'Rugby Football and the Colonial Tours', *The Fortnightly Review*, Vol. 82, 1907
Sewell, E. H. D., 'Rugby Football', *The Fortnightly Review*, Vol. 85, 1909
Sturdee, R. J., 'The Ethics of Football', *The Westminster Review*, Vol. 159, February 1903
Trevor, P., 'Football during the Season', *The Badminton Magazine*, April 1898

Books

Alcock, C. W. (ed.), *The Football Annual*, London, 1868–1900
Alcock, C. W. and Hill, R., *Famous Footballers, 1895/96*, London, 1895
Alken, H., *The National Sports of Great Britain*, London, 1903
Arnold, M., *Culture and Anarchy*, London 1869
Aspin, J., *A Picture of the Manners, Customs, Sports and Pastimes of the Inhabitants of England*, London, 1825
Athletic News Annuals, Manchester 1892–1901

Baines, T., *The Industrial North in the Last Decade of the Nineteenth Century*, Leeds 1928

Barrow FC, Yearbook, Barrow, 1895

Baskerville, A. H., *Modern Rugby Football: New Zealand Methods; Points to the Beginner, the Player, the Spectator*, London, 1907

Bedell, A. W., *An Account of Hornsea in Holderness*, Hull, 1848

Bradby, H. C., *Rugby*, London, 1900

Budd, A., Fry, C. B., Robinson, B. F. and Cook T. A., *Football*, London, 1897

Cassell's Complete Book of Sports and Pastimes, London, 1893

Clarkson, H., *Memories of Merry Wakefield*, Wakefield, 1889

Cooper, G. H., *Spen Valley Rugby Football Reminiscences*, Cleckheaton, 1920

Dickens, C., *Hard Times*, London, 1854

Gallaher, D. and Stead, W. J., *The Complete Rugby Footballer*, London, 1906

Gaskell, E., *North and South*, London, 1855

Goldthorpe, J., *Twenty Years' Records of Leeds FC*, Leeds, 1910

Goulburn, E. M., *The Book of Rugby School*, Rugby, 1856

Halifax FC, *History of Halifax Cricket and Football Club*, Halifax, 1900

Hardy, H. H., *Public School Life – Rugby*, London, 1911

Higson, J., *History of Salford Football Club*, Salford, 1892

Hughes, T., *Tom Brown's Schooldays*, London, 1857

Hull Football Almanack, Hull, 1888

Jackson, H., *The Eighteen Nineties*, London, 1913

Kay's Illustrated Yorkshire Football Guide 1894/95, Bradford, 1894

Lawson, J., *Letters to the Young on Progress in Pudsey During the Last Sixty Years*, Stanningley, 1887

Lennox, Lord W., *Merrie England, Its Sports and Pastimes*, London, 1858

Marshall, Rev. F. (ed.), *Football – the Rugby Union Game*, London, 1892

Masterman, C. F. G., *The Heart of Empire*, London, 1901

Masterman, C. F. G., *The Condition of England*, 1909

Old Rugbeian Society, *The Origin of Rugby Football*, Rugby, 1897

Pike, W. T. (ed.), *The West Riding of Yorkshire at the Opening of the 20th Century*, Brighton, 1902

Price, A. C., *A History of the Leeds Grammar School from its Foundation until the End of 1918*, Leeds, 1919

Pullin, A. W., *Alfred Shaw: Cricketer, His Career and Reminiscences*, London, 1902

Rahilly, Jerome J., *Rugby Football*, London, 1904

'Referee', *History of Barrow Football Club*, Barrow, 1914

Robinson, B., Fletcher, *Rugby Football*, London, 1896

Rochdale Hornets FC, *Grand Bazaar Official Guide and Handbook*, Rochdale, 1901

Rouse, W. H. D., *A History of Rugby School*, London, 1898

Russell, C. E. B., *Manchester Boys*, Manchester 1905

Selfe, Lt Col. S, *Chapters from the History of Rugby School*, Rugby, 1910

Shaw, C. F., *The Gallant Youths*, Batley, 1899

Shearman, M., *Athletics and Football*, London, 1887

Shearman, M., *Football*, London, 1899

Smith, H., *Festivals, Games and Amusements*, London, 1831

Smith, W. (ed.), *Old Yorkshire*, London, 1882

Strutt, J., *The Sports and Pastimes of the People of England*, London, 1801

Terrett, J. J., *HH Asquith and the Featherstone Massacre*, London, 1906

The Rugby Union Football Handbook, London, 1889–1896

The Sportsman, *British Sports and Sportsmen Past and Present*, London, 1908

Vassall, H., *Rugby Football*, London, 1889

Watson, A. E. T. (ed.), *The Year's Sport: A Review of British Sports and Pastimes for the Year 1885*, London, 1886

Whadcoat, J. H., *An Account of the West Yorkshire Educational and Benevolent Institution*, Bradford, 1906

Whellan, W., *The History and Topography of the Counties of Cumberland and Westmoreland*, Pontefract, 1860

Yorkshire Football Handbook, Leeds, 1881/82 and 1885/1886

Yorkshire Lives – Social and Political, London, 1899

Yorkshire Men of Mark, Exeter, 1898

Yorkshire Owl Cricket Annual 1896, Leeds, 1896

Yorkshire Sporting Almanack for 1862, Leeds, 1862

Yorkshire Who's Who, London, 1912

Local Directories

Foster, E., *Barrow & District Yearbook*, Barrow, 1906

Kelly's West Riding Directory, 1889

Roberts, C. J., *Directory of Barrow in Furness*, Barrow, 1886

Slater's Directory of Leeds and District 1892–93, 1893

Slater's Directory of the Warrington, 1887 and 1891

Slater's Directory of the West Riding, 1887 and 1891

White W., *White's Clothing District Directory*, 1881

White, W., *White's General and Commercial Directory of Leeds and the West Riding*, 1870

Publications since 1920

Articles, papers and contributions to books

Adair, D., 'Competing or Complementary Forces? The "Civilising" Process and the Commitment to Winning in Nineteenth Century English Rugby and Association Football', *Canadian Journal of the History of Sport*, Vol. 24, No. 2, December 1993

Arnold, A. J., 'Shall it be Bradford or Leeds? The Origins of Professional Football in the West Riding Textile District', *Publications of the Thoresby Society – Miscellany*, Vol. 19, 1990

Arscott, C. and Wolff, J., 'Cultivated Capital', *History Today* Vol. 37, 1987

Baker, W. J., 'The Making of a Working Class Football Culture in Victorian England', *Journal of Social History*, Vol. 13, No. 2, 1979

Baker, W. J., 'William Webb Ellis and the Origins of Rugby Football: The Life and Death of a Victorian Myth', *Albion*, Vol. 13, 1981

Barlow, S., 'The Diffusion of "Rugby" Football in the Industrialised Context of Rochdale, 1868–90', *International Journal of the History of Sport*, Vol. 10, No. 1, April 1993

Birley, D., 'Sportsmen and the Deadly Game', *British Journal of Sports History*, Vol. 3, December 1986

Briggs, A., 'The View from Badminton' in A Briggs (ed.), *Essays in the History of Publishing: Longman 1724–1974*, London, 1974

Collins, T., 'History, Theory and the "Civilising Process"', *Sport in History*, Vol. 25, No. 2, August 2005

Cunningham, H., 'Leisure and Culture', *The Cambridge Social History of Britain 1750–1950 (Vol. 2)*, Cambridge, 1990

Cunningham, H., 'Leisure' in J. Benson (ed.), *The Working Class in England 1875–1914*, London, 1985

Davies, B., 'Bifurcation in Sport: Some Preliminary Thoughts on the Case of Rugby League', *The Journal of Regional and Local Studies*, Vol. 8, No. 1, Spring 1988

Delaney, T., 'The Great Betrayal at Park Avenue Bradford', *Code 13*, No. 7, June 1988

Delaney, T., 'A Brief History of Brighouse Rangers 1878–1906', *Code 13*, No. 9, December 1988

Dellheim, C., 'Imagining England: Victorian Views of the North', *Northern History* Vol. 22, 1986

Dunning, E. and Sheard, K., 'The Bifurcation of Rugby Union and Rugby League: A Case Study Of Organisational Conflict and Change', *International Review of Sports Sociology*, II, 1976

Elias, N. and Dunning, E., 'Folk Football in Medieval and Early Modern Britain', in E. Dunning (ed.) *The Sociology of Sport*, London, 1971

Elton, A., 'Becoming a City: Leeds, 1893', *Publications of the Thoresby Society, Miscellany*, Second Series, Vol. 3, 1993

Farr, E., 'A History of Morley Northern', *Code 13*, No. 13, December 1989

Gibbons, T., 'Why Are There Two Forms of Rugby?', *Open Rugby*, May 1998

Gould, S. J., 'Creation Myths of Cooperstown' in *Bully for Brontosaurus*, London, 1991

Greenhalgh, P., "The Work and Play Principle": The Professional Regulations of the NRFU, 1898–1905', *International Journal of the History of Sport*, Vol. 9, No. 3, December 1992

Halladay, E., 'Of Pride and Prejudice: The Amateur Question in English Nineteenth Century Rowing', *The International Journal of the History of Sport*, Vol. 4, No. 1, May 1987

Harrison, B., 'Religion and Recreation in Nineteenth Century England', *Past and Present*, No. 38, December 1967

Hendrick, H., 'The Leeds Gas Strike', *Publications of the Thoresby Society, Miscellany*, Vol. 16, Part 2, 1993

Hill, C., 'The Norman Yoke', *Puritanism and Revolution*, London, 1958

Hobsbawm, E. J., 'Labour in the Great City', *New Left Review* 166, November/December 1987

Holt, R., 'Contrasting Nationalisms', *International Journal of the History of Sport*, Vol. 12, No. 2, August 1995

James, D., 'The First Ever Northern Union International', *Code 13*, September 1989

Jowitt, T., *Late Victorian and Edwardian Bradford*, Bradford Centre Occasional Papers, Vol. 2, Leeds, 1980

Kirby, H. T., 'Some Notes on the Bloxam Family of Rugby', *Essays in Honour of Philip B Chatwin*, Oxford, 1962

Maguire, J., 'Images of Manliness and Competing Ways of Living in Late Victorian and Edwardian Britain', *British Journal of Sports History*, Vol. 3, December 1986

Mandle, W. F., 'Games People Played: Cricket and Football in England and Victoria in the Late Nineteenth Century', *Historical Studies*, April 1972

Mandle, W. F., 'W. G. Grace as a Victorian Hero', *Historical Studies*, April 1980

Mangan, J. A., 'Duty unto Death: English Masculinity and Militarism in the Age of the New Imperialism', *International Journal of the History of Sport*, Vol. 12, No. 2, August 1995

Mann, L. and Pearce, D., 'Social Psychology of Sports Spectators', in D Glencross (ed.), *Psychology and Sport*, Sydney 1979

Markey, R., 'Explaining Union Mobilisation in the 1880s and Early 1900s', *Labour History*, No. 83, November 2002

Martens, J., 'They Stooped to Conquer: Rugby Union Football 1895–1914', *Journal of Sport History*, Vol. 20, No. 1, Spring 1993

Mather, T., 'A History of Fleetwood NUFC', *The Greatest Game*, No. 11, September 1992; No. 12, November 1992; and No. 13, February 1993

Metcalfe, A., 'Organised Sport in the Mining Communities of South Northumberland', *Victorian Studies*, No. 25, Summer 1982

Metcalfe, A., 'Football in the Mining Communities of East Northumberland', *International Journal of the History of Sport*, Vol. 5, No. 3, December 1988

Moore, A., 'Opera of the Proletariat: Rugby League, the Labour Movement and Working-Class Culture in New South Wales and Queensland', *Labour History*, No. 79, November 2000

Morris, R. J., 'Middle Class Culture 1700–1914' in D. Fraser (ed.), *A History of Modern Leeds*, Manchester, 1980

Nairn, T., 'The English Working Class' in R. Blackburn (ed.), *Ideology in Social Science*, London, 1972

Nauright, J., 'Sport, Manhood and Empire', *The International Journal of the History of Sport*, Vol. 8, No. 2, September 1991

Oddy, D. J., 'Working Class Diets' *Economic History Review*, Vol. 23, 1970

Reid, D. A., 'The Decline of Saint Monday 1766–1876', *Past and Present*, No. 71, May 1976

Reid, D. A., 'Folk-Football, the Aristocracy and Cultural Change: A Critique of Dunning and Sheard', *The International Journal of the History of Sport*, Vol. 5, No. 2, September 1988

Rhind, N., 'Blackheath Football Club 1862–1870', *Transactions of the Greenwich and Lewisham Antiquarian Society*, Vol. 10, No. 1, 1985

Roberts, E., 'Working Class Standards of Living in Barrow and Lancaster 1890–1914', *Economic History Review*, Vol. 30, 1977

Russell, D., '"Sporadic and Curious": The Emergence of Rugby and Soccer Zones in Yorkshire and Lancashire c1860–1914', *The International Journal of the History of Sport*, Vol. 5, No. 2, September 1988

Stedman-Jones, G., 'Working Class Politics and Working Class Culture in London 1870–1900', *Journal of Social History*, Vol. 7, Summer 1974

Stedman-Jones, G., 'Class Expression Versus Social Control? A Critique of Recent Trends in the Social History of "Leisure"', *History Workshop Journal*, No. 4, Autumn 1977

Storch, R. D., 'The Policeman as "Domestic Missionary": Urban Discipline and Popular Culture in Northern England 1850–1880', *Journal Of Social History*, Vol. 9, 1976

Thompson, F. M. L., 'Social Control in Victorian Britain', *Economic History Review*, Vol. 34, No. 2, 1981

Tranter, N. L., 'The Cappielow Riot and the Composition and Behaviour of Soccer Crowds in Late Victorian Scotland', *The International Journal of the History of Sport*, Vol. 12, No. 3, December 1995

Vamplew, W., 'Ungentlemanly Conduct: The Control of Soccer Crowd Behaviour, 1888–1914' in T. C. Smout (ed.), *The Search for Wealth and Stability*, London, 1979

Vamplew, W., 'Sports Crowd Disorder in Britain 1870–1914', *Journal of Sport History*, Vol. 7, No. 1, 1980

Vamplew, W., 'Paying for Play: the Earnings of Professional Sportsmen in England 1870–1914' in R. Cashman and M. McKernan (eds), *Sport, Money, Morality and the Media*, New South Wales, 1982

Vamplew, W., 'The Economics of a Sports Industry, Scottish Gate Money Football 1890–1914', *Economic History Review*, Vol. 35, November 1982

Vamplew, W., 'Profit or Utility Maximisation? An Analysis of English County Cricket Before 1914' in W. Vamplew (ed.), *The Economic History of Leisure*, Adelaide, 1983

Veitch, C., "Play Up! Play Up! and Win the War!" Football, the Nation and the First World War', *Journal of Contemporary History*, Vol. 20, July 1985

Vincent, G. T., 'Practical Imperialism: The Anglo-Welsh Rugby Tour of New Zealand 1908', *The International Journal of the History of Sport*, Vol. 15, No. 1, April 1998

Walton, J., 'Residential Amenity, Respectable Morality and the Rise of the Entertainment Industry: the Case of Blackpool 1860–1914', *Literature and History*, Vol. 1, 1975

Walton, J., 'The Demand for Working Class Seaside Holidays in Victorian England', *Economic History Review*, Vol. 34, 1982

Walton, J., 'Professor Musgrove's North of England: A Critique', *Journal of Regional and Local Studies*, Vol. 12, No. 2, 1992

Williams, Gareth, 'How Amateur Was My Valley: Professional Sport and National Identity in Wales 1890–1914', *The British Journal of Sports History*, Vol. 2, No. 2, September 1985

Williams, Graham, 'Initiating the Liverpudlians – A History of the first Liverpool City', *Code 13*, No. 13, December 1989

Williams, Graham, 'If At First You Can't Decide: A History of South Shields', *Code 13*, No. 15, June 1990

Wolff, J. and Hrscott, C., 'Cultivated Capital', *History Today*, Vol. 37, 1987

Books

Adams, T., *The Hit Men*, Sydney, 1994

Arlott, J. (ed.), *The Oxford Companion to Sports and Games*, Oxford, 1976

Arnold, A. J., *A Game That Would Pay, A Business History of Professional Football In Bradford*, London, 1988

Auty, T. W., *Centenary History of Headingley Football Club*, Leeds, 1978

Bailey, P., *Leisure and Class in Victorian England*, Second Edition, London, 1987

Balaam, L., *Manchester Football Club 1860–1985*, Manchester, 1985

Bale, J., *Sport and Place*, London, 1982

Barak, M., *A Century of Rugby At Sale*, Sale, 1962

Beard, R., *Muddied Oafs: The Soul of Rugby*, London, 2004

Benson, J., *The Penny Capitalists: A Study of Working Class Entrepreneurs*, Dublin, 1983

Bergin, T. E., *The Game – The Harvard–Yale Football Rivalry 1875–1983*, Yale, 1984

Best, G., *Mid-Victorian Britain 1851–1875*, London, 1979

Birley, D., *The Willow Wand*, London, 1979

Birley, D., *Sport and the Making of Britain*, Manchester, 1993

Birley, D., *Land of Sport and Glory: Sport and British Society 1887–1910*, Manchester, 1995

Briggs, A., *Victorian Cities*, London, 1963

Briggs, A., *Victorian People*, London, 1965

Briggs, A. and Saville, J. (eds), *Essays in Labour History*, London, 1960

Calder, A., *The Myth of the Blitz*, London, 1991

Cartwright, B. F., *A Ton Full Of Memories*, Batley, 1987

Cashman, R. and McKernan, M. (eds) *Sport in History*, Queensland, 1979

Chadwick, S., *Claret and Gold*, Huddersfield, 1945

Chadwick, S., *Northern Union*, Huddersfield, 1946

Clarke, J. and Critcher, C., *The Devil Makes Work: Leisure in Capitalist Britain*, London, 1985

Coffey, J., *Canterbury XIII*, Christchurch, 1987

Cox, R. W., *History of Sport: A Guide to the Literature and Sources of Information*, Cheshire, 1994

Croxford, W. B., *Rugby Union in Lancashire and Cheshire*, Liverpool, 1950

Cunningham, H., *The Volunteer Force*, London, 1975

Cunningham, H., *Leisure in the Industrial Revolution*, London, 1980

Dalby, K., *The Headingley Story 1890–1955*, Leeds, 1955

Dalglish, J. R. A., *Red, Black and Blue, The First 125 Years of Liverpool Football Club*, Swinton, 1983

Davies, A. and Fielding, S. (eds), *Workers' Worlds: Cultures and Communities in Manchester and Salford 1880–1939*, Manchester, 1992

Delaney, T., *The Roots of Rugby League*, Keighley, 1984

Delaney, T., *The Grounds of Rugby League*, Keighley, 1991

Delaney, T., *Rugby Disunion*, Keighley, 1993

Dobbs, B., *Edwardians At Play*, London, 1973

Dunning, E. and Sheard, K., *Barbarians, Gentlemen and Players*, New York, 1979

Dyos, H. J. and Wolff, M. (eds), *The Victorian City: Images and Realities*, London, 1973

Elias, N., *The Civilising Process*, Oxford, 1978

Elton, C., *Hull City – A Complete Record*, Derby, 1989

Ensor, R. C. K., *England 1970–1914*, London, 1936

Fagan, S., *The Rugby Rebellion: The Divide of League and Union*, Sydney, 2005

Farrar, D. and Lush, P. (eds), *Tries in the Valleys*, London, 1998

Farrar, D., Lush, P. and O' Hare, M. *Touch and Go*, London, 1995

Firth, D., *My Dear Victorious Stod*, London, 1977

Firth, G., *Victorian Yorkshire at Play*, Nelson, 1989

Frost, T., *Bradford City – A Complete Record*, Derby, 1988

Gate, R., *Gone North* (two volumes), Ripponden, 1986

Gate, R., *The Struggle For The Ashes*, Ripponden, 1986

Gate, R., *Rugby League, An Illustrated History*, London, 1989

Genovese, E., *Roll, Jordan, Roll: The World the Slaves Made*, London, 1974

Gill, E., *Skipton RUFC Centenary*, Skipton, 1974

Gillett, E. and MacMahon, K. A., *A History of Hull*, Hull, 1980

Golby, J. (ed.), *Culture and Society in Britain 1850–1890*, London, 1986

Golby, J. M. and Purdue, A. W., *The Civilisation of the Crowd*, London, 1984

Gould, S. J., *Bully for Brontosaurus*, London, 1991

Green, B. (ed.), *The Wisden Book of Cricketer's Lives*, London, 1986

Green, M., *The Villagers, A Brief History of Bramley RLFC*, Leeds, not dated

Green, M. and Hoole, L., *The Parksiders, A Brief History of Hunslet RLFC*, Leeds, not dated

Greenland, W. J., *The History of the Amateur Football Alliance*, London, 1965

Guttmann, A., *From Ritual to Record: The Nature of Modern Sports*, New York, 1978

Guttmann, A., *Sports Spectators*, New York, 1986

Haight, G. (ed.), *A Victorian Reader*, New York, 1972

Haley, B., *The Healthy Body in Victorian Culture*, Cambridge, Mass, 1978

Hardcastle, A., *The Thrum Hall Story*, Halifax, 1986

Harding, J., *Billy Meredith*, Derby, 1985

Harding, J., *For the Good of the Game*, London, 1991

Hargreaves, Jennifer (ed.), *Sport, Culture and Ideology*, London, 1982

Hargreaves, John, *Sport Power and Culture: A Social and Historical Analysis of Popular Sports in Britain*, Cambridge, 1986

Harris, H. A., *Sport and Britain*, London, 1975

Harrison, J. F. C., *Late Victorian Britain 1875–1901*, London, 1990

Hartley, M. and Clapham, T., *The Avenue*, Nottingham, 1987

Haynes, J., *From All Black to All Gold*, Christchurch, 1996

Heads, I., *The Kangaroos*, Sydney, 1990

Heads, I., *True Blue*, Sydney, 1992

Hickie, T. V., *They Ran with the Ball: How Rugby Football Began in Australia*, Sydney, 1993

Hickie T. V. and Hughes, A., *The Game for the Game Itself. The History of Sub-District Rugby in Sydney*, Sydney 2004

Hinchliffe, G., *A History of King James's Grammar School in Almondbury*, Huddersfield, 1963

History of the Lancashire Football Association, Blackburn, 1928

Hobsbawm, E. J., *Worlds of Labour*, London, 1984

Hobsbawm, E. J., *Nations and Nationalism Since 1870*, Cambridge, 1990

Hobsbawm, E. J. and Ranger, T. (eds.), *The Invention of Tradition*, London, 1983

Hoggart, R., *The Uses of Literacy*, London, 1957

Holt, R., *Sport and the British*, Oxford, 1989

Holt, R. (ed.), *Sport and the Working Class in Modern Britain*, Manchester, 1990

Hope-Simpson, J. B., *Rugby Since Arnold*, London, 1967

Houghton, W. E., *The Victorian Frame of Mind*, London, 1957

Hughes, G., *One Hundred Years of Scarlett*, Llanelli, 1983

Humphries, S., *Hooligans or Rebels? An Oral History of Working Class Childhood and Youth, 1889–1939*, Oxford, 1981

Hynes, S., *The Edwardian Turn of Mind*, Princeton, 1968

Inglis, K., *The Churches and the Working Classes in Victorian England*, London, 1963

Inglis, S., *The Football Grounds of Great Britain*, London, 1987

Inglis, S., *League Football and the Men Who Made It*, London, 1988

James, C. L. R., *Beyond a Boundary*, London, 1963

Jarred, M. and Macdonald, M., *Leeds United – A Complete Record*, Derby, 1986

Jewell, H. M., *The North–South Divide: The Origins of Northern Consciousness in England*, Manchester, 1994

Johnes, M., *Soccer and Society, South Wales, 1900–1939*, Cardiff, 2002

Jones, G. E., *Modern Wales: A Concise History*, Cambridge, 1984

Joyce, P., *Work, Society and Politics*, Brighton, 1980

Joyce, P., *Visions of the People*, Cambridge, 1991

Kidd, A. J. and Roberts, K. W. (eds), *City, Class and Culture: Studies of Cultural Production and Social Policy in Victorian Manchester*, Manchester, 1985

Korr, C., *West Ham United*, London, 1986

Latham, M., *Buff Berry and The Mighty Bongers*, Chorley, 1995

Latham, M. and Mather, T., *The Rugby League Myth*, Chorley, 1993

Lindley, J. C., *100 Years of Rugby*, Wakefield, 1973

Lorimar, D. A., *Colour, Class and the Victorians*, Leicester, 1978

Lovesey, P., *The Official Centenary of the Amateur Athletics Association*, London, 1979

Lowerson, J., *Sport and the English Middle Classes*, Manchester, 1993

Lowerson, J. and Myerscough, J., *Time to Spare in Victorian England*, Sussex, 1977

McIntosh, P. C., *Sport in Society*, London, 1963

McIntosh, P. C., *Physical Education in England since 1800*, London, 1968

Mackenzie, J. M., *Imperialism and Popular Culture*, Manchester, 1986

McKibbin, R., *The Ideologies of Class*, Oxford, 1990

Macrory, J., *Running With The Ball, The Birth of Rugby Football*, London, 1991

Malcolmson, R. W., *Popular Recreations in English Society 1770–1850*, London, 1975

Mangan, J. A., *Athleticism in the Victorian and Edwardian Public School*, Cambridge, 1981

Mangan, J. A., *The Games Ethic and Imperialism*, London, 1986

Mangan, J. A. (ed.), *Pleasure, Profit, Proselytism*, London, 1988

Mangan, J. A., and Park, R. J. (eds), *From 'Fair Sex' to Feminism: Sport and the Socialisation of Women in the Industrial and Post-Industrial Eras*, London, 1987

Mangan, J. A. and Walvin, J. (eds), *Manliness and Morality: Middle Class Masculinity in Britain and America, 1800–1940*, Manchester, 1987

Marples, M., *A History of Football*, London, 1954

Marsden, A., *Preston Grasshoppers' Centenary Brochure*, Preston, 1969

Marshall, Rev. F. and Tosswill, L. R. (eds), *Football – the Rugby Union Game*, London, 1925

Marx, K. and Engels, F., *On Britain*, Moscow, 1971

Mason, P., *The English Gentleman: The Rise and Fall of an Ideal*, London, 1993

Mason, T., *Association Football and English Society 1863–1915*, Brighton, 1980

Mason, T. (ed.), *Sport in Britain, A Social History*, Cambridge, 1989

Meacham, S., *A Life Apart: The English Working Class 1890–1914*, London, 1977

Meller, H., *Leisure and the Changing City, 1870–1914*, London, 1976

Melling, P., *Man of Amman*, Llandysul, 1993

Messenger, D. M., *The Master*, Sydney, 1982

Mitchell, W. R., *By Gum, Life Were Sparse!*, London, 1981

Montefiore, D., *Cricket in the Doldrums*, Campbelltown, Australia, 1992

Moore, A., *The Mighty Bears. A Social History of North Sydney RLFC*, Sydney, 1996

Moore, A., *Jimmy Devereux's Yorkshire Pudding. Reflections on the Origins of Rugby League in New South Wales and Queensland*, Sydney, 1999

Moorhouse, G., *A People's Game*, London, 1995

Morgan, K. O., *Rebirth of a Nation: Wales 1880–1980*, Oxford, 1981

Morris, R. J. and Rodger, R. (eds), *The Victorian City, A Reader in British Urban History*, Essex, 1993

Musgrove, F, *The North of England. A History from Roman Times to the Present*, Oxford, 1990

Nauright, J. and Chandler, T. (eds), *Making Men*, London, 1996

O'Loghlen, J. F., (ed.), *Rugby League Annual and Souvenir 1928*, Sydney, 1928

Oriard, M., *Reading Football: How the Popular Press Created an American Spectacle*, Chapel Hill, 1993

Owen, O. L., *The History of the Rugby Football Union*, London, 1955

Pearce, C., *The Manningham Mills Strike*, Hull, 1975

Pearson, G., *Hooligan, A History of Respectable Fears*, London, 1983

Pelmear, K., *Rugby Football, an Anthology*, London, 1958

Phillips, C. B. and Smith, J. H., *Lancashire and Cheshire From AD1540*, London, 1994

Phillips, J., *A Man's Country: The Image of the Pakeha Male, A History*, Auckland, 1987

Raine, A., *History of St Peter's School, York*, London, 1926

Read, D., *The English Provinces*, London, 1964

Read, D., *The Age of Urban Democracy*, London, 1979

Roberts, R., *The Classic Slum*, Manchester, 1971

Robertson, J., *Uppies and Doonies*, Aberdeen, 1967

Rubinstein, W. D., *Capitalism, Culture and Decline in Britain 1750–1990*, London, 1993

Ryan, G., *Forerunners of the All Blacks*, Christchurch, 1993

Ryan, G., *The Contest for Rugby Supremacy: Accounting for the 1905 All Blacks*, Christchurch, 2005

Ryan, G. (ed.), *Tackling Rugby Myths: Rugby and New Zealand Society 1854–2004*, Dunedin, 2005

Sandiford, K., *Cricket and the Victorians*, Aldershot, 1994

Service, A., *Saints in Their Glory*, St Helens, 1985

Sissons, R., *The Professionals: A Social History of the Professional Cricketer*, London, 1988

Smith, D. and Williams, G., *Fields of Praise, The Official History of the Welsh Rugby Union, 1881–1981*, Cardiff, 1980

Souvenir History of Swinton, Swinton, 1929

Storch, R. D. (ed.), *Popular Culture and Custom in Nineteenth Century England*, London, 1982

Thompson, E. P., *Customs in Common*, London, 1991

Thompson, F. M. L., *The Rise of Respectable Society*, London, 1988

Thompson, F. M. L. (ed.), *The Cambridge Social History of Britain 1750–1950*, Cambridge, 1990

Thompson, P., *The Edwardians*, London, 1975

Thorburn, S., *The History of Scottish Rugby*, London, 1970

Thornton, A. P., *The Habit of Authority*, London, 1966

Tischler, S., *Footballers and Businessmen*, New York, 1981

Titley, U. A. and McWhirter, R., *A Centenary History of the Rugby Football Union*, London, 1970

Trescatheric, B., *Sport and Leisure in Victorian Barrow*, Barrow, 1983

Vamplew, W., *Pay Up and Play the Game: Professional Sport in Britain 1875–1914*, Cambridge, 1988

Waites, B., *Popular Culture in Late Nineteenth and Early Twentieth Century Lancashire*, Open University course U203, Unit 6, not dated

Waller, P. J., *Town, City and Nation: England 1850–1914*, Oxford, 1983

Walvin, J., *The People's Game*, London, 1975

Walvin, J., *Leisure and Society, 1830–1950*, London, 1978

Walton, J., *Lancashire: A Social History 1558–1939*, Manchester, 1987

Walton, J. and Walvin, J. (eds), *Leisure in Britain, 1780–1939*, Manchester, 1983

Waters, C., *British Socialists and the Politics of Popular Culture*, Manchester, 1990

Wiener, M., *English Culture and the Decline of the Industrial Spirit 1850–1980*, Cambridge, 1981

Williams, Gareth, *1905 and All That*, Llandysul, 1991

Williams, Gareth and Smith, D., *Fields of Praise*, Cardiff, 1980
Williams, Graham, *The Code War*, Harefield, 1994
Williams, R., *Culture and Society 1780–1950*, London, 1958
Williams, R., *The Long Revolution*, London, 1961
Wright, A. R., *British Calendar Customs*, London, 1936
Wynne-Thomas, P., *Give Me Arthur*, London, 1985
Yeo, E. and Yeo, S. (eds), *Popular Culture and Class Conflict 1590–1914*, Brighton, 1981
Young, P., *Manchester United*, London, 1960
Young, P., *Football in Sheffield*, London, 1964
Young, P., *A History of British Football*, London, 1968

Video, CD-Rom and electronic media

Leroy Angel http://www.rfu.com/index.cfm/fuseaction/RFUHome.News-Detail/Story1D/ 11196, accessed on 23 July 2005
Rugby League Tours, Micron Video, Wigan 1988
Oxford English Dictionary Second Edition on CD-Rom, Oxford, 1993

Theses

Arnold, J., *The Influence of Pilkington Brothers (Glass Manufacturers) on the Growth of Sport and Community Recreation in St Helens*, MEd thesis, University of Liverpool, 1977
Blackledge, P., *William Cail, Amateurism and the Rugby Football Union*, MA thesis, University of Northumbria, 1994
Bradley, S., *Leisure and Society in Huddersfield 1868–95, BA thesis*, University of Bristol, 1989
Greenhalgh, P., *The History of the Northern Rugby Football Union 1895–1915*, PhD thesis, University of Lancaster, 1992
Lewis, R. W., *The Development of Professional Football in Lancashire, 1870–1914*, PhD thesis, University of Lancaster, 1993
Martens, J. W., *Rugby Union Football and English Society 1871–1914*, PhD thesis, University of Manitoba, 1988
Taylor, M., *'Proud Preston' A History of the Football League 1900–39*, PhD thesis, De Montfort University, 1997

Index

before

under the

the fact of Puzo's authorsh

Now for the first time it has been

and can take its place among his ca

tional narrative novels. It explores the th

love, revenge and betrayal (including even a Sici

setting complete with a rather familiar Mafia don),

all of which would become central to the trilogy

that catapulted Puzo to international stardom.

The Dark Arena
The Fortunate Pilgrim
The Runaway Summer of Davie Shaw
The Godfather
Fools Die
The Sicilian
The Fourth K
The Last Don
Omerta
The Family

NON-FICTION

The Godfather Papers and Other Confessions
Inside Las Vegas

SIX GRAVES
TO MUNICH

Mario Puzo

Writing as
Mario Cleri

MACLEHOSE PRESS
QUERCUS · LONDON

First published in Great Britain in 2009 by MacLehose Press
This paperback edition first published in 2010 by

MacLehose Press
an imprint of Quercus
21 Bloomsbury Square
London, WC1A 2NS

ISBN 978 1 84916 276 0

Printed and bound in Great Britain by Clays Ltd, St Ives plc

10 9 8 7 6 5 4 3 2 1

Typeset by Ellipsis Books Limited, Glasgow
Printed and bound in Great Britain by Clays Ltd, St Ives plc

SIX GRAVES TO MUNICH

CHAPTER 1

Michael Rogan checked the lurid sign outside Hamburg's hottest nightclub. *Sinnlich! Schamlos! Sündig!* Sensual! Shameless! Sinful! The Roter Peter made no bones about what it was selling. Rogan took a small photograph out of his pocket and studied it by the red light of the swine-shaped door lamp. He had studied the photograph a hundred times, but he was nervous about recognizing the man he was looking for. People changed a great deal in ten years, Rogan knew. He himself had changed.

He went past the obsequiously bowing doorman into the club. Inside it was dark except for the "blue" movie flickering on a small rectangular screen. Rogan threaded his way through the crowded tables, the noisy, alcohol-stinking crowd. Suddenly the house lights came on and framed him against the stage, with naked blonde girls dancing above his head. Rogan's eyes searched the faces of those seated at ringside tables. A waitress touched his arm. She said coquettishly in German, "Is the Herr Amerikaner looking for something special?"

Rogan brushed past her, annoyed at being so easily spotted as an American. He could feel the blood pounding against the silver plate that held his skull together – a danger signal. He would have to do this job quickly and get back to his hotel. He moved on through the club, checking the dark corners, where patrons drank beer from huge steins and impersonally grabbed at the nearest waitress. He glanced into the curtained booths, where men sprawled on leather sofas and studied the girls on stage before picking up the phone to summon their favourite to join them.

Rogan was becoming impatient now. He didn't have much more time. He turned and faced the stage. Behind the nude dancing girls there was a transparent panel in the curtain. Through the panel the patrons could see the next line of girls getting ready to go on stage, and they applauded every time one of the girls took off a bra or a stocking. A voice called out drunkenly, "You darlings, ah, you darlings – I can love you all."

Rogan turned towards the voice and smiled in the darkness. He remembered that voice. Ten years had not changed it. It was a fatty, choking Bavarian voice, thick with false friendliness. Rogan moved swiftly towards it. He opened his jacket and slipped off a leather button that gripped the Walther pistol securely in its shoulder holster. With his other hand he took the silencer out of his jacket pocket and held it as if it were a pipe.

And then he was before the table, before the face of the man he had never forgotten, whose memory had kept him alive the last ten years.

The voice had not deceived him; it was Karl Pfann. The German must have gained fifty pounds and he had lost nearly all his hair, only a few blond strands criss-crossed his greasy pate; but the mouth was as tiny and almost as cruel as Rogan remembered it. Rogan sat down at the next table and ordered a drink. When the house lights went out and the blue movie came on again he slipped the Walther pistol out of its holster, and keeping his hands under the table, fitted the silencer onto the pistol barrel. The weapon sagged out of balance; it would not be accurate beyond five yards. Rogan leaned to his right and tapped Karl Pfann on the shoulder.

The gross head turned, the shiny pate inclined, and the false-friendly voice Rogan had been hearing in his dreams for ten years said, "Yes, *mein Freund*, what do you wish?"

Rogan said in a hoarse voice, "I am an old comrade of yours. We made a business deal on *Rosenmontag*, Carnival Monday, 1945, in the Munich Palace of Justice."

The movie distracted Karl Pfann, and his eyes turned towards the bright screen. "No, no, it cannot be," he said impatiently. "In 1945 I was serving the Fatherland. I became a businessman after the war."

"When you were a Nazi," Rogan said. "When you were a torturer ... When you were a murderer."

The silver plate in his skull was throbbing. "My name is Michael Rogan. I was in American Intelligence. Do you remember me now?"

There was the smash of glass as Karl Pfann's huge body swivelled round and he peered through the darkness at Rogan. The German said quietly, menacingly, "Michael Rogan is dead. What do you want from me?"

"Your life," Rogan said. He swung the Walther pistol out from under the table and pressed it into Pfann's belly. He pulled the trigger. The German's body shuddered with the force of the bullet. Rogan reset the silencer and fired again. Pfann's choking death cry was drowned out by the roar of laughter sweeping through the nightclub as the screen showed a hilarious seduction scene.

Pfann's body slumped over the table. His murder would not be noticed until the movie ended. Rogan slipped the silencer off the pistol and put both pieces in his jacket pockets. He got up and moved silently through the darkened nightclub. The gold-braided doorman saluted him and whistled for a taxi, but Rogan turned his face away and walked down the Allee towards the waterfront. He walked along the

5

waterfront for a long time, until his pulse slowed its wild galloping. In the cold north German moonlight, ruined U-boat pens and rust-covered submarines brought back the terrible ghosts of war.

Karl Pfann was dead. Two down and five to go, Rogan thought grimly. And then ten years of bad dreams would be paid for and he could make peace with the silver plate in his skull, the eternal screams of Christine calling his name, calling for salvation, and the blinding, flashing moment when seven men in a high-domed room of the Munich Palace of Justice had put him to death as if he were an animal. They had tried to murder him, without dignity, as a joke.

The wind along the waterfront cut into his body and Rogan turned up the Reeperbahn, Ropemaker's Walk, passing the police station as he entered Davidstrasse. He was not afraid of the police. The light in the nightclub had been too dim for anyone to have seen him well enough to describe him accurately. Still, to be safe, he ducked into a side street that had a large wooden sign: "Adolescents Forbidden!" It seemed like any other street, until he turned the corner.

He had stumbled on to Hamburg's famous St Pauli Alley, the city area set aside for legal prostitution. It was brilliantly lighted and thronged with strolling men. The gingerbread, three-storey houses seemed ordinary at first glance, except that parties were going on in all of them. The street-level floors had huge showcase windows, revealing the rooms within. Sitting in armchairs, reading, drinking coffee, and chatting, or lying on sofas and staring dreamily at the ceiling, were some of the most beautiful young girls Rogan had ever seen.

A few pretended to be cleaning their kitchens and wore only an apron that came to mid-thigh and had no back at all. Each house had a sign: "30 Marks for One Hour." On a few windows the shades were drawn. Printed in gold on the black shades was the word *Ausverkauft*, "Sold Out," to announce proudly that some well-to-do sport had hired the girl for the whole night.

There was one blonde who was reading at a zinc-topped table in her kitchen. She looked forlorn, never glancing up at the busy street; some coffee had spilled near her open book. Rogan stood outside the house and waited for her to raise her head so that he could see her face. But she would not look up. She must be ugly, Rogan thought. He would pay her thirty marks just so he could rest before he started the long walk back to his hotel. It was bad for him to get excited, the doctors had said, and a woman with an ugly face would not excite him. With that silver plate in his skull Rogan was forbidden to drink hard liquor, make love excessively, or even become angry. They had not said anything to him about committing murder.

When he entered the brightly lighted kitchen he saw that the girl at the table was beautiful. She closed her book regretfully, got up, then took him by the hand and led him to the inner private room. Rogan felt a quick surge of desire that made his legs tremble, his head pound. The reaction of murder and flight hit him full force, and he felt himself becoming faint. He sank down on the bed, and the young girl's flutelike voice seemed to come from far away. "What's the matter with you? Are you ill?"

Rogan shook his head and fumbled with his wallet. He spread a sheaf of bills on the bed and said, "I am buying you for the night. Pull down your shade. Then just let me sleep." As she went back into the kitchen Rogan took a small bottle of pills from his shirt pocket and popped two of them into his mouth. It was the last thing he remembered doing before he lost consciousness.

When Rogan awoke the grey dawn smeared through dusty back windows to greet him. He looked around. The girl was sleeping on the floor beneath a thin blanket. A faint scent of roses came from her body. Rogan rolled over so that he could get out of the bed on the other side. The danger signals were gone. The silver plate no longer throbbed; the headache had vanished. He felt rested and strong.

Nothing had been taken from his wallet. The Walther pistol was still in his jacket pocket. He had picked an honest girl who also had common sense, Rogan thought. He went round to the other side of the bed to wake her up, but she was already struggling to her feet, her beautiful body trembling in the morning cold.

The room smelled strongly of roses, Rogan noticed, and there were roses embroidered on the window curtains and on the bedsheets. There were even roses embroidered on the girl's sheer nightgown. She smiled at him. "My name is Rosalie. I like everything with roses – my perfumes, my clothing, everything."

She seemed girlishly proud of her fondness for roses, as if it gave her a special distinction. Rogan found this amusing. He sat on the bed and beckoned to her. Rosalie came and stood between his legs. He could smell her delicate perfume, and as she slowly took off her silk nightgown he could see the strawberry-tipped breasts, the long white thighs; and then her body was folding around his own like soft silky petals, and her full-lipped mouth bloomed open beneath his own, fluttering helplessly with passion.

CHAPTER 2

Rogan liked the girl so well that he arranged for her to live with him in his hotel for the next week. This involved complicated financial arrangements with the proprietor, but he didn't mind. Rosalie was delighted. Rogan got an almost paternal satisfaction out of her pleasure.

She was even more thrilled when she learned that his hotel was the world-famous Vier Jahreszeiten, the most luxurious hotel in postwar Hamburg, its service in the grand manner of the old Kaiser Germany.

Rogan treated Rosalie like a princess that week. He gave her money for new clothes, and he took her to the theatre and to fine restaurants. She was an affectionate girl, but there was a strange blankness in her that puzzled Rogan. She responded to him as if he were something to love, just as a pet dog is something to love. She stroked his body as impersonally as she would stroke a fur coat, purring with the same kind of pleasure. One day she came back unexpectedly from a shopping trip and found Rogan cleaning his Walther P-38 pistol. That Rogan should own such a weapon was a matter of complete indifference to her. She really didn't care, and she didn't question him about it. Although Rogan was relieved that she reacted this way, he knew it wasn't natural.

Experience had taught Rogan that he needed a week's rest after one of his attacks. His next move was to Berlin, and towards the end of the week he debated whether or not to take Rosalie along to the divided city. He decided against it. Things might end badly, and she would be hurt through no fault of her own. On the last night he told her he would be leaving her in the morning and gave her all the cash in his wallet. With that strange blankness, she took the money and tossed it on the bed. She gave no sign of emotion other than a purely physical one of animal hunger. Because it was their last night together she wanted to make love for as long as possible. She began to take off her clothes. As she did so she asked casually, "Why must you go to Berlin?"

Rogan studied her creamy shoulders. "Business," he said.

"I looked in your special envelopes, all seven of them. I wanted to know more about you." She pulled off her stockings. "The night you met me you killed Karl Pfann, and his envelope and photograph are marked with the number two. The envelope and picture of Albert Moltke are marked 'number one,' so I went to the library and found the Vienna newspapers. Moltke was killed a month ago. Your passport shows you were in Austria at that time. Envelopes three and four are marked with the names of Eric and Hans Freisling, and they live in Berlin.

So you are going to Berlin to kill them when you leave me tomorrow. And you plan to kill the other three men also, numbers five, six, and seven. Isn't that true?"

Rosalie spoke matter-of-factly, as if his plans were not extraordinary in any way. Naked, she sat on the edge of the bed, waiting for him to make love to her. For a bizarre moment Rogan thought of killing her and rejected it; and then he realized that it would not be necessary. She would never betray him. There was that curious blankness in her eyes, as if she had no capacity to distinguish between good and evil.

He knelt before her on the bed and bent his head between her breasts. He took her hand in his, and it was warm and dry; she was not afraid. He guided her hand to the back of his skull, made her run her fingers over the silver plate. It was concealed by hair brushed over it, and part of it was overgrown with a thin membrane of dead, horny skin; but he knew she could feel the metal. "Those seven men did that to me," he said. "It keeps me alive, but I'll never see any grandchildren. I'll never live to be an old man sitting in the sun."

Her fingers touched the back of his skull, not

recoiling from the metal or the horny, dead flesh. "I'll help you if you want me to," she said; and he could smell the scent of roses on her and he thought, knowing it was sentimental, that roses were for weddings, not for death.

"No," he said. "I'll leave tomorrow. Forget about me. Forget you ever saw those envelopes. O.K.?"

"O.K.," Rosalie said, "I'll forget about you." She paused, and for a moment that curious emptiness left her and she asked, "Will you forget about me?"

"No," Rogan said.

CHAPTER 3

Mike Rogan never forgot a thing. At the age of five he told his mother in detail what had happened to him three years earlier when, at the age of two, he'd been seriously ill with pneumonia. He told her the name of the hospital, which his mother no longer remembered; he described the hospital paediatrician, an extraordinarily ugly man who had a marvellous way with children. The paediatrician would even let youngsters play with the star-shaped disfiguring wen on his chin so that they would not be afraid of it. Michael Rogan remembered trying to pull the wen off and the paediatrician letting out a comical "ouch!"

His mother was astounded by and a little fearful of Michael's memory feat, but his father was overjoyed. Joseph Rogan was a hard-working accountant, and he had visions of his son becoming a C.P.A. before he was twenty-one and earning a good living. His thoughts went no further, until little Michael Rogan came home from kindergarten with a note from his teacher. The note informed the Rogans that parents and son should appear at the school principal's office the next day to discuss Michael's academic future.

The interview was short and to the point. Michael could not be permitted to attend kindergarten with the rest of the children. He was a disruptive influence. He corrected the teacher when she left some little detail out of a story. He already knew how to read and write. He would have to be sent to a special school, or take his chances in the higher grades immediately. His parents decided to send him to a special school.

At the age of nine, when the other boys were running into the street with baseball gloves or footballs, Michael Rogan would leave his house carrying a genuine leather briefcase that had his initials and address stamped on it in gold. Inside the briefcase was the text of whatever subject he was studying that particular week. It rarely took him more than a week to master a subject that normally required a year's study. He would simply memorize all the texts by reading them once. And it was only natural that such a boy was considered a freak in his neighbourhood.

One day a group of kids his own age surrounded Michael Rogan. One of them, a chunky blond boy, said to him, "Don't you ever play?" Rogan didn't answer. The blond boy said, "You can play on my side. We're gonna play football."

"All right," Michael said. "I'll play."

That day was a glorious day for him. He found out that he had good physical coordination and that he could hold his own playing football or fighting with other boys. He came home for supper with his expensive leather briefcase smeared with mud. He also had a black eye and puffy, bloody lips. But he was so proud and so happy that he ran to his mother shouting, "I'm going to be on the football team! They picked me to be on the football team!"

Alice Rogan took one look at his battered face and burst into tears.

She tried to be reasonable. She explained to her young son that his brain was valuable, that he should never expose it to any danger. "You have an extraordinary mind, Michael," she said. "Your mind may someday help humanity. You can't be like other boys. What if you should hurt your head playing football? Or fighting with another boy?"

Michael listened and understood. When his father came home that evening he said almost the same thing. So Michael gave up all thoughts of being like ordinary boys. He had a precious treasure to guard for humanity. Had he been older he would have realized that his parents were being pompous and a bit ridiculous about this treasure, but he had not yet acquired that kind of adult judgment.

When he was thirteen the other boys started to humiliate him, taunt him, knock his briefcase from his hands. Michael Rogan, obeying his parents, refused to fight and suffered humiliation. It was his father who began to have doubts about how his son was being brought up.

One day Joseph Rogan brought home huge, puffy boxing gloves and taught his son the art of self-defence. Joseph told him to stick up for himself, to fight if necessary. "It's more important that you grow up to be a man," he said, "than to be a genius."

It was during his thirteenth year that Michael Rogan discovered he was different from ordinary boys in another way. His parents had always taught him to dress neatly and in an adult fashion, because he spent so much of his time studying with adults. One day a group of boys surrounded Rogan and told him they were going to take off his pants and hang them from a lamp-post, a routine humiliation most of the boys had undergone.

Rogan went berserk when they put their hands on him. He sank his teeth into one boy's ear and ripped it partly from the boy's head. He got his hand around the ringleader's throat and throttled him, despite other boys kicking and punching him to make him let go. When some grown-ups finally broke up the fight, three of the group and Rogan had to be hospitalized.

But nobody ever bothered him again. He was shunned not only as a freak but as a violent freak.

Michael Rogan was intelligent enough to know that his rage was not natural, that it sprang from some deeper source. And he came to understand what it was. He was enjoying the fruits of his extraordinary memory, his intellectual powers, without having done anything to deserve them, and he felt guilty about it. He talked of his feelings with his father, who understood and started to make plans for Michael to lead a more normal life. Unhappily, Joseph Rogan died of a heart attack before he could help his son.

Michael Rogan, going on fifteen, was tall, strong, and well coordinated. He was absorbing knowledge on the advanced levels now; and under the complete dominance of his mother, he really believed that his mind was a sacred trust to be guarded for its future use to humanity. By this time he had his M.A. and was studying for his M.S. His mother treated him like a reigning king. That year Michael Rogan discovered girls.

In this he was perfectly normal. But he discovered to his chagrin that girls were afraid of him and treated him with giggling teenage cruelty. He was so intellectually mature that once again he was regarded as a freak by those his age. This drove him back to his studies with renewed fury.

At eighteen he found himself accepted as an equal by the seniors and graduate students at the Ivy League school where he was completing studies for his Ph.D. in mathematics. The girls, too, seemed to be attracted to him now. Big for his age, he was broad through the shoulders, and could easily pass for twenty-two or twenty-three. He learned to disguise his brilliance so that it would not be too frightening, and at last he got into bed with a girl.

Marian Hawkins was a blonde who was dedicated to her studies, but she was also dedicated to all-night parties. She was his steady sex partner for a year. Rogan neglected his studies, drank a great deal of beer, and committed all the natural stupidities of a normal growing boy. His mother was distressed at this turn of events, but Rogan did not let her distress bother him at all. Though he would never admit it to himself, he disliked his mother.

The Japanese attacked Pearl Harbor on the day Rogan was assured of his doctorate. By now Rogan had tired of Marian Hawkins and was looking for a graceful way out. He was tired of training his mind and tired also of his mother. He was hungry for excitement and adventure. On the day after Pearl Harbor he sat down and wrote a long letter to the chief of Army Intelligence. He made a list of his academic awards and achievements and enclosed them with the letter. Less than a week later he received a telegram from Washington, asking him to report for an interview.

The interview was one of the bright moments of his life. He was interrogated by a crew-cut Intelligence captain who looked over the list Rogan had sent with a bored expression. He seemed unimpressed, especially when he learned that Rogan had no background of athletic activity.

Captain Alexander pushed Rogan's papers back into a manila folder and took it into the inner office. He was gone for a while, and when he came back he had a mimeographed sheet in his hand. He put it on the desk in front of him and tapped it with his pencil. "This sheet is covered with a coded message. It's an old, outdated code we no longer use. But I want to see if you can figure it out. Don't be surprised if you find it too difficult; after all, you've had no training." He handed the sheet to Rogan.

Rogan looked it over. It appeared to be a standard cryptographic letter substitution, relatively simple. Rogan had studied cryptography and the theory of codes when he was eleven years old, for mental kicks. He picked up a pencil and got to work, and in five minutes he read the translated message to Captain Alexander.

The captain disappeared into the other room and returned with a manila folder from which he took a sheet of paper containing only two paragraphs. This was a more difficult code, and its brevity made it that much harder to decode. It took Rogan almost an hour to break it. Captain Alexander looked at his translation and disappeared again into the inner office. The next time he came out he was accompanied by a grey-haired colonel, who sat in a corner of the reception room and studied Rogan intently.

Now Captain Alexander handed Rogan three sheets of paper covered with symbols. He smiled a little this time. Rogan recognized that smile, he had seen it on the faces of teachers and specialists who thought they had Rogan in a spot. So he was very careful with the code, and it took him three hours to break it. He was so concentrated on his task that he didn't notice the room filling up with officers, all watching him intently. When Rogan finished he handed his yellow work sheets to the captain. Captain Alexander scanned the translation swiftly and without a word handed it to the grey-haired colonel. The colonel ran his eyes down the paper and then said curtly to the captain, "Bring him to my office."

To Rogan, the whole thing had been an enjoyable exercise, and he was startled to see the colonel looked worried. The first thing he said to Rogan was, "You've made this a bad day for me, young man."

"I'm sorry," Rogan said politely. He didn't really give a damn. Captain Alexander had irritated him.

"It's not your fault," the colonel growled. "None of us thought you could break that last code. It's one of our best, and now that you know it we'll have to change over. After we screen you and accept you in the services maybe we can use the code again."

Rogan said incredulously, "You mean all the codes are that easy?"

The colonel said drily, "To you they are, obviously.

To anybody else they are all that hard. Are you prepared to enter the service immediately?"

Rogan nodded. "This very minute."

The colonel frowned. "It doesn't work that way. You have to be screened for security. And until you are cleared, we'll have to keep you under arrest. You already know too much to be running around loose. But that's just a formality."

The formality proved to be an Intelligence department prison that made Alcatraz seem like a summer camp. But it did not occur to Rogan that this treatment was typical of all Intelligence attitudes. A week later he was sworn into the service as a second lieutenant. Three months later he was in charge of the section responsible for breaking all European codes, except for Russia's. The Russian code was part of the Asian section.

He was happy. For the first time in his life he was doing something dramatic and exciting. His memory, his fabulously brilliant mind, was helping his country to win a great war. He had his pick of young girls in Washington. And soon he was promoted. Life couldn't be better. But in 1943 he had begun to feel guilty again. He felt that he was using his mental ability to avoid front-line action, and he volunteered for the field Intelligence section. His offer was rejected; he was too valuable to be risked.

It was then that he came up with the idea of himself as a walking code switchboard to coordinate the invasion of France from inside that country. He prepared the plan in detail; it was brilliant, and the chiefs of staff approved. And so the brilliant Captain Rogan was parachuted into France.

He was proud of himself, and he knew that his father, too, would have been proud of what he was doing now. But his mother wept because he was endangering his brain, that fabulous brain they had sheltered and nurtured for so long. Rogan shrugged it off. He hadn't yet done anything so marvellous with his brain. Perhaps after the war he would find his real interest and establish his true genius. But he had learned enough to know that raw brilliance needs long years of hard work to develop properly. He would have time after the war. On New Year's Day, 1944, Captain Michael Rogan was parachuted into Occupied France as chief Allied communications officer with the French Underground. He had trained with Britain's S.O.E.

agents, had learned how to operate a secret radio transmitter-receiver, and was carrying a tiny suicide capsule surgically embedded in the palm of his left hand.

His billet hideout was in the house of a French family named Charney in the town of Vitry-sur-Seine, just south of Paris. There Rogan set up his network of couriers and informers and radioed coded information to England. On occasion he received radioed requests for certain details needed for the coming invasion of Europe.

It proved to be a quiet, peaceful life. On fine Sunday afternoons he went on picnics with the daughter of the house, Christine Charney, a long-limbed, sweet-looking girl, with chestnut hair. Christine studied music at the local university. She and Michael Rogan became lovers, and then she became pregnant.

Wearing his beret and flashing his false ID papers, Rogan married Christine Charney at the town hall and they returned to her parents' house to carry out the work of the Underground together.

When the Allies invaded Normandy on 6 June, 1944, Rogan had so much communication traffic on his radio that he became careless. Two weeks later the Gestapo swooped down on the Charney house and arrested everyone inside it. They waited for exactly the right moment. Not only did they arrest the Charney family and Mike Rogan; they also arrested six Underground couriers waiting for messages. Within a month all were interrogated, tried, and executed. All except Michael Rogan and his wife, Christine. From the interrogation of the other prisoners the Germans had learned about Rogan's ability to memorize intricate codes, and they wanted to give him special attention. His wife was kept alive, Rogan was smilingly told, "as a special courtesy." She was then five months pregnant.

Six weeks after their capture, Michael Rogan and his wife were put in separate Gestapo staff cars and driven to Munich. In that city's busy central square stood the Munich Palace of Justice, and in one of those court buildings, Michael Rogan's final and most terrible interrogation began. It lasted for endless days, more days than he could count. But in the years afterwards his fabulous memory spared him nothing. It repeated his agony second by second, over and over again. He suffered a thousand separate nightmares. And it always began with the seven-man interrogation team waiting for him in the high-domed room of the Munich Palace of Justice — waiting patiently and with good humour, for the sport that would give them pleasure.

All seven wore swastika armbands, but two men wore tunics of different shades. From this and the collar insignia, Rogan knew that one of them was with the Hungarian armed forces and the other was with the Italian army. These two took no part in the interrogation at first; they were official observers.

The chief of the interrogation team was a tall, aristocratic officer with deep-set eyes. He assured Rogan that all they wanted was the codes stored in his head, and then Rogan and his wife and the unborn child would live. They hammered at him all that first day, and Rogan stood mute. He refused to answer any questions. Then on the night of the second day he heard Christine's voice screaming for help in the next room. She kept calling his name, screaming, "Michel! Michel!" over and over. She was in agony. Rogan looked at the burning eyes of the chief interrogator and whispered, "Stop that. Stop. I'll tell you everything."

For the next five days he gave them old, discarded code combinations. In some way, perhaps by comparing them with intercepted messages, they learned what he was doing. The next day they seated him in the chair and stood around in a circle. They did not question him; they did not touch him. The man in the Italian uniform disappeared into the other room. A few moments later Rogan heard his wife screaming in agony again. The pain in her voice was beyond belief. Rogan started to whisper that he would tell them everything, anything they wanted to know, but the chief interrogator shook his head. They all sat in silence as the screams pierced the walls and their brains, until Rogan slipped from his chair to the floor, weeping, almost unconscious with grief. Then they dragged him across the floor of the high-domed room and into the next chamber. The interrogator in the Italian uniform was sitting beside a phonograph. The twirling black record sent Christine's screams shrieking through the Palace of Justice.

"You never tricked us," the chief interrogator said contemptuously; "we outwitted you. Your wife died under torture the very first day." Rogan studied their faces carefully. If they let him live he would kill them all some day.

He realized only later that this was exactly the reaction they wanted. They promised to let him live if he would give them the correct codes. And in his desire for vengeance, he did so. For the next two weeks he gave them the codes and explained how they worked. He was sent back to his solitary cell for what seemed many more months. Once a week he would be escorted to the high-domed room and interrogated by the seven men in what he came to realize was a purely routine procedure. There was no way for Rogan to know that during these months the Allied armies had swept across France and into Germany and were now at the gates of Munich. When he was summoned for his final interrogation he could not know that the seven interrogators were about to flee and disguise their identities, disappear into the mass of Germans in a desperate effort to escape punishment for their crimes.

"We are going to set you free; we are going to keep our promise," the aristocratic chief interrogator with the deep-set eyes said to Rogan. That voice rang with sincerity. It was an actor's voice, or an orator's. One of the other men pointed to some civilian clothes lying over the back of a chair. "Take off your rags and change into these."

Unbelieving, Rogan changed his clothes before their eyes. There was even a wide-brimmed fedora, which one of the men jammed on his head. They all grinned at him in a friendly way. The aristocratic officer said in his sincere, bell-toned voice, "Isn't it good to know that you will be free? That you will live?"

But suddenly Rogan knew he was lying. There was something wrong. Only six men were in the room with him, and they were smiling secret, evil smiles. At that moment Rogan felt the cold metal of the gun touch the back of his head. His hat tilted forward as the gun barrel pushed up against its brim, and Rogan felt the sickening terror of a man about to be killed. It was all a cruel charade and they were killing him as they would kill an animal, as a joke. And then a great roar filled his brain, as if he had fallen under water, and his body was torn out of the space it filled, exploded into a black, endless void . . .

That Rogan lived was a miracle. He had been

shot in the back of the head, and his body was thrown on a pile of corpses, other prisoners executed in the courtyard of the Munich Palace of Justice. Six hours later, advance elements of the U.S. Third Army entered Munich, and its medical units found the great pile of bodies. When they came to Rogan they found him still alive. The bullet had deflected off the skull bone, tearing a hole in, but not penetrating, the brain – a type of wound not uncommon with shell fragments but rarely made by small arms.

Rogan was operated on in a forward field hospital and sent back to the United States. He spent another two years in various army hospitals for special treatment. The wound had impaired his sight; he could see only straight ahead, with very little lateral vision. With training, his vision improved enough for him to get a driver's licence and live an ordinary life. But he had come to rely on his hearing more than his sight, whenever possible. At the end of the two years the silver plate put in his skull to hold the shattered bones together seemed a natural part of him. Except in moments of stress. Then it felt as if all the blood in his brain pounded against it.

When he was released the doctors told Rogan

that drinking liquor would be bad for him, that sexual intercourse to excess would do him harm, that it would be better if he did not smoke. He was assured that his intellectual capacities had not been damaged, but that he would need more rest than the average man. He was also given medication for the intermittent headaches. Internal cranial pressure would build up as a result of the damaged condition of his skull and the silver plate.

In brief, his brain was terribly vulnerable to any kind of physical or emotional stress. With care he could live to be fifty, even sixty. He was to follow instructions, take his medication regularly – which included tranquillizers – and report to a V.A. hospital every month for check-ups and changes in medication. His fabulous memory, Rogan was assured, was not impaired in the slightest. And that had proved to be the final irony.

In the ten years that followed, he obeyed instructions, he took his medication, he reported to the V.A. hospital every month. But what finally proved his undoing was his magic memory. At night when he went to bed it was as if a movie unreeled before his eyes. He saw the seven men in the high-domed room of the Munich Palace of Justice in minute detail. He felt his hat brim tilt forward, the gun cold against his neck. The black roaring void swallowed him up. And when he closed his eyes he heard Christine's terrible screams from the next room.

The ten years were a continuous nightmare. When he was released from the hospital he decided to make his home in New York City. His mother had died after he had been reported missing in action, so there was no sense in returning to his home town. And he thought that in New York he might find the proper use for his abilities.

He got a job with one of the mammoth insurance companies. The work was one of simple statistical analysis, but to his amazement he found it was beyond him; he could not concentrate. He was discharged for incompetence, a humiliation that set him back physically as well as mentally. It also increased his distrust of his fellow human beings. Where the hell did they come off, firing him after he had had his head blown apart protecting their skins during the war?

He took a job as a government clerk in the Veterans Administration building in New York. He was given a G.S.-3 grade, which paid him sixty dollars a week, and asked to do only the simplest of tasks in filing and sorting. Millions of new files were being set up on the new veterans of World War II, and it was this that started him thinking about computers. But it was to be two years later before his brain could really work out the complicated mathematical formulae that such computer systems needed.

He lived a drab existence in the great city. His $60 a week was barely enough to cover necessary expenses, such as the little efficiency apartment on the outskirts of Greenwich Village, frozen foods, and whisky. He needed the whisky to get drunk enough so that he would not dream when he slept.

Spending every working day filing dreary documents, he would come home to the shabby apartment and cook frozen foods to warm, tasteless pulp. Then he would drink half a bottle of whisky and sink into a sodden slumber on his rumpled bed, sometimes without taking his clothes off. And still the nightmares came. But the nightmares were not much worse than the reality had been.

In the Munich Palace of Justice they had stripped him of his dignity. They had done what the boys had threatened to do to him when he was thirteen years old, the harsh adult equivalent of taking off his trousers and hanging them on the lamp-post. They had mixed laxatives with his food and that, along with the fear and the thin gruel that was called oatmeal at breakfast and stew at night, made his bowels uncontrollable; the food ran through him. When he was dragged out of his cell for the daily interrogation at the long table he could feel the seat of his pants sticky against his buttocks. He could smell the stench. But worse, he could see the cruel grins on the faces of his inter-rogators, and he would feel ashamed as a little boy feels ashamed. And yet in some way it made him feel closer to the seven men who were torturing him.

Now years later, alone in his apartment, he would relive the physical indignities. He was shy and would not go out of the apartment to meet people, nor would he accept invitations to parties. He met a girl who worked as a clerk in the V.A. building, and with a tremendous effort of will made himself respond to her obvious interest. She came to his apartment for a drink and dinner and made it plain that she was willing to stay the night. But when Rogan went to bed with her, he was impotent.

It was a few weeks after this that his supervisor

called him into the personnel office. The supervisor was a World War II veteran who thought that his job of supervising thirty file clerks proved he was mentally superior to the men under him. Trying to be kind to Rogan he said, "Maybe this work is just a little too hard for you right now; maybe you should do some kind of physical work, like running the elevator. You know what I mean?"

The very fact that it was well intentioned made it more galling to Rogan. As a disabled veteran he had a right to appeal his discharge. The personnel officer at the conference advised him not to do so. "We can prove that you're just not bright enough to do this job," he told Rogan. "We have your Civil Service exam marks, and they just barely qualify you. So I think you'd be wise to take the medical discharge from government service. Then maybe if you go to night school you can do a little better."

Rogan was so astonished that he burst out laughing. He reasoned that part of his file must be missing, or that these people thought he had filled out his forms falsely. That was it, he thought, as he saw them smiling at him. They thought he had faked everything in his educational files. Rogan laughed again and walked out of the personnel office, out of the building, out of the insultingly drab job that he could not even perform properly. He never went back, and one month later he received his employment discharge in the post. He was reduced to living on his disability pension, which he had previously never touched.

With more time on his hands, he drank more. He took a room near the Bowery and became one of the countless derelicts who spent the day drinking cheap wine until they became unconscious. Two months later he was back in the Veterans Administration as a patient. But not for his head wound. He was suffering from malnutrition and so dangerously debilitated that a common cold might finish him off.

It was while he was in the hospital that he ran into one of his childhood friends, Philip Houke, who was being treated for an ulcer. It was Houke, now a lawyer, who got Rogan his first job with computers. It was Houke who brought Rogan into some contact with humanity again, by reminding him of his former brilliance.

But it was a long, hard road coming back. Rogan stayed in the hospital for six months, the first three to "dry out." The final three months he underwent new tests on his skull injury, plus special mental-fatigue tests. For the first time a complete and correct diagnosis was made: Michael Rogan's brain retained its almost superhuman memory capacity and some of its creative brilliance. But it could not stand up to long uninterrupted use or extended stress without blurring with fatigue. He would never be able to put in the long hard hours of concentration that creative research demanded. Even simple tasks requiring long consecutive hours of work were now out of the question.

Instead of this news dismaying him, Michael Rogan was pleased that finally he knew exactly where he stood. He was also relieved of his guilt, for he was no longer responsible for a "treasure to humanity." When Philip Houke arranged for him to work with one of the new computer firms, Rogan found that unconsciously his mind had been working on computer construction problems ever since he had been a file clerk for the V.A. So in less than a year he solved many of the technical construction problems with his knowledge of maths. Houke demanded a partnership in the firm for Rogan, and became his financial adviser. In the next few years Rogan's computer firm became one of the top ten in the country. Then it went public, and its shares tripled in value within a year. Rogan became known as the genius in the field, and was asked to advise on administrative procedures when the separate service departments were consolidated into the Defense Department. He also became a millionaire. Ten years after the war he was a success, despite the fact that he could not work more than an hour a day.

Philip Houke took care of all his business affairs and became his best friend. Houke's wife tried to get Rogan interested in her unmarried girl friends, but none of the affairs ever became serious. His fabulous memory still worked against him. On bad nights he still heard Christine screaming in the Munich Palace of Justice. And he felt again the wet stickiness on his buttocks as the seven interrogators watched him with their contemptuous grins. He could never start a new life, he thought, not with another woman.

During those years Rogan kept track of every trial of war criminals in postwar Germany. He subscribed to a European newspaper clipping service, and when he started to collect patent royalties he retained a German private detective agency in Berlin to send him photographs of all accused war criminals no matter how low their rank. It seemed a hopeless task to find seven men whose names he did not know and who were surely making every effort to stay hidden among Europe's millions.

His first break came when the private detective agency sent him a photograph of a dignified-looking Austrian city official, with the caption "Albert Moltke acquitted. Retains electoral position despite former Nazi ties." The face was the face of one of the seven men he sought.

Rogan had never forgiven himself for his carelessness in transmitting radio messages on D-Day, the carelessness that had led to the discovery and the destruction of his Underground group. But he had learned from it. Now he proceeded cautiously and with the utmost precision. He increased his retainer to the detective firm in Germany and instructed them to keep Albert Moltke under close surveillance for a year. At the end of that time he had three more photographs, with names and addresses, three more dossiers of the men who had murdered his wife and tortured him in the Munich Palace of Justice. One was Karl Pfann, in the export-import business in Hamburg. The other two were brothers, Eric and Hans Freisling, who owned a mechanic's shop and petrol station in West Berlin. Rogan decided that the time had come.

He made his preparations very carefully. He had his company appoint him as its European sales representative, with letters of introduction to computer firms in Germany and Austria. He had no fear of being recognized. His terrible wound and his years of suffering had changed his appearance a great deal; and besides, he was a dead man. So far as his interrogators knew, they had killed Captain Michael Rogan.

Rogan took a plane to Vienna and set up his business headquarters there. He checked into the Sacher Hotel, had a fine dinner, with the renowned *Sachertorte* for dessert, and sipped brandy in the hotel's famous Red Bar. Later he took a walk through the twilit streets, listening to the zither music emanating from the cafés. He walked for a long time, until he was relaxed enough to return to his room and sleep.

During the next two weeks, through friendly Austrians he met at two computer firms, Rogan got himself invited to the important parties in Vienna. Finally, at a municipal ball, which the city bureaucrats had to attend, he met Albert Moltke. He was surprised that the man had changed so much. The face had mellowed with good living and good food. The hair was silver grey. The whole attitude of his body suggested the politician's surface politeness. And on his arm was his wife, a slender, cheerful-looking woman, obviously much younger than he was and obviously much in love with him. When he noticed Rogan staring at him, Moltke bowed politely, as if to say, "Yes, thank you for voting for me. I remember you very well, of course. Come and see me any time in my office." It was the bow of an expert politician. No wonder he beat the rap when he'd been tried as a war criminal, Rogan thought. And he took some pleasure in knowing that it was the acquittal and the resultant photograph in the newspapers that had sentenced Albert Moltke to death.

Albert Moltke had bowed to the stranger, though

his feet were killing him and he was wishing with all his heart that he was back home beside his own fireplace drinking black coffee and eating *Sachertorte*. These fêtes were a bore, but after all the *Partei* had to raise election funds somehow. And he owed it to his colleagues after they had supported him so loyally during the late troubled times. Moltke felt his wife, Ursula, press his arm, and he bowed again to the stranger, feeling vaguely that it was someone important, someone he should remember more clearly.

Yes, the *Partei* and his dear Ursula had rallied round when he had been accused as a war criminal. And after he had been acquitted the trial turned out to be his best piece of luck. He had won election to one of the local councils, and his political future, though limited, was assured. It would be a good living. But then the disturbing thought came as it always came: What if the *Partei* and Ursula found out the charges were true? Would his wife still love him? Would she leave him if she knew the truth? No, she could never believe him capable of such crimes, no matter what the proof. He could hardly believe it himself. He had been a different man then – harder, colder, stronger. In those times one had to be like that to survive. And yet . . . and yet . . . how could it be? When he tucked his two young children in bed his hands sometimes hesitated in the act of touching them. Such hands could not touch such innocence. But the jury had freed him. They had acquitted him after weighing all the evidence, and he could not be tried again. He, Albert Moltke, was forever innocent, according to law. And yet . . . and yet . . .

The stranger was coming towards him. A tall, powerfully built man, with an oddly shaped head. Handsome, in a dark German way. But then Albert Moltke noticed the well-tailored suit. No, this man was an American, obviously. Moltke had met many of them since the war, in the transaction of business. He smiled his welcome and turned to introduce his wife, but she had wandered off a few steps and was talking to someone else. And then the American was introducing himself. His name sounded something like Rogar, and this, too, was vaguely familiar to Moltke. "Congratulations on your promotion to the *Recordat.* And congratulations on your acquittal some time ago."

Moltke gave him a polite smile. He recited his standard speech. "A patriotic jury did its duty and decided, fortunately for me, for an innocent fellow German."

They chatted awhile. The American suggested that he could use some legal help on setting up his computer business. Moltke became interested. He knew that the American really meant he wanted to bypass a few city taxes. Moltke, knowing from past experience that this could make him rich, took the American by the arm and said, "Why don't we get a little bit of fresh air, take a little stroll?" The American smiled and nodded. Moltke's wife did not see them leave.

As they walked through the city streets the American asked casually, "Don't you remember my face?"

Moltke grimaced and said, "My dear sir, you do seem familiar, but I meet a lot of people, after all." He was a little impatient; he wished the American would get down to business.

With a slight sense of uneasiness, Moltke realized that now they were walking in a deserted alley.

Then the American leaned close to Moltke's ear and whispered something that almost made his heart stop beating: "Do you remember *Rosenmontag*, 1945? In Munich? In the Palace of Justice?"

And then Moltke remembered the face; and he was not surprised when the American said, "My name is Rogan." With the fear that flooded through him there was overwhelming shame, as if for the first time he truly believed in his own guilt.

Rogan saw the recognition in Moltke's eyes. He steered the little man deeper into the alley, feeling Moltke's body trembling, trembling under his arm. "I won't hurt you," he said. "I only want some information about the other men, your comrades. I know Karl Pfann and the Freisling brothers. What were the names of the other three men, and where can I find them?"

Moltke was terrified. He started running clumsily down the alley. Rogan ran beside him, sprinting easily, as if the two of them were trotting together for exercise. Coming up on the Austrian's left side, Rogan drew the Walther pistol from his shoulder holster. Still running, he fitted the silencer on to the barrel. He felt no pity; he considered no mercy. Moltke's sins were etched in his brain, committed a thousand times in his memory. It had been Moltke who had smiled when Christine screamed in the next room, and who had murmured, "Come, don't be so much a hero at your poor wife's expense. Don't you want your child to be born?" So reasonable, so persuasive, when he knew that Christine was already dead. Moltke was the least of them but the memories of him had to die. Rogan fired two shots into Moltke's side. Moltke swooped forward in a falling glide; and Rogan kept running, out of the alley and on to a main street. The next day he took a plane to Hamburg.

In Hamburg it had been easy to track down Karl Pfann. Pfann had been the most brutal of the interrogators, but in such an animal-like way that Rogan had despised him less than the others. Pfann had acted according to his true nature. He was a simple man, stupid and cruel. Rogan had killed him with less hatred than he had killed Moltke. It had gone exactly according to plan. What had not gone according to plan was Rogan's meeting the German girl Rosalie, with her flower fragrance and her curious lack of emotion and her amoral innocence.

*

Now lying beside her in his Hamburg hotel room, Rogan ran his hands lightly over her body. He had told her everything, sure that she would not betray him – or perhaps in the hope that she would, and so end his murdering quest. "Still like me?" he asked.

Rosalie nodded. She held his hand to her breast. "Let me help you," she said. "I don't care about anyone. I don't care if they die. But I care about you – a little bit. Take me to Berlin and I'll do anything you want me to."

Rogan knew she meant every word. He looked into her eyes and was troubled by the childlike innocence he saw there, and the emotional blankness, as if murdering and making love were, to her, equally permissible.

He decided to take her along. He liked having her around, and she would be a real help. Besides, there didn't seem to be anything or anyone else she cared about. And he would never involve her in the actual executions.

The next day he took her shopping on the Esplanade and in the arcade of the Baseler Hospiz. He bought her two new outfits that set off the pale-rose skin, the blue of her eyes. They went back to the hotel and packed, and after supper they caught the night flight to Berlin.

CHAPTER 4

Several months after the war ended, Rogan had been flown from his V.A. hospital in the United States to U.S. Intelligence headquarters in Berlin. There he had been asked to look at a number of suspected war criminals to see if any of them were men who had tortured him in the Munich Palace of Justice. His case was now file number A23,486 in the archives of the Allied War Crimes Commission. Among the suspects were none of the men he remembered so clearly. He could not identify a single one, so he was flown back to the V.A. hospital. But he had spent a few days wandering around the city, the rubble of countless homes giving him a measure of savage satisfaction.

The great city had changed in the years since then. The West Berlin authorities had given up trying to clear away the seventy million tons of ruins which the Allied bombers had created during the war. They had pushed the rubble into small artificial hills, then had planted flowers and small shrubs over them. They had used the rubble to fill foundations for towering new apartment houses, built in the most modern space-conserving style. Berlin was now a huge, steel-grey rat warren of stone, and at night that warren showed the most vicious nests of vice spawned by ravaged postwar Europe.

With Rosalie, Rogan checked into the Kempinski Hotel on the Kurfürstendamm and Fasanenstrasse, perhaps the most elegant hotel in Western Germany. Then he made a few telephone calls to some of the firms with which his company did business, and he set up an appointment with the private detective agency that had been on his payroll for the past five years.

For their first lunch together in Berlin, he took Rosalie to a restaurant called the Ritz that served the finest Oriental food. He noticed with amusement that Rosalie ate a huge amount of food with huge enjoyment. They ordered bird's nest soup, which looked like a tangle of vegetable brains stained with black blood. Her favourite dish was a combination of red lobster pieces, white pork chunks, and brown shards of nutmegged beef, but she found the barbecued spare ribs and the chicken with tender snow peas delicious. She sampled his shrimp with black bean sauce and nodded her approval. All of it was accompanied by several helpings of fried rice and innumerable cups of hot tea. It was an enormous lunch, but Rosalie put it away without any effort. She had just discovered that there was other food in the world besides bread, meat, and potatoes. Rogan, smiling at her pleasure, watched her finish off what was left on the silver-covered platters.

In the afternoon they went shopping along the Kurfürstendamm, whose brightly lit store windows trailed off into grey, empty store fronts as the boulevard approached the Berlin Wall. Rogan bought Rosalie an expensive gold wristwatch with a clever roof of precious stones that slid back when its owner wanted to know the time. Rosalie squealed with delight, and Rogan thought wryly that if the way to a man's heart was through his stomach, then the way to a woman's heart was paved with gifts. But when she leaned over to kiss him, when he felt her soft, fluttering mouth on his own, his cynicism vanished.

That evening he took her to the Eldorado Club, where the waiters dressed as girls and the girls dressed as men. Then on to the Cherchelle Femme, where pretty girls on the stage stripped as casually as if they were in their own private bedrooms, with intimate wriggles and vulgar scratches. Finally the girls danced before huge mirrors wearing only long black hose and saucy red caps on their heads. Rogan and Rosalie ended up at the Badewanne in Nürnberger Strasse. They drank champagne and ate small, thick white sausages from large platters, using their fingers and wiping their hands on the tablecloth, like everyone else.

By the time they got back to their hotel suite

Rogan was almost sick with sexual desire. He wanted to make love immediately, but Rosalie, laughing, pushed him away and disappeared into the bedroom. Frustrated, Rogan took off his jacket and tie and started to mix a drink at the little bar that was part of every suite. In a few minutes he heard Rosalie call, "Michael," in her soft, almost adolescent-sweet voice. He turned towards her.

On her blonde head was a new hat he had bought her in Hamburg, a lovely creation of green ribbon. On her legs were long black net stockings that reached almost to the tops of her thighs. Between the green hat and black stockings was Rosalie – in the flesh. She came towards him slowly, smiling that intently happy smile of a woman roused to passion.

Rogan reached for her. She eluded his grasp, and he followed her into the bedroom, hastily pulling off the rest of his clothes on the way. When he reached for her this time, she did not move away. And then they were on the king-size bed, and he could smell the rose fragrance of her body, feel the petal-velvet skin as together they sank into an act of love that blotted out the hoarse night noises of Berlin, the plaintive cries of the animals imprisoned in the Tiergarten just below their windows, and the ghostly images of murder and revenge that haunted Rogan's vulnerable brain.

CHAPTER 5

Rogan wanted his first contact with the Freisling brothers to be casual. The next day he rented a Mercedes, drove it to the brothers' gas station, and had the car checked. He was attended to by Hans Freisling, and when Rogan went to the office to pay his bill, Eric was there, in a leather chair, checking oil-storage accounts.

The brothers had both aged well, perhaps because

they had been unattractive to begin with. Age had tightened their loose, sly mouths; their lips were not so thick. They had become smarter in their dress and less vulgar in their speech. But they had not changed in their treachery, though it was now petty larceny instead of murder.

The Mercedes had been checked out that day by the rental agency and was in perfect condition. But Hans Freisling was charging him twenty marks for some minor mechanical adjustments and telling him his fan belt would have to be replaced. Rogan smiled and asked him to replace it. While this was being done he chatted with Eric, and mentioned that he was in the computer manufacturing business and would be staying in Berlin for some time. He pretended not to see the sly, greedy interest on Eric Freisling's face. When Hans came in to tell him that the fan belt had been changed, Rogan tipped him generously and drove away. After he parked the Mercedes in front of his hotel he checked under the hood. The fan belt had not been changed.

Rogan made it a point to visit the gas station every few days in the Mercedes. The two Freislings, other than chiselling him on gas and oil, were showing an extraordinary friendliness. They had some other angle to work on him, Rogan knew, and wondered what it was. Certainly they had him pegged for a pigeon. But then he had plans for them too, he thought. Before he killed them, however, he would have to get from them the identity and whereabouts of the other three, especially the chief interrogator. Meanwhile he did not want to appear anxious and scare them off. He threw his money around as bait and waited for the Freislings to make their move.

The next weekend the hotel desk called early on Sunday evening to inform him that two men wished to come to his room. Rogan grinned at Rosalie. The brothers had taken the bait. But it was Rogan who was surprised. The two men were strangers. Or rather, one was a stranger. The taller of the two Rogan recognized almost immediately as Arthur Bailey, the American Intelligence agent who had interrogated Rogan about his "execution" and had asked him to identify suspects in Berlin more than nine years before. Bailey was studying Rogan with impassive eyes as he showed his identification.

"I just read up on your file, Mr Rogan," Bailey said. "You don't look anything like your photographs any more. I didn't recognize you at all when I first saw you again."

"When was that?" Rogan asked.

"At the Freisling gas station a week ago," Bailey said. He was a lanky midwestern type, his drawl as unmistakably American as were his clothes and posture. Rogan wondered why he hadn't noticed him at the gas station.

Bailey smiled gently at him. "We think the Freislings are East German agents, just as a sideline. They are hustlers. So when you showed up there and got friendly we checked you out. Called Washington, checked your visas and all that. Then I sat down and read your file. Something else clicked, and I went to the back files of the daily papers. And finally I figured it all out. You managed to track down those seven men in Munich, and now you've come back to knock them off. There was Moltke in Vienna and Pfann in Hamburg. The Freisling brothers are next on your list – right?"

"I'm here to sell computers," Rogan said warily. "That's all."

Bailey shrugged. "I don't care what you do; I'm not responsible for law enforcement in this country.

But I'm telling you now: Hands off the Freisling brothers. I've put in a lot of time to get the goods on them, and when I do I'll bust up a whole East German spy set-up. I don't want you knocking them off and leaving me with a blind trail."

Suddenly it was clear to Rogan why the Freisling brothers had been so friendly to him. "Are they after my data on the new computers?" he asked Bailey.

"I wouldn't be surprised," he said. "Computers – the new ones – are on the embargo list to Red countries. But I'm not worried about that; I know what you want to give them. And I'm warning you: You do, and you have me for an enemy."

Rogan stared at him coldly. "I don't know what you're talking about, but let me give you some advice: Don't get in my way or I'll run right over you. And there isn't a damn thing you can do to me. I've got pipelines right into the Pentagon. My new computers are more important to them than any crap you can drag up with a two-bit spy apparatus."

Bailey gave him a thoughtful look, then said, "O.K., we can't touch you, but how about the girl friend?" He jerked his head towards Rosalie sitting on the sofa. "We can sure as hell cause her a little trouble. In fact, one phone call and you'll never see her again."

"What the hell are you talking about?"

Bailey's lean, angular face took on an expression of mock surprise. "Didn't she tell you? Six months ago she escaped from a mental hospital on the Nordsee. She was committed in 1950 for schizophrenia. The authorities are still looking for her – not very hard, but looking. One phone call and the police pick her up. Just remember that." Bailey paused, and then said slowly, "When we don't need those two guys any more I'll tell you. Why don't you skip them and go after the others that are still left?"

"Because I don't know who the other three are. I'm counting on the Freisling brothers to tell me."

Bailey shook his head. "They'll never talk unless you make it worth their while, and they're tough. You'd better leave it to us."

"No," Rogan said. "I have a sure-fire method. I'll make them talk. Then I'll leave them to you."

"Don't lie, Mr Rogan. I know how you'll leave them." He put out his hand to shake Rogan's. "I've done my official duty, but after reading your file I have to wish you luck. Watch out for those Freisling brothers; they're a pair of sly bastards."

When Bailey and his silent partner had closed the door behind them Rogan turned to Rosalie. "Is it true what they said about you?"

Rosalie sat up straight, her hands folded in her lap. Her eyes gazed steadily into Rogan's. "Yes," she said.

They didn't go out that evening. Rogan ordered food and champagne to be sent up to their room, and after they finished they went to bed. Rosalie cradled her golden head in his arm and took puffs from his cigarette. "Shall I tell you about it?" she asked.

"If you want to," Rogan said. "It doesn't really make any difference, you know — your being sick."

"I'm all right now," she said.

Rogan kissed her gently. "I know."

"I want to tell you," she said. "Maybe you won't love me afterwards, but I want to tell you."

"It doesn't matter," Rogan insisted; "it really doesn't."

Rosalie reached out and turned off the bedside table lamp. She could speak more freely in the dark.

CHAPTER 6

How she had wept that terrible day in the spring of 1945. The world had come to an end when she was a daydreaming fourteen-year-old maiden. The great dragon of war had carried her away.

She left her home early that morning to work on the family's rented garden plot on the outskirts of her home town of Bublingshausen in Hesse. Later, she was digging the dark earth when a great shadow fell across the land. She looked up and saw a vast armada of planes blotting out the sun, and she heard the thunder of their bombs dropping on the optical works of Wetzlar. Then the bombs, overflowing as water overflows a glass, spilled into her own harmless medieval village. The badly frightened girl buried her face in the soft wormy earth as the ground trembled violently. When the sky no longer roared with thunder and the shadow had lifted from the sun, she made her way back to the heart of Bublingshausen.

It was burning. The gingerbread houses, like toys torched by a wanton child, were melting down into ashes. Rosalie ran down the flowered streets she had known all her life, picking her way through smouldering rubble. It was a dream, she thought; how could all the houses she had known since childhood vanish so quickly?

And then she turned into the street that approached her home in the *Hintergasse*, and she saw a row of naked rooms, tier on tier. And it was magic that she could see the houses of her neighbours and friends without any shielding walls – the bedrooms, the dining rooms, all set before her like a play on the stage. And there was her mother's bedroom and her own kitchen that she had known all the fourteen years of her life.

Rosalie moved towards the entrance, but it was blocked by a hill of rubble. Sticking out of the vast pile of pulverized brick she saw the brown-booted feet and checked trouser legs that were her father's. She saw other bodies covered with red and white dust; and then she saw the one solitary arm pointing with mute agony towards the sky, on one grey finger the plaited gold band that was her mother's wedding ring.

Dazed, Rosalie sank down into the rubble. She felt no pain, no grief – only a peculiar numbness. The hours passed. Dusk was beginning to fall when she heard the continuous rumble of steel on crumbled stone. Looking up, she saw a long line of American tanks snaking through what had been Bublingshausen. They passed through the town and there was silence. Then a small Army truck with a canvas canopy came by. It stopped, and a young American soldier jumped down out of the driver's seat. He was blond and fresh-faced. He stood over her and said in rough German, "Hey, *Liebchen*, you want to come with us?"

Since there was nothing else to do, and since everyone she knew was dead, and since the garden she had planted that morning would not bear fruit for months, Rosalie went with the soldier in his canopied truck.

They drove until dark. Then the blond soldier took her into the back of the truck and made her lie down on a pile of army blankets. He knelt beside her. He broke open a bright green box and gave her a piece of hard round cheese and some chocolate. Then he stretched out beside her.

He was warm, and Rosalie knew that as long as she felt this warmth she could never die, never lie beneath the smouldering pile of rubbled brick where her mother and father now were. When the young soldier pressed against her and she felt the hard column of flesh against her thigh, she let him do whatever he wanted. Finally he left her huddled in the pile of blankets, and he went to the front and started to drive again.

During the night the truck stopped and other soldiers came into the back of it to lie on the blankets with her. She pretended to be asleep and let them, too, do as they wished. In the morning the truck continued on, then stopped in the heart of a great ruined city.

The air was sharper and colder. Rosalie recognized the dampness of the north, but though she had often read about Bremen in her school books she did not recognize this vast wasteland of bombed-out ruins as the famous merchant city.

The blond soldier helped her out of the truck and into a building whose lower floor was still intact. He took her into a huge dining room crammed with military gear and containing a black stove with a roaring fire. In the corner of the room was a bed with brown blankets. The blond soldier led her to the bed and told her to lie down on it. "My name is Roy," he said. And then he lowered himself upon her.

Rosalie spent the next three weeks in that bed. Roy curtained it with blankets so that it became a small private chamber. There Rosalie received an endless procession of faceless men who pushed themselves inside her. She didn't care. She was alive and warm. She was not cold beneath the rubble.

On the other side of the blanket curtain she could hear a great many male voices laughing, she could hear the shuffling of cards and the clink of bottles against glass. When one soldier left and another took his place, she always welcomed the new man with a smile and open arms. On one occasion a soldier peeped round the curtain and whistled with admiration when he saw her. She was already fully developed at fourteen, already a woman.

The soldiers treated her like a queen. They brought her heaped plates of food she had not tasted since before the war. The food seemed to stoke her body with unslakeable passion. She was a treasure of love, and they pampered her as they used her body. Once, the blond Roy who had picked her up in his truck said with concern, "Hey, baby, you wanta get some sleep? I'll chase everybody out." But she shook her head. For as long as her faceless lovers came through the curtain of blankets, she could believe it was all a dream — the hard flesh, her father's checked legs sticking out of the rubble, the wedding-banded hand pointing towards the sky. It could never come true.

But one day some other soldiers came, pistols on their hips, white helmets on their heads. They made her dress, then took her down to a truck loaded with other young girls, some joking, some crying. Rosalie must have fainted in the truck, for the next thing she knew she was lying in a hospital bed. Very dimly and from far away she saw a doctor looking at her intently. He had on a white jacket, but beneath it was an American uniform.

Lying on the cool white bed she heard the doctor say, "So this is the babe who has everything. Pregnant, too. We'll have to abort her. All that penicillin and fever killed the foetus. Such a beautiful kid, too."

Rosalie laughed. She knew she was dreaming beside her garden patch outside Bublingshausen, waiting to walk home to her father and mother. Perhaps there would be a letter from her older brother who was fighting in the East against Russia. But her dream was taking so long to end. She was frightened now, the dream was too terrible. She began to cry, and finally she was truly awake . . .

Two doctors stood beside her hospital bed; one German, one American. The American smiled. "So you're back with us, young lady, that was close. Can you talk now?"

Rosalie nodded.

The American doctor said, "Do you know you

put fifty American soldiers in the hospital with V.D.? You did more damage than a whole German regiment. Now – have you been with soldiers anywhere else?"

The German doctor leaned over to translate. Rosalie raised herself up on one arm, covers clutched modestly to her breast. She asked him gravely, "Then it's not a dream?" She saw his bewildered look. She started to weep. "I want to go home to my mother," she said. "I want to go home to Bublingshausen."

Four days later she was committed to the insane asylum at Nordsee.

In the darkness of their Berlin hotel room, Rogan pulled her close to him. He understood now about her emotional blankness, her apparent lack of any moral values. "Are you all right now?" he asked.

"Yes," she said. "Now I am."

CHAPTER 7

Rogan drove the Mercedes to the Freislings' gas station the next day and asked them to make some modifications on its body. Specifically he wanted the huge trunk in the rear to be made airtight. While the work was being done he became very chummy with the brothers, told them about his computer work and how his company was looking for an opportunity to sell their ideas to the countries behind the Iron Curtain. "Legally, of course, only legally," Rogan said in a tone of voice that implied he was just saying it for the record but that he would welcome a profitable crooked deal.

The two brothers smiled slyly. They understood. They questioned him more closely about his work. They asked him if he would be interested in making a tourist visit to East Berlin in their company. Rogan was delighted. "Of course," he said eagerly, and pressed them for a specific date. But they smiled and said, *"Langsam, langsam.* Slowly, slowly."

Several times they had seen Rosalie with him, and they had drooled over her beauty. Once when Rogan had gone into the office to pay a bill, he had come out to find Eric Freisling, with his head inside the Mercedes, talking earnestly to Rosalie. As they drove away Rogan asked Rosalie, "What did he say to you?"

Rosalie answered impassively, "He wanted me to sleep with him and spy on you."

Rogan didn't say anything. As he parked in front of the hotel Rosalie asked, "Which brother was it that talked to me? What is his name?"

"Eric," Rogan said.

Rosalie smiled at him sweetly. "When you kill them let me help you kill Eric."

The next day Rogan was busy making his own personal modifications on the Mercedes. He spent the rest of the week driving around Berlin and thinking out his plans. How would he make the Freisling brothers give him the names of the last three men? One day he went past the huge parking area of Berlin's main railway station. Thousands of cars were parked there. Rogan grinned. A perfect cemetery.

To build an image of being a big spender who had crude tastes – which in turn might suggest a moral corruptness – Rogan took Rosalie to the more expensive and disreputable nightclubs, night after night. He knew that the Freisling brothers, perhaps even the East German counterintelligence apparatus, would be checking him out.

When the Freislings arranged an East Berlin tourist visa for him and Rosalie, he expected the contact to be made then. He had in his pocket a sheaf of computer blueprints for sale. But no contact was made. They saw the concrete Headquarters Bunker in which Hitler had died. The Russians had tried to blow it up, but the concrete walls were so thick, so solid with cement and steel, that it had proved impossible to destroy. So this historic bomb shelter, which had witnessed the suicide of the most feared madman of all time, was now a grassy mound in the middle of a children's playground.

Strolling farther on through the Hansa quarter bristling with huge, grey, avant-garde apartment buildings, they were repelled by one of the new architectural gimmicks in the building complex. All its pipes for garbage, toilet waste, water, ended exposed in a huge glass terminal building, so that they looked like a nest of malignant steel snakes. Rosalie shuddered. "Let's go home," she said. She did not like the new world any better than the old.

Back in West Berlin they hurried to their hotel. Rogan unlocked the door to their suite and opened it for Rosalie, patting her round bottom as she went by. He followed her inside and heard her surprised gasp as he closed the door. He wheeled round.

They were waiting for him. The two Freisling brothers sat behind the coffee table, smoking cigarettes. It was Hans who spoke. "Herr Rogan, do not be alarmed. You understand that in our business one has to be careful. We did not wish anyone to know we had contacted you."

Rogan went forward to shake their hands. He smiled reassuringly. "I understand," he said. He understood more. That they had come early to search his room. To find out if he was a plant. To perhaps find and steal the blueprints so they would not have to pay cash for them — Communist cash they could then put in their own pockets. But they had been out of luck and forced to wait. The blueprints were in his jacket pocket. More important, the seven envelopes, plus the gun and silencer, were in a small bag that he had checked into the hotel storage cellar.

Hans Freisling smiled. The last time he had smiled like that, his brother Eric had crept up behind Rogan to fire the bullet in his skull. "We wish to purchase some of your computer blueprints, in strict confidence of course. Are you agreeable?"

Rogan smiled back. "Have supper with me here tomorrow evening," he said. "You understand I have to make some arrangements. I do not keep everything I need in this room."

Eric Freisling smiled slyly and said, "We understand." He wanted Rogan to know that they had searched the suite; he wanted him to know that they were not men to be trifled with.

Rogan looked at him steadily. "Come tomorrow evening at eight," he said. He ushered them out of the room.

That night he could not respond to Rosalie, and when she finally fell asleep, Rogan lit a cigarette and waited for the familiar nightmare to come. He was on his third cigarette when it started.

And then in his mind a dark curtain was drawn aside and he was in the high-domed room of the Munich Palace of Justice. Far away in the limitless shadows of his brain seven men took their eternal shapes. Five of them were blurred; but two – Eric and Hans Freisling – were very clear, very distinct, as if they were standing in a spotlight. Eric's face was as he had looked into it that fatal day, the slack heavy mouth, the sly, snapping black eyes, the thick nose, and stamped over all the features, a brutish cruelty.

The face of Hans Freisling was similar to Eric's, but with cunning rather than cruelty in the expression. It was Hans who advanced on the young prisoner Rogan and encouraged him with false kindliness. It was Hans who looked directly into Rogan's eyes and reassured him. "Dress in those nice clothes," Hans had whispered. "We are going to set you free. The Americans are winning the war and some day you can help us. Remember how we spared your life. Change your clothes now. Quickly."

And then, trustfully, Rogan changed his clothing, gratefully he smiled at the seven murderers of his wife. When Hans Freisling put out his hand in friendship, the young prisoner Rogan reached out to grasp it. Only then did the faces of the five other men become clear with their furtive, guilty grins. And he thought: *"Where is the seventh man?"* And at that moment the brim of his new hat tilted forward over his eyes. He felt the cold metal of the gun barrel against the back of his neck. He felt his hair bristle with terror. And just before the bullet exploded in his skull he heard his cry for mercy, the long shrieking "Ahhhhhhhh." And the last thing he saw was Hans Freisling's sly smile of delight.

He must have cried out loud. Rosalie was awake. His whole body was shaking, absolutely out of control. Rosalie got up out of bed, and using a smooth cloth towel, she wiped his face with cooling alcohol.

Then she bathed his whole body with it. Next, she ran the tub full of hot water and made him sit in the steaming bath. She sat on its marble rim as he soaked. Rogan could feel his body stop shaking, the pounding of blood against the metal plate in his skull easing off.

"Where did you learn all this?" he asked her.

Rosalie smiled. "The last three years in the asylum I was used as a nursing aid. I was almost well then. But it took me three years to get up enough courage to run away."

Rogan took her cigarette and puffed on it. "Why didn't they release you?"

She smiled down on him sadly. "They had no-one to release me to," she said. "I have no-one in the world." She paused for a long moment. "Except you."

The following day was a very busy one for Rogan. He gave Rosalie five hundred dollars' worth of marks and sent her out shopping. Then he went out to do some necessary chores. Making sure he was not followed, he drove to the outskirts of Berlin and parked the Mercedes. He went into a pharmacy and bought a small funnel and some chemicals. At a hardware store he bought wires, a small glass mixing bowl, nails, tape, and a few tools. He drove the Mercedes to a deserted side street, its ruins not yet rebuilt, and worked on the interior of the car for almost three hours. He disconnected all the wiring that operated the rear brake lights, and ran other wires into the car trunk. He bored holes into the airtight trunk, and then put tiny hollow rubber tubing into the holes. He mixed the chemicals, then put them in the small funnel and placed it over the piece of hollow tubing that now came up from the floor to the steering wheel. It was all very ingenious, and Rogan hoped it would work. He shrugged. If it didn't, he'd have to use the pistol and its silencer again. And that could be dangerous. It would hook him up with the other killings when the police compared ballistic tests. Rogan shrugged again. The hell with it, he thought. By the time they got all the evidence together his mission would be completed.

He drove back to the hotel and parked in the special area reserved for guests. Before he went up to his room he drew his suitcase from the storage cellar. Rosalie was already waiting in their suite. It hadn't taken her long to spend the money. She modelled the seductive Paris gown she had bought, which scarcely covered her breasts. "If that doesn't distract those two bastards nothing will," Rogan said, with an exaggerated leer. "Now are you sure you know what you have to do tonight?"

Rosalie nodded, but he briefed her again, slowly and thoroughly. "Do you think they will tell you what you want to know?" Rosalie asked.

"I think so," Rogan said with a grim smile. "One way or the other." He picked up the telephone and ordered dinner for four to be sent up to the room at eight o'clock.

The Freisling brothers were punctual, they arrived with the food trolley. Rogan dismissed the waiter, and as they ate they discussed the terms of their deal. When they had finished eating he poured four glasses of *Pfefferminz* liqueur, half brandy, half peppermint. "Ah, my favourite drink," Hans Freisling said. Rogan smiled. He had remembered the smell of peppermint in the interrogation room, the bottle Hans had carried around with him.

When Rogan capped the bottle he dropped in the drug pellets. He did it quickly and expertly; the brothers were not aware of what he was doing, though they were looking directly at him. With their natural suspiciousness, they were waiting for him to drink first. "*Prosit*," Rogan said, and drank. The sweet liqueur almost made him sick. The two brothers drained their glasses, and Hans licked his thick lips greedily. Rogan passed him the bottle. "Help yourself," he said. "I must go and get the documents. Allow me." He went past them into the bedroom. As he did so he saw Hans fill his glass and drain it. Eric was not drinking. But then Rosalie leaned over, her creamy breasts showing. She filled Eric's glass for him and let her hand fall on his knee. Eric lifted the glass and drank, his eyes on Rosalie's breasts. Rogan closed the door of the bedroom behind him.

He opened the suitcase and took out the Walther pistol and its silencer. Quickly he fitted them together. Then holding the gun in plain view, he opened the door and walked back into the other room.

The drug in the liqueur was a slow-acting one, not a knockout drug. It was designed to cripple the victim's reflexes so that he would move and react very slowly. It was similar to the effect that too much alcohol has on a man's physical coordination, throwing it out of balance, yet leaving him the illusion that he is performing better than ever. So the Freisling brothers were not yet aware of what was happening to their bodies. When they saw the gun in Rogan's hands they both jumped up from their seats, but they moved in slow motion.

Rogan pushed them back on to their chairs. He sat down opposite them. From his jacket pocket he took a flattened bullet, tarnished with age, and threw it on the coffee table between them.

"You, Eric," Rogan said. "You fired that bullet into the back of my skull ten years ago. In the Munich Palace of Justice. Do you remember me now? I'm the little playmate you sneaked up on while I was changing my clothes – and while your brother Hans kept telling me that I was going to be freed. I've changed a lot. Your bullet changed the shape of my head. But look hard. Do you recognize me now?" He paused, then said grimly, "I've come back to finish our little game together."

Mentally dulled by the drug, they both wore looks of blank incomprehension and stared at Rogan. It was Hans who first showed recognition, whose face first showed the natural shock, fear, and terrified surprise. Then they tried to flee, moving like men under water. Rogan reached over and again gently pushed them back in their seats. He frisked them for weapons. They had none.

"Don't be afraid," Rogan said, deliberately imitating Hans' voice. "I'm not going to harm you." He paused. "Of course I'll turn you in to the authorities, but all I want from you now is a little information. As a long time ago you wanted some from me. I cooperated then, didn't I? I know you'll be just as intelligent."

Hans answered first, his voice thick with the drug but still sly. "Of course we'll cooperate; we'll tell you anything we know."

"But first we'll make a bargain," Eric growled sullenly.

As long as they kept sitting still the brothers seemed to function normally. Now Hans leaned forward and said with ingratiating friendliness, "Yes. What do you wish to know, and what will you do for us if we cooperate?"

Rogan said quietly, "I want to know the names of the other men who were with you in the Munich Palace of Justice. I want to know the name of the torturer who killed my wife."

Eric leaned over, parallel to his brother, and said slowly, contemptuously, "So you can kill us all like you killed Moltke and Pfann?"

"I killed them because they would not give me the other three names," Rogan said. "I offered them a chance to live as I now give you a chance to live." He signalled now to Rosalie. She brought over pads and pencils and handed them to the brothers.

Hans looked surprised, then grinned. "I will tell you right now. Their names are—" Before Hans could utter another word Rogan jumped up and smashed the German's mouth with the butt of his pistol. Hans' mouth became a dark hole out of which bloody pieces of gum bubbled, and bits of broken teeth. Eric tried to come to his brother's defence, but Rogan pushed him back into the chair. He did not trust himself to hit Eric. He was afraid he wouldn't stop until the man was dead.

"I don't want to hear any lies," Rogan said. "And to make sure you don't lie to me, you'll each – separately – write down the names of the other three men who were in the Munich Palace of Justice. You'll also put down where each man is living now. I'm especially interested in the chief interrogator. I also want to know which man actually killed my wife. When you've finished, I'll compare your separate lists. If both have the same names, you won't be killed. If the information does not tally, if you have different names listed, you'll both be killed immediately. That's the deal. It's up to you."

Hans Freisling was gagging, clawing pieces of broken teeth and bits of gum from his smashed mouth. He couldn't speak. Eric asked the final question: "If we cooperate, what will you do to us?"

Rogan tried to sound as earnest and sincere as possible. "If you both write down the same information, I won't kill you. I'll accuse you as war criminals, however, and turn you in to the proper authorities. Then you'll have to stand trial and take your chances."

He was amused by the secret looks they gave each other and knew just what they were thinking. Even if arrested and tried, even if convicted, they could appeal and get out on bail. Then they figured they could defect to East Germany and thumb their noses at justice. Rogan, pretending not to notice the looks they exchanged, pulled Hans out of his chair and moved him to the other end of the coffee table so that neither one could see what his brother was writing down. "Get busy," he said. "And it had better be good. Or you'll both die here in this room, tonight." He pointed the Walther pistol at Eric's head while keeping Hans in full view. With the silencer, the pistol was a frightening-looking weapon.

The brothers began to write. Hampered by the drug, they wrote laboriously, and it seemed a long time before first Eric, then Hans, finished. Rosalie, who had sat on the coffee table between them to make certain they could not signal to each other, picked up their pads to hand them to Rogan. He shook his head. "Read them to me," he said. He kept the pistol pointed at Eric's head. He had already decided to kill him first.

Rosalie read Eric's list aloud. "Our commanding officer was Klaus von Osteen. He is now chief justice in the Munich courts. The other two were observers. The man from the Hungarian army was Wenta Pajerski. He is now a Red party chief in Budapest. The third man was Genco Bari. He was an observer from the Italian army. He now lives in Sicily."

Rosalie paused. She switched the pads to read what Hans had written. Rogan held his breath. "Klaus von Osteen was the commanding officer. He was the one who killed your wife." Rosalie paused at the look of anguish that passed over Rogan's face. Then she continued reading.

The information tallied, both brothers had put down essentially the same information, the same names, although only Hans had named Christine's murderer. And as Rogan compared the two pads he realized that Eric had given the minimum of information, whereas Hans had included extra details such as Genco Bari being a Mafia member, probably a big man in the organization. Rogan, however, had the feeling that the brothers had held back something he should know about. They were exchanging sly, congratulatory looks.

Again Rogan pretended not to notice. "O.K.," he said. "You did the smart thing, so I'm going to keep my part of the bargain. Now I must turn you over to the police. We'll leave this room together and go down the back stairs. Remember, don't try to run. I'll be right behind you. If you recognize anyone when we get outside, don't try to signal them."

The two men looked unconcerned; Eric was smirking at Rogan quite openly. Rogan was a fool, they thought. Didn't the Amerikaner realize the police would release them immediately?

Rogan played it very straight and very dumb. "One other thing," he said. "Downstairs I'm going to put you in the trunk of my car." He saw the fear in their faces. "Don't be frightened and don't make a fuss. How can I control you if I have to drive the car?" he asked reasonably. "How else can I conceal you from any friends who may be waiting for you outside when I drive out of the parking lot?"

Eric snarled, "We made the trunk of that car an air-sealed chamber. We'll suffocate. You plan to kill us anyway."

"I've had special air holes drilled into the trunk since then," Rogan said blandly.

Eric spat on the floor. He made a sudden grab for Rosalie and held her in front of him. But the drug had so weakened him that Rosalie easily twisted out of his grasp. And as she wrenched free one of her long painted fingernails went into Eric's eye. He screamed and held his hand to his left eye. Rosalie stepped out of the line of fire.

Up to this moment Rogan had controlled his anger. Now his head began to throb with familiar pain. "You dirty bastard," he said to Eric. "You put down as little information as possible. You didn't tell me it was Klaus von Osteen who killed my wife. And I'm willing to bet you helped him. Now you don't want to get into the trunk of the car because you think I'm going to kill you. All right, you son of a bitch. I'm going to kill you right now. Right here in this hotel room. I'm going to beat you to a bloody pulp. Or maybe I'll just blow your head off."

It was Hans who brought peace. Almost tearfully, through his puffed and bloody lips, he said to his brother, "Be calm, do what the American wishes us to do. Don't you see he has gone mad?"

Eric Freisling looked searchingly at Rogan's face. "Yes," he said then. "I will do what you wish."

Rogan stood very still. Rosalie came up beside him and touched him as if to bring him back to sanity. And his terrible anger began to subside. He said to her, "You know what you have to do after we leave?"

"Yes."

Rogan herded the two brothers out of the room and down the back stairs of the hotel. He kept the gun in his pocket. When they went out of the rear entrance that led to the parking lot, Rogan whispered directions until they came to where the Mercedes was parked. Rogan made them kneel in the gravel at his feet while he unlocked the trunk. Eric got into it first, awkwardly, the drug still affecting his movements. He gave Rogan a last distrustful look. Rogan pushed him to the floor. As Hans crawled into the spacious trunk his mouth tried to form a smile; it was an obscene leer because of his smashed lips and fragmented teeth. He said meekly, humbly, "You know, I'm glad this happened. All these years what we did to you has been on my conscience. I think it will be very good for me, psychologically, to be punished."

"Do you really think so?" Rogan said politely, and slammed the trunk lid down over them.

CHAPTER 8

Rogan drove the Mercedes around Berlin for the next couple of hours. He made sure a supply of air was going through the rubber hosing and into the trunk. This was to give Rosalie time to do her part. She had to go down to the hotel ballroom, where she would drink, flirt, and dance with the unattached men so that later everyone would remember her having been there. This would give her an alibi.

Near midnight Rogan pulled the wire attached to the steering wheel. This would cut off the air and feed carbon monoxide into the trunk. In thirty minutes or less the Freisling brothers would be dead. Rogan now drove towards the Berlin railway station.

But after fifteen minutes Rogan stopped the car. He had intended to kill them as they had tried to kill him in the Munich Palace of Justice, without warning and still hoping for freedom. He had meant to slaughter them like animals, but he could not.

He got out of the car, went around to the back, and banged on the trunk lid. "Hans ... Eric," he called. He didn't know why he used their first names, as if they had become friends. He called out again, in a low urgent voice, to warn them they were going into the eternal darkness of death, so that they could compose whatever souls they had, say whatever prayers possible to make themselves ready for the black void. Again he banged on the trunk, louder this time, but there was no answer. He realized suddenly what must have happened. In their drugged condition they had probably died shortly after Rogan had switched to the carbon monoxide. To make sure that they were dead and not shamming, Rogan unlocked the trunk and raised the lid.

Evil they had been, no loss to the world, but in their last moments they had found some spark of humanity. In their final agony the two brothers had turned to each other and died in each other's arms. Their faces had lost all slyness and cunning. Rogan stared at them for a long time. It was a mistake, he thought, to have killed them together. Accidentally, he had been merciful.

He locked the trunk and drove on to the railway station. He swung the car into the vast car park, filled with thousands of vehicles, and parked it in the section he thought most likely to remain filled, near the east entrance. Then he got out of the Mercedes and started towards his hotel. As he walked he let the keys to the Mercedes slip out of his hand and into the gutter.

He walked all the way back to the hotel, and so it was nearly three in the morning before he let himself into his hotel suite. Rosalie was waiting up for him. She brought him a glass of water to take with his pills, but Rogan could feel the blood pounding in his head, louder and louder. The familiar sickish, sweet taste was in his mouth, and then he felt the fearsome spinning vertigo, and he was falling ... falling ... falling ...

CHAPTER 9

It was three days before Rogan became conscious of his surroundings. He was still in the hotel suite, lying in his bed, but the bedroom had the antiseptic smell of a hospital. Rosalie was hovering over him, instantly at his side when she saw he was awake. Peering over her shoulder was a peevish-faced man with a beard who resembled the comical German doctor in films.

"Ah" – the doctor's voice was a harsh voice –

"you have finally found your way back to us. Fortunate, very fortunate. Now I must insist you go to the hospital."

Rogan shook his head. "I'm O.K. here. Just give me a prescription for some more of my pills. No hospital is going to help me."

The doctor adjusted his spectacles and stroked his beard. Despite the facial camouflage he looked young, and he was obviously disturbed by Rosalie's beauty. Now he turned to scold her. "You must give this fellow some peace. He is suffering from nervous exhaustion. He must have complete rest for at least two weeks. Do you understand me?" The young doctor angrily tore a sheet from his prescription pad and handed it to her.

There was a knock on the door of the hotel suite, and Rosalie went to answer it. The American Intelligence agent Bailey came in, followed by two German detectives. Bailey's long Gary Cooper face was sour. "Where's your boy friend?" he asked Rosalie. She nodded towards the bedroom door. The three men moved towards it.

"He's sick," Rosalie said. But the three men went into the bedroom.

Bailey did not seem surprised to find Rogan in bed. Neither did he seem to have any sympathy for the sick man. He looked down at Rogan and said flatly, "So you went ahead and did it."

"Did what?" Rogan asked. He was feeling fine now. He grinned up at Bailey.

"Don't bullshit me," Bailey snapped angrily. "The Freisling brothers have disappeared. Just like that. They left their gas station closed; their stuff is still in their apartment; their money is still in the bank. That means only one thing: They're dead."

"Not necessarily," Rogan said.

Bailey waved his hand impatiently. "You'll have to answer some questions. These two men are from the German political police. You'll have to get dressed and come down to their headquarters."

The young bearded doctor spoke up. His voice was angry, commanding. "This man cannot be moved."

One of the German detectives said to him, "Watch yourself. You don't want all those years in medical school to be wasted on a pick and shovel."

Instead of frightening the doctor, this made him angrier. "If you move this man he may very well die. I will then personally press charges of manslaughter against you and your department."

The German detectives, astonished at this defiance, did not say another word. Bailey studied the doctor and said, "What's your name?"

The doctor bowed, almost clicked his heels, and said, "Thulman. At your service. And what is your name, sir?"

Bailey gave him a long intimidating stare, then in obvious mockery, he bowed and clicked his heels together. "Bailey," he said. "And we are going to take this man down to the Halle."

The doctor gave him a look of contempt. "I can click my heels together louder than you when I am barefooted, you poor imitation of a Prussian aristocrat. But that is beside the point. I forbid you to move this man because he is ill; his health will be severely endangered. I do not think you can afford to disregard my warnings."

Rogan could see that the three men were baffled. He was, too. Why the hell was this doctor sticking his neck out for him?

Bailey said sarcastically, "Will it kill him if I ask him a few questions right here and now?"

"No," said the doctor, "but it will tire him."

Bailey made an impatient gesture and turned his lanky frame towards Rogan. "Your visas for travel in Germany are being revoked," he said. "I've had that arranged. I don't care what you do in any other country, but I want you out of my territory. Don't try to come back with phoney papers. I'll have my eye on you as long as you're in Europe. Right now you can thank this doctor for saving your ass." Bailey walked out of the bedroom, the two German detectives followed, and Rosalie ushered all three out of the suite.

Rogan grinned at the doctor. "Is it true – I really can't be moved?"

The young doctor stroked his beard. "Of course. However, you may move yourself, since then there would be no psychological stress on your nervous system." He smiled at Rogan. "I dislike seeing healthy men, especially policemen, bully sick people. I don't know what you are up to, but I'm on your side."

Rosalie saw the doctor to the door, then came back and sat on the bed. Rogan put his hand over hers. "Do you still want to stay with me?" he asked. She nodded. "Then pack all our things," Rogan said.

"We'll leave for Munich. I want to meet Klaus von Osteen before the others. He's the most important one."

Rosalie bowed her head to his. "They will kill you after all," she said.

Rogan kissed her. "That's why I have to take care of von Osteen first. I want to make sure of him. I don't mind so much if the other two get away." He gave her a gentle push. "Start packing," he said.

They caught a morning flight to Munich and checked into a small *Pension* where Rogan hoped they might not be noticed. He knew that Bailey and the German police would trace him to Munich, but it would take them a few days to discover his whereabouts. By then his mission would be completed and he would be out of the country.

He rented a small Opel while Rosalie went to the library to read up on von Osteen in the newspaper file and to locate his home address.

When they met for dinner, Rosalie had a full report. Klaus von Osteen was now the highest-ranking judge of the Munich courts. He had started off as the wastrel son of a famous noble family related to the English royal family. Though he had been a German officer during the war, there was no record of his having joined the Nazi party. Shortly before the end of the war he had been severely wounded and that had apparently turned him into a new man at the age of forty-three. Back in civilian life he had studied law and had become one of the best lawyers in Germany. He had then entered the political arena as a moderate and a supporter of the American entente in Europe. Great things were expected of him; it was possible that he might even become the chancellor of West Germany. He had the support of the German industrialists and the American occupation authorities, and a magnetic influence over the working classes as a superb orator.

Rogan nodded grimly. "That sounds like the guy. He had a terrific voice, sincere as hell. The bastard really covered his tracks, though."

Rosalie said anxiously, "Are you sure this is the right man?"

"It's the right one; it has to be," Rogan said. "How could Eric and Hans hit on the same name unless it was the truth?" He paused. "We'll go to his house right after dinner. When I see his face I'll recognize him, no matter how much he's changed. But it's him, all right. He was a real aristocrat."

They drove to von Osteen's address, using a city map as a guide. Von Osteen's house was in a fashionable suburb, and it was a mansion. Rogan parked the car and they went up the stone steps to the huge baronial doors. There was a wooden knocker in the shape of a wild boar's head. Rogan slammed it twice against the wooden panel. In a moment the door was opened by an old-fashioned German butler, grossly fat, obsequious. Very coldly he said, *"Bitte, mein Herr."*

"We have come to see Klaus von Osteen," Rogan said. "On confidential business. Just tell him that Eric Freisling sent us."

The butler's voice was less cold. He evidently recognized the Freisling name. "It is regrettable," he said. "Judge von Osteen and the family are on vacation in Switzerland, and then they plan to go to Sweden and Norway and finally England. They will not be back for nearly a month."

"Damn," Rogan said. "Can you tell me where they are staying right now – their address?"

The butler smiled, his face creasing into ridges

of ruddy suet. "No," he said. "Judge von Osteen is not following a schedule. He can be reached only through official channels. Do you wish to leave a message, sir?"

"No," Rogan said. He and Rosalie returned to the car.

Back in their room, Rosalie asked, "What will you do now?"

"I'll have to gamble," he said. "I'll go to Sicily and track down Genco Bari. If everything works out O.K., I'll fly to Budapest and see about Wenta Pajerski. Then I'll come back to von Osteen here in Munich."

Rosalie said, "What about your entry visa? Bailey will have that cancelled."

Rogan said drily, "I used to be in the spy business too. I'll find a way to get a phoney passport or a phoney visa. And if Bailey gets too close, I'll just have to forget he's a fellow American."

Rosalie said, "What about me?"

He didn't answer her for a long time. "I'm making arrangements so that you'll get enough money to live on every month. A trust fund that will go on, no matter what happens."

"You're not taking me with you?" Rosalie asked.

"I can't," Rogan said. "I'd have to get you papers. And I'd never be able to lose Bailey if I took you along."

"Then I'll wait for you here in Munich," she said.

"O.K. But you have to get used to the idea of my not being around some time. The chances are a million to one against my making it all the way. They'll nail me for sure when I get von Osteen."

Gratefully she leaned her head against his shoulder. "I don't care," she said. "Just let me wait for you; please let me wait for you."

He stroked her blonde hair. "Sure, sure," he said. "Now will you do something for me?"

She nodded.

"I was looking at the map," Rogan said. "We can drive to Bublingshausen in four hours. I think it would be good for you to see it again. Will you go back?"

He felt her whole body go tense, her back arch in terror. "Oh, no," she said. "Oh, no!"

He held her quivering body close. "We'll drive through very quickly," he said. "You'll see how it is. Now. Then maybe you won't see so clearly how it was before. Maybe everything will blur. Try. I'll drive through very fast, I promise. Remember, that's the first thing you told the doctor – that you wanted to go back to Bublingshausen?"

Her body had stopped shaking. "All right," she said. "I'll go back. With you."

CHAPTER 10

The next morning they loaded the Opel with Rogan's things. They had decided that from Bublingshausen they would drive on to Frankfurt where Rogan could catch a plane to Sicily and look for Genco Bari. Rosalie would take the train back to Munich and wait for Rogan there. Rogan had reassured her. "When I finish in Sicily and Budapest I'll come back here for Osteen. And I'll come straight to the *Pension*, first thing." In this he had lied. He planned to see her again only if he killed von Osteen and managed to stay free.

The Opel sped along the German roads. Rosalie sat as far away from Rogan as possible, huddled against her door, head turned away. Near midday Rogan asked, "Do you want to stop for lunch?" She shook her head. As they came nearer and nearer to Bublingshausen, Rosalie hunched farther and farther down in her seat. Rogan swung the Opel off the main *Autobahn*, and then they were entering the city of Wetzlar, whose great optical works had been the original target of the American bombers that had killed her father and mother. The Opel moved slowly through the heavy city traffic, then finally came to the yellow sign, with its arrow pointed towards the suburban road, that read: "Bublingshausen." Rosalie buried her face in her hands so that she would not be able to see.

Rogan drove slowly. When they entered the village he studied it carefully. There were no scars of war. It had been completely rebuilt, only the houses were no longer made of gingerbread wood, but of concrete and steel. Children played in the streets. "We're here," he said. "Look up."

Rosalie kept her head in her hands. She didn't answer. Rogan made the car go very slowly, easier to control, then he reached over and pulled Rosalie's blonde head out of her hands, forcing her to look at her childhood village.

What happened then surprised him. She turned on him with anger and said, "This is not my village. You've made a mistake. I don't recognize anything here." But then the street made a turn, heading out towards open country, and there were the fenced-in plots of ground, private gardens, each gate with its owner's name printed on a varnished yellow board. Wildly Rosalie turned her head to look back at the village, then at the gardens. He could see the recognition dawning in her eyes. She started fumbling with the door handle and Rogan stopped the car. Then Rosalie was out and running across the road on to the grassy earth of the gardens, running awkwardly. She stopped and looked up into the sky, and then finally she turned her head towards Bublingshausen. Rogan could see her body arch with her inward agony, and when she crumpled to the ground he got out of the car and ran to her.

She was sitting awkwardly, legs splayed out, and

she was weeping. Rogan had never seen anyone weep with such grief. She was wailing like a small child, wailing that would have been comical if it had not been so powerfully wrung from her guts. She tore at the earth with her painted fingernails, as if she were trying to inflict pain on it. Rogan stood beside her, waiting, but she gave no sign that she knew he was there.

Two young girls, no more than fourteen, came down the road from Bublingshausen. They carried gardening sacks over their arms and they chatted gaily together. They entered the gates of their families' gardens and began digging. Rosalie raised her head to watch them, and they gave her curious, envious glances. Envious of her fine clothes, envious of the obviously wealthy man who stood beside her. Rosalie stopped weeping. She tucked her legs beneath her and put a hand on Rogan's leg to make him sit on the grass beside her.

Then she cradled her head against his shoulder and wept quietly for a very long time. He understood that finally now, for the first time, she could grieve for her lost father and mother, her brother in his cold Russian grave. And he understood that as a young girl she had gone into some terrible shock that prevented her from consciously accepting her loss, but that had instead driven her into schizophrenia and the asylum. She had a chance now to get over it, Rogan thought.

When she had finished weeping, Rosalie sat for a while staring at the village of Bublingshausen and then at the two young girls digging in their gardens. The girls kept glancing up at Rosalie, devouring her expensive clothes with their eyes, coolly inspecting her beauty.

Rogan helped Rosalie to her feet. "Those two girls envy you," he said.

She nodded and smiled sadly. "I envy them."

They drove on to Frankfurt and Rogan returned the car to the rental agency office at the airport. Rosalie waited with him until take-off time. Before he walked down the ramp, she said to him, "Can't you forget the rest of them; can't you let them live?"

Rogan shook his head.

Rosalie clung to him. "If I lost you now it would be the end of me. I know it. Please let the others go."

Rogan said gently, "I can't. Maybe I could forget about Genco Bari and the Hungarian, Wenta Pajerski. But I could never forgive Klaus von Osteen. And since I have to kill him, I have to kill the others. That's the way it is."

She still clung to him. "Let von Osteen go," she said. "It doesn't matter. Let him stay alive and then you'll stay alive, and I'll be happy, I can live happily."

"I can't," he said.

"I know. He killed your wife and he tried to kill you. But everybody was trying to kill each other then." She shook her head. "Their crime against you was murder. But it was everybody's crime then. You would have to kill the whole world to get your revenge."

Rogan pushed her away from him. "I know all that, everything you've just said. I've thought about it all these years. I might have forgiven them for killing and torturing Christine. I might have forgiven them for torturing and trying to kill me. But von Osteen did something that I can never forgive. He did something to me that makes it impossible for me to live on the same planet with him, as long as he's alive. He destroyed me without bullets, without even raising his voice. He was crueller than all the others." Rogan paused, and he could feel the blood begin to pound against the plate in his skull. "In my dreams I kill him, and then I bring him back to life so I can kill him again."

They were calling the number of his flight over the loudspeaker. Rosalie kissed him hurriedly and whispered, "I'll wait in Munich for you. In the same *Pension*. Don't forget me."

Rogan kissed her eyes and mouth. "For the first time I hope I come through it alive," he said. "Before, I didn't care. I won't forget you." He turned and walked down the ramp to the plane.

CHAPTER 11

Flying over Germany in twilight, Rogan could see how the country had rebuilt itself. The rubbled cities of 1945 had sprung back with more factory smokestacks, taller steel spires. But there were still ugly scabs of burned-out sections visible from the sky, the pockmarks of war.

He was in Palermo and checked into its finest hotel before midnight, and already starting his search.

He had asked the hotel manager if he knew anyone in the city by the name of Genco Bari. The hotel manager had shrugged and spread his arms wide. Palermo, after all, had over 400,000 people. He could hardly be expected to know all of them, could he, *signore?*

The next morning, Rogan contracted a firm of private detectives to track down Genco Bari. He gave them a generous retainer and promised them a large bonus if they were successful. Then he made the rounds of those official bureaux he thought might help him. He went to the United States consulate, the Sicilian chief of police, the publishing office of Palermo's biggest newspaper. None of them knew anything of or anyone named Genco Bari.

It seemed impossible to Rogan that his search would not be successful. Genco Bari must be a wealthy man, a man of substance, since he was a member of the Mafia. Then he realized that this was the hitch. Nobody, no-one at all would give him information on a Mafia chief. In Sicily the law of *omertà* ruled. *Omertà*, the code of silence, was an ancient tradition of these people: Never give information of any kind to any of the authorities. The punishment for breaking the code was swift and sure death, and not to be risked to satisfy the mere curiosity of a foreigner. In the face of *omertà*, the police chief and the firm of private detectives were helpless in their quest for information. Or perhaps they, too, did not break the unwritten law.

At the end of the first week, Rogan was about to move on to Budapest when he received a surprise caller at his hotel. It was Arthur Bailey, the Berlin-based American Intelligence agent.

Bailey held out a protesting hand, a friendly smile on his face. "I'm here to help," he said. "I found out you've got too much drag in Washington to be pushed around, so I might as well. Of course I have my selfish motive, too. I want to keep you from accidentally ruining a lot of our groundwork in setting up information systems in Europe."

Rogan looked at him thoughtfully for a long moment. It was impossible to doubt the man's sincerity and warm friendliness. "Fine," he said at last. "You can start off helping me by telling me where to find Genco Bari." He offered the lean American a drink.

Bailey sat down, relaxed, and sipped his Scotch.

"Sure, I can tell you that," he said. "But first you have to promise that you'll let me help you all the way. After Genco Bari you'll go after Pajerski in Budapest and then von Osteen in Munich, or vice versa. I want you to promise to follow my advice. I don't want you caught. If you are, you'll wreck Intelligence contacts it's taken the United States years and millions of dollars to set up."

Rogan didn't smile or act particularly friendly. "O.K. Just tell me where Bari is — and make sure I get a visa for Budapest."

Bailey sipped his drink. "Genco Bari is living in his walled estate just outside the village of Villalba in central Sicily. The necessary Hungarian visas will be waiting for you in Rome whenever you're ready. And in Budapest I want you to contact the Hungarian interpreter at the United States consulate. His name is Rakol. He'll give you all the help you need and arrange your exit from the country. Fair enough?"

"Sure," Rogan said. "And when I get back to Munich do I contact you, or will you contact me?"

"I'll contact you," Bailey said. "Don't worry, I'll be able to find you."

Bailey finished his drink. Rogan saw him to the elevator and Bailey said casually, "After you killed those first four guys, that gave us enough of a lead to break your Munich Palace of Justice case wide open. That's how I know about Bari, Pajerski, and von Osteen."

Rogan smiled politely. "That's what I figured," he said. "But since I found them by myself, it doesn't matter what you found out. Right?"

Bailey gave him an odd look, shook hands, and just before getting into the elevator said, "Good luck."

As Bailey knew the whereabouts of Genco Bari, Rogan realized that everyone else must have known too – the police chief, the private detectives, probably even the hotel manager. Genco Bari was one of the big Mafia leaders of Sicily; his name was no doubt known throughout the country.

He rented a car to drive the fifty-odd miles to Villalba. It struck him that he would quite possibly never leave this island alive, and that the last criminals would remain unpunished. But that didn't seem to matter so much now. As it did not matter that he had made up his mind not to see Rosalie again. He had arranged for her to receive money from his estate once she had been in touch with the office. She would forget about him and make a new life. Nothing mattered at the moment except killing Genco Bari. And Rogan thought about that man in the Italian uniform. The only man of the seven in the high-domed room in the Munich Palace of Justice who had treated him with any genuine warmth. And yet he, too, had taken part in the final betrayal.

On that final terrible morning in the Munich Palace of Justice, Klaus von Osteen had smiled in the shadows behind his great desk, as Hans and Eric Freisling had urged Rogan to change into his "freedom clothes." Genco Bari had said nothing; he'd merely looked at him with gentle pitying eyes. Finally he had crossed the room and stood in front of Rogan. He had helped Rogan knot his tie, had patted it securely inside Rogan's jacket. He had distracted Rogan so that Rogan had never seen Eric Freisling slip behind him with the gun. Bari, too, had taken a hand in the final humiliating cruelty of the execution. And it was because of Bari's humanity that

Rogan could not forgive him. Moltke had been a selfish, self-serving man; Karl Pfann, a brutal animal. The Freisling brothers were evil incarnate. What they had done could be expected, springing as it did out of their very natures. But Genco Bari had exuded a human warmth, and his taking part in torture and execution was a deliberate, malignant degeneracy; unforgivable.

Now driving through the starry Sicilian night, Rogan thought of all the years he had dreamed of his revenge. How it had been the one thing that had kept him from dying. And when they had thrown him on the pile of corpses stacked outside the Munich Palace of Justice, even then when his shattered brain oozed blood and flickered with only a tiny spark, how that tiny spark had been kept alive by the energy of sheer hatred.

And now that he was no longer with Rosalie, now that he planned not to see her again, his memories of his dead wife seemed to flood back into his being. He thought, Christine, Christine, you would have loved this starry night, the balmy air of Sicily. You always trusted and liked everyone. You never understood the work I was doing, not really. You never understood what would happen to all of us if we were captured. When I heard your screams in the Munich Palace of Justice, it was the surprise in your screams that made them so terrifying. You could not believe that human beings did such terrible things to their fellow human beings.

She had been beautiful: long legs for a French girl, with rounded thighs; a slim waist and small shy breasts that grew bold beneath his hand; lovely soft brown hair like overflowing silk, and charmingly serious eyes. Her lips, full and sensual, had had the same character and honesty as he'd seen in her eyes.

What had they done to her before she died? Bari, Pfann, Moltke, the Freislings, Pajerski, and von Osteen? How had they made her scream so; how had they killed her? He had never asked any of the others because they would have lied to him. Pfann and Moltke would have made it seem less terrible; the Freisling brothers would have invented gory details to make him suffer even now. Only Genco Bari would tell him the truth. For some reason Rogan was sure of this. He would finally learn how his pregnant wife had died. He would learn what had caused those terrible screams, the screams that the torturers had recorded and preserved so carefully.

CHAPTER 12

He reached the town of Villalba at 11:30 P.M. and was surprised to find it brilliantly lighted, hundreds of coloured lanterns strung in arches over every street. From gaily decorated wooden booths lining the cobblestone pavements, villagers offered hot sausages for sale, and wine, and thick Sicilian pizza squares with oily anchovies buried in a rich bed of tomato sauce. The smell filled the night air and made Rogan ravenous. He stopped the car and devoured a sandwich of sausage until his mouth felt on fire from the hot spicy meat. Then he moved to the next booth to buy a glass of tart red wine.

He had come to Villalba on the birthday of the town's patron saint, Saint Cecilia. As was the custom, the people of the town were celebrating the birthday of their saint with a great fiesta that would last three days. Rogan had arrived on the evening of the fiesta's second day. By this time everybody, including some of the small children, was drunk on the new, tart Sicilian wine. They greeted Rogan with open arms. And when they heard him speak his almost perfect Italian the wine merchant, a huge fat man with big moustaches who said his name was Tullio, embraced Rogan.

They drank together. Tullio wouldn't let him go, refused to take money for the wine. Other men gathered round. Some brought long loaves of bread stuffed with sweet fried peppers; others gnawed on smoked eels. Children danced in the streets. Then down the main avenue came three elaborately dressed girls, shining black hair piled high, strolling arm in arm and giving the men provocative looks. These

were the fiesta *putains*, the festival whores, specially
picked and imported to pluck the virginity of all the
young men who had come of age this year, and thus
protect the honour of the local girls.

The men around the wine booth melted away,
joining the long trail of young men following the
three fiesta *putains*.

The fiesta would be a great cover, Rogan thought.
He might be able to do the job this very night and
be out of town by morning. He asked Tullio, "Can
you tell me where the house of Genco Bari is
located?"

The change in the huge Sicilian was immediate.
His face froze into a blank mask. All friendliness
vanished. "I do not know any Genco Bari," he said.

Rogan laughed. "I am an old war comrade of
his, and he invited me to visit him here in Villalba.
Never mind, I'll find it myself."

Tullio immediately unfroze. "Ah, you are invited
to his fiesta also? The whole village is invited. Come,
I'll go with you myself." And though there were at
least five customers waiting for wine, Tullio motioned
them away and shuttered the wooden booth. Then
he took Rogan by the arm and said, "Put yourself

in my hands and you will never forget this night as long as you live."

"I hope so," Rogan said politely.

The villa of Genco Bari, on the outskirts of the town, was surrounded by a high stone wall. The two huge iron grille gates had been swung open, and the grounds of the just visible mansion were decorated with coloured streamers that went from tree to tree. Genco Bari was holding open house for the villagers, most of whom worked on his farmlands. Rogan followed Tullio inside the gates.

Long garden tables were laden with great bowls of macaroni, fruit, and homemade ice cream. Women filled glasses from wine casks resting on the lawn, and offered the red-purple liquid to anyone who passed by. The whole surrounding countryside seemed to be attending the fête here on the grounds of the Mafia leader's estate. On a raised platform three musicians began a wild piping dance tune. And on the same raised platform, seated on a throne-like carved chair, was the man Rogan had come to kill.

The Mafia leader shook hands with everyone. He smiled graciously. But Rogan almost did not recognize him. The fleshy tanned face had changed to a bony waxen death's-head the colour of the faded ice-cream Panama hat that adorned the shrunken head. Amidst the gaiety of the fiesta, Genco Bari was the white mask of death. There was no doubt: Rogan would have to move fast to claim his revenge, or a more impersonal executioner would do the job.

Men and women formed into a square to dance to the music. Rogan became separated from Tullio as he was swept into the vortex of the dance. He seemed to descend into a whirling funnel of human bodies that spewed him out into the open air, hand in hand with a young Sicilian girl. Other couples were peeling off from the whirling crowd and disappearing into the bushes. Rogan's girl danced behind a huge wine barrel and drank from a great silver pitcher on top of it. Then she held up the pitcher for Rogan to drink.

She was beautiful. Her full sensuous mouth was stained purple from wine. Her flashing dark eyes, her clear olive skin, consumed the lantern light in their own greater fire. Her full breasts, spilling over the low-cut blouse, pulsated with her eager breathing, and her plump thighs strained against the silk skirt, the hungry flesh not to be denied or contained. She watched Rogan drink, pushing her body up to his; then she led him through dark tree-lined lanes, away from the festivities, to the rear of the stone mansion. He followed her up a flight of outside stone steps that spiralled along the walls and ended at a balcony. Then they were going through inky glass doors to an inside bedroom.

The girl turned and held up her mouth to Rogan. Her breasts were heaving with passion, and Rogan put his hands on them as if to still their movement. Her arms twined around his body, pressing him close.

For a moment Rogan thought of Rosalie. He had made up his mind that he would not see her again, that he would not let her share what he was sure would be his capture or death. Now, by making love to this girl, the decision would become final in his mind. And more important, the girl was the key to penetrating Genco Bari's mansion; he was in it right now. With the girl, who was growing impatient.

She was pulling him on to the bed, tugging at his clothes. Her skirt was hiked up to her stomach, and Rogan could see her marvellous full-fleshed thighs, feel her hot skin burning his own. In minutes they were coiled about each other like two snakes, twisting on the bed, straining and plunging, their naked bodies slippery with sweat, until finally they rolled on to the cool stone floor. Locked in each other's arms they fell asleep there, woke, drank red wine from a jug, got back on the bed, made love again, and fell asleep for a final time.

When Rogan woke up in the morning he had the worst hangover of his life. He felt as if his whole body was filled with sweet rotten grapes. He groaned, and the naked girl next to him cooed sympathetically, reached down beneath the bed, and lifted up the half-empty jug of wine they had been drinking the night before.

"This is the only cure," she said. She drank from the jug and handed it to Rogan. He put it to his lips and the fruity wine washed the ache out of his head. He kissed the girl's heavy breasts. They seemed to give off the fragrance of grapes; her whole body exuded the aroma of the wine, as if she herself were the very essence of it.

Rogan smiled at her. "And who are you?" he asked.

"I am Mrs Genco Bari," she said. "But you may call me Lucia." At that moment there was a knock on the bolted door. She smiled at him. "And that is my husband come to reward you."

Lucia went to unbolt the door while Rogan reached to where his jacket hung on a chair, groping for his Walther pistol. Before he could find it the door swung open and Genco Bari came into the room. Behind his frail, wasted figure loomed two Sicilian peasants, shotguns cradled in their arms. One of the peasants was Tullio. He stared at Rogan impassively.

Genco Bari sat at his wife's dressing table. He smiled in a kindly way at Rogan. "Have no fear; I am not the typical, jealous Sicilian husband," he said. "As you see, it is obvious I can no longer fulfil my husbandly duties. I am a more worldly man than my fellow peasants, and so I permit my wife to satisfy her very natural needs. But never with someone from this village, and always with discretion. Last night I am afraid my poor Lucia became carried away by the new wine and her passion. But no matter. Here is your reward." He tossed a purse stuffed with money on the bed. Rogan did not move to take it.

Genco Bari turned to his wife. "Lucia, did he acquit himself well?"

Lucia flashed Rogan a brilliant smile and nodded. "Like a fine bull," she said mischievously.

Bari laughed, or rather he tried to laugh. But since there was no flesh on his face, it was merely a grimace of loose bones and skin and teeth. "You must forgive my wife," he said to Rogan. "She is a simple peasant girl with forthright, lusty ways. That is why I married her three years ago when I learned I was dying. I thought I could hold on to life by feasting on her body. But that soon ended. And then when I saw her suffering I broke all the traditions of our land. I permitted her to have lovers. But under conditions dictated by me, so that my honour and the honour of my family would remain untarnished. So let me warn you now: If you boast of this to anyone in Sicily, I will set my ferrets after you and you will never lie with women again."

Rogan said curtly, "I don't need that money, and I never tell stories about women."

Genco Bari stared at him intently. "There is something familiar about your face," he said. "And you speak Italian almost like a native. Have our paths ever crossed?"

"No," Rogan said. He was looking at Bari with

pity. The man weighed no more than seventy pounds. His face was a skin-covered skull.

Genco Bari said musingly, as if talking to himself, "You were searching for me when you were in Palermo. Then the American agent Bailey set you on my trail. Tullio here" – he jerked his head at the armed guard – "tells me that at his wine booth you were inquiring where I lived and that I had invited you here. So we must know each other." He leaned towards Rogan. "Have you been sent here to kill me?" He smiled his ghastly smile. He flung out his arms jestingly. "You are too late," he said. "I am dying. There is no point in your killing me."

Rogan said quietly, "When you remember who I am, I'll answer that question."

Bari shrugged. "It doesn't matter," he said. "But until I do remember, I insist that you remain a guest here at my villa. Take a little holiday. You will amuse my wife, and perhaps you can spare an hour each day to chat with me. I am always curious about America. I have many friends there. Say yes to my request; you won't be sorry for it."

Rogan nodded, then shook the hand outstretched to him. When Bari and his guards had left the bedroom Rogan asked Lucia, "How long does your husband have to live?"

Lucia shrugged. "Who knows? A month, a week, an hour. I feel very sorry for him, but I am young; I have my life to live, so perhaps it is better for me if he dies soon. But I will weep for him. He is a very kind man. He has given my parents a farm, and he has promised to leave his whole estate to me when he dies. I would have gone without lovers. It was he who insisted. Now I am glad." She came and sat on Rogan's lap, ready for more of the same.

Rogan spent the next week at Genco Bari's villa. It became obvious that he could never hope to escape Sicily after he killed Bari. The Mafia organization would intercept him easily at the Palermo airport. His only hope was to kill Bari in such a way that his body would not be discovered for at least six hours. That would give him time to get on the plane.

He spent part of each day making plans and cultivating Bari. He found the Mafia Don extremely likeable, courteous, and helpful. They became almost good friends in that week. And although he went horseback riding and on amorous picnics with Lucia, he found his conversations with Genco Bari more entertaining. Lucia's sexual appetite and grape smell were overwhelming. It was with relief that Rogan settled down every evening to share Genco Bari's light supper and glass of grappa. Bari had changed completely from the murderer he had been twenty years before. He treated Rogan like a son, and he was extremely interesting, especially when telling strange stories about the Mafia in Sicily.

"Do you know why no stone wall in Sicily is over two feet high?" he asked Rogan. "The government in Rome felt that too many Sicilians were ambushing each other from behind stone walls, so they thought that if they reduced the height of the walls they would reduce the number of murders. How foolish. Nothing will stop people from killing each other. Don't you agree?" And he gave Rogan a sharp look. Rogan merely smiled. He did not want to be led into any philosophical discussions about murder.

Bari told Rogan stories about the old Mafia feuds and protection rackets. How every branch of industry had its own Mafia branch clinging like a leech and sucking blood. That there was even a branch of the Mafia that collected protection money from young men who serenaded their ladies beneath their balconies. The whole island was unbelievably corrupt. But you could live in peace — if you, too, were a member of the Mafia.

Bari had become a farmer in 1946, because he had refused to have anything to do with the traffic in narcotics that sprang up after the war. "I was an evil man in those days," Genco Bari told Rogan with a deprecating smile. "I was violent. But I never harmed a woman, and I would never deal in narcotics. That is *infamità*. I always kept my honour. Even murderers and thieves have their honour."

Rogan smiled politely. Bari had forgotten about the Munich Palace of Justice, and he had forgotten the screams of Christine preserved on the brown wax phonograph cylinder. It was time to remind him.

By the end of the week Rogan had thought of a plan that would let him kill Bari and make a clean getaway. He proposed to the Mafia Don that they both go for a picnic in Rogan's car. They would drive out into the country with a basket of food and jugs of wine and grappa and sit in the shade of a tree. The outing would do the ailing man good.

Bari smiled at Rogan. "That would be very fine. It is very thoughtful of you to waste your time on an old wreck like me. I'll give orders to have your car stocked with food and drink. Shall we take Lucia with us?"

Rogan frowned and shook his head. "She's too lively, and men can't talk with women around. I like your company too much to have it spoiled by a female's idle chatter." Bari laughed and they were agreed; they would leave early the next morning and return late in the evening. Genco Bari had some business in a few small villages that could be taken care of along the way. Rogan was glad to see that these villages were on the road to Palermo.

They started off the next morning with Rogan driving and Genco Bari, his skull-like face shielded by his inevitable cream-coloured Panama hat, seated next to him. They drove a few hours on the main road to Palermo, and then Bari directed Rogan to take a side road that wound up in the hilly regions. The road ended in a narrow trail, and Rogan had to stop the car.

"Bring the food and wine," Genco Bari said. "We'll picnic beneath the rocks."

Rogan carried the basket to where Bari was standing in the shadow of the hill. There was a red-checked tablecloth to spread over the ground, and on top of that he put the covered dishes of fried aubergine, cold sausage, a loaf of crusty bread wrapped in a white napkin. There were wide short glasses for the wine, and Bari poured from the jug. When they had finished eating, Bari offered Rogan a long, thin black cigar. "Sicilian tobacco, rare, but the best in the world," Bari said. He flared his lighter and lit Rogan's cigar for him, then said in exactly the same tone of voice, "Why are you going to kill me today?"

Rogan, surprised, took a quick glance around to see if he had been led into a trap. Genco Bari shook his head. "No, I have not taken any precautions to guard my life. It is of no value to me any longer. But I still like to satisfy my curiosity. Who are you and why do you wish to kill me?"

Rogan said slowly, "You told me once that you had never done violence to a woman. But you helped to kill my wife." Bari looked puzzled, so Rogan went on. "On *Rosenmontag*, 1945, in the Munich Palace of Justice. You fixed my tie before Eric Freisling shot me in the back of the head. But you never killed me. You never killed me. I stayed alive. The Freisling brothers are dead, Moltke and Pfann are dead. After I kill you I have only Pajerski and von Osteen to punish, and then I can die happy."

Genco Bari puffed on his cigar, stared at Rogan for a long time. "I knew you would have an honourable motive for killing me. You are so obviously an honourable man. All week I could see you planning how to kill me and then get safely on your plane in Palermo. So I've helped you. Leave my body here and go forward. Before anyone knows what has happened, you will be in Rome. Then I suggest you leave Italy as quickly as possible. The Mafia has a long arm."

"If you hadn't straightened my tie, if you hadn't distracted me so that Eric could sneak up behind me, I might not kill you," Rogan said.

On Bari's emaciated face was a look of surprise. Then he smiled sadly. "I never meant to trick you," he said. "I thought you knew you were going to die. And so I wanted you to feel a human touch, to comfort you in those last few moments without betraying myself to my fellow murderers. You see, I do not excuse myself from that deed. But I must insist to you now: I had nothing to do with your wife's death or with her screams."

The Sicilian sun was directly overhead and the rock overhanging them gave no shade. Rogan felt the sick anticipation rising in his stomach. "Was it von Osteen who killed her?" he said. "Tell me who tortured her, and I swear by her memory and her soul that I will let you go free."

Genco Bari stood up. For the first time in their relationship he was harsh and angry. "You fool," he said, "haven't you realized I want you to kill me? You are my deliverer, not my executioner. Every day I suffer terrible pain that no drugs can completely banish. The cancer is in every cell of my body, but it can't kill me. As we did not succeed in killing you in the Munich Palace of Justice. I may live in this pain for years to come, cursing God. I knew from the very first day that you wanted to kill me. I helped you in every way to find an opportunity." He smiled at Rogan. "This sounds like a rather grim joke, but I will only tell you the truth about your wife if you promise to kill me."

Rogan said harshly. "Why don't *you* just kill yourself?"

147

He was surprised when Genco Bari bowed his head then raised it to look directly into his eyes. Almost with shame, the Italian whispered, "It would be a mortal sin. I believe in God."

There was a long silence. They were both standing. Finally Rogan said, "Tell me if it was von Osteen who killed my wife, and I promise to end yours."

Genco Bari spoke slowly. "It was the leader of our group, Klaus von Osteen, who had the screams recorded to torture you with later. He was a strange, terrible man, no other man I have ever known would have thought of such a thing at such a time. For it wasn't planned, you know. It was all an accident. So he had to think of the recording right there, right on the spur of the moment, as the girl was dying."

Rogan said hoarsely, "Then who tortured her? Who killed her?"

Genco Bari looked directly into his eyes and said gravely, "You did."

Rogan felt the blood pounding in his head, the skull around the silver plate throbbing with pain. He said thickly, "You lousy bastard, you tricked me.

You're not going to tell me who did it." He took the Walther pistol from his jacket and pointed it at Bari's stomach. "Tell me who killed my wife."

Again Genco Bari looked directly into Rogan's eyes and said gravely, "You did. She died giving birth to a dead child. None of us touched her. We were sure she knew nothing. But von Osteen recorded her screams to frighten you with."

"You're lying," Rogan said. Without even thinking he pulled the trigger of the Walther pistol. The report echoed against the rocks like thunder, and Genco Bari's frail form was hurled to the ground almost five feet from where he had been standing. Rogan walked to where the dying man was crumpled against a rock. He put the pistol against Bari's ear.

The dying man opened his eyes and nodded gratefully; he whispered to Rogan, "Don't blame yourself. Her screams were terrible because all pain, all death, is equally terrible. You too must die again, and it will not be less terrible." His breath was coming in bloody ribbons of spit. "Forgive me, as I forgive you," he said.

Rogan held the man in his arms, not firing again, waiting for him to die. It took only a few minutes, and he had plenty of time to catch his plane in Palermo. But before he left he covered Genco Bari's body with a blanket from the car. He hoped it would be found soon.

CHAPTER 13

At Rome Rogan caught a flight to Budapest. Arthur
Bailey had kept his promise and the visas were
waiting for him. Rogan took along some whisky
and stayed drunk on the plane. He couldn't forget
what Genco Bari had told him: that Christine had
died in childbirth; that he, Rogan, had been responsible for her death. But could a death so

common to women since time began cause the terrible screams of pain he had heard on the phonograph in the Munich Palace of Justice? And that cruel bastard von Osteen making the record. Only a genius of evil could think of something so inhuman on the spur of the moment. Rogan forgot his own feelings of guilt for a moment as he thought of killing von Osteen and the pleasure it would give him. He thought of letting Pajerski's execution wait, but he was already on the plane bound for Hungary; Arthur Bailey had already arranged things for him in Budapest. Rogan smiled grimly. He knew something Bailey didn't know.

In Budapest, more than a little drunk, Rogan went directly to the United States consulate and asked to see the interpreter. This was all according to Arthur Bailey's instructions.

A small nervous man with a toothbrush moustache led him to the inner chambers. "I am the interpreter," he said. "Who sent you to me?"

"A mutual friend named Arthur Bailey," Rogan told him.

The little man ducked away into another room. After a few moments he came back and said in a frightened, timid voice, "Please follow me, sir. I will take you to someone who will help you."

They entered a room in which a burly man with thinning hair waited for them. He shook Rogan's hand with vigour and introduced himself as Stefan Vrostk. "I am the one who will aid you in your mission," he said. "Our friend Bailey has requested I give it my personal attention." With a wave of his hand he dismissed the little interpreter.

When they were alone in the room, Vrostk began to speak in an arrogant manner. "I have read about your case. I have been briefed on what you have done. I have been informed on your future plans." He spoke as if he were a man of great importance; he was, obviously, a man of overwhelming conceit.

Rogan sat back and just listened. Vrostk went on. "You must understand that here behind the Iron Curtain things are very different. You cannot hope to operate so flagrantly as you have done. Your record as an agent in World War II does show you are prone to carelessness. Your network was destroyed because you did not take proper precautions when you used your clandestine radio. Isn't that true?" He gave Rogan a patronizing smile. But Rogan continued to look at him impassively.

Vrostk was a little nervous now, but this did not lessen his arrogance one bit. "I will point out Pajerski to you — where he works, his living habits, how he is guarded. The actual execution you must do yourself. I will then arrange to have the underground spirit you out of the country. But let me impress upon you that you are to do nothing without consulting me. You will do nothing without my approval. And you must accept without questioning my plans for your escape from this country once you have completed your mission. Do you understand this?"

Rogan could feel the anger mounting to his head. "Sure," he said. "I understand. I understand everything perfectly. You work for Bailey, don't you?"

"Yes," Vrostk said.

Rogan smiled. "O.K.; then I'll follow your orders. I'll tell you everything before I do it." He laughed again. "Now show me where I can get my hands on Pajerski."

Vrostk smiled paternally. "First we must have you checked into a hotel where you will be safe. Take a little nap, and this evening you and I shall dine at the Café Black Violin. And there you shall see Pajerski. He dines there every evening, plays chess there, meets his friends there. It is his hangout, as you say in America."

In the small side-street hotel Vrostk had found for him, Rogan sat in a stuffed chair and made his own plans. In doing so he thought about Wenta Pajerski and everything the raw-boned Hungarian had done to him in the Munich Palace of Justice.

The face was huge, red, and warty as a hog's, yet Pajerski had been only casual in his cruelty, and sometimes he had been kind. He had halted the interrogation to give Rogan a drink of water or a cigarette, slipped mint wafers into his hand. And though Rogan knew that Pajerski was deliberately playing the role of the "good guy," the classic "nice cop" who makes some prisoners talk where nothing else will, he could not even now help feeling the glow of gratitude the act of kindness in itself inspired.

Whatever the motive, the sugary mints had been real, the sweet bits of chocolate broke his suffering.

The water and cigarettes were miraculous gifts of life. They lived. They entered his body. So why not let Pajerski live? He remembered the hulking man's vitality, his obvious joy in the good things of life that were material. The physical pleasure he took in eating, drinking, and even in the tortures demanded by the interrogation. But he had laughed when Eric Freisling was creeping up behind Rogan to fire the bullet into his skull. Pajerski had enjoyed that.

Rogan remembered something else. On the afternoon of the first interrogation in the Munich Palace of Justice, they had played the recording of Christine's screams from the next room. Rogan had twisted and cried out in agony. Pajerski had sauntered out of the high-domed room saying jokingly to Rogan, "Be at ease; I go to make your wife scream with pleasure instead of pain."

Rogan sighed. They had all played their parts so well. They had succeeded in tricking him every time. They had failed in only one thing: They had not killed him. And now it was his turn. It was his turn to materialize suddenly out of the darkness, bearing torture and death in his hands. It was his turn to know and see everything, and their turn to guess and fear what would happen next.

CHAPTER 14

That night Rogan went with Stefan Vrostk to the Black Violin. It proved to be exactly the kind of place he would have imagined as being Wenta Pajerski's favourite hangout. The food was good and the plates were heaped high. The drinks were strong and cheap. The waitresses were handsomely buxom, cheerful, lusty, and had a dozen sly ways of presenting their plump bottoms to be pinched. The accordion music was bouncy, and the atmosphere was hazy with pungent tobacco smoke.

Wenta Pajerski entered at exactly 7.00 P.M. He had not changed at all, just as animals never look older after maturity, until they reach an extreme age. And Wenta Pajerski was an animal. He pinched the first waitress so hard she let out a little scream of pain. He drank a huge tankard of beer in one slug, choking it down in his refusal to stop and draw a breath. Then he sat at a large round table, reserved for him, and was soon joined by male cronies. They laughed and joked and drank French cognac by the bottle. Meanwhile a blonde waitress brought an oblong carved chest to the table. With great relish, Pajerski opened it up and took out chess pieces. The chest itself opened up into a chess board. Pajerski appropriated the white pieces for himself, with their advantage of moving first, without giving his opponent the usual hidden choice between black and white. This was an insight into the giant Hungarian's character. He had not changed.

Rogan and Vrostk watched Pajerski's table all evening. Pajerski played chess until nine, drinking all the while. At exactly nine the blonde waitress took away the chess set and brought dinner to the table.

Pajerski ate with such animal gusto that Rogan felt almost sorry he had to be killed. It was like killing some happy-go-lucky unreasoning animal. Pajerski lifted the soup bowl to his lips to lap up the last dregs. He used a huge spoon, instead of a fork, to shovel mountains of gravy-soaked rice into his cavernous mouth. He drank his wine from the bottle, with an impatient gurgling thirst. Then he let out a wave of belches that rolled across the room.

When he was finished, Pajerski paid for everyone's dinner, pinched the waitress's behind, and shoved a huge tip of crumpled paper money down inside her dress so that he could squeeze her breast. Everybody put up with his behaviour; they were obviously either very fond of him or very afraid of him. His male companions followed him out on to the dark streets, marching arm in arm, talking loudly. When they passed an open café whose music rolled out into the open, Wenta Pajerski did a bearlike waltz down the street, whirling his nearest companion in his arms.

Rogan and Vrostk followed them until they disappeared into an ornately faced building. Then

Vrostk hailed a cab, and they drove to the consulate. Vrostk gave Rogan the Hungarian's dossier to read. "This will fill you in on the rest of Pajerski's evening," he said. "We won't have to follow him everywhere. He does the same thing every night."

The dossier was short but informative. Wenta Pajerski was the executive officer of the Communist secret police in Budapest. He worked hard all day in the town hall administration building. He also had his living quarters in this building. Both office and living quarters were heavily guarded by special details of the secret police. He always left the building punctually at 6:30 P.M., but was escorted by guards in plain clothes. At least two official guards were among the men who walked down the street with him.

Wenta Pajerski was the only one of the seven torturers who had remained in the same kind of work. Ordinary citizens suspected of activities against the State disappeared into his office and were never seen again. He was believed responsible for the kidnapping of West German scientists. Pajerski was high on the list of Cold War criminals the West would like to see liquidated. Rogan smiled grimly.

He understood Bailey's cooperation and why Vrostk was so anxious that everything be checked out with him. The repercussions of Pajerski's murder would shake the whole city of Budapest.

The dossier also explained the ornate building Pajerski had entered with his friends. It was the most expensive and exclusive brothel, not only in Budapest but in the whole area behind the Iron Curtain as well. After caressing every girl in the parlour, Pajerski never took fewer than two upstairs for his pleasure. An hour later he would reappear in the street, puffing on an enormous cigar, looking as content as a bear ready to hibernate. But both inside the house and out, his guards stuck as close to him as possible, without interfering with his pleasures. He was not vulnerable in that area.

Rogan closed the dossier and looked up at Vrostk. "How long has your organization been trying to kill him?" he asked.

Vrostk grimaced. "What makes you think that?"

Rogan said, "Everything in this dossier. Earlier today you gave me a lot of crap about how you're the big boss of this operation because you're so much better an agent than I am. I took it. But you're not my boss. I'll tell you what you have to know, and I'll count on you to get me out of the country after I kill Pajerski. But that's all. And I'll give you some good advice: Don't pull any fast ones on me – none of those tricky Intelligence moves. I'd kill you as soon as I'd kill Pajerski. Sooner. I like him better." Rogan gave the man a brutally cold smile.

Stefan Vrostk flushed. "I didn't mean to offend you earlier," he said. "I meant it well."

Rogan shrugged. "I haven't come all this way to be jerked around like a puppet. I'll pull your chestnuts out of the fire; I'll kill Pajerski for you. But don't ever try to bull me again." He got out of his chair and walked out of the door. Vrostk followed him and conducted him out of the consulate, then held out his hand. Rogan ignored it and walked away.

He could not explain why he had got so tough with Vrostk. Perhaps it was the feeling that only an accident of time and history had prevented Vrostk from being one of the seven men in the high-domed room of the Munich Palace of Justice. But it was also that he distrusted Vrostk even now. Anyone who acted so imperiously in small matters had to be weak.

Not trusting anyone else, Rogan checked out the dossier by personal observation. For six days he frequented the Café Black Violin and memorized Pajerski's every move. The dossier proved to be correct in every particular. But Rogan noticed something that was not in the dossier. Pajerski, like many genial giants, always looked for an advantage. For example, he always took the white pieces, without fail, in his chess games. He had a nervous habit of scratching his chin with the pointed crown of his king piece. Rogan also noted that though the chess set was the property of the Black Violin, it was not loaned to other patrons until Pajerski had finished with it for the evening.

The Hungarian also passed a café whose music delighted him, and he would invariably go into his bearlike dance when he heard the music from that café. The dance took him usually thirty yards ahead of his guards to a street corner, which he then turned. For perhaps one minute he was out of the guards' sight, alone and vulnerable. Vrostk wasn't such a hot agent, Rogan thought, not if that one vulnerable minute was not recorded in the dossier. Unless it had been deliberately omitted.

Rogan kept checking. He thought the brothel a likely place to catch Pajerski unguarded. But he found that two men from the secret police invariably took their posts outside the bedroom door while Pajerski took his exercise within.

The problem was admittedly difficult. Pajerski's living and working quarters were impregnable. Only in the evening was he slightly vulnerable. When he danced round that corner there would be a minute to kill him and escape. But a minute would not be enough to evade the guards following. In his mind Rogan kept reviewing Pajerski's every move, searching for a fatal chink in the man's security armour. On the sixth night he fell asleep with the problem still unsolved. What made it even more difficult was that Pajerski had to know why he was being killed before he died. For Rogan this was essential.

In the middle of the night he woke up. He had had a dream in which he played chess with Wenta Pajerski, and Pajerski kept saying to him, "You stupid Amerikaner, you have had a checkmate for three moves." And Rogan had kept staring at the board looking for the elusive winning move, staring at the huge white king carved out of wood. Smiling slyly, Pajerski picked up the white king and used its pointed crown to scratch his chin. It was a hint. Rogan sat up in bed. The dream had given him his answer. He knew how he would kill Pajerski.

The next day he went to the consulate and asked to see Vrostk. When he told the agent what tools and other equipment he would need Vrostk looked at him in astonishment, but Rogan refused to explain. Vrostk told him it would take at least the rest of the day to get everything together. Rogan nodded. "I'll come by tomorrow morning to pick it up. Tomorrow night your friend Pajerski will be dead."

CHAPTER 15

In Munich every day was the same for Rosalie. She had settled into the *Pension* to wait for Rogan's return. She checked the Munich airport schedules and found that there was a daily flight from Budapest, arriving at 10.00 P.M. After that, every night she waited at the gate to check the passengers coming off the Budapest plane. She sensed that Rogan might not come back to her, that he would not want her involved in his murder of von Osteen. But since he was the only man, the only human being she cared about, she went every evening to the airport. She prayed that he had not died in Sicily; and then as time went on, she prayed that he had not died in Budapest. But it didn't matter. She was prepared to make her evening pilgrimage for the rest of her life.

During the second week she went shopping in the central square of Munich. That was where the Palace of Justice was situated. It had miraculously escaped damage during the war and now housed the criminal courts of the city. Nazi concentration camp commandants and guards were being tried for their war crimes in those courtrooms at almost every session.

On an impulse, Rosalie went into the massive building. In the cool, dark hall she studied the public bulletin boards to see if von Osteen was sitting as judge that day. He was not. Then a little notice caught her eye. The municipal court system was advertising for a nurse's aide to work in the emergency hospital room of the court.

Again on an impulse, Rosalie applied for the position. Her training in the asylum had given her the necessary basic skills, and she was immediately taken on. There was a great shortage of medical personnel in all postwar German cities.

The emergency hospital room was in the basement of the Municipal Palace of Justice. It had its own private entrance, a small door that led into the huge inner courtyard. With a shock of horror, Rosalie realized that it was in this courtyard that the wounded Rogan had been thrown on to a pile of corpses.

The emergency room was astonishingly busy. Wives of convicted criminals sentenced to long terms in prison collapsed and were brought down to be revived. Elderly swindlers on trial suffered heart attacks. Rosalie's duties were more clerical than medical. She had to record every case in a huge blue book on the admittance desk. The young doctor on duty was immediately taken by her beauty and asked her to dinner. She refused him with a polite smile. Some of the sleek attorneys accompanying their sick clients to the medical room asked her if she would be interested in working in their offices. She smiled at them and politely said she would not.

She was interested in only one man in the Munich

Palace of Justice: Klaus von Osteen. When he sat in court she attended the trial by taking a very late lunch hour and skipping lunch.

He was not the man she had imagined. He had a dignified ugliness, but his voice was kind and gentle. He treated accused criminals with the utmost courtesy and a trace of genuine, merciful pity. She heard him sentence a man found guilty of a particularly violent and sadistic crime, and he had not indulged in the usual righteousness of a judge meting out punishment. He had let the convicted man keep his dignity.

One day she found herself directly behind him on a street near the Munich Palace of Justice, and she trailed him as he limped down the street. One of his legs was shorter than the other. He was accompanied by a detective guard who moved a few steps behind him and seemed very alert. But von Osteen himself seemed preoccupied. Despite this preoccupation, he was extraordinarily courteous to people who greeted him in the street and to the chauffeur of the official car that was assigned him.

Rosalie noticed that the man had an extraordinary magnetism. The respect shown him by his fellow judges, the clerks of the court, and the lawyers testified to von Osteen's force of character. And when a woman laden with bundles collided with him in the street, von Osteen helped her to pick up her bundles, though he was grimacing with pain. He did it with genuine courtliness. It was hard to believe that this was the man Rogan hated so much.

Rosalie found out as much as she could about von Osteen so that she would have the information for Rogan when he arrived in Munich. She learned that von Osteen had a wife who was a power in the social life of Munich and an aristocrat in her own right. She was much younger than von Osteen. They did not have any children. She learned that von Osteen had more political control of the city than any other official, including the burgomeister. He was also backed by the U.S. State Department officials as a proven democrat, both anti-Nazi and anti-Communist.

Despite all this, it was enough for her to know that Rogan hated the man to make all von Osteen's virtues count for nothing. She kept a notebook on von Osteen's habits, to make it easier for Rogan to kill him.

And every night at 10.00 she waited at the airport for the flight from Budapest, certain that Rogan would return.

CHAPTER 16

When Rogan woke up on his final day in Budapest, his first act was to destroy the dossiers he had compiled on the seven men. Then he went through his belongings to see if there was anything he wanted to keep. But there was nothing except his passport.

He packed everything else and carried his bags to the railway station. He checked the bags into an empty coin locker, then left the station. Crossing over one of the many bridges in the city, he casually dropped the locker key into the river. Then he went to the consulate.

Vrostk had gathered everything he needed. Rogan checked the items — the small jeweller's drill and chipping tools, the tiny wires, the timing device, the liquid explosive, and some special electronic parts of tiny size. Rogan smiled and said, "Very good."

Vrostk preened himself. "I have a very efficient organization. It was not easy to get all these things on such short notice."

"To show my appreciation," Rogan said, "I'm going to buy you a late breakfast at the Café Black Violin. Then we'll come back here and I'll go to work with this stuff. And I'll also tell you what I'm going to do."

At the café they ordered coffee and brioches. Then, to Vrostk's obvious surprise, Rogan called for the chess set. The waitress brought it over, and Rogan set up the pieces, taking the whites for himself.

Vrostk said in an annoyed voice, "I have no time for such foolishness. I must get back to my office."

"Play," Rogan said. Something in his voice made Vrostk suddenly quiet. He let Rogan make the first move and then moved his black pawn. The game was soon over. He beat Rogan easily and the pieces were dumped back into the set for the waitress to carry away. Rogan gave a large tip. Outside the café he hailed a taxi to take them back to the consulate. He was in a hurry now; every moment was valuable.

In Vrostk's office Rogan sat down at the table that had the special equipment on it.

Vrostk was angry; it was the bullying anger of a small-minded man. "What is the meaning of all this foolishness?" he asked. "I demand to know."

Rogan put his right hand into his jacket pocket, pulled it out again clenched. He thrust it at Vrostk and then opened it. Lying in his palm was the white king.

Rogan worked intently at the table for nearly three hours. He drilled a hole in the bottom of the king, and then took the bottom out entirely. Working very carefully, he hollowed out the inside of the chess piece and packed it with liquid explosive, wires, and the tiny electronic parts. When he was finished he put the bottom back on, and then with buffing cloth and enamel he hid all scratches and chips. He held the chess piece in his hand, trying to see if the extra weight was too obvious. He did notice a little difference, but he reasoned that this was because he was looking for the difference. The piece would pass.

He turned to Vrostk. "At eight o'clock tonight this thing will blow up in Pajerski's face. I've got it fixed so that nobody else will get hurt. There's just enough to kill the man holding the piece. And Pajerski always scratches his chin with it. That and the timing device will set off the explosive. If I see someone else holding it, I'll interfere and deactivate it. But I've watched Pajerski, and I'm sure he'll be the guy who'll have the piece in his hand at eight tonight. Now I want you to have your underground people pick me up at the corner two blocks from the café. I'm counting on your organization to get me out of the country."

"You mean you're going to stay in the café until Pajerski is killed?" Vrostk asked. "That's sheer madness. Why not leave beforehand?"

"I want to make sure nobody else gets killed," Rogan said. "And before he dies, I also want Pajerski to know who killed him and why, and I can't do that unless I'm there."

Vrostk shrugged. "It's your affair. As for my people picking you up two blocks from the café, that's too dangerous for them. I'll have a black Mercedes limousine waiting for you in front of the consulate here. It will be flying the consulate flag. What time do you want it to be ready?"

Rogan frowned. "I may change the timing on the explosive, or it may possibly go off ahead of time if Pajerski keeps scratching his chin with it too much. Better have the car waiting for me at seven-thirty and tell them to expect me at ten minutes past eight. I'll be on foot, and I'll just get into the car without any fuss. I assume they know me by sight. You've shown me to them?"

Vrostk smiled. "Of course. Now I suppose you and I will have a late lunch and a game of chess at the Black Violin so that you can return the white king."

Rogan smiled. "You're getting smarter all the time."

Over coffee they played the second game of chess, and Rogan won easily. When they left the café, the booby-trapped white king was safely back with its fellow chess pieces.

That evening Rogan left his small hotel room at exactly 6.00. The Walther pistol was tucked under his arm and buttoned securely into its holster. The silencer was in his left jacket pocket. His passport and visas were in his inside jacket pocket. He walked slowly and leisurely to the Café Black Violin and took his usual small corner table. He unfolded a newspaper, ordered a bottle of Tokay, and told the waitress he would order food later.

He had drunk half the bottle when Wenta Pajerski came roaring into the café. Rogan looked at his watch. The giant Hungarian was right on schedule; it was 7.00 P.M. He watched Pajerski pinch the blonde waitress, yell to his waiting friends, and have his first drink. It was about time for him to call for his chess set, but he ordered a second drink. Rogan felt himself go tense. Would this be the first night that Pajerski would pass up his chess games? For some reason it seemed to have slipped his mind this evening. But then, without his calling for it, the waitress brought the chess set to Pajerski's table, waiting expectantly for the pinch that would reward her forethought.

It almost looked as if Pajerski would wave her away. But then he grinned, his warty piggy face becoming a mass of joviality. He pinched the blonde waitress so hard that she gave a little scream of pain.

Rogan called to the waitress and asked her for a pencil and a piece of notepaper. He looked at his watch. It read 7:30. On the rough brown notepaper he wrote: "I will turn your screams of pleasure into pain. *Rosenmontag*, 1945, in the Munich Palace of Justice."

He waited until his watch read 7:55, then he called a waitress over and handed her the note. "Give this to Mr Pajerski," he said. "Then come right back to me and I will give you this." He showed her a banknote that was more than her weekly salary. He didn't want her standing near Pajerski when the booby trap went off.

Pajerski was scratching his chin with the white king when the waitress handed him the note. He read it slowly, translating the English audibly, his lips moving. He raised his eyes to stare directly at Rogan. Rogan stared back at him, smiling slightly. His watch read 7:59. And then as he saw the recognition slowly dawn in Pajerski's eyes the white king exploded.

The explosion was deafening. Pajerski had been holding the chess piece in his right hand under his chin. Rogan had been staring into his eyes. Then suddenly Pajerski's eyes disappeared in the explosion, and Rogan found himself staring into two empty bloody sockets. Pieces of flesh and bone spattered all over the room, and then Pajerski's head, its flesh shredded, slumped over on flaps of skin that were still holding the neck to the body. Rogan slipped out of his seat and left the café by the kitchen door. The screaming, stampeding crowd took no notice of him.

Out on the street he walked one block to a main avenue and hailed a taxi. "To the airport," he told the driver; then, just to make sure, he said, "Take the street that goes past the American consulate."

He could hear the whine of police car sirens speeding to the Café Black Violin. In a few minutes his taxi was on the broad avenue that led past the consulate. "Don't go so fast," he told the driver. He leaned back so that he could not be seen from the street.

There was no Mercedes limousine waiting there. The street was empty of all vehicles, which was in itself unusual. But it had a hell of a lot of pedestrians, waiting to cross at corners and window shopping. And most of the pedestrians were big burly men. To Rogan's experienced eye they had secret police written all over them. "Speed it up to the airport," he told the driver.

It was then that he noticed what seemed like a physical coldness in his chest. It was as if his whole body were being touched by death. He felt the chilliness spread. But he was not cold. He did not feel any real physical discomfort. It was simply as if he himself had become some sort of host to death.

He had no trouble getting on the plane. His visa was in order, and there was no sign of any special police activity at the airport. His heart beat swiftly when he boarded the aircraft, but again there were no complications. The plane took off, climbed, and then it levelled off and headed for the German border and Munich.

That night Rosalie left her job as nurse's aide in the Munich Palace of Justice at 6.00 P.M. The young doctor who worked with her insisted she have dinner with him. Afraid of losing her job, she agreed. He made sure the meal took a long time by ordering several courses. It was after 9.00 P.M. when they finished. Rosalie looked at her watch. "You must excuse me; I have an important engagement at ten," she said, and started to gather up her coat and gloves.

The young doctor had a disappointed look on his face. It did not occur to Rosalie that she could miss meeting the plane one night and keep her escort company for the rest of the evening. If she missed meeting the Budapest plane even one time, it would mean she thought Rogan was dead. She walked out of the restaurant and hailed a taxi. By the time she got to the airport it was nearly ten. By the time she ran through the terminal to the Budapest plane arrival gate, passengers were already coming out. Out of habit, she lit a cigarette as she watched them. And then she saw Rogan and her heart nearly broke.

He looked dreadfully ill. His eyes were sunken, the muscles of his face were rigid, and there was a fearful stiffness in his body movements. He had not seen her, and she started running towards him, calling his name through her sobs.

Rogan heard the clicking of a woman's heels on

marble, heard Rosalie calling his name. He started to turn away, then turned back to catch her as she rushed into his arms. And then he was kissing her wet face and her lovely eyes as she whispered, "I'm so happy, I'm so happy. I came here every night, and every night I thought you might have died and I'd never know and I'd be coming here for the rest of my life."

Holding her close, feeling her warmth, Rogan felt the icy chill that had been part of his body begin to melt away, as if he were coming alive again. He knew then that he would have to keep her with him.

CHAPTER 17

They took a taxi to the *Pension*, and Rosalie led Rogan
up to the room she'd had while she was alone in
Munich. It was a comfortable place, half bedroom,
half living room, with a small green sofa curved
into its middle. There was a vase of wilted roses on
the table, some of their scent still hung in the air.
Rogan reached out for Rosalie as soon as they had
locked the door behind them. They quickly undressed

and went to bed, but their love-making was too frantic, too filled with tension.

They smoked a cigarette together in the darkness, and then Rosalie began to weep. "Why can't you stop now?" she whispered. "Why can't you just stop?"

Rogan didn't answer. He knew what she meant. That if he let Klaus von Osteen go free his life, and hers, could start again. They would stay alive. If he went after von Osteen the chances of his escaping were small. Rogan sighed. He could never tell another human being what von Osteen had done to him in the Munich Palace of Justice, it was too shameful. Shameful in the same way that their attempt to kill him had been shameful. He knew only one thing! He could never live on earth as long as von Osteen was alive. He could never sleep a night through without nightmares as long as von Osteen was alive. To balance his own private world he had to kill the seventh and last man.

And yet, in a strange way, he dreaded the moment when he would see von Osteen again. He had to remind himself that now von Osteen would be the victim, von Osteen would shriek with fear, von Osteen would collapse in terror. But it was hard to imagine all this. For back in those terrible days when the seven men had tortured him in the Munich Palace of Justice, in those nightmare days when Christine's screams from the next room had set his body trembling with anguish, Rogan had come to regard Klaus von Osteen finally as God, had almost come fearfully to love him.

Rosalie had fallen asleep, her face still wet with tears. Rogan lit another cigarette. His mind, his invincible memory, and all the agonies of remembrance imprisoned him once again in the high-domed room of the Munich Palace of Justice.

In the early morning hours the jail guards would come into his cell with small rubber clubs and a battered tin bucket for his vomit. They would use the rubber clubs to beat his stomach, his thighs, his groin. Pinned helplessly against the iron bars of his cell, Rogan felt the black bile gush into his mouth, and he'd retch. One of the guards would skilfully catch the vomit in the tin bucket. They never asked any questions. They beat him automatically, just to set the proper tone for the day.

Another guard wheeled in a breakfast tray on which stood a chunk of black bread and a bowl of greyish, lumpy gruel they called oatmeal. They made Rogan eat, and since he was always hungry, he gobbled the oatmeal and gnawed at the bread, which was rubbery stale. After he had eaten, the guards would stand around in a circle as if they were going to beat him again. Rogan's physical fear, his body organs weakened by malnutrition and torture, made it impossible for him to control his bowels at this moment. They opened against his will: He could feel the seat of his pants becoming sticky as the oatmeal oozed out of him.

As the foul stench filled the cell the guards dragged him out of his prison and through the halls of the Munich Palace of Justice. The marble halls were deserted this early in the morning, but Rogan would be ashamed of the trail of tiny brown dots he left behind him. His bowels were still open, and though he keyed up all his nervous energy to close them, he could feel both pants legs go damp. The stench followed him down the halls. But now the swelling bruises on his body blotted out his shame until he had to sit down before his seven interrogators, and then the sticky mess plastered against the length of his lower back.

*

The guards shackled his arms and legs to a heavy wooden chair and put the keys on the long mahogany table. As soon as one of the seven interrogators arrived to begin the day's work, the guards left. Then the other members of the interrogation team would saunter in, some of them holding their breakfast coffee cups in their hands. During the first week, Klaus von Osteen always arrived last. This was the week that "normal" physical torture was used on Rogan.

Because of the complicated nature of the information Rogan had to give, the intricate codes and the mental energy required to recall his memorized digital patterns, physical torture proved to be too shattering to the thought process. After torture Rogan could not have given them the codes even if he had wanted to. It was Klaus von Osteen who first understood this and ordered all physical persuasion held to a "gentle" minimum. Afterwards von Osteen was always the first member of the interrogation team to arrive in the morning.

In the early morning hours, von Osteen's beautifully chiselled aristocratic face was pale with shaving talcum, his eyes still gentle with sleep. Older than Rogan by a generation, he was the father every young man would like to have: distinguished-looking, without being foppish; sincere, without being oily or unctuous; grave, yet with a touch of humour; fair, yet stern. And in the weeks that followed, Rogan, worn down by physical fatigue, lack of proper food and rest, the constant torturing of his nerves, came to feel about von Osteen as if he were a protective father figure who was punishing him for his own good. His intellect rejected this attitude as ridiculous. The man was the chief of his torturers, responsible for all his pain. And yet emotionally, schizophrenically, he waited for von Osteen each morning as a child awaits his father.

The first morning von Osteen arrived before the others he put a cigarette in Rogan's mouth and lit it. Then he spoke, not questioning, but explaining his own position. He, von Osteen, was doing his duty for the Fatherland by interrogating Rogan. Rogan was not to think it was a personal thing. He had an affection for Rogan. Rogan was almost young enough to be the son he never had. It distressed him that Rogan was being stubborn. What possible purpose could such childish defiance have? The secret codes in Rogan's brain would no longer be used by the Allies, that was certain. A sufficient time had elapsed to render useless any information he gave them. Why could not Rogan end this foolishness and save them all suffering? For the torturers suffered with the tortured. Did he think they did not?

Then he reassured Rogan. The questioning would end. The war would end. Rogan and his wife Christine would be together again and happy again. The fever of war and murder would be over, and human beings would not have to fear each other any longer. Rogan was not to despair. And von Osteen would pat Rogan's shoulder comfortingly.

But when the other interrogators sauntered into the room von Osteen's manner would change. Again he became the chief interrogator. His deep-set eyes bored into Rogan's eyes. His melodious voice became harsh, strident. Yet curiously enough it was the harshness of a strict father with a note of love for his wayward child. There was something so magnetic, so powerful in von Osteen's personality that Rogan believed the role von Osteen played: that the interrogation was just; that he, Rogan, had brought the physical pain upon himself.

Then had come the days when he heard Christine's screams from the next room. On those days von Osteen had not arrived early in the morning, had always arrived last. And then there was that terrible day when they had let him into the next room and showed him the phonograph and the spinning record that preserved Christine's agony. Von Osteen had said smilingly, "She died on the first day of torture. We've tricked you." And Rogan, hating him at that moment with such intensity, had become ill, bile spilling out of his mouth on to his prison clothing.

Von Osteen had lied even then. Genco Bari said that Christine had died during childbirth, and Rogan believed Bari. But why did von Osteen lie? Why did he wish his people to seem more evil than they actually were? And then Rogan, remembering, realized the brilliant psychology behind von Osteen's every word and deed.

The hatred he felt for those who had killed his wife had made him want to stay alive. He wanted to stay alive so that he could kill them all and smile down at their own tortured bodies. And it was this hatred, this hope for revenge, that had crumbled his resistance and in the following months made him start giving his interrogators all the secret codes he could remember.

Von Osteen started coming early again, the first one in the interrogation room. Again he began to console Rogan, his voice magnetic with understanding. After the first few days he always unshackled Rogan's arms and legs and brought him coffee and cigarettes for breakfast. He kept assuring Rogan that he would be set free as soon as the codes were completed. And then one morning he came in very early, closed and locked the door of the high-domed room behind him, and said to Rogan, "I must tell you a secret which you must promise not to reveal." Rogan nodded. Von Osteen, his face grave and friendly, said, "Your wife is still alive. Yesterday she gave birth to a baby boy. They are both doing well, they are both being well cared for. And I give you my solemn word of honour that the three of you will be united when you have finished giving us all the information we need. But you must not breathe a word of this to the others. They may cause trouble, since I am exceeding the bounds of my authority by making you this promise."

Rogan was stunned. He searched von Osteen's face to see if the man was lying. But there was no doubting the kind sincerity in the German's eyes, the gentle goodness that seemed to be the very essence of his facial bones. Rogan believed. And the thought that Christine was alive, that he would see her beautiful face again, that he would hold her soft slender body in his arms again, that she was not dead and under the earth – all this made him break down and weep. Von Osteen patted him on the shoulder, saying softly in his hypnotic voice, "I know, I know. I am sorry I could not tell you sooner. It was all a trick you see, part of my job. But now it's no longer necessary and I wanted to make you happy."

He made Rogan dry his tears, and then he unlocked the door to the interrogation room. The other six men were waiting outside, coffee cups in their hands. They seemed angry at being shut out, angry that their leader was in some way allied to their victim.

That night in his cell Rogan dreamed of Christine and the baby son he had never seen. Oddly enough the baby's face was very clear in his dream, fat and pink-cheeked, but Christine's face was hidden in shadows. When he called to her she came out of the shadows, and he could see her, see that she was happy. He dreamed of them every night.

Five days later it was *Rosenmontag*, and when von Osteen came into the room he was carrying an armful of civilian clothing. He smiled a genuinely happy smile and said to Rogan, "Today is the day I keep my promise to you." And then the other six men crowded into the room. They congratulated Rogan as if they were professors who had helped him graduate from school with honours. Rogan started putting on the clothes. Genco Bari helped to knot his tie, but Rogan kept his eyes on von Osteen, asking a mute question with his eyes, asking if he would see his wife and child. And von Osteen understood and nodded his head, secretively, reassuringly. Someone clapped the fedora on Rogan's head.

As he stood there looking at their smiling faces he realized one of them was missing. Then he felt the cold muzzle of the gun against the back of his neck and the hat tilted forward over his eyes. In that one millionth of a second he understood everything and sent a last despairing look at von Osteen, crying out in his mind, "Father, Father, I believed. Father,

I forgave all your torture, your treachery. I forgive you for murdering my wife and giving me hope. Save me now. Save me now." And the last thing he saw before the back of his skull exploded was von Osteen's gentle face contorting into a devil's mocking laugh.

Now lying in bed beside Rosalie, Rogan knew that killing von Osteen just once would not be enough to satisfy him. There should be a way of bringing him back to life and killing him over and over again. For von Osteen had searched out the very essence of the humanity in both of them, and for no more than a joke, betrayed it.

When Rogan awoke the next morning Rosalie already had breakfast waiting for him. The room had no kitchen, but she used a hot plate to make coffee and had bought some rolls. While they ate she told him that Klaus von Osteen was not sitting in court that day but would be sentencing a convicted prisoner the next morning. They reviewed everything she knew about von Osteen – what she'd told Rogan before he'd gone to Sicily and what she'd learned later. Von Osteen was a powerful political figure in Munich and had the backing of the U.S.

State Department for a higher climb to power. As a judge, von Osteen had a twenty-four-hour guard at his home and when he went outside. He was without personal guards only in the Munich Palace of Justice, which swarmed with its own complement of security police. Rosalie also told Rogan about her job as a nurse's aide in the Munich Palace of Justice.

Rogan smiled at her. "Can you get me in there without my being seen?"

Rosalie nodded. "If you must go there," she said.

Rogan didn't answer for a moment. Then he said, "Tomorrow morning."

After she had gone off to work, Rogan went out to do his own errands. He bought the gun-cleaning packet he needed to disassemble and oil the Walther pistol. Then he rented a Mercedes and parked it a block away from the *Pension*. He went back up to the room and wrote some letters, one to his lawyer in the States, another to his business partners. He put the letters in his pocket to post after Rosalie came home from work. Then he took apart the Walther pistol, cleaned it thoroughly, and put it back together again. He put the silencer in a bureau drawer.

He wanted to be absolutely accurate this last time, and he was not sure he could get close enough to compensate for the loss of accuracy the silencer caused.

When Rosalie came home he asked, "Is von Osteen sitting tomorrow for sure?"

"Yes." She paused a moment, then asked, "Shall we go out to eat, or do you want me to bring something into the room?"

"Let's go out," Rogan said. He dropped his letters into the first post box they passed.

They had dinner at the famous Brauhaus where the beer steins never held less than a quart and twenty kinds of sausages were served as appetizers. The evening paper, *Tagenblatt*, had a story about the killing of Wenta Pajerski in Budapest. The democratic underground believed responsible for the murder had been smashed by a series of secret police raids, the paper reported. Fortunately, the bomb had injured no-one but the intended victim.

"Did you plan it that way?" Rosalie asked.

Rogan shrugged. "I did my best when I booby-trapped the chess piece. But you can never tell. I was worried one of those waitresses might get a stray fragment. A lucky thing Pajerski was a big guy. He soaked it all up."

"And now there is only von Osteen," Rosalie said. "Would it make any difference if I told you that he seems like a good man?"

Rogan laughed harshly. "It wouldn't surprise me," he said. "And it doesn't make any difference."

They didn't speak about it, but they both knew it could well be their last evening together. They didn't want to go back to their room with its green sofa and narrow bed. So they drifted from one great barn-like beer hall to another, drinking schnapps, listening to the happy Germans singing, watching them gulp countless quarts of beer at long wooden tables. The huge Bavarians wolfed links of fat little sausages and washed them down with towering, frothy steins of golden beer. Those who were momentarily sated fought their way through thick, malt-reeking crowds to the marbled bathrooms, to make use of the special vomiting bowls big enough to drown in. They vomited up all they had consumed, then fought their way back to the wooden tables and clamoured for more sausages and beer, only to return to the bathrooms and get rid of it once again.

They were disgusting, but they were alive and warm, so warm their heat made the huge beer halls hot as ovens. Rogan kept drinking schnapps while Rosalie switched to beer. Finally, having drunk enough to be sleepy, they started walking to their *Pension*.

When they passed the parked Mercedes, Rogan told Rosalie, "That's the car I rented. We'll take it to the court house tomorrow morning and park it near your entrance. If I don't come out you just drive away and leave Munich. Don't come looking for me. O.K.?"

"O.K.," she said. Her voice was tremulous, so he held her hand to keep her from crying. She pulled her hand away, but it was only to take the key from her purse. They entered the *Pension*, and as they mounted the stairs she took his hand again. She released it only to unlock the door to their room. She entered and switched on the lights. Behind her, Rogan heard her gasp of fright. Seated on the green sofa was the Intelligence agent Arthur Bailey; closing the door behind them was Stefan Vrostk. Vrostk held a gun in his right hand. Both men were smiling a little.

"Welcome home," Bailey said to Rogan. "Welcome back to Munich."

CHAPTER 18

Rogan smiled reassuringly at Rosalie. "Go and sit down. Nothing is going to happen. I've been expecting them." He turned to Bailey. "Tell your fink to stash his weapon and you do the same. You're not going to use them. And you're not going to stop me from doing what I have to do."

Bailey put away his gun and motioned to Vrostk. He said to Rogan very slowly, very sincerely, "We came to help you out. I was just worried that maybe you'd gone kill-crazy. I thought you might just start blasting away if you found us here, so I figured I'd get the drop and then explain."

"Explain away," Rogan said.

"Interpol is on to you," Bailey said. "They've hooked you up with all the murders, and they're processing copies of all your passport photos. They traced you to Munich; I got the teletype in my Munich branch office just an hour ago. They think you're here to kill somebody, and they're trying to find out who. That's the only thing you've got going for you. That nobody knows who you're after."

Rogan sat on the bed opposite the dusty green sofa. "Come off it, Bailey," he said. "You know who I'm after."

Bailey shook his head. His lean, handsome face took on a worried look. "You've become paranoiac," he said. "I've helped you all along. I haven't told them anything."

Rogan leaned back on the pillow. His voice was very calm. "I'll give you this much credit. At the beginning you didn't know who the seven men in the Munich Palace of Justice were. But by the time

I came back you had a dossier on every one of them. When I saw you a few months ago, the time you came to tell me to lay off the Freisling brothers, you knew all seven. But you were not going to let me know. After all, an Intelligence network operating against the Communists is more important than an atrocity victim getting his revenge. Isn't that how you Intelligence guys figure?"

Bailey didn't answer. He was watching Rogan intently. Rogan went on: "After I killed the Freisling brothers you knew nothing would stop me. And you wanted Genco Bari and Wenta Pajerski knocked off. But I was never supposed to get away from Budapest alive." He turned to Vrostk. "Isn't that right?"

Vrostk flushed. "All arrangements were made for your escape. I cannot help it if you are a headstrong person who insists on going his own way."

Rogan said contemptuously, "You lousy bastard. I went by the consulate just to check you out. There was no car waiting, and the whole neighbourhood was crawling with cops. You tipped them off. I was never supposed to get to Munich; I was supposed to die behind the Iron Curtain. And that would have solved all your Intelligence problems."

"You're insulting me," Bailey said. "You're accusing me of having you betrayed to the Communist secret police." His voice held a tone of such sincere outrage that Rosalie glanced doubtfully at Rogan.

"You know, if I were still a kid in the war you would have fooled me just now. But after the time I spent in the Munich Palace of Justice I see through guys like you. I had you all the way, Bailey; you never fooled me for a second. In fact, when I came to Munich I knew you'd be waiting, and I thought of tracking you down and killing you first. Then I figured it wouldn't be necessary. And I didn't want to kill someone just because he got in my way. But you're no better than those seven men. If you'd been there you'd have done what they did. Maybe you have. How about it, Bailey? How many guys have you tortured? How many guys have you murdered?"

Rogan paused to light a cigarette. He looked directly into Bailey's eyes when he started to speak again. "The seventh man, the chief interrogator, the man who tortured my wife and recorded her screams, is Judge Klaus von Osteen. The highest-ranking federal judge in Bavaria. The politician with the brightest future, maybe the next chancellor of

West Germany. Backed by our State Department. And in the pocket of the American Intelligence apparatus. So you can't afford to have him killed by me, and you certainly can't have him arrested for war crimes."

Rogan stubbed out his cigarette. "To keep me from killing von Osteen, to keep the story of his being a Gestapo man a secret, I had to be destroyed. You ordered Vrostk to betray me to the Hungarian secret police. Isn't that right, Bailey? Simple, airtight, clean-handed, just the way you sincere Intelligence types like it."

Vrostk said in his arrogant-sounding voice, "What is to stop us from silencing you now?" Bailey gave his subordinate a weary look of impatience. Rogan laughed.

"Bailey, tell your fink why he can't," Rogan said, amused. When Bailey remained silent Rogan went on, speaking directly to Vrostk. "You're too stupid to figure out what I've done, but your boss knows. I've sent letters to people in the States I can trust. If I die, von Osteen will be exposed, American diplomacy will be discredited. American Intelligence here in Europe will get it in the neck from Washington. So you can't kill me. If I'm captured – same thing. Von Osteen will be exposed, so you can't inform on me. You have to settle for breaking even. You have to hope that I kill von Osteen and nobody ever finds out why. I won't insist on your helping me. That would be asking too much."

Vrostk's mouth hung open in shock. Bailey stood up to go. "You've got it figured out pretty good," he said to Rogan. "Everything you said is true, I won't deny it. Vrostk took his orders from me. But everything I did was part of my job, to get my job done. What the hell do I care about your getting your revenge, getting your justice, when I can help our country control Germany through von Osteen? But you've made all the right moves, so I have to stand aside and let you do what you have to do. And I have no doubt that you'll get to von Osteen, even though there'll be a thousand cops looking for you tomorrow morning. But you've forgotten one thing, Rogan: You'd better escape after you kill him."

Rogan shrugged. "I don't give a damn about that."

"No, and you don't give much of a damn what happens to your women either." He saw that Rogan had not understood. "First, your pretty little French wife that you let them kill, and now this *Fräulein* here." He jerked his head towards Rosalie, who was sitting on the green sofa.

Rogan said quietly, "What the hell are you talking about?"

Bailey smiled for the first time. He said softly, "I mean that if you kill von Osteen and then you get killed, I put your girl through the wringer. She gets accused as an accessory to your murders, or she gets put away in that insane asylum. The same thing happens if von Osteen lives and gets exposed by your letters after you're dead. Now, I'll give you an alternative. Forget about killing von Osteen and I'll get you and the girl immunity for everything you've done. I'll get it fixed so the girl can enter the States with you when you go back. Think it over." He started to leave.

Rogan called after him. His voice was shaky. For the first time that evening he seemed to have lost some of his confidence. "Tell me the truth, Bailey," Rogan said. "If you had been one of the seven men in the Munich Palace of Justice, would you have done the things to me that they did?"

Bailey considered the question seriously for a

moment; then he said quietly, "If I really believed it would help my country win the war, yes, I would have." He followed Vrostk out of the door.

Rogan got up and went to the bureau. Rosalie saw him fit the rifled metal of the silencer on the spine of the Walther pistol and said in an anguished voice, "No, please don't. I'm not afraid of what they'll do to me." She moved towards the door, as if to stop him from going out. Then she changed her mind and sat on the green sofa.

Rogan watched her for a moment. "I know what you're thinking," he said, "but didn't I let Vrostk and Bailey get away with trying to kill me in Budapest? Everybody in that profession is some kind of special animal, not a human being. They're all volunteers; nobody forces them into those jobs. They know what their duties will be. To torture, betray, and murder their fellow human beings. I don't feel any pity for them."

She did not answer; she bowed her head into her hands. Rogan said gently, "In Budapest I risked my life to be sure no-one else was hurt except Pajerski. I was ready to give up everything, even my chance of punishing von Osteen, so that none of the innocent bystanders would be injured by me. Because those bystanders were innocent. These two men are not. And I won't have you suffer because of me."

Before she could answer, before she could raise her head, he went out of the room. She could hear his footsteps going swiftly down the stairs.

Rogan drove off in the rented Mercedes and turned on to a main avenue, his foot pressed down on the gas. At this hour there was little traffic. He was hoping that Bailey and Vrostk didn't have their own car, that they had come to the *Pension* in a taxi and would now be on foot and trying to catch another taxi.

He had gone no more than one block on the avenue when he saw them walking along together. He drove on one more block, then parked the car and started walking back along the avenue to meet them. They were still a hundred feet away when they turned into the entrance of the Fredericka Beer Hall. Damn, he thought, he'd never be able to get at them in there.

He waited outside for an hour, hoping that they would have a few quick beers and then come out. But they did not reappear and he decided, finally, to go inside.

The beer hall was not full, and he saw Bailey and Vrostk right away. They had a long wooden table to themselves and they sat there gobbling down white sausages. Rogan took a seat near the door, where he would be shielded from them by a full table of beer drinkers who were still going strong.

As he watched Bailey and Vrostk drink, he was surprised at their appearance and behaviour, and then amused at his surprise. Till now he had always seen them when they wore their masks of duty, careful not to reveal any weakness. Here he saw them relaxed, their disguises put aside.

The arrogant Vrostk evidently loved fat women. Rogan saw Vrostk pinch all the plump waitresses and let the skinny ones go by untouched. When a really hefty girl passed him, carrying a tray loaded with empty beer steins, Vrostk could not contain himself. He tried to embrace her, and the glasses went flying all over the wooden table; the waitress gave him a good-natured push that sent him staggering into Bailey's lap.

The lean Arthur Bailey was a finicky glutton. He was devouring plate after plate of white sausages, leaving a little stringy tail of casing from each. He washed each mouthful of sausage down with a gulp of beer. He was totally absorbed in what he was doing. Suddenly he lunged towards one of the bathrooms.

Vrostk followed him, weaving drunkenly. Rogan waited a moment, then he, too, followed. He went through the doorway and was in luck; Bailey and Vrostk were the only occupants.

But he could not shoot; he could not take his Walther pistol from his jacket pocket. Bailey was bent helplessly over one of the huge white vomit bowls, puking up everything since breakfast. Vrostk was gently holding Bailey's head so that it would not dip into the bowl's contents.

Caught with their defences down, they were curiously touching. Rogan backed out before they could see him, and left the beer hall. He drove the Mercedes to the *Pension*, parked it, and went up to the room. The door was not locked. Inside Rosalie was sitting on the green sofa, waiting for him. Rogan took off the silencer and threw it back into the bureau drawer. He went and sat beside Rosalie on the sofa.

"I couldn't do it," he said. "I don't know why, but I couldn't kill them."

CHAPTER 19

Next morning, while he drank his coffee he wrote down the name of his lawyer in the States and gave it to her. "If you do get into any kind of trouble, write to this man," Rogan said. "He'll come to help you out."

That he had not killed Bailey and Vrostk had in some way resigned Rosalie to Rogan's hunting down von Osteen. She did not try to make him change his mind; she accepted what he had to do. But she wanted him to rest for a few days. He looked ill and very tired. Rogan shook his head. He had waited too many years; he did not want to wait another day.

He had a slight headache. He could feel pressure on the part of his skull covered by the silver plate. Rosalie gave him water to wash down the pills he always carried with him. She watched him check the Walther pistol and put it in his jacket pocket. "Aren't you using the silencer?" she asked.

"It makes the gun too inaccurate," he said. "I'd have to get within fifteen feet to be sure of hitting him. And maybe I won't be able to get that close."

She understood what he really meant: that he had no hope of escaping; that it would be useless to silence the murder weapon. Before they went out of the door she made him hold her in his arms, but there was no way he could comfort her.

He had her drive the car, not trusting his uncertain lateral vision at an important time like this. His damaged optical nerve was at its worst in moments of stress, and he wanted to be able partially to shield his face with his hand as he moved through the city. Munich would be full of police looking for him.

They drove past the courthouse steps, through the square Rogan remembered so well, with its florid columned buildings. Rosalie parked the Mercedes a short distance from the side entrance. Rogan got out of the car and entered the majestic archway into the courtyard of the Palace of Justice.

He walked over the cobblestones that had once been stained with his blood and whose crannies had swallowed the tiny blasted fragments of his skull. Stiff with tension, he followed Rosalie into the emergency medical clinic and watched her slip into her white nurse's tunic. She turned to him and said quietly, "Are you ready?"

Rogan nodded. She took him up an interior staircase that led into a dark cool hall floored with marble. Great oak doors studded the sides of the corridor at intervals of fifty feet, the doors to the courtrooms. Deep niches next to each door contained suits of armour. Some of the niches were empty, the armour looted during the war and not yet replaced.

As he passed the courtroom doors Rogan could see the accused – petty thieves, burglars, rapists, pimps, murderers, and innocents – waiting for justice.

He walked down the long corridor, his head pounding with the fearful emotion that filled the air like a malevolent electric current. They came to a wooden stand that held a placard: *Kriminalgericht,* and underneath: *Bundesgericht von Osteen, Präsidium.*

Rosalie was pulling at his arm. "In this courtroom," she whispered. "Von Osteen will be the middle one of three judges."

Rogan went in past a bailiff and took a seat in a back row. Rosalie sat beside him.

Slowly Rogan raised his head to look at the three judges on their platform at the lower end of the huge courtroom. A spectator seated in front of him obscured his view, and he tilted his head to get a better look. None of the judges looked familiar. "I don't see him," he whispered to Rosalie.

"The judge in the middle," she whispered.

Rogan stared intently. The judge in the middle bore no resemblance to von Osteen. Von Osteen's features were aristocratic, aquiline; this man's features were lumpy. Even his forehead was narrower. No man could have changed so much. He whispered to Rosalie, "That's not von Osteen; he doesn't look anything like him."

Slowly Rosalie turned to face him. "You mean he's not the seventh man?"

Rogan shook his head. He saw gladness in her eyes and did not understand. Then she whispered, "But he *is* von Osteen. That's certain. I know that for a fact."

He felt dizzy suddenly. They had tricked him after all. He remembered the Freisling brothers' sly smiles when they had given him the information about von Osteen. He remembered something confident in Bailey's manner when they talked about von Osteen, something that had amused the Intelligence agent. And now he understood the look of gladness in Rosalie's eyes: He would never find the seventh man and so would abandon his search and live out his life. This was what she had hoped for.

The silver plate in his skull began to ache, and the hatred for the whole world that soured his blood drained the strength from his body and he started to slump towards Rosalie. She caught him as he began to black out, and a stout bailiff, seeing what had happened, helped to carry Rogan out of the courtroom and down to the emergency clinic. Rosalie stayed on the side where Rogan had his gun, feeling the shape of it through the cloth of his jacket. In the clinic she made him lie on one of the four beds and put a screen around him. Then she held up his head and pushed the pills down his throat. In a few minutes the colour returned to Rogan's cheeks and he opened his eyes.

She spoke to him softly, but he didn't answer, and finally she had to leave him there to attend to someone who had come in for minor medical aid.

Rogan stared at the ceiling. He tried to force his brain to think things out. There was no way the Freisling brothers could have been lying when they put down the same names of their wartime colleagues. And Bailey had admitted that it was von Osteen who was the man Rogan sought. Was it possible, then, that Rosalie had lied to him? No. For Rosalie, it was impossible. There was just one thing to do: Find Bailey and make him tell the truth. But only after he had rested; he felt too weak now. Rogan closed his eyes. He slept for a little while. When he woke up he thought he was in one of his familiar nightmares.

From the other side of the screen came the voice of the chief interrogator who had so long ago tortured him and betrayed his humanity. The voice was powerfully magnetic, ringing with sympathy. It was inquiring after the man who had fainted in the courtroom. Rogan could hear Rosalie, her tone respectful, reassuring the visitor that the man had been overcome by the heat and would shortly be well again. She thanked the Honourable Judge for his kindness in asking after the health of her patient.

When the door closed Rosalie came round the screen and found Rogan sitting up in bed. There was a grim smile on his face. "Who was that?" he asked, wanting to make sure.

"Judge von Osteen," Rosalie said. "He came to ask how you were. I told you what a kind man he was. I always felt he couldn't be the one you were looking for."

Rogan said softly, "That's what the brothers were smiling about, and Bailey too. They knew I would never recognize von Osteen, just as they hadn't recognized me. But his power was all in his voice, and I'd never forget that." He saw her look of dismay. "Is Judge von Osteen sitting this afternoon, after lunch?" he asked.

Rosalie sat down on the bed, with her back to him. "Yes."

Rogan patted her shoulder, his fingers drawing strength from her young body. He could feel the exultant joy running through him. In a few hours it would all be over; he would never dream his terrible dreams again. But he would need all his strength. He told Rosalie what shots to give him from her drug supply in the clinic locker. As she prepared the needle he thought about the change in von Osteen's appearance.

Remembering von Osteen's proud features, Rogan knew the man would not have had voluntary facial surgery merely to escape danger. In the years since they had last seen each other von Osteen had gone through his own hell of suffering. But it didn't matter; nothing mattered any more, Rogan thought. Before the day was over both their worlds would end.

CHAPTER 20

Superior Federal Judge Klaus von Osteen sat on the high bench, two fellow judges flanking him. He saw the mouth of the prosecuting attorney move, but he could not make any sense out of the words. Haunted by his own guilt, his own fear of punishment, he could not concentrate on the case before him. He would have to agree with the verdict of his two fellow judges.

A flash of movement in the rear of the courtroom caught his eye, and his heart contracted painfully. But it was just a couple taking their seats. He tried to see the man's face, but the head was bent down and away. Now the defence attorney was listing excuses for his client. Von Osteen tried to focus his attention on what the man was saying. He concentrated. Suddenly there was a commotion in the rear of the courtroom. By a great effort of will von Osteen kept himself from standing up. He saw a woman in white and one of the bailiffs half carry a slumping man out through the doorway. It was not an uncommon occurrence in these courtrooms where people were subjected to such cruel stress.

The incident disturbed him. With a crook of his finger he summoned one of the clerks to the bench and whispered instructions. When the clerk returned and told him that a friend of the nurse employed by the court had fainted and had been taken to the emergency room, von Osteen sighed with released tension. And yet there was something strange about such a thing happening at just this time.

When the court recessed for lunch, von Osteen decided to go down to the emergency room and inquire after the man's condition. He could have sent a clerk, but he wanted to see for himself.

The nurse was a very pretty girl and fine-mannered. He noted with approval that she was far superior to the usual type employed in such government positions. She motioned to a screen around one of the hospital beds and told him that the man was recovering; it had been a mild fainting spell, nothing serious. Von Osteen stared at the screen. He was almost overcome by the urge to walk behind that screen and look into the man's face, to resolve all his fears. But such an act would be extraordinary, and besides, the nurse was in his way. She would have to move aside. He said a few words to her with mechanical politeness and left the room. For the first time since he had become a judge in the Munich Palace of Justice he walked through the courtyard, turning his head so that he would not see the interior wall against which the bodies had been stacked on that terrible day long ago. Leaving the courtyard, he walked down the main avenue where his chauffeured limousine waited to take him to his home for lunch.

The detective guard sat in the front with the

chauffeur, and von Osteen smiled with amusement. The guard would be almost no protection against a determined assassin, merely another victim. When the car rolled into the driveway of his home he noticed that his house guard had been increased. They would help. It would force the assassin to make his attempt somewhere else, and Marcia would be safe.

His wife was waiting for him in the dining room. The table was set with white napery that had a faint tinge of blue in the curtained light. The silver sparkled, and the bowls of bright flowers were arranged with the skill of an artist. He said jokingly to his wife, "Marcia, I wish the food were as good as the setting." She made a face of mock displeasure. "Always the judge," she said.

Looking at his wife, von Osteen thought, Would she believe in my guilt if it all came out? And he knew that if he denied everything she would believe him. She was twenty years his junior, but she truly loved him. Of that he had no doubts. Von Osteen ran his hand over his face. The surgery had been excellent, the best available in Germany, but close up the many scars and seams in his flesh were clearly visible. He wondered if that was why she kept the rooms curtained against too bright a light and the lamps dim.

After lunch she made him lie down on the sitting-room sofa for an hour's rest. She took a seat opposite him, a book in her lap.

Klaus von Osteen closed his eyes. He could never confess to his wife; she believed in him. And after all, he had received his punishment. A few weeks after *Rosenmontag*, 1945, a shell had fragmented his face. He had always accepted his terrible wound without bitterness, for in his mind it atoned for the crime he had committed against the young American agent in the Munich Palace of Justice.

How could he explain to anyone that as a staff officer, a nobleman, a German, he had come to recognize the degradation of his country, its dishonour. And like a man who is married to a drunkard and who decides to become a drunkard himself to show his love for her, so he, too, had become a torturer and a murderer to remain a German. But had it really been that simple?

In those years since the war he had lived a truly good life, and it had been natural to him. As a judge he had been humane, never cruel. He had left his past behind him. The records of the Munich Palace of Justice had been carefully destroyed; and up until a few weeks ago he had felt little remorse for his wartime cruelties.

Then he had learned of Pfann and Moltke being killed, and the Freisling brothers too. A week ago the American Intelligence officer Arthur Bailey had come to his home and told him about Michael Rogan. Rogan had murdered the men who had been von Osteen's underlings in the Munich Palace of Justice when he had been a judge without the sanction of law. Von Osteen remembered Michael Rogan. They had not killed him after all.

Arthur Bailey had reassured him. Rogan would never accomplish his final murder, American Intelligence would see to that. They would also keep von Osteen's war atrocities a secret. Von Osteen knew what this meant. If he ever came to political power in West Germany he would be subject to blackmail by American Intelligence.

Lying on the sofa he reached out to touch his wife, not opening his eyes. It was only when he learned that Rogan was alive that von Osteen began to dream about him. He had nightmares of Rogan leaning over him, the back of his skull bleeding, the blood dripping on to von Osteen's face. He had nightmares of a phonograph record blaring out the screams of Rogan's young wife.

What was the truth? Why had he tortured Rogan and then killed him? Why had he recorded the screams of that pretty girl dying in childbirth? And why had he finally betrayed Rogan, led him on to hope for life, led him on to believe his wife was still alive?

He remembered the first day of the interrogation, the look on Rogan's face. It was an innocent, good face, and it had irritated him. It was also the face of a young man to whom nothing terrible had yet happened.

On that same day von Osteen had gone to visit the prisoner's wife and found that she had been taken to the medical room, in childbirth. Walking towards the room, he had heard the young girl's screams of pain, and when the doctor had told him the girl was dying von Osteen had decided to have the screams recorded to frighten Rogan into talking.

What a clever man he had been, von Osteen

thought. He was clever in everything. Clever in evilness; and after the war, living with his ruined face, clever in goodness. And being clever, he now knew why he had destroyed Rogan so completely.

He had done so, von Osteen realized, because evil and good must always try to destroy each other; and it must follow that in the world of war and murder, evil must triumph over good. And so he had destroyed Rogan, slyly led him on to trust and hope. And at that final moment when Rogan had begged for mercy with his eyes von Osteen had laughed, his laughter drowned by the roar of the bullet exploding into Rogan's skull. He had laughed at that moment because the sight of Rogan, with his hat tilted forward over his brow, had been genuinely comical; and death itself, in those terrible days of 1945, was merely a burlesque.

"It's time." His wife was touching his closed eyes. Von Osteen rose from the sofa and his wife helped him into his jacket. Then she walked with him to the limousine. "Be merciful," she said.

It caught him unawares. He looked at her, his eyes dazed with incomprehension. She saw this and said, "On that poor wretch you will have to sentence this afternoon."

Suddenly von Osteen had the overwhelming urge to confess his crimes to his wife. But the car was wheeling slowly away from the house on its way back to the Munich Palace of Justice. Already under sentence of death, but hoping for a reprieve, von Osteen could not bring himself to confess.

CHAPTER 21

Arthur Bailey paced the office of the C.I.A. communications centre in the U.S. Army headquarters outside Munich. Early that morning he had sent a coded radiogram to the Pentagon explaining the entire situation regarding von Osteen and Rogan. He had recommended that no action be taken by his organization. Now he was waiting impatiently for the answer.

It was nearly midday before a reply was received. The clerk took it into the top-secret decoding room, and half an hour later the message was placed in Bailey's hands. It stunned him. It instructed him to have von Osteen guarded and to inform the German police of Rogan's intentions. This course of action would be so disastrous, Bailey thought, that he decided to use the radiophone to the Pentagon. The code signature on the reply was that of a former German teammate of Bailey's, Fred Nelson. They couldn't speak too freely over the radiophone, but maybe Bailey could get his message across to Nelson. And he sure as hell had to hurry. Rogan might be right behind Judge von Osteen this minute.

It took him ten minutes to get a connection. After identifying himself he said cautiously, "Do you people know what the hell you're doing with those instructions you sent me? You could blow the whole political set-up sky high."

Nelson's voice was cool and noncommittal. "That decision came from the top in Intelligence. It's been cleared by the State people. So just go ahead and follow orders."

Bailey said disgustedly, "They're all crazy." His

voice sounded so worried that Nelson took pity on him.

"That one aspect you're worried about," Nelson said guardedly, "that's being taken care of."

Nelson was referring to the letters Rogan had sent to his friends in the States. "Yes, I understand," Bailey said. "What was done about that?"

"We've kept a file on him since your first report. We know everybody he might correspond with, and we've placed a postal intercept on the post of every person he knows."

Bailey was genuinely surprised. "Can you get away with that in the States? I didn't think of that at all."

"National security. We can do anything." Nelson sounded sardonic. "Will this guy let himself be taken alive?"

"No."

"He'd better not be," Nelson said, and broke the connection.

Bailey cursed himself for having called instead of just following instructions. He knew what Nelson's last remark meant. He had to make sure that Rogan was not captured alive, or not allowed to remain alive after he was captured. They didn't want him talking about von Osteen.

Bailey got into the waiting staff car and told the driver to take him to the Palace of Justice in Munich. He didn't think Rogan had had enough time to make his move, but he wanted to make sure. Then he would pick up Vrostk, and they would both go to the *Pension* and finish Rogan off.

CHAPTER 22

In the emergency clinic of the Munich Palace of Justice, Rogan prepared for his final meeting with Klaus von Osteen. He combed his hair and straightened his clothing; he wanted to look as presentable as possible so as not to stand out in the crowd. He patted his jacket pocket on the right side to make sure the Walther pistol was still there, though he could feel its weight.

Rosalie took a bottle of colourless liquid from her mobile tray and poured some on a thick square of gauze. She put the gauze in Rogan's left-hand pocket. "If you start to feel faint, hold it to your mouth and breathe in," she said.

He bent down to kiss her, and she said, "Wait until he finishes with his court; wait till the end of the day."

"I'll have a better chance if I catch him coming back from lunch. Be in the car." He touched her cheek lightly. "There's a good chance I'll get away."

Sad-eyed, they smiled at each other with pretended confidence; then Rosalie took off her white tunic and tossed it on a chair. "I'll go now," she said, and without another word, without a backward look, she left the clinic and walked through the courtyard to the street beyond. Rogan watched her before he, too, left the clinic and climbed the interior stairs to the main-floor corridor of the Munich Palace of Justice.

The corridor was filled with convicted people waiting to learn their punishments, and with them were families and friends, as well as the defenders and dispensers of justice. They gradually began disappearing into the individual courtrooms, until the cool dark hall was empty. There was no sign of von Osteen.

Rogan walked down the hall to the courtroom where von Osteen had sat that morning; he was late. The court was already in session, and had been for some minutes. It was ready to sentence the criminal before it. Von Osteen, as president of the court, sat between his two fellow judges. They all wore black robes, but only von Osteen wore the high conical hat of ermine and mink that designated the chief judicial officer, and his figure seemed to exert a dread fascination on everyone in the courtroom.

He was about to sentence the convicted criminal before him. The decision was announced in that magnificent persuasive voice that Rogan remembered so well. It was a life sentence for the poor wretch before him.

Rogan felt an enormous relief that his search was ended. He walked a hundred feet past the doors of the courtroom and stepped into one of the empty niches in the wall of the corridor, a niche that for a thousand years had held the armour of a German warrior. He stood there for nearly an hour before the people in the courtroom came out of the oaken doors into the corridor.

He saw a black-robed figure exit from the courtroom through a small side door. Von Osteen was coming towards him through the shadowy corridor. He looked like an ancient priest prepared for sacrifice, black robes flapping, the conical hat of ermine and mink like a bishop's mitre, holy and untouchable. Rogan waited, blocking the corridor. He drew the Walther pistol and held it before him.

They were face to face now. Von Osteen peered through the shadowy light and whispered, "Rogan?" And Rogan felt an overwhelming joy that this last time he was recognized, that his victim knew the crime for which he must die. He said, "You condemned me to death once."

He heard the hypnotic voice say, "Rogan, Michael Rogan?" And von Osteen was smiling at him and saying, "I'm glad you've finally come." He reached up and touched his furred hat. "You are far more terrible in my dreams," he said. Rogan fired.

The pistol shot clanged through the marble corridors like some great bell. Von Osteen staggered back. He held up both hands as if to bless Rogan.

Rogan fired again. The black-robed figure began to sag, the conical hat making the fall majestic, sacrilegious. People ran into the corridor from the adjoining courtrooms, and Rogan fired one last bullet into the body lying on the marbled floor. Then, with the pistol in his hand, he ran out of the side exit into the sunlit square. He was free.

He saw the waiting Mercedes just a hundred paces away and started for it. Rosalie was standing beside the car, looking tiny, as if she were at the end of a long tunnel. Rogan started running. He was really going to make it, he thought; it was all over, and he was going to make it. But a middle-aged, moustached policeman, directing traffic, had seen the gun in Rogan's hand and rushed from his post to intercept him. The policeman was unarmed. He stood in Rogan's path and said, "You are under arrest; you cannot brandish a weapon in public."

Rogan brushed him aside and walked towards the Mercedes. Rosalie had disappeared now; she must be inside the car starting the motor. Rogan desperately wanted to reach her. The policeman followed him, grasping his arm, saying, "Come now, be sensible. I am a German police officer, and I place you under arrest." He had a thick Bavarian accent that made his voice sound friendly. Rogan hit him in the face. The policeman staggered back, then ran after him clumsily, trying to herd Rogan into the Palace of Justice with his heavy body, yet afraid to use physical force because of the pistol in Rogan's hand. "I am a police officer," he said again, astonished, unable to believe that anyone would refuse to obey his lawful commands. Rogan turned and shot him through the chest.

The policeman fell against him, looked up into his eyes, and said, with surprise, with innocent horror, *"O wie gemein Sie sind."* The words rang in Rogan's mind. "Oh, how wicked you are." He stood there, paralysed, as the policeman fell dying at his feet.

Frozen in the sunlit square, Rogan's own body seemed to disintegrate, the strength running out of it. But then Rosalie was beside him, taking his hand and making him run. She pushed him into the Mercedes and then roared out of the square. She drove wildly through the streets of Munich to reach the safety of their room. Rogan's head had tilted to the right, away from her, and she saw with horror a trickle of blood seeping out of his left ear, the blood running against gravity, propelled by an inner pump gone awry.

They were at the *Pension*. Rosalie stopped the car and helped Rogan get out. He could barely stand. She took the soaked gauze out of his left jacket pocket and held it to his mouth. His head jerked up and she could see the scarlet snake of blood trickling from his left ear. He was still clutching the Walther pistol in his right hand, and people in the street were staring at them. Rosalie led him into the building and helped him up the stairs. The spectators would surely call the police. But for some reason, Rosalie wanted him behind closed doors, shielded from everybody's eyes. And when they were alone and safe she led Rogan to the green sofa and made him lie down and put his head in her lap.

And Rogan, feeling the ache of the silver plate in his skull, knowing he would never dream his terrible dreams again, said, "Let me rest. Let me sleep before they come." Rosalie stroked his brow, and he could smell the fragrance of roses on her hand. "Yes," she said. "Sleep a little."

A short time later the Munich police entered the room and found them so. But the seven men in the high-domed room of the Munich Palace of Justice had finally killed Rogan after all. Now, ten years later, his damaged brain had exploded in a massive haemorrhage. Blood had poured from every aperture of his head – from his mouth, his nose, his ears, his eyes. Rosalie sat quietly, her lap a basin filled with Rogan's blood. As the police came forward she started to weep. Then slowly she bowed her head to bless Rogan's cold lips with a final kiss.